Ready® Common Core | 7 Reading INSTRUCTION
Teacher Resource Book

Advisors

Crystal Bailey, Math Impact Teacher, Eastern Guilford Middle School, Guilford County Schools, Gibsonville, NC

Leslie Blauman, Classroom Teacher, Cherry Hills Village Elementary, Cherry Creek School District, Cherry Hills Village, CO

Max Brand, Reading Specialist, Indian Run Elementary, Dublin City School District, Dublin, OH

Kathy Briguet, Retired Curriculum Coordinator for K-12 Literacy, Forest Lake Area Schools, Forest Lake, MN; Adjunct Instructor, Reading Instruction in the Elementary Grades, University of Minnesota, Minneapolis, MN

Helen Comba, Supervisor of Basic Skills & Language Arts, School District of the Chathams, Chatham, NJ

Cindy Dean, Classroom Teacher, Mt. Diablo Unified School District, Concord, CA

Randall E. Groth, Ph.D., Associate Professor of Mathematics Education, Salisbury University, Salisbury, MD

Jennifer Geaber, Kingston Hill Academy Charter School, South Kingstown, RI

Bill Laraway, Classroom Teacher, Silver Oak Elementary, Evergreen School District, San Jose, CA

Susie Legg, Elementary Curriculum Coordinator, Kansas City Public Schools, Kansas City, KS

Sarah Levine, Classroom Teacher, Springhurst Elementary School, Dobbs Ferry School District, Dobbs Ferry, NY

Nicole Peirce, Classroom Teacher, Eleanor Roosevelt Elementary, Pennsbury School District, Morrisville, PA

Donna Phillips, Classroom Teacher, Farmington R-7 School District, Farmington, MO

Kari Ross, Reading Specialist, MN

Sunita Sangari, Math Coach, PS/MS 29, New York City Public Schools, New York, NY

Shannon Tsuruda, Classroom Teacher, Mt. Diablo Unified School District, Concord, CA

Mark Hoover Thames, Research Scientist, University of Michigan, Ann Arbor, MI

Acknowledgments

Project Manager: Susan James
Revising Editor: Rob Hill
Cover Designer and Illustrator: Julia Bourque
Book Designer: Mark Nodland

Managing Editor: Nicole VanderLinden
Director–Product Development: Daniel J. Smith
Vice President–Product Development: Adam Berkin

Table of Contents

Unit 2: Key Ideas and Details in Literature

Unit 3: Craft and Structure in Informational Text

Unit 4: Craft and Structure in Literature

Unit 5: Integration of Knowledge and Ideas in Informational Text

Unit 6: Integration of Knowledge and Ideas in Literature

Language Handbook

Conventions of Standard English

Knowledge of Language

Ready® Common Core Program Overview

Ready® Common Core is an integrated program of assessment and data-driven instruction designed to teach your classroom the Common Core State Standards (CCSS) for English Language Arts. The program teaches and assesses all the tested CCSS in the Reading and Language strands. You can use the program in a supplemental way to address specific standards where your students need instruction and practice, or in a more comprehensive way to engage students in all the CCSS.

Built for the Common Core. Not just aligned.

Differentiated Instruction and Assessments

***Ready Common Core Instruction*—**provides differentiated instruction and independent practice of key concepts and skills that builds student confidence. Interim reading assessments give frequent opportunities to monitor progress. A Language Handbook gives instruction and practice on the Common Core Language standards.

Ready Assessments provides extensive practice on the high-rigor items required by the Common Core, giving you a measure of student growth. The three full-length tests will strengthen students' skills, build their confidence, and ensure that they are ready to show their mastery of the Common Core.

Teacher Resource Book and Teacher Toolbox

Ready Common Core Teacher Resource Books support teachers with strong professional development, step-by-step lesson plans, and best practices for implementing the CCSS.

Ready Common Core Teacher Toolbox (Teacher Toolbox sold separately) provides online lessons, prerequisite lessons from previous grades, and targeted best-practice teaching strategies.

i-Ready® Diagnostic

Built on the Common Core and integrated with the ***Ready*** program, ***i-Ready Diagnostic*** helps teachers track student growth, pointing teachers toward the correct ***Ready*** lessons to use for remediation. See page A22 for details. (***i-Ready*** sold separately.)

Features

 Built with brand-new content

 Uses a research-based gradual-release instructional model

 Employs higher-rigor test questions, requiring students to cite text-based evidence to support answers

 Includes complex, authentic texts from a wide range of genres

 Embeds thoughtful professional development

 Integrates teaching of language arts standards at point of use

 Engages students with high-interest themes for passages, drawing in commonly studied science and social studies topics

NEW 2014 Edition

- More high-rigor test items reflecting latest guidance from Smarter Balanced and PARCC
- New Language Handbook covering the CCSS Language strand
- Updated item Depth of Knowledge (DOK) levels based on latest guidance

Supporting the Implementation of the Common Core

The Common Core State Standards (CCSS) were developed to make sure that by the time students graduate from high school, they are college- and career-ready. Therefore, the creators of the standards started with the expectations they had for students at the end of 12th grade and worked down to kindergarten. As a result of this backward design approach, the CCSS are more rigorous than most current standards. The creators of the standards want students at every grade to be creative and critical readers and writers. At the end of each grade, students are expected to independently read and comprehend increasingly complex text. Not only are most current textbooks lacking alignment to the CCSS, they also lack the levels of complex text identified in the CCSS. **Ready® Common Core** is here to help.

Because every Common Core reading standard has been addressed with a clear, thoughtful pedagogy, you can use the **Ready** program as the main structure of a year-long program. Any other materials aligned to the CCSS can be easily woven into the curriculum.

Each **Ready** lesson covers the entirety of a particular skill, so classrooms can work through any lesson independently from the rest of the book. This gives teachers in states transitioning to the CCSS enormous flexibility, knowing that **Ready** lessons can be pulled out and applied to any implementation plan.

Keep Up to Date with *Ready®* Teacher Toolbox

The online **Ready** Teacher Toolbox gives you access to a host of multilevel resources, such as instructional support, online lessons, and lessons for prerequisite skills. (See pages A20 and A21 for more.) You can access the latest version of **Ready Assessments** there, as well.

Smarter Balanced Assessment Consortium (SBAC) and the Partnership for Assessment of Readiness for College and Career (PARCC) are state-led consortia developing assessments aligned to the Common Core. They are creating higher-rigor, innovative item types and assessments that can measure a student's mastery of the Common Core. (See page A14 to see the higher-level DOK items in **Ready**, matching the consortia approach.) To match the differing approaches of the two consortia, we have created custom versions of **Ready Assessments**, one for PARCC and one for SBAC.

The situation will be changing rapidly as the consortia complete their work. We will make sure that **Ready Assessments** addresses the most recent information released by the consortia. You can ensure you have access to the latest updates by visiting the **Ready** Teacher Toolbox (*www.teacher-toolbox.com*).

Helpful Resources for the Transition to the Common Core

http://www.corestandards.org/
The main website for the Common Core. Here you'll find the full text of the standards, plus frequently asked questions and resources.

http://www.smarterbalanced.org/ and http://www.parcconline.org
The testing consortium creating Common Core assessments for future implementation.

http://www.ascd.org/common-core-state-standards/common-core.aspx
A helpful list of all of ASCD's resources on the Common Core, as well as link to ASCD's free EduCore digital tool, which was funded by a grant from the Bill & Melinda Gates Foundation. A repository of evidence-based strategies, videos, and supporting documents that help educators transition to the Common Core.

http://www.reading.org/resources/ResourcesByTopic/CommonCore-resourcetype/CommonCore-rt-resources.aspx
Links to helpful articles about the Common Core from *Reading Today Online*.

Answering the Demands of the Common Core with *Ready*®

THE DEMANDS OF THE COMMON CORE	HOW *READY*® DELIVERS
Text Complexity: Students must engage with texts of sufficient complexity to prepare them for college and career.	All texts in **Ready** have been carefully leveled to meet Common Core requirements for complexity. See more on page A11.
Intentional, Close Reading: Careful, close readings of complex texts teach students how to gather evidence and build knowledge.	All **Ready** lessons contain activities requiring close reading, re-reading, and frequent interactions with text. On-page guidance models the good habits that successful readers employ. See more on page A12.
Text-based Evidence: Students' interpretations and comprehension of the text must be supported by the words in the text.	All the questions and activities in **Ready** lessons require students to cite evidence directly from the text. Instruction and hints throughout the lesson reinforce the importance of quoting from the text to substantiate interpretations.
Wide Range of Genres, Emphasis on Nonfiction: Students must read a true balance of authentic literary and informational texts. Success in college and the real world requires that students master the skills needed to read a wide range of genres.	**Ready** passages encompass the range of genres and text types cited in the Common Core, including articles, poems, historical text, technical text, scientific text, and dramas. 50% of **Ready** lessons focus on informational texts. See more on page A13.
Building Content Knowledge: Students should view reading as an opportunity to learn new information. As much as possible, therefore, have students read text on related topics that allow them to deepen their understanding.	All passages in a **Ready** lesson are thematically linked. Many of the themes relate to grade-appropriate science and social studies content, others to high-interest, appealing topics. Theme activities provide opportunities for students to see relationships between topics and deepen their content knowledge.
High-Quality Texts: It's important that students are exposed to well-crafted texts that are worth reading closely and exhibit exceptional craft and thought or provide useful information.	**Ready** lessons include authentic texts that students will see in the real world, including text and images from websites, and newspaper and magazine articles from such publications as *The New York Times*, *National Geographic*, and *Highlights*.
Integrated ELA Instruction: Use the texts as a source of rich language arts instruction, as opposed to isolated skill instruction.	**Ready** integrates Speaking & Listening, Writing, and Language activities with every Reading lesson.
Use of Technology and Digital Media: Students learn to use technology thoughtfully and efficiently to enhance their reading.	Specific **Ready** Media Features and lessons allow students to integrate audio and visual media into their reading experience. They learn to evaluate the pros and cons of various media and to employ the best medium to achieve a particular purpose.

The Importance of Text Complexity

Research has shown that the complexity levels of the texts in current classrooms are far below what is required for college- and career-readiness. A major emphasis of the Common Core State Standards is for students to encounter appropriately complex texts at each grade level in order to develop the mature language skills and conceptual knowledge they need for success in school and life. Instructional materials should meet this challenge with texts of appropriate complexity at each grade level.

A Three-Part Model for Measuring Text Complexity

No single formula can provide an accurate measure of text complexity. For that reason, the CCSS has developed a balanced three-part model that takes into account the following three ways of assessing text complexity:

Qualitative Measures:
The purpose of the text, the structure and clarity of the language, and background knowledge demands

Quantitative Measures:
Standard readability formulas, such as Lexile and Flesch-Kincaid

Reader–Task Consideration:
Including the reader's motivation and experience, as well as the complexity of the task assigned and questions posed

Text Complexity in *Ready*®

All passages in **Ready** conform to the leveling criteria outlined by the CCSS. We used quantitative formulas to place texts within the grade-level bands recommended by the Standards, which are more rigorous than those of the past. We also had an experienced team of teachers and literacy specialists apply the qualitative and reader–task measures described above. Through the scaffolded instruction in **Ready**, students develop the strategies they will need to comprehend this challenging text.

Academic Vocabulary

The CCSS categorize types of vocabulary in a three-tier model similar to the one developed by Beck, McKeown, & Kucan in *Bringing Words to Life*. (Beck, McKeown, & Kucan, 2002) Tier One Vocabulary are the words of everyday speech. Tier Two (which CCSS calls "general academic vocabulary") are the words a reader encounters in rich, complex texts of all types. Tier Three (which CCSS calls "domain specific") are the words particular to a field of study, such as science or history. While Tier Three words are often explicitly defined in a subject-area text, this is not the case with Tier Two words. Their meanings are often subtle, yet they are the most important words for students to learn, since they are generalizable, or applicable to a wide variety of texts.

Unlike reading programs of the past, in which difficult vocabulary was "pretaught" before reading, CCSS emphasizes the use of text-based strategies, such as context and word structure, to determine word meaning. **Ready** provides this type of instruction in the Teacher Resource Book lessons by identifying challenging Tier Two words in a passage and giving the teacher explicit text-based strategies to support students in unlocking their meanings.

Close-Up on Close Reading

What Is Close Reading?

The purpose of a close reading is to unlock the meanings of a text and to probe an author's motivations for writing it. To achieve these goals, readers must

- reread the text (in whole or in part),
- write down questions and observations relevant to the text's meaning and purpose, and
- mark up the text to identify details that help answer those questions and develop those observations.

Internalizing and mastering such close-reading strategies prepares students for college and careers, which is a key goal of the Common Core: "[Research] links the close reading of complex text—whether the student is a struggling reader or advanced—to significant gains in reading proficiency." (PARCC, 2011)

How Do We Apply Close Reading Instruction in *Ready® Common Core*?

Short, rich, complex text: Readers use close-reading strategies with challenging text that are hard to fully comprehend on a first reading. It's this type of complex text you'll find in *Ready*. *Ready* uses short text because we agree with reading experts that "When students are introduced to a . . . strategy through close reading, it's wise to use a short piece of text. Constraining the amount of text under investigation helps students see how to apply that . . . strategy and limits the amount of time required to teach [it]." (Fisher, Frey, & Lapp, 2012)

Multiple readings: In Guided Practice, we explicitly emphasize multiple readings (see page A28). For the first reading, students focus on literal comprehension. In the second reading, students apply close-reading strategies to unlock meaning and practice the lesson's featured standard. Fisher, Frey, & Lapp describe the value of multiple readings: "Sophisticated readers understand that the nature of some text requires that they be read more than once. . . . First and foremost, close reading requires a willingness to return to the text to read part or even all of it more than once." (Fisher, Frey, & Lapp, 2012)

Marking up the text: Our Close Reading activities guide students to mark up the text, helping them remember and make sense of what they read. We prompt students to mark specific evidence in the text that provide answers to the text-dependent questions they will need to answer. As Fisher, Frey, & Lapp describe it, "[b]y annotating texts . . . students learn to slow down their reading to mine the depths of the concepts, arguments, and metaphors used by the writer." (Fisher, Frey, & Lapp, 2012)

Teaching for transfer: Students must take what they learn from the study of one text and apply it to the next. To encourage this transfer, we remove the scaffolds in our Common Core Practice section. See page A30 for a tip activating these metacognitive strategies.

Monitoring Student Progress in *Ready® Instruction*

These ongoing assessment features in the *Ready* program keep you informed about student progress:

Student Lesson

- **Common Core Practice:** Each lesson ends with Common Core Practice. Use these results to identify how well students mastered the specific standard. If students scored poorly, review the lesson and use reteaching support in the Teacher Resource Book.

- **Interim Assessment:** Use the Interim Assessments and Performance Tasks at the end of each unit to see how well students can integrate the skills and strategies covered in that unit.

Full-Length Assessments

- **Ready Assessments:** Three full-length assessments allow you to benchmark student progress on each CCSS throughout the year.

Teacher Resource Book

- **Error Alerts:** This easy-to-use feature allows you to quickly identify and address common misconceptions students experience when applying the targeted standard.

Genres and Themes in *Ready*®

To succeed in college and the world outside the classroom, students must master reading a wide range of genres. *Ready*® ensures students read rich texts linked in meaningful ways by including a variety of genres and by organizing each lesson under a theme. The following chart shows the themes and genres for grade 7 lessons.

Lesson	Theme	Genres
1: Analyzing the Development of Central Ideas	Careers	Biography, Social Studies
2: Summarizing Informational Texts	Invasive Species	Public Document, Science
3: Citing Evidence to Make Inferences	The Competitive Spirit	History, Speech
4: Analyzing Interactions in a Text	Inventors and Inventions	Biography, History
5: Citing Evidence to Support Inferences	The Element of Surprise	Short Story
6: Analyzing the Interaction of Story Elements	Imagination and Ingenuity	Fantasy, Historical Fiction
7: Determining Theme	Setting a New Course	Realistic Fiction
8: Summarizing Literary Texts	Myths and Legends	Legend, Myth
9: Analyzing Word Meanings	Little Creatures, Big Impact	Science
10: Analyzing Text Structure	What Makes Us *Us*?	Science
11: Determining Point of View	Catastrophes	Editorial, Science
12: Determining Word Meanings	The City and the Country	Lyric Poem
13: Analyzing Rhyme and Repetition	Honoring Heroes	Drama, Lyric Poem, Realistic Fiction
14: Analyzing the Structure of a Poem	A Family Scrapbook	Lyric Poem, Narrative Poem, Ode, Sonnet
15: Analyzing the Structure of Drama	Anne Frank: Diary to Drama	Drama
16: Analyzing Point of View	Perspectives	Allegory, Realistic Fiction
17: Evaluating an Argument	Energy and Our Future	Economics, Persuasive Essay, Speech
18: Comparing and Contrasting Texts	Facing the Challenges	Persuasive Essay, Report, Science
19: Comparing and Contrasting Genres	A Time of Transition	Historical Fiction, History, Speech

Depth of Knowledge Levels in *Ready*®

The following table shows the **Ready**® lessons and sections with higher-complexity items, as measured by Webb's Depth of Knowledge index.

Lesson	Section	Item	DOK	Lesson	Section	Item	DOK
				Depth of Knowledge Levels for Higher-Rigor Items in *Ready Common Core*			
1	Guided Practice	3	3	13	Guided Instruction	—	3
1	Common Core Practice	3	3	13	Guided Practice	1	3
1	Common Core Practice	4	3	13	Guided Practice	2	3
3	Guided Practice	3	3	13	Guided Practice	3	3
3	Common Core Practice	4	3	13	Common Core Practice	1	3
4	Guided Instruction	—	3	13	Common Core Practice	2	3
4	Guided Practice	3	3	13	Common Core Practice	3	3
4	Common Core Practice	3	3	13	Common Core Practice	4	3
4	Common Core Practice	4	3	14	Guided Instruction	—	3
Unit 1	Interim Assessment	1A	3	14	Guided Practice	3	3
Unit 1	Interim Assessment	1B	3	14	Common Core Practice	4	3
Unit 1	Interim Assessment	4	3	15	Guided Practice	3	3
Unit 1	Interim Assessment	6	3	15	Common Core Practice	4	3
Unit 1	Interim Assessment	8	3	16	Guided Practice	1	3
Unit 1	Interim Assessment	9	3	16	Guided Practice	3	3
Unit 1	Interim Assessment	10	3	16	Common Core Practice	3	3
5	Guided Practice	3	3	16	Common Core Practice	4	3
5	Common Core Practice	4	3	Unit 4	Interim Assessment	1	3
6	Guided Practice	3	3	Unit 4	Interim Assessment	3	3
6	Common Core Practice	4	3	Unit 4	Interim Assessment	4A	3
7	Guided Practice	3	3	Unit 4	Interim Assessment	4B	3
7	Common Core Practice	4	3	Unit 4	Interim Assessment	6	3
Unit 2	Interim Assessment	1	3	Unit 4	Interim Assessment	8	3
Unit 2	Interim Assessment	2A	3	Unit 4	Interim Assessment	9	3
Unit 2	Interim Assessment	2B	3	Unit 4	Interim Assessment	10	3
Unit 2	Interim Assessment	4	3	17	Guided Instruction	—	3
Unit 2	Interim Assessment	6	3	17	Guided Practice	3	3
Unit 2	Interim Assessment	8	3	17	Common Core Practice	4	3
Unit 2	Interim Assessment	9	3	18	Guided Instruction	—	3
9	Guided Instruction	—	3	18	Guided Practice	1	3
9	Guided Practice	1	3	18	Guided Practice	2	3
9	Guided Practice	2	3	18	Guided Practice	3	4
9	Guided Practice	3	3	18	Common Core Practice	1	3
9	Common Core Practice	1	3	18	Common Core Practice	3	3
9	Common Core Practice	2	3	18	Common Core Practice	4	4
9	Common Core Practice	3	3	Unit 5	Interim Assessment	1	3
9	Common Core Practice	4	3	Unit 5	Interim Assessment	2	3
10	Guided Practice	3	3	Unit 5	Interim Assessment	4	3
10	Common Core Practice	3	3	Unit 5	Interim Assessment	5	3
10	Common Core Practice	4	3	Unit 5	Interim Assessment	6	3
11	Guided Instruction	—	3	Unit 5	Interim Assessment	7A	3
11	Guided Practice	1	3	Unit 5	Interim Assessment	7B	3
11	Guided Practice	2	3	Unit 5	Interim Assessment	8	4
11	Guided Practice	3	3	Unit 5	Interim Assessment	9	4
11	Common Core Practice	1	3	19	Guided Instruction	—	3
11	Common Core Practice	2	3	19	Guided Practice	1	3
11	Common Core Practice	3	3	19	Guided Practice	2	3
11	Common Core Practice	4	3	19	Guided Practice	3	4
Unit 3	Interim Assessment	2	3	19	Common Core Practice	1	3
Unit 3	Interim Assessment	4	3	19	Common Core Practice	3	3
Unit 3	Interim Assessment	5	3	19	Common Core Practice	4	4
Unit 3	Interim Assessment	8	3	Unit 6	Interim Assessment	1	3
Unit 3	Interim Assessment	9	3	Unit 6	Interim Assessment	3	3
Unit 3	Interim Assessment	10	3	Unit 6	Interim Assessment	4	3
12	Guided Instruction	—	3	Unit 6	Interim Assessment	5A	3
12	Guided Practice	1	3	Unit 6	Interim Assessment	5B	3
12	Guided Practice	2	3	Unit 6	Interim Assessment	5C	3
12	Guided Practice	3	3	Unit 6	Interim Assessment	6	4
12	Common Core Practice	2	3	Unit 6	Interim Assessment	7	3
12	Common Core Practice	3	3	Unit 6	Interim Assessment	8	4
12	Common Core Practice	4	3	Unit 6	Interim Assessment	9	4

Cognitive Rigor Matrix

The following table combines the hierarchies of learning from both Webb and Bloom. For each level of hierarchy, descriptions of student behaviors that would fulfill expectations at each of the four DOK levels are given. For example, students can show how they evaluate by citing evidence or checking multiple sources, but there isn't a lower-rigor (DOK 1 or 2) way of truly assessing this skill.

Depth of Thinking (Webb) + Type of Thinking (Revised Bloom)	DOK Level 1 Recall & Reproduction	DOK Level 2 Basic Skills & Concepts	DOK Level 3 Strategic Thinking & Reasoning	DOK Level 4 Extended Thinking
Remember	• Recall, locate basic facts, definitions, details, events			
Understand	• Select appropriate words for use when intended meaning is clearly evident	• Specify, explain relationships • Summarize • Identify central ideas	• Explain, generalize, or connect ideas using supporting evidence (quote, text evidence, example . . .)	• Explain how concepts or ideas specifically relate to other content domains or concepts
Apply	• Use language structure (pre/suffix) or word relationships (synonym/antonym) to determine meaning	• Use content to identify word meanings • Obtain and interpret information using text features	• Use concepts to solve non-routine problems	• Devise an approach among many alternatives to research a novel problem
Analyze	• Identify the kind of information contained in a graphic, table, visual, etc.	• Compare literary elements, facts, terms, events • Analyze format, organization, & text structures	• Analyze or interpret author's craft (e.g., literary devices, viewpoint, or potential bias) to critique a text	• Analyze multiple sources or texts • Analyze complex/abstract themes
Evaluate			• Cite evidence and develop a logical argument for conjectures based on one text or problem	• Evaluate relevancy, accuracy, & completeness of information across texts/sources
Create	• Brainstorm ideas, concepts, problems, or perspectives related to a topic or concept	• Generate conjectures or hypotheses based on observations or prior knowledge and experience	• Develop a complex model for a given situation • Develop an alternative solution	• Synthesize information across multiple sources or texts • Articulate a new voice, alternate theme, new knowledge or perspective

SBAC, 2012; adapted from Hess et al., 2009

Using *Ready® Common Core*

The ***Ready®*** program provides rigorous instruction on the Common Core State Standards using a proven-effective gradual-release approach that builds student confidence. It also prepares students for more complex assessment items with full-length assessments and interim assessments. With the Teacher Resource Book, you get strong support, step-by-step lesson plans, and best-practice tips to learn new approaches to teaching the Common Core. The Teacher Toolbox gives you access to invaluable, easy-to-use resources to differentiate instruction with a host of online materials, all in one place.

Using as a Supplement to a Textbook

The textbook you use in your classroom may not have been developed for the Common Core. It may not have all the resources you'll need to meet these challenging standards. In addition, the passages in textbooks don't reflect the levels of text complexity required by the Common Core, and the activities and questions don't reflect their rigor. By supplementing with ***Ready***, you'll be able to address all of these gaps and deficiencies.

Using with a Balanced Literacy/Reading Workshop Curriculum

Because every standard in ***Ready Common Core*** has been addressed with a clear, thoughtful pedagogy, you can use the ***Ready*** program as the main structure of a year-long English language arts program. Any other materials aligned to the Common Core can be woven into the curriculum, using the four easy steps on this page as your map.

Using with *i-Ready® Diagnostic*

If you are an ***i-Ready*** subscriber, you can administer the ***i-Ready Diagnostic*** as a cross-grade-level assessment to pinpoint instructional needs and address them with ***Ready Common Core Instruction***. For more on this, see page A22.

1 Measure Growth

- Use Assessment 1 from ***Ready Assessments*** to establish a baseline for measurement and to focus instructional plans. Use Assessments 2 and 3 to measure growth as students work through the program. These tests give students practice with more complex items that match the rigor of the Common Core.

2 Instruct

- Administer each ***Ready Common Core Instruction*** lesson, using the Pacing Guide on page A17 as a guide. Language Handbook lessons are also listed to show how the Reading and Language lessons can be used together.

- At any time during the instructional program, refer to the Teacher Toolbox to review prerequisite skills and access lessons from previous grades for remediation.

3 Monitor Progress

- Use the Interim Assessments at the end of each ***Ready Instruction*** unit to pinpoint student progress on the standards they have most recently learned and diagnose problem areas.

4 Differentiate Instruction

Provide differentiated instruction for your students using the rich and varied resources in the Teacher Toolbox. Here you'll find links to prerequisite skills from earlier grades of ***Ready***, as well as links to highly interactive animated modules that will deepen students' understanding of skills and strategies. See page A20 for more on using the Teacher Toolbox.

Year-Long Pacing Guide for Grade 7

Week	*Ready® Common Core Instruction* Lesson	Days	Minutes per Day	Language Handbook Lesson(s) (allow 20 minutes per lesson)
1	Assessment 1	3	60	
2	Lesson 1: Analyzing the Development of Central Ideas	5	30–45	11
3	Lesson 2: Summarizing Informational Texts	5	30–45	12
4	Lesson 3: Citing Evidence to Make Inferences	5	30–45	13
5	Lesson 4: Analyzing Interactions in a Text	5	30–45	14
	Unit 1 Interim Assessment	1	30–45	
6	Lesson 5: Citing Evidence to Support Inferences	5	30–45	–
7	Lesson 6: Analyzing the Interaction of Story Elements	5	30–45	–
8	Lesson 7: Determining Theme	5	30–45	9
9	Lesson 8: Summarizing Literary Texts	5	30–45	–
	Unit 2 Interim Assessment	1	30–45	
10	Lesson 9: Analyzing Word Meanings	5	30–45	15
11	Lesson 10: Analyzing Text Structure	5	30–45	16
12	Lesson 11: Determining Point of View	5	30–45	17
	Unit 3 Interim Assessment	1	30–45	
13	Assessment 2	3	60	
14	Lesson 12: Determining Word Meanings	5	30–45	1
15	Lesson 13: Analyzing Rhyme and Repetition	5	30–45	2
16	Lesson 14: Analyzing the Structure of a Poem	5	30–45	3
17	Lesson 15: Analyzing the Structure of Drama	5	30–45	4
18	Lesson 16: Analyzing Point of View	5	30–45	5
	Unit 4 Interim Assessment	1	30–45	
19	Lesson 17: Evaluating an Argument	5	30–45	6
20	Lesson 18: Comparing and Contrasting Texts	5	30–45	7
	Unit 5 Interim Assessment	1	30–45	
21	Media Feature 1: Comparing Text to Other Media	5	30–45	8
22	Lesson 19: Comparing and Contrasting Genres	5	30–45	–
	Unit 6 Interim Assessment	1	30–45	
23	Media Feature 2: Comparing Media Techniques	5	30–45	10
24	Assessment 3	3	60	

Teaching with *Ready® Common Core Instruction*

Ready® Common Core Instruction was created to help students develop proficiency with the Common Core State Standards (CCSS). Each lesson uses scaffolded instruction, beginning with modeled and guided instruction, and then gradually releasing the student into fully independent practice of the skills and strategies behind the Common Core. Use in conjunction with the Teacher Toolbox, which allows you to access additional resources—see page A20 for more information.

Weekly Pacing

Year-Long Program: Use *Ready Common Core Instruction* as the foundation of a year-long English language arts program or a year-long supplement to your basal program. The Year-Long Sample Week (below) shows a model schedule for teaching one Reading lesson per week. The Year-Long Sample Week, *Ready Common Core* Language Handbook table on page A19 shows a model schedule for teaching five Language lessons per week. Use the Year-Long Pacing Guide on page A17 for a specific week-to-week schedule integrating Reading and Language instruction.

Intensive Test Preparation: Target *Ready Common Core Instruction* lessons based on *Ready Assessment* results to focus learning during test-preparation. The Intensive Test Preparation chart on page A19 models teaching two Reading lessons (lessons A and B here) per week.

Year-Long Sample Week, *Ready Common Core Instruction*

	Day 1	Day 2	Day 3	Day 4	Day 5
Core	**Part 1: Introduction** (20 minutes, includes Tap Students' Prior Knowledge from TRB)	**Part 2: Modeled Instruction** (25 minutes)	**Part 3: Guided Instruction** (45 minutes, includes Answer Analysis discussion from TRB)	**Part 4: Guided Practice** (45 minutes, includes Answer Analysis discussion and Integrating Standards activities from TRB)	**Part 5: Common Core Practice** (45 minutes)	**Part 5: Common Core Practice** Answer Analysis: discussion of test results (20 minutes, from TRB) Integrating Standards activities (25 minutes, from TRB)
Optional		Genre Focus (TRB)	Tier Two Vocabulary (TRB)	ELL Support (TRB)	Theme Connection (TRB)	Additional Activities (TRB)

Key:

👪 *Whole Class/Small Group*

👤 *Individual*

Lessons Built for the Common Core

Each grade level in *Ready® Common Core English Language Arts Instruction* provides targeted instruction on the Common Core State Standards for ELA.

Ready Instruction, covers the following strands:

- Reading Standards for Literature: Key Ideas and Details, Craft and Structure, Integration of Knowledge and Ideas

- Reading Standards for Informational Text: Key Ideas and Details, Craft and Structure, Integration of Knowledge and Ideas

The Ready Language Handbook covers the following strands within the CCSS Language Standards:

- Conventions of Standard English

- Knowledge of Language

- Vocabulary Acquisition and Use

The correlations chart beginning on page A39 provides an in-depth look at how *Ready Common Core Instruction* correlates to the CCSS. The passages and questions in *Ready Instruction* reflect the rigor and complexity required by the Common Core.

Intensive Test Preparation, *Ready Common Core Instruction*

	Day 1	Day 2	Day 3	Day 4	Day 5
In Class	*Lesson A* Introduction (15 minutes) Modeled Instruction (30 minutes)	*Lesson A* Guided Instruction (15 minutes) Guided Practice (30 minutes)	*Lesson B* Introduction (15 minutes) Modeled Instruction (30 minutes)	*Lesson B* Guided Instruction (15 minutes) Guided Practice (30 minutes)	*Lesson A* Review concepts and skills (20 minutes) *Lesson B* Review concepts and skills (20 minutes)
Homework (optional)		*Lesson A* Common Core Practice		*Lesson B* Common Core Practice	

Year-Long Sample Week, *Ready Common Core* Language Handbook

Day 1	Day 2	Day 3	Day 4	Day 5
Introduction (10–15 minutes)	**Introduction** (10–15 minutes)	**Introduction** (10–15 minutes)	**Introduction** (10–15 minutes)	**Introduction** (10–15 minutes)
Guided Practice (10–15 minutes)	**Guided Practice** (10–15 minutes)	**Guided Practice** (10–15 minutes)	**Guided Practice** (10–15 minutes)	**Guided Practice** (10–15 minutes)
Common Core Practice (10–15 minutes)	**Common Core Practice** (10–15 minutes)	**Common Core Practice** (10–15 minutes)	**Common Core Practice** (10–15 minutes)	**Common Core Practice** (10–15 minutes)

Connecting with the *Ready*® Teacher Toolbox

Designed for use with ***Ready*® *Common Core Instruction***, the Teacher Toolbox provides a host of multilevel resources teachers can use to differentiate instruction. If you purchased the Teacher Toolbox, you should have received an insert with access codes and information. Please contact Customer Service at (800)-225-0248 if you need this information. Visit *www.teacher-toolbox.com* to get started.

The Common Core builds on skills covered in the previous year's standards. Of course, many students will not have mastered those standards, and most students could use a review. ***Ready Common Core*** allows you to access lessons from previous ***Ready*** grades through the Teacher Toolbox.

How Do I Use the Teacher Toolbox?

Lessons are conveniently organized to match your print materials, making it easy to find additional resources for teaching the skills and standards associated with each lesson. All of these resources are perfect for use with any interactive whiteboard or other computer projection screen.

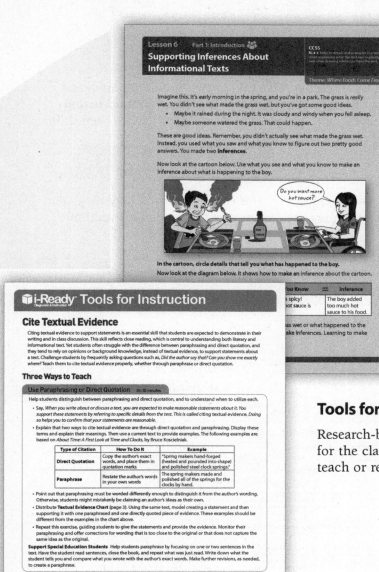

Ready® Lessons

Ready® lessons make it easy for teachers to focus on particular skills, or even reteach skills that students may not have mastered at earlier grade levels. What you get:

- Every lesson in this book is available as an individual PDF file, which you can project for whole-class and small-group use.

- Prerequisite student lesson PDFs—and the accompanying Teacher Resource Book lesson—from prior grades are available to administer as remediation.

- All three full-length **Ready Assessments** are available for easy measurement of student growth.

Tools for Instruction

Research-based, best-practice routines and activities for the classroom and small groups provide ways to teach or review standards and prerequisite skills.

Guided Interactive Tutorials

Guided interactive tutorials give teachers another engaging way to provide whole-class or small-group instruction. Lessons follow a consistent structure of explicit instruction and guided practice. Immediate corrective feedback continuously supports students.

Using *i-Ready*® Diagnostic with *Ready*® Common Core

If you have already purchased *i-Ready*® *Diagnostic*, you can use its robust reporting to monitor students' overall and domain-specific reading proficiency as they move through *Ready*® *Common Core Instruction*. Specifically, use the Student Profile report and the Instructional Grouping report to identify Next Step skills for student instruction.

Available for Grades K–8

Student Profile Report

The **Student Profile** report shows teachers students' performance levels for each strand and why they are struggling. Plus, it provides detailed recommendations and resources to support teacher-led instruction.

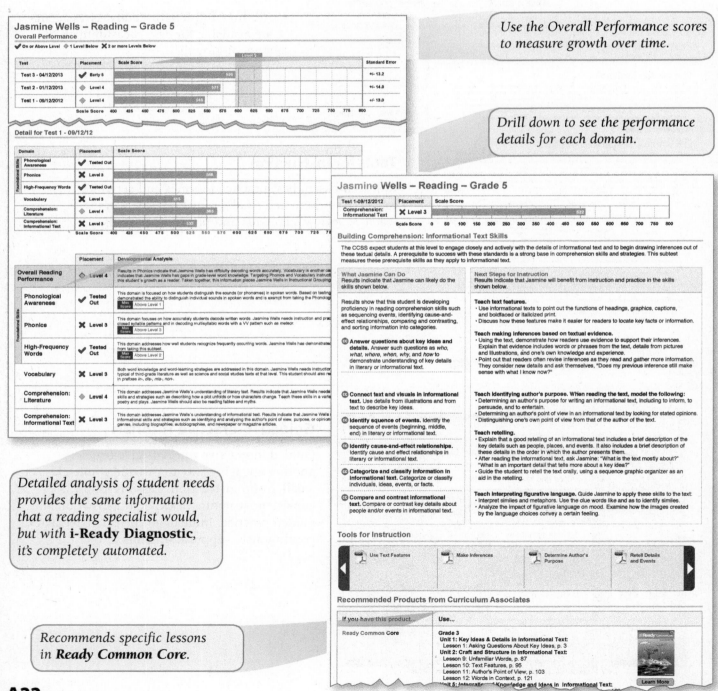

Use the Overall Performance scores to measure growth over time.

Drill down to see the performance details for each domain.

*Detailed analysis of student needs provides the same information that a reading specialist would, but with **i-Ready Diagnostic**, it's completely automated.*

*Recommends specific lessons in **Ready Common Core**.*

Instructional Grouping Profile

The **Instructional Grouping Profile** report shows teachers exactly how to group students so that students who are struggling with the same skills get the most out of small-group instruction. The report also gives effective instructional recommendations and resources for each group profile.

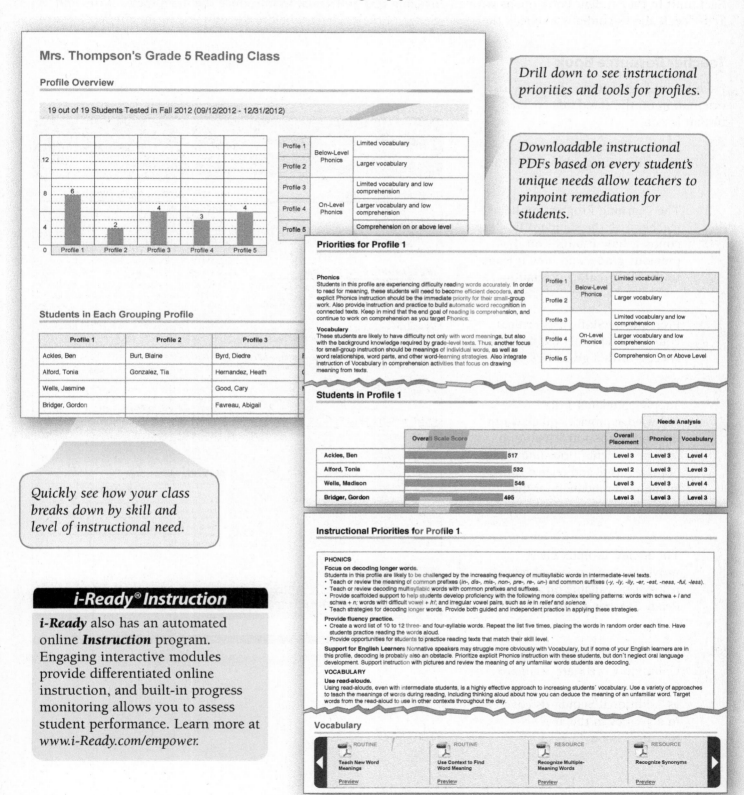

Mrs. Thompson's Grade 5 Reading Class

Profile Overview

19 out of 19 Students Tested in Fall 2012 (09/12/2012 - 12/31/2012)

Profile 1	Below-Level Phonics	Limited vocabulary
Profile 2		Larger vocabulary
Profile 3	On-Level Phonics	Limited vocabulary and low comprehension
Profile 4		Larger vocabulary and low comprehension
Profile 5		Comprehension on or above level

Students in Each Grouping Profile

Profile 1	Profile 2	Profile 3
Ackles, Ben	Burt, Blaine	Byrd, Diedre
Alford, Tonia	Gonzalez, Tia	Hernandez, Heath
Wells, Jasmine		Good, Cary
Bridger, Gordon		Favreau, Abigail

Drill down to see instructional priorities and tools for profiles.

Downloadable instructional PDFs based on every student's unique needs allow teachers to pinpoint remediation for students.

Quickly see how your class breaks down by skill and level of instructional need.

Priorities for Profile 1

Phonics
Students in this profile are experiencing difficulty reading words accurately. In order to read for meaning, these students will need to become efficient decoders, and explicit Phonics instruction should be the immediate priority for their small-group work. Also provide instruction and practice to build automatic word recognition in connected texts. Keep in mind that the end goal of reading is comprehension, and continue to work on comprehension as you target Phonics.

Vocabulary
These students are likely to have difficulty not only with word meanings, but also with the background knowledge required by grade-level texts. Thus, another focus for small-group instruction should be meanings of individual words, as well as word relationships, word parts, and other word-learning strategies. Also integrate instruction of Vocabulary in comprehension activities that focus on drawing meaning from texts.

Profile 1	Below-Level Phonics	Limited vocabulary
Profile 2		Larger vocabulary
Profile 3	On-Level Phonics	Limited vocabulary and low comprehension
Profile 4		Larger vocabulary and low comprehension
Profile 5		Comprehension On or Above Level

Students in Profile 1

	Overall Scale Score	Overall Placement	Needs Analysis Phonics	Needs Analysis Vocabulary
Ackles, Ben	517	Level 3	Level 3	Level 4
Alford, Tonia	532	Level 2	Level 3	Level 3
Wells, Madison	546	Level 3	Level 3	Level 4
Bridger, Gordon	495	Level 3	Level 3	Level 3

Instructional Priorities for Profile 1

PHONICS
Focus on decoding longer words.
Students in this profile are likely to be challenged by the increasing frequency of multisyllabic words in intermediate-level texts.
- Teach or review the meaning of common prefixes (*in-, dis-, mis-, non-, pre-, re-, un-*) and common suffixes (*-y, -ly, -ily, -er, -est, -ness, -ful, -less*).
- Teach or review decoding multisyllabic words with common prefixes and suffixes.
- Provide scaffolded support to help students develop proficiency with the following more complex spelling patterns: words with schwa + *l* and schwa + *n*; words with difficult vowel + *r/r/*; and irregular vowel pairs, such as *ie* in *relief* and *science*.
- Teach strategies for decoding longer words. Provide both guided and independent practice in applying these strategies.

Provide fluency practice.
- Create a word list of 10 to 12 three- and four-syllable words. Repeat the list five times, placing the words in random order each time. Have students practice reading the words aloud.
- Provide opportunities for students to practice reading texts that match their skill level.

Support for English Learners Nonnative speakers may struggle more obviously with Vocabulary, but if some of your English learners are in this profile, decoding is probably also an obstacle. Prioritize explicit Phonics instruction with these students, but don't neglect oral language development. Support instruction with pictures and review the meaning of any unfamiliar words students are decoding.

VOCABULARY
Use read-alouds.
Using read-alouds, even with intermediate students, is a highly effective approach to increasing students' vocabulary. Use a variety of approaches to teach the meanings of words during reading, including thinking aloud about how you can deduce the meaning of an unfamiliar word. Target words from the read-aloud to use in other contexts throughout the day.

Vocabulary

ROUTINE	ROUTINE	RESOURCE	RESOURCE
Teach New Word Meanings	Use Context to Find Word Meaning	Recognize Multiple-Meaning Words	Recognize Synonyms
Preview	Preview	Preview	Preview

i-Ready® Instruction

i-Ready also has an automated online **Instruction** program. Engaging interactive modules provide differentiated online instruction, and built-in progress monitoring allows you to assess student performance. Learn more at *www.i-Ready.com/empower.*

Features of *Ready® Common Core Instruction*

This section guides teachers to the key features of the Student Book and Teacher Resource Book. Numbered boxes call out and describe the key features. Use this section to familiarize yourself with the overall structure of a *Ready® Common Core ELA Instruction* lesson.

Each unit in the Student Book opens with an engaging text and visual to introduce the main focus of the unit. A Self-Check allows students to check their knowledge of each standard before the unit and again after each lesson.

Teacher Resource Book

Each lesson begins with a full page of orientation on the standards covered in that lesson.

1 Lesson Objectives identifies specific skills goals for students.

2 The Learning Progression helps teachers see the standard in context, how it builds on the previous grade, and how it leads to the next year's expectations.

3 Prerequisite Skills lists critical concepts and skills required for success with a given lesson.

4 Tapping Students' Prior Knowledge provides quick warm-ups and discussion activities to activate students' prior knowledge of prerequisite and related skills, laying the foundation for the featured standard.

5 The *Ready* Toolbox chart provides an overview of related resources available online in the *Ready* Teacher Toolbox.

6 CCSS Focus identifies the Common Core State Standard featured in the lesson, as well as Additional Standards covered in activities in the Teacher Resource Book.

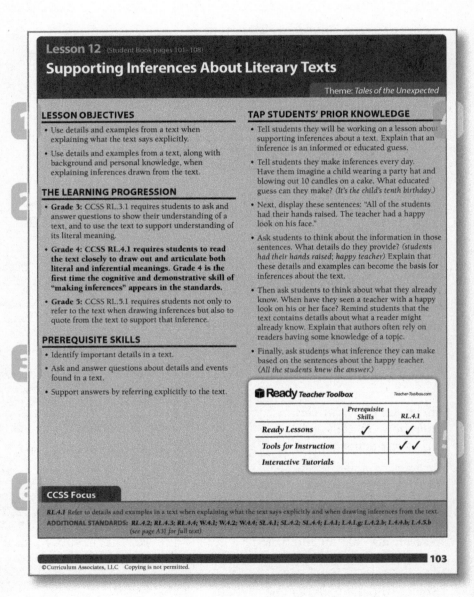

Lesson 12 (Student Book pages 101–108)

Supporting Inferences About Literary Texts

Theme: *Tales of the Unexpected*

LESSON OBJECTIVES

- Use details and examples from a text when explaining what the text says explicitly.
- Use details and examples from a text, along with background and personal knowledge, when explaining inferences drawn from the text.

THE LEARNING PROGRESSION

- **Grade 3:** CCSS RL.3.1 requires students to ask and answer questions to show their understanding of a text, and to use the text to support understanding of its literal meaning.
- **Grade 4: CCSS RL.4.1 requires students to read the text closely to draw out and articulate both literal and inferential meanings. Grade 4 is the first time the cognitive and demonstrative skill of "making inferences" appears in the standards.**
- **Grade 5:** CCSS RL.5.1 requires students not only to refer to the text when drawing inferences but also to quote from the text to support that inference.

PREREQUISITE SKILLS

- Identify important details in a text.
- Ask and answer questions about details and events found in a text.
- Support answers by referring explicitly to the text.

TAP STUDENTS' PRIOR KNOWLEDGE

- Tell students they will be working on a lesson about supporting inferences about a text. Explain that an inference is an informed or educated guess.
- Tell students they make inferences every day. Have them imagine a child wearing a party hat and blowing out 10 candles on a cake. What educated guess can they make? (*It's the child's tenth birthday.*)
- Next, display these sentences: "All of the students had their hands raised. The teacher had a happy look on his face."
- Ask students to think about the information in those sentences. What details do they provide? (*students had their hands raised; happy teacher*) Explain that these details and examples can become the basis for inferences about the text.
- Then ask students to think about what they already know. When have they seen a teacher with a happy look on his or her face? Remind students that the text contains details about what a reader might already know. Explain that authors often rely on readers having some knowledge of a topic.
- Finally, ask students what inference they can make based on the sentences about the happy teacher. (*All the students knew the answer.*)

Ready *Teacher Toolbox*		Teacher-Toolbox.com
	Prerequisite Skills	RL.4.1
Ready Lessons	✓	✓
Tools for Instruction		✓ ✓
Interactive Tutorials		

CCSS Focus

RL.4.1 Refer to details and examples in a text when explaining what the text says explicitly and when drawing inferences from the text.
ADDITIONAL STANDARDS: RL.4.2; RL.4.3; RL.4.4; W.4.1; W.4.2; W.4.4; SL.4.1; SL.4.2; SL.4.4; L.4.1; L.4.1.g; L.4.2.b; L.4.4.b; L.4.5.b
(*see page A31 for full text*)

103

©Curriculum Associates, LLC   Copying is not permitted.

Introduction

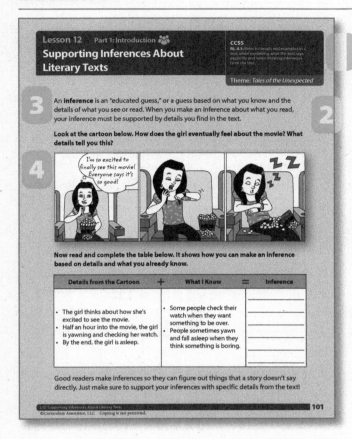

The Introduction builds student confidence and motivation by gradually introducing students to the lesson standard. Most pages begin by having students explore how they apply the strategy in non-text based ways. This page is meant to be teacher directed.

Student Book

1 The CCSS covered in the lesson are given, and the theme for the lesson is identified.

2 This page gives a student-friendly overview of the skills, concepts, strategies, and vocabulary of the covered standard(s).

3 Key vocabulary appears in boldface.

4 Visual aids—such as cartoons, tables, charts, and graphic organizers—engage struggling readers and visual learners.

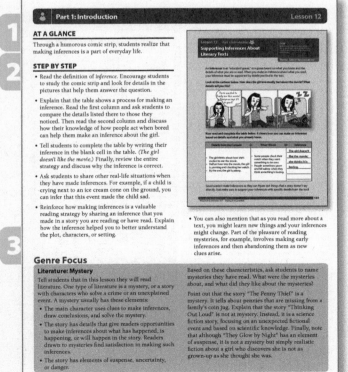

Teacher Resource Book

1 At a Glance provides a brief overview of what students do in each lesson part.

2 Step by Step provides an explicit walk-through of the steps for guiding students through each lesson part.

3 Genre Focus provides a student-friendly introduction to one of the genres featured in the lesson.

Modeled Instruction

The teacher models how a good reader goes about the process of answering a question. The teacher begins by reading the passage aloud, and then, using the think-aloud support in the Teacher Resource Book, guides students through answering the question. Depending on the support your students need, you may choose to do this page together with the class or first have students independently complete the activity, and then review it together.

Student Book

1 The genre for each passage is identified by the Genre tab.

2 Students begin by applying the strategy to a short piece of text.

3 Clearly stated steps walk students through the thought process for responding to the question.

Teacher Resource Book

1 A detailed Think Aloud models the thought process for answering the question.

2 The ELL Support feature targets language concepts that students who are learning English may need reinforcement on, including compound words, prefixes, suffixes, contractions, homophones, multiple-meaning words, and regular and irregular verbs.

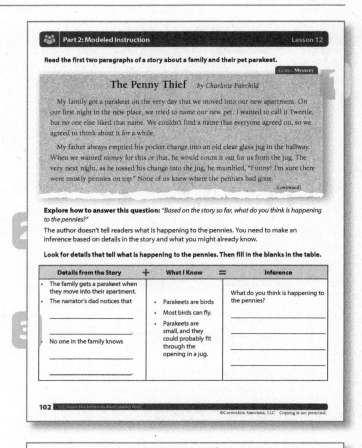

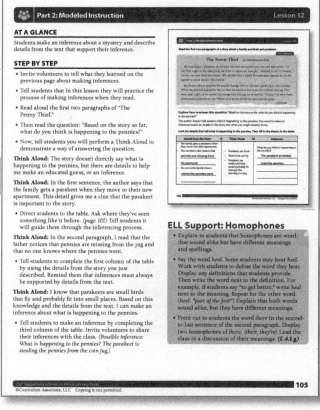

A26

Guided Instruction

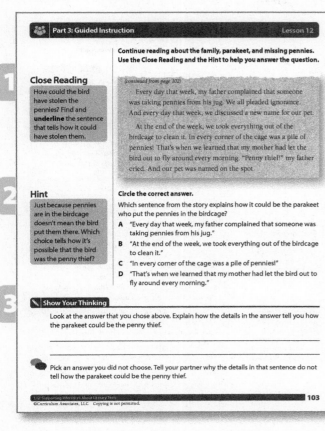

Students work through a sample question. The Close Reading and Hint provide strong guidance. After students respond to the question independently and respond to the Show Your Thinking prompt, partners discuss the reasons for their answers. Finally, the teacher discusses the steps leading to the correct answer, and discusses why the other choices are not correct.

Student Book

1. Close Reading encourages students to interact with the text, often directing them to mark up the text by underlining, circling, or note-taking.

2. The Hint provides clues to help students respond to a specific question.

3. Show Your Thinking challenges students to explain why the answer they chose is correct. A thoughtful open-ended question is posed for discussion.

Teacher Resource Book

1. Answer Analysis explains why an answer is correct and identifies the types of errors students commonly make in choosing incorrect answer choices.

2. Error Alert addresses common errors or misconceptions that lead students to an incorrect answer.

3. Tier Two Vocabulary gives guidance on helping students use text-based strategies to understand a given word. Tier Two (or general academic) words are more common in complex texts than in speech. Since they occur in many types of reading, a knowledge of Tier Two words is a powerful aid to comprehension.

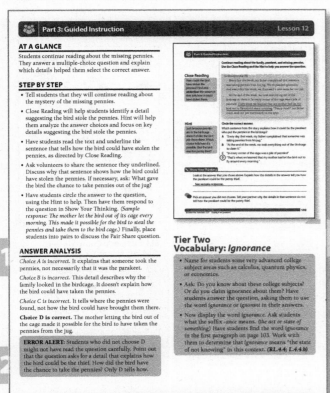

Guided Practice

The Study Buddy, Close Reading, and Hints provide guidance as students read a longer passage and answer several questions. After an initial reading with students, the teacher checks literal comprehension by asking the questions in the Teacher Resource Book. After the second reading, students and teacher discuss the Study Buddy and Close Reading activities, then students use the Hints to answer the questions.

Student Book

1 Students apply the targeted reading strategy to a longer piece of text.

2 The Study Buddy is the student's reading coach, modeling strategies proficient readers use to access text.

3 Close Reading activities continue to guide students.

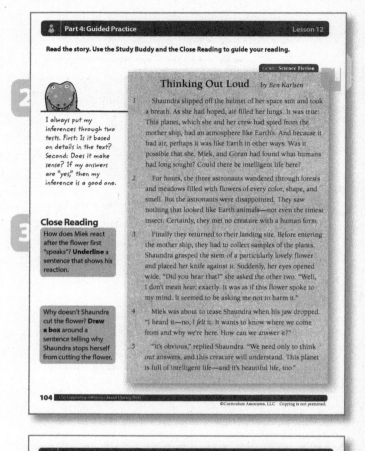

Teacher Resource Book

1 Written by experienced teachers, Tips provide thoughtful and practical suggestions on how to deepen students' understanding and appreciation of the target strategy.

2 ELL Support continues to appear at point of use.

3 Multi-paragraph, full-page passages are read and then reread, enforcing the good habits of close reading.

Teaching Tip: Read the Study Buddy prompt together with students and discuss how it relates to the text.

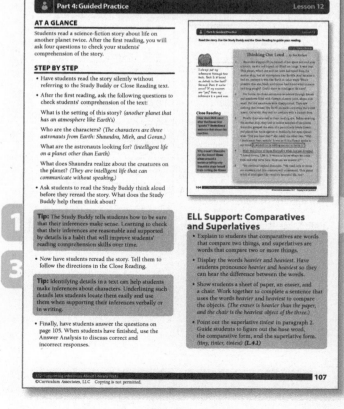

A28

Guided Practice

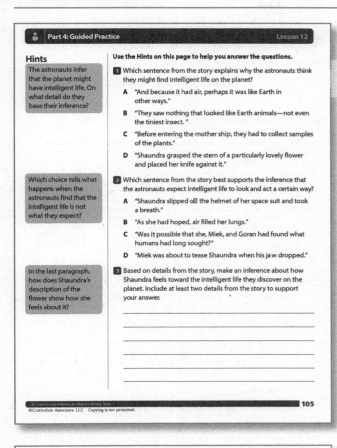

Student Book

1 Students answer a series of multiple-choice and/or short-response questions on the targeted skill.

2 Clues in the Hints draw students back to the text to find text-based evidence.

Teaching Tip: As you review the answers to each question in the Guided Practice, ask students how the Close Reading activity helps them answer the question. Probe how and why the parts of the text they marked up are evidence that they can cite in their answer.

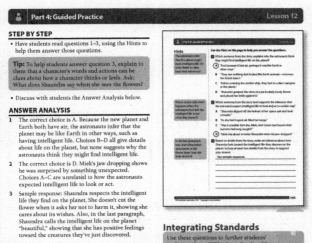

Teacher Resource Book

1 The Tip helps teachers extend one or more of the Hints.

2 Answer Analysis provides detailed discussion of why each answer choice is correct or incorrect, as well as a sample answer for the open-ended questions.

3 Reteaching reinforces and deepens students' learning by using a graphic organizer to visually depict and verify the correct answer to one of the questions.

4 Integrating Standards helps teachers integrate standard instruction by providing specific questions and short activities that apply standards in addition to the targeted one. Standard codes are provided at point of use.

Common Core Practice

Scaffolding is removed. Students work independently to read a longer passage and answer a series of multiple-choice and short-response questions. Students mark their answers directly in the Student Book by filling in bubbles in an Answer Form. After students have completed the questions, they record the number of questions they answered correctly in the scoring box on the right side of the Answer Form. The teacher can use the Answer Analysis to review correct and incorrect answers, encouraging students to discuss the thought process they used in their responses.

Student Book

1 Students apply the targeted strategy to a longer and more difficult text.

> **Teaching Tip:** To encourage students to transfer the skills they've learned, have students ask themselves the following four questions, formulated by reading expert Nancy Boyles, as they reflect on the Common Core Practice passage. (Boyles, 2012/13)
>
> • What is the author telling me here?
>
> • Are there any hard or important words?
>
> • What does the author want me to understand?
>
> • How does the author play with language to add to meaning?

Teacher Resource Book

1 The Answer Form on the facsimile of the Student Book pages has the bubbles filled in for easy scoring.

2 Theme Connection provides short questions and activities that help students make connections among the lesson passages and build content knowledge about the lesson theme.

3 Answer Analysis provides detailed discussion of why each answer choice is correct or incorrect, as well as a sample answer for the open-ended questions.

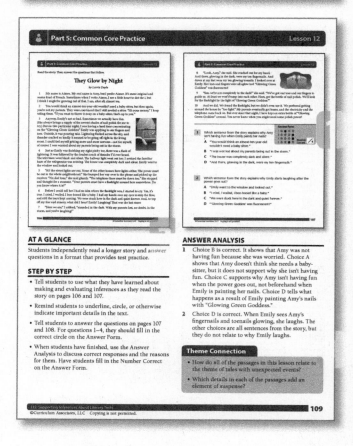

Common Core Practice

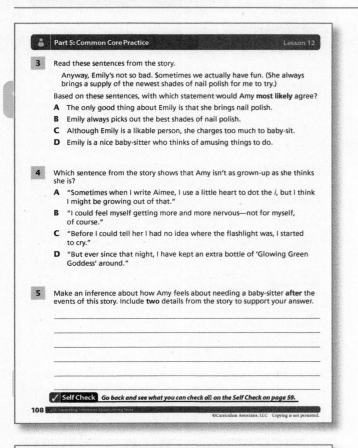

Student Book

1 Students answer multiple-choice and open-ended questions on the Common Core Practice passage.

2 Students are reminded to update their Self Check, located at the beginning of every unit, to reflect the learning accomplished in the lesson.

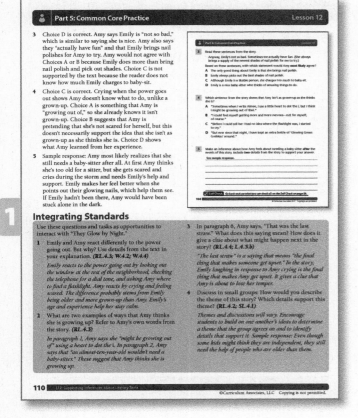

Teacher Resource Book

1 Integrating Standards helps teachers integrate all ELA standards instruction, including appropriate Language, Speaking & Listening, and Writing standards by providing specific questions and short activities that apply to the Common Core Practice passage. Standard codes are provided at point of use.

Additional Activities

Additional Activities provides short activities that allow you to expand on the passages in the lesson with meaningful standards-based Writing, Language, and Speaking & Listening activities. Standards codes are identified at point of use next to each activity, allowing you to easily integrate standards instruction.

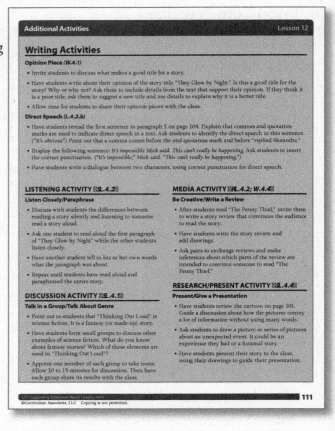

Interim Assessments

Interim Assessments are given at the end of each unit to assess students' understanding of the unit standards and to measure progress.

- Questions include both multiple-choice and short-response items that assess all of the unit's standards.

- A Performance Task—Extended Response asks students to write a longer essay about some aspect of the passage, citing evidence from the text to support their response. This item reflects how the testing consortia apply extended-response essays as a part of their performance-based events.

- In the Teacher Resource Book, correct answers are indicated on the Answer Form. Correct and incorrect answers are fully explained in Answer Analysis.

- Rubrics for the short-response items and Performance Task guide teachers in assigning a score to these items. Sample Responses provide examples of what a top-scoring response should include.

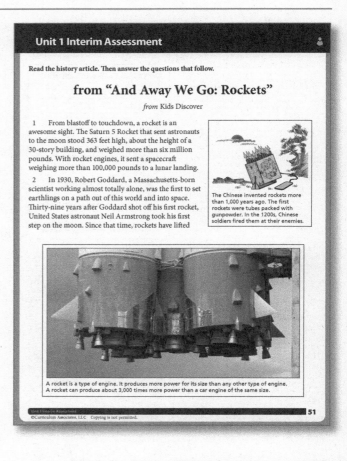

Features of the *Ready® Common Core* Language Handbook

The **Ready Common Core** Language Handbook was created to help students develop proficiency with the Common Core State Standards for Language. Each lesson uses scaffolded instruction, beginning with an introduction and guided practice and then moving students into fully independent practice of the skills and strategies behind the Common Core. This section shows the key features of the Student Book and Teacher Guide.

Student Book

Introduction

The Introduction builds student confidence and motivation by introducing students to the lesson standard. This part of the lesson is meant to be teacher directed.

1 The CCSS covered in the lesson are given.

2 This section gives a student-friendly overview of the skills, concepts, strategies, and vocabulary of the covered standard(s).

3 Key vocabulary appears in boldface.

4 Visual aids, such as tables and charts, engage struggling readers and visual learners.

Guided Practice

The Guided Practice activity allows students to apply what they have learned in the Introduction. Students may work with partners in this part of the lesson.

5 The direction lines clearly identify how to complete the activity.

6 The Hint provides guidance to help students complete the activity.

7 Students apply the targeted language concept as they respond to a variety of activities, such as fill in the blanks, circling, and sentence completion.

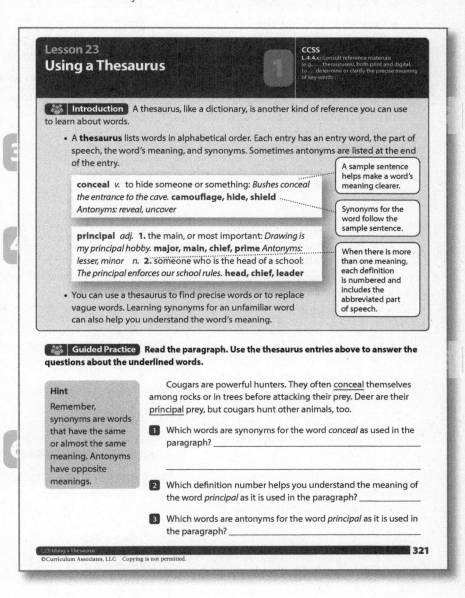

Common Core Practice

In the Common Core Practice section the scaffolding is removed. Students work independently.

8 Students answer multiple-choice questions related to the targeted standard. One lesson has short-response items.

9 Students mark their answers directly in the Student Book by filling in bubbles in an Answer Form. For short-response items, students write on writing lines.

10 Students record the number of questions they answered correctly in the scoring box. The lesson with short-response items has no scoring box.

Student Book

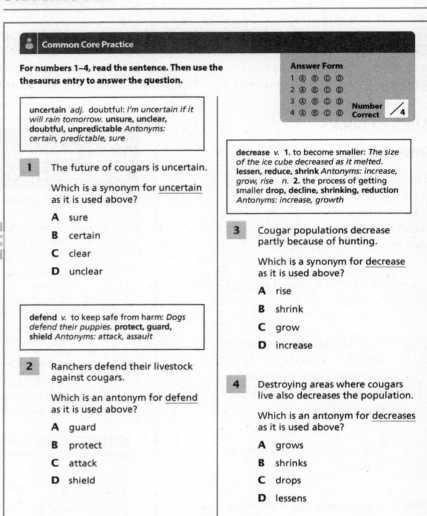

Common Core Practice

For numbers 1–4, read the sentence. Then use the thesaurus entry to answer the question.

Answer Form
1 Ⓐ Ⓑ Ⓒ Ⓓ
2 Ⓐ Ⓑ Ⓒ Ⓓ
3 Ⓐ Ⓑ Ⓒ Ⓓ **Number Correct** /4
4 Ⓐ Ⓑ Ⓒ Ⓓ

uncertain *adj.* doubtful: *I'm uncertain if it will rain tomorrow.* **unsure, unclear, doubtful, unpredictable** *Antonyms: certain, predictable, sure*

1 The future of cougars is uncertain.

Which is a synonym for <u>uncertain</u> as it is used above?

A sure
B certain
C clear
D unclear

defend *v.* to keep safe from harm: *Dogs defend their puppies.* **protect, guard, shield** *Antonyms: attack, assault*

2 Ranchers defend their livestock against cougars.

Which is an antonym for <u>defend</u> as it is used above?

A guard
B protect
C attack
D shield

decrease *v.* **1.** to become smaller: *The size of the ice cube decreased as it melted.* **lessen, reduce, shrink** *Antonyms: increase, grow, rise* *n.* **2.** the process of getting smaller **drop, decline, shrinking, reduction** *Antonyms: increase, growth*

3 Cougar populations decrease partly because of hunting.

Which is a synonym for <u>decrease</u> as it is used above?

A rise
B shrink
C grow
D increase

4 Destroying areas where cougars live also decreases the population.

Which is an antonym for <u>decreases</u> as it is used above?

A grows
B shrinks
C drops
D lessens

322 L23: Using a Thesaurus

A34

Supporting Research

Overview

Ready® Common Core Instruction is founded on research from a variety of federal initiatives, national literacy organizations, and literacy experts. As a result, this program may be used in support of several instructional models.

Ready® Uses . . .	Examples	Research Says . . .
Instructional Strategies		
Close Reading Close reading refers to the slow, deliberate reading of short pieces of text, focusing solely on the text itself, to achieve a deep understanding.	**SB:** Study Buddy and Close Reading features help students focus on the most important elements of the text.	"The Common Core State Standards place a high priority on the close, sustained reading of complex text. . . . Such reading focuses on what lies within the four corners of the text." (Coleman & Pimentel, Revised Publishers' Criteria, 2012, p. 4)
Multiple Readings Through reading a text more than once, students are able to access different levels of its meaning.	**TRB:** In Guided Practice, students read the text first, with follow-up discussion to confirm literal understanding before delving into more complex questions.	"[Close reading] often requires compact, short, self-contained texts that students can read and re-read deliberately and slowly to probe and ponder the meanings of individual words, the order in which sentences unfold, and the development of ideas over the course of the text." (Coleman & Pimentel, Revised Publishers' Criteria, 2012, p. 4)
Text-Dependent Questions Questions that are text-dependent can be answered only by information contained in the text itself, not personal opinion or background knowledge.	**SB:** Questions in each section of the *Ready* lesson are text-dependent. Students are required to support answers with evidence from the text.	"When examining a complex text in depth, tasks should require careful scrutiny of the text and specific references to evidence from the text itself to support responses." (Coleman & Pimentel, Revised Publishers' Criteria, 2012, p. 6)
Citing Textual Evidence The Common Core State Standards require students to provide evidence directly from the text to support their inferences about a text.	**SB:** Questions in the *Ready* lessons and Interim Assessments specifically require students to cite evidence from the text to support their answers.	"Students cite specific evidence when offering an oral or written interpretation of a text. They use relevant evidence when supporting their own points in writing and speaking..." (Common Core State Standards, 2010, p. 7)
Building Content Knowledge Reading multiple texts on a single topic builds knowledge and an increasingly deeper understanding of the topic.	**SB:** Passages in each lesson focus on a single topic or theme. Informational topics align with grade-level science and social studies curricula as well as high-interest grade level topics. **TRB:** The Theme Connection feature helps students make connections among lesson passages. Additional Activities allow students to expand their understanding of the lesson topic.	"Students establish a base of knowledge across a wide range of subject matter by engaging with works of quality and substance." (Common Core State Standards, 2012, p. 7)

Ready® Uses . . .	Examples	Research Says . . .
Instructional Strategies (continued)		
Direct Instruction Scripted lesson plans include explicit step-by-step instruction of reading and learning strategies and lesson objectives.	**SB:** The Introduction gives an overview of the lesson content. Step-by-step directions for answering questions are provided in Modeled Instruction. **TRB:** In the Step-by-Step section, explicit instructions are provided for the teacher.	"The research demonstrates that the types of questions, the detailed step-by-step breakdowns, and the extensive practice with a range of examples . . . will significantly benefit students' comprehension." (Gersten & Carnine, 1986, p. 72)
Scaffolded Instruction Scaffolded instruction is the gradual withdrawal of support through modeled, guided, and independent instruction.	**SB:** Graphic organizers, Study Buddy, and Close Reading provide support in earlier parts of the lesson, allowing students to achieve independence by the Common Core Practice section. **TRB:** The gradual-release model of Modeled/Guided Instruction and Guided Practice provides appropriate support that is gradually withdrawn as students gain mastery of the standard.	"Scaffolded instruction optimizes student learning by providing a supportive environment while facilitating student independence." (Larkin, 2002)
Prior Knowledge Prior knowledge activities activate knowledge from previous experiences.	**TRB:** Tap Prior Knowledge at the beginning of each lesson engages students in a discussion to connect the new skill to what they already know.	"Research clearly emphasizes that for learning to occur, new information must be integrated with what the learner already knows." (Rumelhart, 1980)
An Integrated Model of Literacy The processes of communication (reading, writing, listening, and speaking) are closely connected, a fact which should be reflected in literacy instruction.	**TRB:** Integrating Standards provides opportunities to apply Common Core State Standards beyond the target one. Additional Activities expand the lesson to include activities in the areas of Writing, Language, Listening & Speaking, Research, and Media.	"While the Standards delineate specific expectations in reading, writing, speaking, listening, and language, each standard need not be a separate focus for instruction. Often, several standards can be addressed by a single, rich task." (Common Core State Standards, 2010, p. 5)
Instructional Features		
Complex Text A major emphasis of the Common Core State Standards is for students to encounter appropriately complex texts at each grade level in order to develop the skills and conceptual knowledge they need for success in school and life.	**SB:** All passages in *Ready* conform to the leveling criteria outlined by the CCSS. (See page A11 of this document for more information on these criteria.)	"To grow, our students must read lots, and more specifically, they must read lots of 'complex' texts—texts that offer them new language, new knowledge, and new modes of thought." (Adams, 2009, p. 182)

Ready® Uses . . .	Examples	Research Says . . .
Instructional Features (continued)		
Balance of Informational and Literary Text; Emphasis on Literary Nonfiction at Grades 6–8 The Common Core State Standards align with the requirements of the National Assessment of Educational Progress (NAEP) in calling for a greater emphasis on informational text.	**SB:** Six units in each grade alternate Literary and Informational text. Nonfiction units at grades 6–8 include essays, speeches, opinion pieces, biographies, journalism, and other examples of literary nonfiction. **TRB:** The Genre Focus feature introduces the characteristics of each genre.	"Most of the required reading in college and workforce training programs is informational in structure and challenging in content . . . . the Standards follow NAEP's lead in balancing the reading of literature with the reading of informational texts. . . ." (Common Core State Standards, 2010, pp. 4–5. See also National Assessment Governing Board, 2008)
Answer Explanations for Students As a part of scaffolded instruction, students receive immediate feedback on their answer choices and the reasoning behind correct and incorrect answers.	**TRB:** In the Guided Instruction, Guided Practice, and Common Core Practice sections of each lesson, as well as in the Interim Assessments, answer explanations are given for each question.	Research (Pashler et al. 2007) has shown that when students receive direct instruction about the reasons why an answer choice is correct or incorrect, they demonstrate long-term retention and understanding of newly learned content.
ELL Support Some teaching strategies that have been proven to be effective for English learners include scaffolded instruction, use of graphic organizers, and modeling of language by teachers and peers.	**SB:** Features such as graphic organizers, Close Reading, Study Buddy, Hints, and Pair/Share partner discussions support English learners throughout the lesson. **TRB:** ELL Support boxes provide linguistic instruction at appropriate points.	"Graphic organizers facilitate ELLs' comprehension through visual illustrations of key terms, vocabulary, ideas, and the relationship among them." (Sigueza, 2005) Researchers state that one of the best practices for teaching ELL students is to model standard pronunciation and grammar. (Mohr & Mohr, 2007)
General Academic Vocabulary (Tier Two) General academic, or Tier Two, words are words a reader encounters in rich, complex texts of all types.	**TRB:** Tier Two Vocabulary boxes at point of use support the teacher in helping students use text-based strategies to figure out the meanings of challenging words.	"Tier Two words are frequently encountered in complex written texts and are particularly powerful because of their wide applicability to many sorts of reading. Teachers thus need to be alert to the presence of Tier Two words and determine which ones need careful attention." (Common Core State Standards, Appendix A, 2010, p. 33. The three-tier model of vocabulary is based on the work of Beck, McKeown, & Kucan, 2002, 2008)
Graphic Organizers Graphic organizers are visual representations of a text's organization of ideas and concepts.	**SB:** In the introduction, a graphic organizer is presented to represent the concepts and ideas of the lesson.	"Graphic organizers can provide students with tools they can use to examine and show relationships in a text." (Adler, 2004)

A37

References

Adams, M. J. (2009). The challenge of advanced texts: The interdependence of reading and learning. In Hiebert, E. H. (ed.), *Reading more, reading better: Are American students reading enough of the right stuff?* (pp. 183–189). New York, NY: Guilford.

Adler, C. R. (2004). Seven strategies to teach students text comprehension. Accessed at: *http://www.readingrockets.org/article/3479.*

Beck, I. L., McKeown, M. G., & Kucan, L. (2002). *Bringing words to life: Robust vocabulary instruction.* New York, NY: Guilford.

Beck, I. L., McKeown, M. G., & Kucan, L. (2008). *Creating robust vocabulary: Frequently asked questions and extended examples.* New York, NY: Guilford.

Boyles, N. (2012/2013). Closing in on close reading. *Educational Leadership, 70*(4), 36–41.

Coleman, D., & Pimentel, S. (2012). *Revised Publishers' Criteria for the Common Core State Standards in English Language Arts and Literacy, Grades 3–12.* Accessed at: *http://www.corestandards.org/resources.*

Fisher, D., Frey, N., & Lapp, D. (2012). *Text complexity: Raising rigor in reading.* Washington, DC: International Reading Association.

Gersten, R., & Carnine, D. (1986). Direct instruction in reading comprehension. *Educational Leadership, 43*(7), 70–79.

Hess, K. K., Carlock, D., Jones, B., & Walkup, J. R. (2009). *What exactly do "fewer, clearer, and higher standards" really look like in the classroom? Using a cognitive rigor matrix to analyze curriculum, plan lessons, and implement assessments.* Accessed at: *http://www.nciea.org/cgi-bin/pubspage.cgi?sortby=pub_date.*

Larkin, M. (2002). *Using scaffolded instruction to optimize learning.* ERIC Digest ED474301 2002-12-00. Retrieved from *www.eric.ed.gov.*

Mohr, K., & Mohr, E. (2007). *Extending English language learners' classroom interactions using the response protocol.* Accessed at: *http://www.readingrockets.org/article/26871.*

National Assessment Governing Board. (2008). *Reading framework for the 2009 National Assessment of Educational Progress.* Washington, D.C.: U.S. Government Printing Office.

National Governors Association Center for Best Practices and Council of Chief State School Officers. (2010). *Common Core State Standards for English Language Arts and Literacy in History/Social Studies, Science, and Technical Subjects.* Accessed at: *http://www.corestandards.org/the-standards.*

————. *English Language Arts Appendix A.* Accessed at: *http://www.corestandards.org/the-standards.*

Partnership for Assessment of Readiness for College and Careers. (2011). *PARCC model content frameworks: English language arts/literacy grades 3–11.* Accessed at: *http://www.parcconline.org/parcc-model-content-frameworks.*

Pashler, H., Bain, P., Bottge, B., Graesser, A., Koedinger, K., McDaniel, M., & Metcalfe, J. (2007). *Organizing instruction and study to improve student learning* (NCER 2007–2004). Washington, D.C.: National Center for Education Research, Institute of Education Sciences, U.S. Department of Education. Retrieved from *http://ncer.ed.gov.*

Rumelhart, D. E. (1980). Schemata: the building blocks of cognition. In Spiro, R. J., Bruce, B. C., & Brewer Erlbaum, W. F. (eds.), *Theoretical issues in reading comprehension* (pp. 33–58).

Sigueza, T. (2005). Graphic organizers. *Colorín Colorado!* Accessed at: *http://www.colorincolorado.org/article/13354.*

Smarter Balanced Assessment Consortium. (2012). *General Item Specifications.* Accessed at: *http://www.smarterbalanced.org/wordpress/wp-content/uploads/2012/05/TaskItemSpecifications/ItemSpecifications/GeneralItemSpecifications.pdf.*

Correlation Charts

Common Core State Standards Coverage by *Ready® Instruction*

The chart below correlates each Common Core State Standard to each **Ready® Common Core Instruction** lesson that offers comprehensive instruction on that standard. Use this chart to determine which lessons your students should complete based on their mastery of each standard.

Common Core State Standards for Grade 7—Reading Standards	*Ready Common Core* Student Lesson(s)	Additional Coverage in Teacher Resource Book Lesson(s)
Reading Standards for Literature		
Key Ideas and Details		
RL.7.1 Cite several pieces of textual evidence to support analysis of what the text says explicitly as well as inferences drawn from the text.	5	6–8, 12–16, 19
RL.7.2 Determine a theme or central idea of a text and analyze its development over the course of the text; provide an objective summary of the text.	7, 8	5, 6, 12–16, 19
RL.7.3 Analyze how particular elements of a story or drama interact (e.g., how setting shapes the characters or plot).	6	5, 7, 8, 15, 16, 19
Craft and Structure		
RL.7.4 Determine the meaning of words and phrases as they are used in a text, including figurative and connotative meanings; analyze the impact of rhymes and other repetitions of sounds (e.g., alliteration) on a specific verse or stanza of a poem or section of a story or drama.	12, 13	5–8, 14–16, 19
RL.7.5 Analyze how a drama's or poem's form or structure (e.g., soliloquy, sonnet) contributes to its meaning.	14, 15	12, 13, 16
RL.7.6 Analyze how an author develops and contrasts the points of view of different characters or narrators in a text.	16	5, 8, 12, 13
Integration of Knowledge and Ideas		
RL.7.7 Compare and contrast a written story, drama, or poem to its audio, filmed, staged, or multimedia version, analyzing the effects of techniques unique to each medium (e.g., lighting, sound, color, or camera focus and angles in a film).	Media Feature 2	5, 7, 8, 12–16, 19
RL.7.9 Compare and contrast a fictional portrayal of a time, place, or character and a historical account of the same period as a means of understanding how authors of fiction use or alter history.	19	15
Range of Reading and Level of Text Complexity		
RL.7.10 By the end of the year, read and comprehend literature, including stories, dramas, and poems, in the grades 6–8 text complexity band proficiently, with scaffolding as needed at the high end of the range.	All Lessons	
Reading Standards for Informational Text		
Key Ideas and Details		
RI.7.1 Cite several pieces of textual evidence to support analysis of what the text says explicitly as well as inferences drawn from the text.	3	1, 2, 4, 9–11, 17, 18
RI.7.2 Determine two or more central ideas in a text and analyze their development over the course of the text; provide an objective summary of the text.	1, 2	3, 4, 9–11, 17
RI.7.3 Analyze the interactions between individuals, events, and ideas in a text (e.g., how ideas influence individuals or events, or how individuals influence ideas or events).	4	1–3, 9, 11, 18

Common Core State Standards © 2010. National Governors Association Center for Best Practices and Council of Chief State School Officers. All rights reserved.

Common Core State Standards for Grade 7—Reading Standards	Ready Common Core Student Lesson(s)	Additional Coverage in Teacher Resource Book Lesson(s)
Reading Standards for Informational Text (continued)		
Craft and Structure		
RI.7.4 Determine the meaning of words and phrases as they are used in a text, including figurative, connotative, and technical meanings; analyze the impact of a specific word choice on meaning and tone.	9	1–4, 10, 11, 17, 18
RI.7.5 Analyze the structure an author uses to organize a text, including how the major sections contribute to the whole and to the development of the ideas.	10	1, 2, 9, 11, 18
RI.7.6 Determine an author's point of view or purpose in a text and analyze how the author distinguishes his or her position from that of others.	11	3, 9, 10, 17, 18
Integration of Knowledge and Ideas		
RI.7.7 Compare and contrast a text to an audio, video, or multimedia version of the text, analyzing each medium's portrayal of the subject (e.g., how the delivery of a speech affects the impact of the words).	Media Feature 1	1, 4, 9, 11, 17, 18
RI.7.8 Trace and evaluate the argument and specific claims in a text, assessing whether the reasoning is sound and the evidence is relevant and sufficient to support the claims.	17	2, 10, 18
RI.7.9 Analyze how two or more authors writing about the same topic shape their presentations of key information by emphasizing different evidence or advancing different interpretations of facts.	18	1, 9
Range of Reading and Level of Text Complexity		
RI.7.10 By the end of the year, read and comprehend literary nonfiction in the grades 6–8 text complexity band proficiently, with scaffolding as needed at the high end of the range.	All Lessons	
Language Standards		
Conventions of Standard English		
L.7.1 Demonstrate command of the conventions of standard English grammar and usage when writing or speaking.	—	6, 7, 13–15, 19
L.7.1a Explain the function of phrases and clauses in general and their function in specific sentences.	L1–L3	1, 9, 18
L.7.1b Choose among simple, compound, complex, and compound-complex sentences to signal differing relationships among ideas.	L4–L6	2, 8
L.7.1c Place phrases and clauses within a sentence, recognizing and correcting misplaced and dangling modifiers.	L7, L8	3, 10, 15
L.7.2a Use a comma to separate coordinate adjectives (e.g., *It was a fascinating, enjoyable movie* but not *He wore an old [,] green shirt*).	L9	4, 10
L.7.2b Spell correctly.	—	5, 12
Knowledge of Language		
L.7.3a Choose language that expresses ideas precisely and concisely, recognizing and eliminating wordiness and redundancy.	L10	6
Vocabulary Acquisition and Use		
L.7.4a Use context (e.g., the overall meaning of a sentence or paragraph; a word's postion or function in a sentence) as a clue to the meaning of a word or phrase.	L11	1–19
L.7.4b Use common, grade-appropriate Greek or Latin affixes and roots as clues to the meaning of a word (e.g., *belligerent, bellicose, rebel*).	L12	1, 2, 4, 5, 7, 9–12, 16, 18, 19
L.7.4c Consult reference materials (e.g., dictionaries, glossaries, thesauruses), both print and digital, to find the pronunciation of a word or determine or clarify its precise meaning or its part of speech.	L13, L14	1, 8, 11, 14, 17, 18

*Lesson numbers such as L12 refer to the Language Handbook.

A40

Common Core State Standards for Grade 7—Reading Standards	*Ready Common Core* Student Lesson(s)	Additional Coverage in Teacher Resource Book Lesson(s)
Language Standards *(continued)*		
Vocabulary Acquisition and Use *(continued)*		
L.7.4d Verify the preliminary determination of the meaning of a word or phrase (e.g., by checking the inferred meaning in context or in a dictionary).	—	3, 5, 6, 8–13, 15–18
L.7.5 Demonstrate understanding of figurative language, word relationships, and nuances in word meanings.	—	3, 12
L.7.5a Interpret figures of speech (e.g., literary, biblical, and mythological allusions) in context.	L15	8, 14, 16, 19
L.7.5b Use the relationship between particular words (e.g., synonym/ antonym, analogy) to better understand each of the words.	L16	1, 17
L.7.5c Distinguish among the connotations (associations) of words with similar denotations (definitions) (e.g., *refined, respectful, polite, diplomatic, condescending*).	L17	7, 11

Additional Coverage of Common Core ELA Standards, Grade 7	*Ready Common Core* Teacher Resource Book Lesson(s)

Writing Standards

Text Types and Purposes

W.7.1	Write arguments to support claims with clear reasons and relevant evidence.	1, 2, 4, 9, 16–18
W.7.1b	Support claim(s) with logical reasoning and relevant evidence, using accurate, credible sources and demonstrating an understanding of the topic or text.	4
W.7.2	Write informative/explanatory texts to examine a topic and convey ideas, concepts, and information through the selection, organization, and analysis of relevant content.	3, 6, 7, 15
W.7.3	Write narratives to develop real or imagined experiences or events using effective technique, relevant descriptive details, and well-structured event sequences.	1, 3, 5–8, 11–13, 16

Production and Distribution of Writing

W.7.4	Produce clear and coherent writing in which the development, organization, and style are appropriate to task, purpose, and audience.	2, 3, 5, 6, 11–14, 16, 17
W.7.5	With some guidance and support from peers and adults, develop and strengthen writing as needed by planning, revising, editing, rewriting, or trying a new approach, focusing on how well purpose and audience have been addressed.	13, 15–19
W.7.6	Use technology, including the Internet, to produce and publish writing and link to and cite sources as well as to interact and collaborate with others, including linking to and citing sources.	9

Research to Build and Present Knowledge

W.7.7	Conduct short research projects to answer a question, drawing on several sources and generating additional related, focused questions for further research and investigation.	2, 4, 5, 8, 10, 11, 19
W.7.8	Gather relevant information from multiple print and digital sources, using search terms effectively; assess the credibility and accuracy of each source; and quote or paraphrase the data and conclusions of others while avoiding plagiarism and following a standard format for citation.	1–3, 6–8, 10, 12, 13, 15, 18
W.7.9a	Apply grade 7 Reading standards to literature (e.g., "Compare and contrast a fictional portrayal of a time, place, or character and a historical account of the same period as a means of understanding how authors of fiction use or alter history").	8, 14, 15, 19
W.7.9b	Apply grade 7 Reading standards to literary nonfiction (e.g. "Trace and evaluate the argument and specific claims in a text, assessing whether the reasoning is sound and the evidence is relevant and sufficient to support the claims").	10

Speaking and Listening Standards

Comprehension and Collaboration

SL.7.1	Engage effectively in a range of collaborative discussions (one-on-one, in groups, and teacher-led) with diverse partners on *grade 7 topics, texts, and issues,* building on others' ideas and expressing their own clearly.	1–19
SL.7.2	Analyze the main ideas and supporting details presented in diverse media and formats (e.g., visually, quantitatively, orally) and explain how the ideas clarify a topic, text, or issue under study.	1, 5, 8, 12, 17
SL.7.3	Delineate a speaker's argument and specific claims, evaluating the soundness of the reasoning and the relevance and sufficiency of the evidence.	7, 12, 13

Presentation of Knowledge and Ideas

SL.7.4	Present claims and findings, emphasizing salient points in a focused, coherent manner with pertinent descriptions, facts, details, and examples; use appropriate eye contact, adequate volume, and clear pronunciation.	1–8, 10–14, 16, 18
SL.7.5	Include multimedia components and visual displays in presentations to clarify claims and findings and emphasize salient points.	6, 8–10, 15, 16
SL.7.6	Adapt speech to a variety of contexts and tasks, demonstrating command of formal English when indicated or appropriate.	3–5, 11, 13–15, 19

Additional Coverage of Reading Standards for Literacy in History/Social Studies and Science and Technical Subjects, Grade 7	Ready Common Core Student Book Lesson(s)
Reading Standards for Literacy in History/Social Studies	
Key Ideas and Details	
RH.6-8.1 Cite specific textual evidence to support analysis of primary and secondary sources.	3, 4
RH.6-8.2 Determine the central ideas or information of a primary or secondary source; provide an accurate summary of the source distinct from prior knowledge or opinions.	1
Craft and Structure	
RH.6-8.6 Identify aspects of a text that reveal an author's point of view or purpose (e.g., loaded language, inclusion or avoidance of particular facts).	11
Integration of Knowledge and Ideas	
RH.6-8.7 Integrate visual information (e.g., in charts, graphs, photographs, videos, or maps) with other information in print and digital texts.	Media Feature 1
RH.6-8.8 Distinguish among fact, opinion, and reasoned judgment in a text.	17
Reading Standards for Literacy in Science and Technical Subjects	
Key Ideas and Details	
RST.6-8.2 Determine the central ideas or conclusions of a text; provide an accurate summary of the text distinct from prior knowledge or opinions.	2
Craft and Structure	
RST.6-8.4 Determine the meaning of symbols, key terms, and other domain-specific words and phrases as they are used in a specific scientific or technical context relevant to grades 6–8 texts and topics.	9
RST.6-8.5 Analyze the structure an author uses to organize a text, including how the major sections contribute to the whole and to an understanding of the topic.	10

Interim Assessment Answer Keys and Correlations

The charts below show the answers to multiple-choice items in each unit's Interim Assessment along with the page numbers for sample responses to constructed-response items. The charts also display the depth-of-knowledge (DOK) index, standard(s) addressed, and corresponding *Ready® Common Core Instruction* lesson(s) for every item. Use this information to adjust lesson plans and focus remediation.

	Ready Common Core Interim Assessment Answer Keys and Correlations			

Unit 1: Key Ideas and Details in Informational Text

Question	Key	DOK[1]	Standard(s)	*Ready Common Core* Student Lesson(s)
1A	A	3	RI.7.2	1
1B	D	3	RI.7.1	3
2	A	2	RI.7.3	4
3	B	2	RI.7.3	4
4	C	3	RI.7.1	3
5	D	2	RI.7.2	2
6	B	3	RI.7.2	1
7	D	2	RI.7.2	2
8	See page 38.	3	RI.7.1	3
9	See page 38.	3	RI.7.3	4
10	See page 38.	3	RI.7.2	1

Unit 2: Key Ideas and Details in Literature

Question	Key	DOK	Standard(s)	*Ready Common Core* Student Lesson(s)
1	B	3	RL.7.1	5
2A	A	3	RL.7.2	7
2B	See page 77.	3	RL.7.1	5
3	C	2	RL.7.3	6
4	B	3	RL.7.1, RL.7.3	5, 6
5	D	2	RL.7.2	7
6	See page 77.	3	RL.7.1	5
7	See page 77.	2	RL.7.2	8
8	See page 77.	2	RL.7.3	6
9	See page 77.	3	RL.7.2, RL.7.3	6, 8

Unit 3: Craft and Structure in Informational Text

Question	Key	DOK	Standard(s)	*Ready Common Core* Student Lesson(s)
1	D	2	RI.7.4	9
2	B	3	RI.7.6	11
3	B	2	RI.7.5	10
4	C	3	RI.7.5	10
5	A	3	RI.7.6	11
6	A	2	RI.7.5	10
7A	D	2	RI.7.4	9
7B	A	2	RI.7.4	9
8	See page 107.	3	RI.7.4	9
9	See page 107.	3	RI.7.6	11
10	See page 107.	3	RI.7.5	10

[1]Depth of Knowledge measures:
1. The item requires superficial knowledge of the standard.
2. The item requires processing beyond recall and observation.

3. The item requires explanation, generalization, and connection to other ideas.
4. The item requires analysis, synthesis, or evaluation of multiple sources or texts.

Unit 4: Craft and Structure in Literature

Question	Key	DOK	Standard(s)	Ready Common Core Student Lesson(s)
1	C	3	RL.7.4	12
2	A	2	RL.7.4	12
3	C	3	RL.7.4	13
4A	C	3	RL.7.6	16
4B	A	3	RL.7.6	16
5	D	2	RL.7.5	14
6	See page 155.	3	RL.7.5	14
7	See page 155.	2	RL.7.4	12
8	See page 155.	3	RL.7.5, RL.7.6	15, 16
9	See page 155.	3	RL.7.5, RL.7.6	15, 16
10	See page 155.	3	RL.7.5, RL.7.6	15, 16

Unit 5: Integration of Knowledge and Ideas in Informational Text

Question	Key	DOK	Standard(s)	Ready Common Core Student Lesson(s)
1	B	3	RI.7.8	17
2	D	3	RI.7.9	18
3	C	2	RI.7.9	18
4	D	3	RI.7.8	17
5	A	3	RI.7.9	18
6	See page 178.	3	RI.7.8	17
7A	See page 178.	3	RI.7.8	17
7B	See page 178.	3	RI.7.8	17
8	See page 178.	4	RI.7.9	18
9	See page 178.	4	RI.7.8, RI.7.9	17, 18

Unit 6: Integration of Knowledge and Ideas in Literature

Question	Key	DOK	Standard(s)	Ready Common Core Student Lesson(s)
1	A	3	RL.7.9	19
2	C	2	RL.7.9	19
3	D	3	RL.7.9	19
4	C	3	RL.7.9	19
5A	B	3	RL.7.9	19
5B	See page 195.	3	RL.7.9	19
5C	See page 195.	3	RL.7.9	19
6	See page 196.	4	RL.7.9	19
7	See page 196.	4	RL.7.9	19
8	See page 196.	4	RL.7.9	19
9	See page 196.	4	RL.7.9	19

Analyzing the Development of Central Ideas

Theme: *Careers*

LESSON OBJECTIVES

- Determine two or more stated or implied central ideas of an informational text.

- Analyze how facts, details, and other evidence develop a central idea.

THE LEARNING PROGRESSION

- **Grade 6:** CCSS RI.6.2 requires students to determine and analyze the development of just one central idea.

- **Grade 7: CCSS RI.7.2 builds on the Grade 6 standard by having students determine and analyze the development of two or more central ideas over the course of a text.**

- **Grade 8:** CCSS RI.8.2 requires students to investigate further the relationship between central and supporting ideas in helping authors develop a text.

PREREQUISITE SKILLS

- Determine a central idea of a text.

- Analyze how a central idea is conveyed through important details in a text.

- Understand the connections between details in a text.

TAP STUDENTS' PRIOR KNOWLEDGE

- Ask students what they've learned about analyzing key details to determine the central idea of a text. Ask students what a central idea is. (*A central idea tells what a whole paragraph or section is mainly about.*) What are details? (*Details are facts, evidence, and other information that support the central idea.*) Explain that students will be learning more about how authors use details to develop central ideas.

- Remind students that authors don't always state the central idea directly. Ask students to explain how they figure out what the central idea is if it is unstated. (*Pay attention to supporting details. Ask yourself what those details tell more about.*)

- Present this text: "To be an Emergency Medical Technician, you must keep your head in emergencies. You will be trained to check people for signs of injuries and to perform certain procedures. Then you must decide if advanced medical care is necessary and transport people to hospitals."

- Help students explain what the central idea might be in that paragraph. (*Sample response: To become an Emergency Medical Technician takes medical training and the ability to stay calm in emergencies.*)

- Review that supporting details are clues to help students determine a stated or unstated central idea in the text. Identifying central ideas can help students understand the points an author is making.

⬛ Ready *Teacher Toolbox*

teacher-toolbox.com

	Prerequisite Skills	RI.7.2
Ready Lessons	✓	✓
Tools for Instruction		✓
Interactive Tutorials		✓

CCSS Focus

RI.7.2 Determine two or more central ideas in a text and analyze their development over the course of the text ….

ADDITIONAL STANDARDS: **RI.7.1, RI.7.3, RI.7.4, RI.7.5, RI.7.7, RI.7.9; L.7.1a, L.7.4a, L.7.4b, L.7.4c, L.7.5b; W.7.1, W.7.3, W.7.8; SL.7.1, SL.7.2, SL.7.4** (*See page A39 for full text.*)

AT A GLANCE

By studying an illustration, students practice determining the central idea and its supporting details.

STEP BY STEP

- Read the first paragraph that includes the definitions of *central idea* and *supporting details*.

- Then have students study the illustration and read the caption. Encourage them to think about what central idea is shown and to circle parts of the illustration and caption that are details supporting this central idea.

- Explain that the web shows a central idea and how it is supported by details. Read the central idea and both supporting details, and ask students to compare them to the parts of the illustration or caption they have circled.

- Then discuss the connection between each supporting detail and the central idea.

- Reinforce the importance of identifying a central idea and supporting details by describing a newspaper article you have read recently. Explain how you used the supporting details to identify the author's central ideas in order to help you understand the important point the writer was making about the topic.

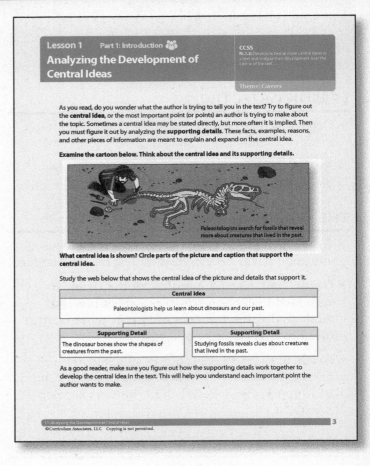

Genre Focus

Informational Texts: Biography

Tell students that in this lesson they will read two biographies. Explain that a biography is an informational text that tells about the events in the life of a real person, written by another person. Biographies usually share these characteristics:

- include facts, anecdotes, and details about all or part of the person's life history

- may tell about a famous person who achieved great things or may tell about anyone

- highlight important experiences in a person's life to reveal more about his or her personality, thoughts, opinions, and motivations

Based on these characteristics, ask students to tell about biographies they have read, including the name of the person being featured and what could be learned from his or her experiences. Students may mention books about famous people in history, science, the arts, or sports.

Tell students that they will be reading "Martha Graham: Modern Dance Innovator," a biography of a famous dancer. Explain that other informational texts in this lesson include a social studies account describing deep-sea treasure hunters and a biography about Suni Williams, the astronaut.

AT A GLANCE

Students read an social studies account about deep-sea divers and then use supporting details to determine the central idea of a paragraph.

STEP BY STEP

- Invite volunteers to tell what they learned on the previous page about identifying a central idea. Explain that in this lesson, students will determine central ideas in informational texts.

- Read aloud "Deep-Sea Treasure Hunters."

- Then read the questions: "What is the central idea of paragraph 2? What details are given to support it?"

- Tell students you will use a Think Aloud to demonstrate a way of answering the questions.

Think Aloud: The author doesn't directly tell the central idea of the paragraph, so I'll determine the central idea by thinking about what all the supporting details have in common. Paragraph 1 names two types of career divers, and paragraph 2 begins by discussing divers who study sunken treasure. This paragraph tells more about that type of diver.

- Direct students to the idea web, and remind them that it shows a central idea and how it is supported by details. Help students complete the central idea in the idea web based on the career path that is described in paragraph 2. Then discuss the supporting details in the paragraph.

Think Aloud: What important idea do I learn about this type of deep-sea diver? The second sentence says that they "often locate, map, and study shipwrecks." This detail tells me what these divers do. The text also says they "learn many things about the lives of the ship's passengers." This is also a supporting detail. It tells me why these types of divers go deep-sea diving.

- Have students add a second supporting detail to the idea web. Then ask students to suggest other supporting details from paragraph 2 that support the central idea. Encourage students to add more supporting details to the idea web as necessary.

- Have students work in groups to complete the activity at the bottom of the page. Invite volunteers to describe how their webs compared with their classmates' webs.

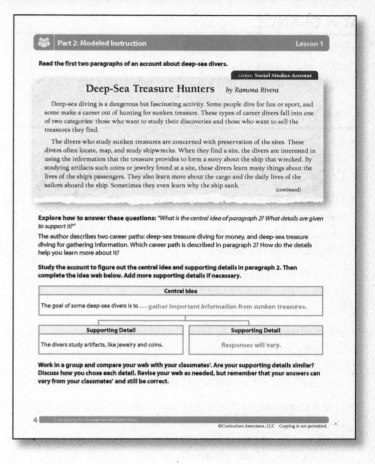

Tier Two
Vocabulary: *Preservation*

- Point out the word *preservation* in paragraph 2. Ask students to identify the base word (*preserve*) and suffix (*-tion*); discuss what this suffix does. (*It forms nouns from verbs.*)

- Guide students to identify context clues that help them determine the meaning of *preserve* as used in the text (*to keep safe or maintain in its original condition*).

- Then have students use their understanding of the word parts to determine the meaning of *preservation.* (*The verb* preserve *changes to a noun, so* preservation *is the act of preserving things or sites.*) Ask why the preservation of ocean artifacts and other historic items is important. **(RI.7.4; L.7.4a, L.7.4b, L.7.4c)**

AT A GLANCE

Students continue reading the account about deep-sea divers. They answer a multiple-choice question and analyze details to help them determine a central idea.

STEP BY STEP

- Tell students they will continue reading the account about deep-sea divers and find details that support the account's central ideas about deep-sea diving.

- Close Reading helps students recognize that each paragraph in an account may have its own central idea. The Hint will help students look for details that support specific ideas.

- Have students read the account and circle the first central idea and underline the second central idea, as directed by Close Reading.

- Ask volunteers to explain the ideas they chose and to tell why they are central to the account. If necessary, ask, "What motivates the second type of deep-sea diver? What rules must all deep-sea divers follow?"

- Have students explain how the text details develop the central idea of divers searching for profit. Guide students to see that the details develop the central idea by describing more about this type of diver.

ANSWER ANALYSIS

Choice A is incorrect. It is true that divers spend a lot of time searching for treasure, but this does not connect to the idea that they must respect the oceans.

Choice B is incorrect. Physical training is a requirement of a diver's job, but it does not support the idea that people must respect the power and dangers of oceans.

Choice C is correct. Identifying legal sites before collecting artifacts shows respect for ocean treasures.

Choice D is incorrect. While profit is what motivates some deep-sea divers, that does not support the idea that they need to respect the oceans and their treasures.

ERROR ALERT: Students who did not choose C might have been confused by the other answer choices, all of which are facts from the text. Remind students that even though the choices are true, they don't necessarily answer the question.

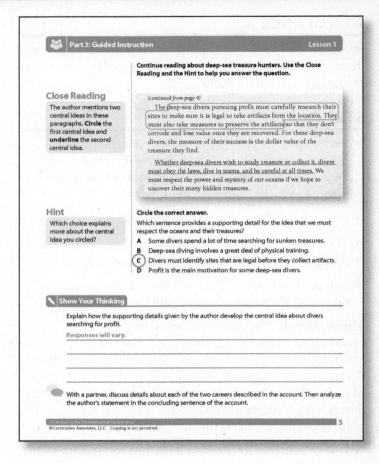

ELL Support: Prefixes

- Explain that many English words have prefixes. A prefix is a group of letters that is added to the beginning of a word to change its meaning.

- Direct students to the words *recovered* and *uncover* on this page. Have students identify the prefixes (*re-*, *un-*) and the base word. (*cover*) Explain that the suffix *re-* means "again." Explain to students that adding the prefix *re-* to *cover* has changed the meaning to "found again."

- Repeat the activity with *uncover*, pointing out that the prefix *un-*, meaning "the opposite of," changes the meaning of *cover* to "the opposite of being covered." **(L.7.4b)**

AT A GLANCE

Students read a biography twice about Suni Williams. After the first reading, you will ask three questions to check your students' comprehension of the text.

STEP BY STEP

- Have students read the biography silently without referring to the Study Buddy or Close Reading text.

- Ask the following questions to ensure students' comprehension of the text:

  What did Suni Williams dream of doing when she was a child? (*She dreamed of walking on the moon.*)

  How did Suni Williams follow in her brother's footsteps? (*They both went to the U.S. Naval Academy.*)

  What did Williams eventually train to become? (*She trained to become a member of the* International Space Station *crew.*)

- Ask students to reread the text and look at the Study Buddy think aloud. What does the Study Buddy help them think about?

Tip: The Study Buddy tells students to identify central ideas as they read by asking themselves questions about what the author wants them to know. Asking themselves questions will help students check that they understand important ideas in the text.

- Have students answer the questions and follow the directions in the Close Reading.

Tip: Close Reading directs students to a quote from Suni Williams. Say that understanding what the person said is important to reading a biography. Paying attention to quotes will help students better understand the person's attitudes and motivations.

- Finally, have students answer the questions on page 7. Use the Answer Analysis to discuss correct and incorrect responses.

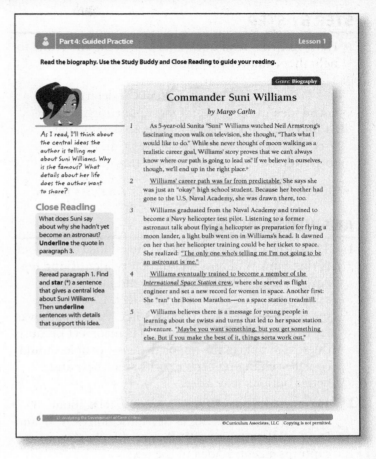

Part 4: Guided Practice   Lesson 1

Read the biography. Use the Study Buddy and Close Reading to guide your reading.

Genre: Biography

Commander Suni Williams

by Margo Carlin

1   As 5-year-old Sunita "Suni" Williams watched Neil Armstrong's fascinating moon walk on television, she thought, "That's what I would like to do." While she never thought of moon walking as a realistic career goal, Williams' story proves that we can't always know where our path is going to lead us? If we believe in ourselves, though, we'll end up in the right place.

2   Williams' career path was far from predictable. She says she was just an "okay" high school student. Because her brother had gone to the U.S. Naval Academy, she was drawn there, too.

3   Williams graduated from the Naval Academy and trained to become a Navy helicopter test pilot. Listening to a former astronaut talk about flying a helicopter as preparation for flying a moon lander, a light bulb went on in Williams's head. It dawned on her that her helicopter training could be her ticket to space. She realized: "The only one who's telling me I'm not going to be an astronaut is me."

4   Williams eventually trained to become a member of the International Space Station crew, where she served as flight engineer and set a new record for women in space. Another first: She "ran" the Boston Marathon—on a space station treadmill.

5   Williams believes there is a message for young people in learning about the twists and turns that led to her space station adventure. "Maybe you want something, but you get something else. But if you make the best of it, things sorta work out."

As I read, I'll think about the central ideas the author is telling me about Suni Williams. Why is she famous? What details about her life does the author want to share?

Close Reading

What does Suni say about why she hadn't yet become an astronaut? **Underline** the quote in paragraph 3.

Reread paragraph 1. Find and **star** (*) a sentence that gives a central idea about Suni Williams. Then **underline** sentences with details that support this idea.

6   L1: Analyzing the Development of Central Ideas   ©Curriculum Associates, LLC   Copying is not permitted.

ELL Support: Idioms

- Direct students to the phrase "a light bulb went on" in paragraph 3. Explain that this is an example of an idiom. An idiom is a phrase that has a meaning that cannot be figured out from the meanings of the individual words.

- Explain that this idiom does not literally mean that turning on a light bulb created light from a lamp. It means someone suddenly had a good idea. The light coming on represents the good idea.

- Encourage students to think of times when they suddenly had a good idea. Have them use the idiom to describe the experience. (*L.7.5a*)

STEP BY STEP

- Have students read questions 1–3, using the Hints to help them answer the questions.

> **Tip:** Question 3 requires students to determine a central idea in the text and its supporting details. Remind students to pay attention to details that describe Williams's actions, feelings, and motivations to help them answer this question.

- Discuss with students the Answer Analysis below.

ANSWER ANALYSIS

1 The correct choice is A. One central idea of the text is that Suni Williams had difficulty identifying her career path. Williams probably did face difficult challenges, so Choice B is incorrect. Choice C is incorrect because the text says her "career path was far from predictable." Choice D is incorrect because the text supports the opposite idea—people should consider changing career paths since new and better options may arise.

2 The correct choice is C. This quote tells about Williams not believing in herself. Choices A, B, and D are all details about Williams's life, but none captures a central idea of the text.

3 Sample response: A central idea is that you have to believe in yourself if you want to achieve your dreams. Supporting details include that Williams watches Neil Armstrong and wants to walk on the moon, she says she's the only one holding her back from becoming an astronaut, and she becomes a member of the *International Space Station* crew.

RETEACHING

Use a chart to organize an answer to question 3. Draw the chart below, leaving the boxes blank. Work with students to fill in the boxes, using information from the text. Sample responses are provided.

Central Idea: You have to believe in yourself if you want to achieve your dreams.		
Supporting Detail: Williams wants to walk on the moon.	**Supporting Detail:** Williams says she's the only one holding her back.	**Supporting Detail:** Williams becomes a member of the space station crew.

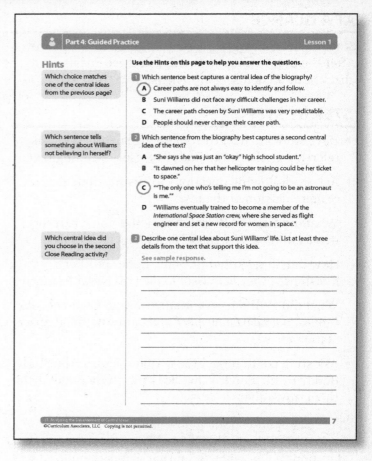

Hints

Which choice matches one of the central ideas from the previous page?

Which sentence tells something about Williams not believing in herself?

Which central idea did you choose in the second Close Reading activity?

Use the Hints on this page to help you answer the questions.

1 Which sentence best captures a central idea of the biography?

A Career paths are not always easy to identify and follow.

B Suni Williams did not face any difficult challenges in her career.

C The career path chosen by Suni Williams was very predictable.

D People should never change their career path.

2 Which sentence from the biography best captures a second central idea of the text?

A "She says she was just an "okay" high school student."

B "It dawned on her that her helicopter training could be her ticket to space."

C "The only one who's telling me I'm not going to be an astronaut is me.'"

D "Williams eventually trained to become a member of the *International Space Station* crew, where she served as flight engineer and set a new record for women in space."

3 Describe one central idea about Suni Williams' life. List at least three details from the text that support this idea.

See sample response.

_____
_____
_____
_____
_____
_____
_____
_____
_____

L1: Analyzing the Development of Central Ideas
©Curriculum Associates, LLC   Copying is not permitted.   7

Integrating Standards

Use these questions to further students' understanding of "Commander Suni Williams."

1 How did Neil Armstrong's moon walk influence young Suni Williams? *(RI.7.3)*

Suni Williams was fascinated with the moon walk, and she dreamed of one day walking on the moon. She carried that dream with her as she grew up, and she eventually followed her heart and went to space as part of the space station crew.

2 What evidence supports the idea that Suni Williams wants to inspire young people? *(RI.7.1)*

The idea that Suni Williams wants to inspire young people is supported by the detail that she "believes there is a message for young people in learning about the twists and turns that led to her space station adventure." Because she thinks there is a message for young people in her story, it suggests that she hopes to inspire them.

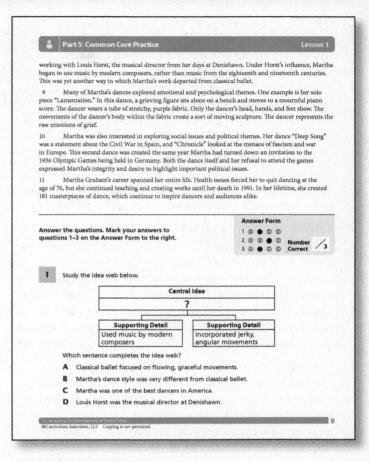

AT A GLANCE

Students independently read a longer biography and answer questions in a format that provides test practice.

STEP BY STEP

- Tell students to use what they have learned about reading closely and analyzing the development of central ideas to read the biography on pages 8 and 9.

- Remind students to pay attention to supporting details that relate to the biography's central ideas.

- Tell students to answer the questions on pages 9 and 10. For questions 1–3, they should fill in the correct circle on the Answer Form.

- When students have finished, use the Answer Analysis to discuss correct responses and the reasons for them. Have students fill in the Number Correct on the Answer Form.

ANSWER ANALYSIS

1   Choice B is correct. Both supporting details tell how Martha's dance style was different from classical ballet. Choice A describes classical ballet, so the details in the web aren't supportive of that idea. Choice C, that Martha was one of the best dancers in America, may be a central idea of the text, but the details in the web do not support that idea. Choice D is a detail included in the text, not a central idea. **(DOK 2)**

Theme Connection

- How do all the texts in this lesson relate to the theme of careers?

- What is one fact or idea you learned about careers from each text in this lesson?

2 Choice C is correct. An innovator is someone who introduces new methods and ideas. Her method of muscle control is described as fresh and new, so this supports the idea of Graham as an innovator. Choice A actually contradicts this idea, suggesting that Graham held back her creativity. Choice B is incorrect. The detail that Graham was in charge of her classes allowed her to be an innovator, but no other detail suggests she did so. Choice D is incorrect because although it was significant that Graham formed her own dance company, this was not necessarily unique and innovative. *(DOK 2)*

3 Choice B is correct. Being the first choreographer to collaborate with other modern artists to create dances shows that Graham was an innovator. Choice A further supports the fact that Graham chose dancing as a career, and Choice C shows that she worked hard, but neither shows that she was an innovator. Choice D supports the idea that Graham was honored, but it does not explain why. *(DOK 3)*

4 Sample response: Many of the dances Martha created explored emotional, psychological, social, and political themes. One of her dances "looked at the menace of fascism and war in Europe," which is a political theme. Another was meant to represent the emotion of grief. *(DOK 3)*

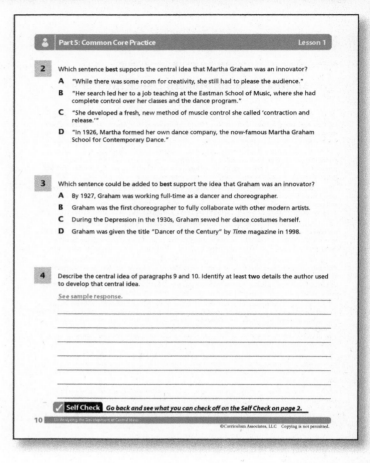

Integrating Standards

Use these questions and tasks as opportunities to interact with "Martha Graham: Modern Dance Innovator."

1 How did Martha's father's profession influence her ideas about dance? *(RI.7.3)*

Her father was a doctor who specialized in nervous disorders. The text says he was interested in how illnesses "could be revealed through the way a patient's body moved." Martha believed dance could also be used to express what people felt inside. She incorporated this idea into her choreography.

2 What text structure has the author used to organize this text? *(RI.7.5)*

This text is a biography, which tells the story of a person's life. It is organized chronologically. The biography begins with her birth in 1894, describes important parts of her life in the order in which they happened, and then ends with her death in 1991.

3 How does the description of classical ballet and Martha's style of dance differ from dance performances you have seen? *(RI.7.7)*

This biography describes dance with vivid, descriptive words and phrases, such as "wildly emotional" and "jerky, trembling movements." It is hard to describe these dances with words alone. I am able to imagine them based on dance performances I've seen.

4 Based on text details, write a narrative of an exchange between two audience members at one of Martha's early performances. *(W.7.3)*

Narratives will vary. Students should draw on information from the text about why the audience disliked Martha's early performances.

5 Discuss in small groups: How did the major events going on in the world contribute to and influence Martha's work? *(SL.7.1)*

Discussions will vary. Remind students to use details from the text to support their ideas.

Writing Activities

Write Reader's Theater *(W.7.3)*

- Briefly discuss what students learned about the life of Martha Graham in "Martha Graham: Modern Dance Innovator." Ask what Graham emphasized in her modern dances and what innovations she introduced.

- Ask students to write a reader's theater script based on an event in Graham's life. Explain that reader's theater is a simplified play; the script tells the story. Encourage students to base the dialogue on details from the essay and to include what Graham might have said and done as well as how others might have reacted to her.

Phrases and Clauses *(L.7.1a)*

- Remind students that a phrase is a group of words that stands together as a unit. A clause is a grammatical construction that includes a subject and predicate but may or may not be a complete sentence.

- Direct students to paragraph 2 of "Deep-Sea Treasure Hunters." Point to the third sentence and read aloud the first clause: "When they find a site." This clause has a subject *(they)* and a predicate *(find a site)*, but it is not a complete thought because of the word *when*. It needs the rest of the sentence to make sense.

- Have students identify other phrases and clauses in this lesson's texts. Then have them write a paragraph about a career of their choice using at least three phrases or clauses. Have volunteers share their paragraphs.

LISTENING ACTIVITY *(SL.7.2)*

Listen Closely/Ask and Answer Questions

- Have volunteers read aloud paragraphs from "Martha Graham: Modern Dance Innovator." Ask other students to listen closely for details about her life.

- Then have students ask and answer questions about Martha Graham based on facts, examples, and evidence in the text.

DISCUSSION ACTIVITY *(RI.7.9; SL.7.1)*

Talk in a Group/Compare Texts

- Ask students to compare and contrast two or more of this lesson's texts.

- Have students form small groups to compare and contrast the central ideas and supporting details. Are there similarities between how the authors describe each career? How do people in each text learn something important about themselves? What is different about each?

- Appoint one member of each group to take notes. Allow 10–15 minutes for discussion, and then have each group share its results with the class.

MEDIA ACTIVITY *(RI.7.7)*

Be Creative/Watch a Dance Performance

- Direct students to video recordings of one of Martha Graham's dance performances mentioned in the text, such as "Lamentation."

- Students should watch the video, keeping in mind how it compares to the experience of reading about a dance performance.

- Have students compare and contrast the two experiences, and tell how watching the video helped them to better understand the biography.

RESEARCH ACTIVITY *(W.7.8; SL.7.4)*

Research and Present/Give a Presentation

- Ask students to use this lesson's texts as a starting point to research careers. What kind of education is required? What kinds of jobs are available? Encourage them to gather relevant information from multiple print and digital sources.

- Remind students to assess the credibility of each source and to quote or paraphrase their information.

- Students should present their findings orally to the class. Have them create a bibliography or reference list that includes all of their sources.

Summarizing Informational Texts

LESSON OBJECTIVES

- Identify the central ideas in an informational text and the important details that support these ideas.

- Summarize an informational text by restating in one's own words the central ideas and important details.

- Provide an objective summary free of personal opinions or judgments.

THE LEARNING PROGRESSION

- **Grade 6:** CCSS RI.6.2 requires students to use central ideas and supporting details to summarize a text and also to omit personal opinions or judgments from the summary.

- **Grade 7: CCSS RI.7.2 builds on the Grade 6 standard by requiring students to determine and analyze the development of two or more central ideas over the course of a text, as well as to summarize the text objectively.**

- **Grade 8:** CCSS RI.8.2 requires students to further investigate the relationship between central and supporting ideas and summarize the text objectively.

PREREQUISITE SKILLS

- Identify a central idea.

- Identify supporting details.

- Summarize a text by identifying key points, without offering biased commentary on those points.

TAP STUDENTS' PRIOR KNOWLEDGE

- Tell students that they will be working on a lesson about summarizing central ideas and supporting details in informational texts. First, ask students to define *central idea*. (*A central idea is what the text is mostly about.*) Remind students that a text may have more than one central idea and that each paragraph or section has its own central idea.

- Next, ask students to define supporting details. (*These are facts, ideas, examples, and opinions that help explain the central idea.*)

- Tell students to think about how they find the central idea in an informational text. (*Pay attention to what the author says at the beginning of a text. Often, authors state the central idea early on in a text.*) Then ask students how they find supporting details that answer questions about the central idea. Guide students to recall that supporting details answer *who, what, where, when, how,* and *why.*

- Tell students that summarizing is a complex strategy in which they extract the most important ideas from a text and present them concisely in their own words. Explain that good summaries do not include personal opinions or judgments about the text, but rather they include only the most important information from the article. Being able to summarize a text will help students remember what they have read.

Ready *Teacher Toolbox*   *teacher-toolbox.com*

	Prerequisite Skills	*RI.7.2*
Ready Lessons	✓	✓
Tools for Instruction	✓	✓
Interactive Tutorials		✓

CCSS Focus

RI.7.2 … provide an objective summary of the text.

ADDITIONAL STANDARDS: RI.7.1, RI.7.3, RI.7.4, RI.7.5, RI.7.8; L.7.1b, L.7.4a, L.7.4b; W.7.1, W.7.4, W.7.7, W.7.8; SL.7.1, SL.7.4
(See page A39 for full text.)

AT A GLANCE

Students read a short news report and identify the central idea and important details using a graphic organizer. They use this information to write a summary of the report.

STEP BY STEP

- Read aloud the paragraph that includes the definitions of *summary* and *objective*. Remind students that a good summary includes the central idea and the most important supporting details in the reader's own words.

- Have students read the news report and think about what it is mostly about, or what its central idea is. Ask them to underline the important details in the report that support this central idea.

- Next, point out the chart. Explain that a chart is a good tool to use to organize central ideas and important details when reading informational texts. Read aloud the central idea and the important details from the chart. Have students compare the details to the information they underlined.

- Then have students read the summary of the report. Discuss how this is a good summary because it is short, restates the central idea and important details, and uses the reader's own words.

- Read aloud the last paragraph. Ask students to explain why good summaries should be free of personal opinions or judgments.

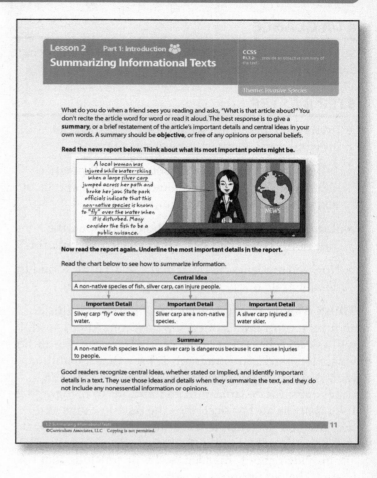

Genre Focus

Informational Texts: Public Documents

Tell students that in this lesson they will read informational texts. One type of informational text is a public document. Government agencies often publish documents to inform the public about events or situations. These documents often include:

- An opener, or lead, that tells who or what the document is about.

- Key details that answer the questions *who, what, where, when, why,* and *how.*

Ask students to name government agencies that might publish public documents. (*Environmental Protection*

Agency, Center for Disease Control, Food and Drug Administration) Have students discuss why these agencies would publish public documents. Ask: *What kinds of information might the public need to know?*

Explain that the first text they will read is a public document written by the government to inform the public about invasive shellfish and plant species affecting U.S. waterways. Students will also read a scientific account about an invasive plant and another account about a non-native snake that is affecting Florida. Students will practice their summarizing skills using the information from these accounts.

AT A GLANCE

Students read a government bulletin, identify important details, and summarize the text.

STEP BY STEP

- Invite students to tell what they learned on the previous page about summarizing a text.

- Tell students that in this lesson they will practice identifying the central idea and important details of texts and write their own summaries.

- Read aloud "The Invaders." Then read aloud the question: "How can I best summarize this bulletin?"

- Now tell students that you will use a Think Aloud to demonstrate a way of answering the question.

Think Aloud: To summarize this bulletin, I'll think about the central idea of each paragraph. After I read, I will ask myself, "What is the central message the author wants to share?" In paragraph 1, I see that the author identifies two types of invasive organisms found in waterways: the Asiatic clam and milfoil. In paragraph 2, I see that the author describes the Asiatic clams as invasive and destructive, causing damage to industrial and agricultural facilities. I see that additional details are provided about this idea, so I will conclude that this is what the paragraph is mostly about.

- Direct students to the missing information below the text and review that it is similar to the chart they completed. Point out the central idea of paragraph 2.

Think Aloud: Now I will ask myself: "What additional details, such as facts or examples, does the author provide that are important to the central idea?" I will underline these details as I reread.

- Have students underline the important details and fill in the missing information at the bottom of the page. Invite volunteers to share what they recorded.

- Then have student pairs take turns summarizing the bulletin. Remind students that their summaries should include the central idea and important details restated in their own words and should not include opinions.

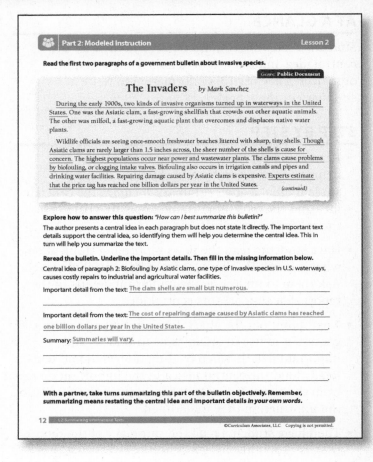

Tier Two Vocabulary: *Aquatic*

- Direct students to the word *aquatic* in sentences 2 and 3 of the bulletin. Tell students that the word *aquatic* is formed from the Latin root word *aqua* meaning "water." Have students use this root information, along with the context of the sentences, to tell what the word *aquatic* means. Guide students to understand that *aquatic* means "of or related to water." **(RI.7.4; L.7.4b)**

- Then have students use a dictionary to find other words that have the root word *aqua*. (*aquarium, aquamarine*) **(L.7.4c)**

AT A GLANCE

Students continue reading the bulletin about invasive species. They answer a multiple-choice question and identify opinions and judgments in a sample summary.

STEP BY STEP

• Tell students that they will continue reading the bulletin about another invasive aquatic species.

• Remind students that Close Reading will help them identify the central idea of the text. The Hint will help them recognize a summary that includes important details and does not include opinions.

• Have students read this section of the bulletin. Then ask them to write margin notes about the central idea of the text, as directed by Close Reading.

• Ask volunteers to share the implied central idea they wrote. Discuss how students determined the central idea. If necessary, ask: "What do all of the supporting details in this paragraph have in common?"

• Have students circle the answer to the question, using the Hint to help them. Then have students respond to the Show Your Thinking, pointing out clue words and phrases that indicate an opinion in an incorrect answer choice.

ANSWER ANALYSIS

Choice A is incorrect. This response includes opinion words such as *annoying* and *should be.* Good summaries should not include the reader's opinions.

Choice B is incorrect. This response includes one important detail from the text, but it does not explain how the plant spreads.

Choice C is incorrect. This response includes opinion words such as *ruins* and *heartlessly,* and does not include important details about how the plant spreads.

Choice D is correct. This summary includes important details about how the plant spreads and why it is harmful, and it does not include opinion statements.

ERROR ALERT: Students who did not choose D may have difficulty recognizing words and phrases that indicate an opinion or judgment. Guide students to see that each choice except D includes words that tell the writer's feelings about milfoil.

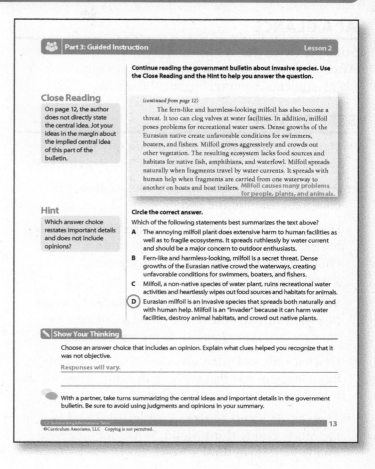

Tier Two Vocabulary: *Fragments*

• Point out the word *fragments* in each of the last two sentences. Have students use context clues to figure out what *fragments* means. Ask students to name the clues in the sentences that helped them determine the meaning of the word. *(Clues may include "travel by water currents" and "carried...on boats and boat trailers.")* **(RI.7.4; L.7.4a)**

• Then have students rewrite the last two sentences using related words in place of *fragments,* such as *parts, pieces,* or *particles.*

AT A GLANCE

Students twice read a scientific account about kudzu. After the first reading, you will ask three questions to check students' comprehension of the text.

STEP BY STEP

- Have students read the account silently without referring to the Study Buddy or Close Reading text.

- Ask the following questions to ensure students' comprehension of the text:

  How did kudzu come to the United States? (*It was brought to the 1876 Centennial Exposition in Philadelphia, Pennsylvania, by the Japanese government.*)

  Why did Americans start planting kudzu? (*People thought it was decorative, they used it as forage for animals, and they planted it to prevent erosion.*)

  In what ways is kudzu invasive? (*It grows quickly, it has a long tap root that makes it difficult to remove, and it is able to smother existing plants.*)

- Then ask students to reread paragraph 1 and look at the Study Buddy think aloud. What does the Study Buddy help them think about?

TIP: The Study Buddy guides students to underline details that describe why kudzu was considered "pretty" and why it was considered to be a "pest." Explain that identifying these important details will help guide them as they write their summaries.

- Have students read the rest of the account. Tell them to follow the directions in the Close Reading.

TIP: Point out that marking important details is an effective way to determine which details support the central ideas. Encourage students to first identify the central idea, either stated or unstated, and then look for important details that support the central ideas.

- Finally, have students answer the questions on page 15. When students have finished, use the Answer Analysis to discuss correct and incorrect responses.

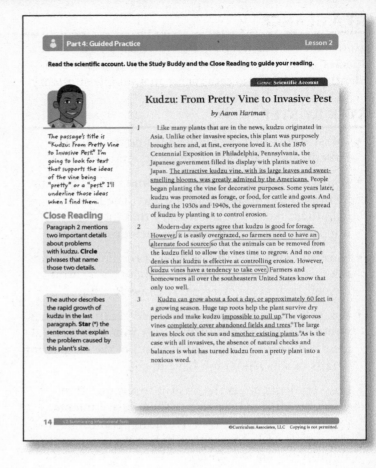

ELL Support: Suffixes

- Explain to students that many English words have suffixes. A suffix is a group of letters that is added to the end of a word to change the word's meaning.

- Work with students to show how the meaning of a word changes with a suffix. Point out the word *invasive* in sentence 2. Have students identify the suffix. (*-ive*) Explain that this suffix means "inclined to, or having the qualities of." Then tell students that the base word of *invasive* is *invade*, which means "to attack or intrude on." Ask students to define *invasive* ("*inclined to attack or intrude on*").

- Then have students find other words in the account with the suffix *-ive*: *attractive, decorative,* and *effective*. Have partners work together to write definitions of each word. (**L.7.4b**)

STEP BY STEP

- Have students read questions 1–3, using the Hints to help them answer the questions.

TIP: If students have trouble answering question 1, remind them of the details they circled in Close Reading. Have them compare the details they circled with the answer choices to help them select the correct answer.

- Discuss with students the Answer Analysis below.

ANSWER ANALYSIS

1. Choice B is correct. This response states the central idea and important details of the paragraph. Choice A does not include important details about using kudzu as forage and to control erosion. Choice C includes an opinion statement. Choice D is not supported by details in the account.

2. Choice A is correct. It restates the central ideas of paragraphs 1 and 3. The words "most troublesome invasive plant species" in Choice B indicate an opinion, which should not be included in a summary. Choice C is incorrect because the text states that there are no natural checks and balances to control the plant. Choice D is a supporting detail, not a central idea.

3. Sample response: Though once considered a desirable plant, kudzu has invasive tendencies that make it a harmful weed. Kudzu is only of limited value as animal forage. It is an effective erosion controller, but it can take over in an undesirable way. This happens because the United States has no natural checks and balances.

RETEACHING

Use a chart to verify the correct answer to question 1. Draw the chart below and work with students to fill in the boxes. Sample responses are provided.

Central Idea: Kudzu has beneficial and harmful characteristics.		
Detail: It is good for forage but it is easily overgrazed.	**Detail:** It can control erosion.	**Detail:** It has a tendency to take over.
Summary: Kudzu is only of limited value as animal forage. It is also an effective erosion controller, but it can take over in an undesirable way.		

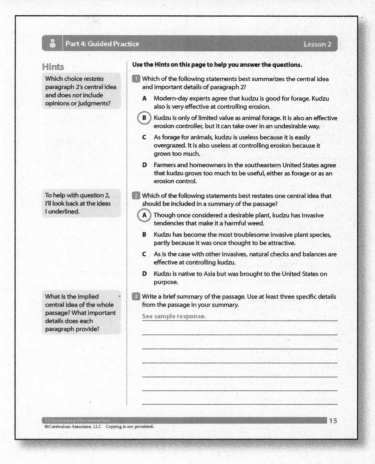

Integrating Standards

Use these questions to further students' understanding of "Kudzu: From Pretty Vine to Invasive Pest."

1. Is kudzu mostly beneficial or mostly destructive? Cite evidence from the account to support your answer. *(RI.7.1)*

   Kudzu is mostly destructive. Even though kudzu has some benefits, such as being "good for forage" and "effective at controlling erosion," kudzu is a "pest" and a "noxious weed." These harmful characteristics make kudzu more destructive than beneficial.

2. Explain how kudzu causes damage to fields and trees. *(RI.7.3)*

   Kudzu grows rapidly, quickly covering fields and trees. Its large leaves smother existing plants, and its long roots make it impossible to pull up.

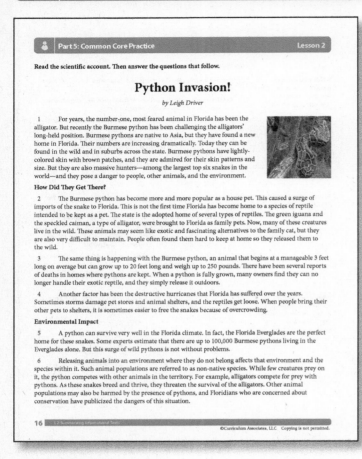

Part 5: Common Core Practice   Lesson 2

Read the scientific account. Then answer the questions that follow.

Python Invasion!

by Leigh Driver

1   For years, the number-one, most feared animal in Florida has been the alligator. But recently the Burmese python has been challenging the alligators' long-held position. Burmese pythons are native to Asia, but they have found a new home in Florida. Their numbers are increasing dramatically. Today they can be found in the wild and in suburbs across the state. Burmese pythons have lightly-colored skin with brown patches, and they are admired for their skin patterns and size. But they are also massive hunters—among the largest top six snakes in the world—and they pose a danger to people, other animals, and the environment.

How Did They Get There?

2   The Burmese python has become more and more popular as a house pet. This caused a surge of imports of the snake to Florida. This is not the first time Florida has become home to a species of reptile intended to be kept as a pet. The state is the adopted home of several types of reptiles. The green iguana and the speckled caiman, a type of alligator, were brought to Florida as family pets. Now, many of these creatures live in the wild. These animals may seem like exotic and fascinating alternatives to the family cat, but they are also very difficult to maintain. People often found them hard to keep at home so they released them to the wild.

3   The same thing is happening with the Burmese python, an animal that begins at a manageable 3 feet long on average but can grow up to 20 feet long and weigh up to 250 pounds. There have been several reports of deaths in homes where pythons are kept. When a python is fully grown, many owners find they can no longer handle their exotic reptile, and they simply release it outdoors.

4   Another factor has been the destructive hurricanes that Florida has suffered over the years. Sometimes storms damage pet stores and animal shelters, and the reptiles get loose. When people bring their other pets to shelters, it is sometimes easier to free the snakes because of overcrowding.

Environmental Impact

5   A python can survive very well in the Florida climate. In fact, the Florida Everglades are the perfect home for these snakes. Some experts estimate that there are up to 100,000 Burmese pythons living in the Everglades alone. But this surge of wild pythons is not without problems.

6   Releasing animals into an environment where they do not belong affects that environment and the species within it. Such animal populations are referred to as non-native species. While few creatures prey on it, the python competes with other animals in the territory. For example, alligators compete for prey with pythons. As these snakes breed and thrive, they threaten the survival of the alligators. Other animal populations may also be harmed by the presence of pythons, and Floridians who are concerned about conservation have publicized the dangers of this situation.

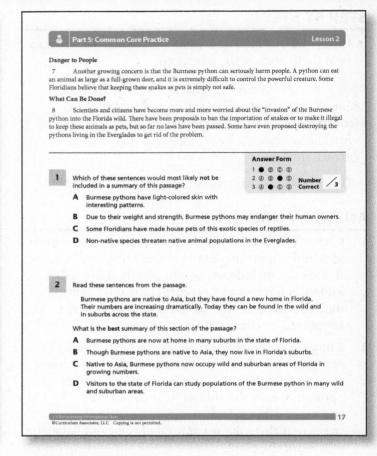

Part 5: Common Core Practice   Lesson 2

Danger to People

7   Another growing concern is that the Burmese python can seriously harm people. A python can eat an animal as large as a full-grown deer, and it is extremely difficult to control the powerful creature. Some Floridians believe that keeping these snakes as pets is simply not safe.

What Can Be Done?

8   Scientists and citizens have become more and more worried about the "invasion" of the Burmese python into the Florida wild. There have been proposals to ban the importation of snakes or to make it illegal to keep these animals as pets, but so far no laws have been passed. Some have even proposed destroying the pythons living in the Everglades to get rid of the problem.

Answer Form
1 ● Ⓑ Ⓒ Ⓓ
2 Ⓐ Ⓑ ● Ⓓ   Number
3 Ⓐ ● Ⓒ Ⓓ   Correct   /3

1   Which of these sentences would most likely **not** be included in a summary of this passage?

A   Burmese pythons have light-colored skin with interesting patterns.

B   Due to their weight and strength, Burmese pythons may endanger their human owners.

C   Some Floridians have made house pets of this exotic species of reptiles.

D   Non-native species threaten native animal populations in the Everglades.

2   Read these sentences from the passage.

> Burmese pythons are native to Asia, but they have found a new home in Florida. Their numbers are increasing dramatically. Today they can be found in the wild and in suburbs across the state.

What is the **best** summary of this section of the passage?

A   Burmese pythons are now at home in many suburbs in the state of Florida.

B   Though Burmese pythons are native to Asia, they now live in Florida's suburbs.

C   Native to Asia, Burmese pythons now occupy wild and suburban areas of Florida in growing numbers.

D   Visitors to the state of Florida can study populations of the Burmese python in many wild and suburban areas.

AT A GLANCE

Students independently read a longer account and answer questions in a format that provides test practice.

STEP BY STEP

- Tell students to use what they have learned about reading closely, identifying central ideas and supporting details, and summarizing a text to read the text on pages 16 and 17.

- Remind students to underline or circle important points as they read.

- Tell students to answer the questions on pages 17 and 18. For questions 1–3, they should fill in the correct circle on the Answer Form.

- When students have finished, use the Answer Analysis to discuss correct responses and the reasons for them. Have students fill in the Number Correct on the Answer Form.

ANSWER ANALYSIS

1   The correct answer is A. Although the account does describe the Burmese python, this is not an important detail supporting the central idea about the invasion of pythons in Florida. Choices B, C, and D all include important details that support the central idea and should be included in a summary. **(DOK 2)**

Theme Connection

- How do all the texts in this lesson relate to the theme of invasive species?

- What is one fact that you learned about invasive species from each text?

2   The correct answer is C. This summary includes the section's central idea and important details without including an opinion. Choice A only includes one important detail and leaves out the information that pythons can also be found in the wild. Choice B only restates the first sentence of this section. Choice D includes additional information that is not supported by the text. **(DOK 2)**

3   Choice B is correct. This statement summarizes the central idea of the section "Environmental Impact," explaining why pythons are a threat to Florida wildlife. Choices A, C, and D each state an important detail from the account, but they do not state a central idea. **(DOK 2)**

4   Sample response: Burmese pythons pose a threat to animals and people in the Florida Everglades. The pythons were brought to Florida as pets, but some were released or escaped into the wild. There, the pythons bred. Scientists believe the Everglades may hold up to 100,000 pythons. Scientists are trying to control the spread of Burmese pythons by educating the public about the threat, proposing import bans, and destroying pythons they find in the wild. So far, however, no official action has been taken to rid Florida of this growing environmental threat. **(DOK 2)**

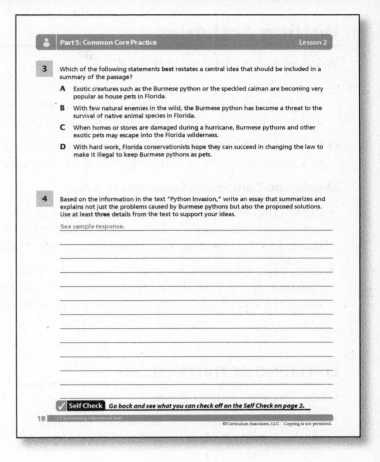

Integrating Standards

Use these questions and tasks as opportunities to interact with "Python Invasion!"

1   Why is the Burmese python considered a popular house pet by many people? **(RI.7.1)**

Some people admire the python's beautiful markings and are fascinated by their large size. People also think they are "exotic," making them a more exciting and unusual pet compared to common dogs and cats.

2   What text features does the author use to organize the information in this account? How does this structure help the author develop her central ideas? **(RI.7.5)**

The author organizes the information in this account by using headings to tell what each section of the account will be about. This structure enables the author to make it clear to the reader what the central idea of each section is and allows readers to see how each central idea builds on the overall idea about how pythons have invaded Florida, as stated in paragraph 1 and the title.

3   How does the author feel about the proliferation of pythons in the Florida environment? Write your answer, including two details from the text to support your claim. **(RI.7.8; W.7.4)**

The author thinks that the pythons are bad for the Florida environment. She states that the pythons are dangerous to humans because of their large size and strength. She also states that the pythons are competing for prey with native Florida animals, such as the alligator, and "threaten the survival of the alligators."

4   Reread the last section of the account. In small groups, evaluate each suggestion for stopping the "invasion" of the python in Florida. Which suggestion is most reasonable? **(SL.7.1)**

Discussions will vary. Students should discuss each suggestion thoroughly, building on one another's ideas as they determine which suggestion is the most reasonable. Remind students to pose questions and comments that keep the discussion on topic.

Writing Activities

Write an Argumentative Letter (W.7.1)

• Write a letter to a local Florida newspaper telling what you think would be the best solution to the python overpopulation problem. Do you think the pythons should be destroyed? Should the pythons be rounded up and kept in a segregated area? Should laws be passed to prevent more pythons from entering Florida as pets?

• Remind students that they should first state their opinion and then provide at least three convincing reasons to support their claim. Encourage them to cite evidence from the text.

Simple and Compound Sentences (L.7.1b)

• Reread the last two sentences in paragraph 2 of "Python Invasion!" Explain that these two sentences are compound sentences. Each contains two complete thoughts that are connected by coordinating conjunctions, *but* and *so*. Discuss how these compound sentences help to show the relationship between ideas.

• Then have students separate each compound sentence into two simple sentences and discuss how the relationship between the ideas changes. Have students give examples of when they would use compound sentences and simple sentences in their own writing.

LISTENING ACTIVITY (SL.7.1)

Listen Closely/Connect Ideas

• Have small groups review the central idea and important details in "Kudzu: From Pretty Vine to Invasive Pest."

• Have one student restate the central idea of paragraph 1. Then have students take turns telling important details that support the central idea.

• Each student listens closely, repeating the central idea and details that were already stated before adding another supporting detail from the text.

MEDIA ACTIVITY (RI.7.8; W.7.1)

Be Creative/Make a Poster

• Have students review the illustration of a news report on page 11. Review that it conveys information to a public audience.

• Challenge students to make a poster that conveys an important message about invasive species to the public. For example, they may make a poster that discourages people from having pet pythons.

• Have students use facts from the texts and illustrations on their posters.

DISCUSSION ACTIVITY (SL.7.1)

Talk in a Group/Extending Scientific Concepts

• Have students review each of the invasive species they read about in this lesson's texts.

• Have small groups of students compare and contrast the species. How was the way the species were introduced similar? What is different about the harm that each species might cause to its new environment?

• Allow 10 to 15 minutes for discussion. Then have each group share its results with the class.

RESEARCH ACTIVITY (W.7.7, W.7.8; SL.7.4)

Research and Present/Give a Presentation

• Review the invasive species students have read about and tell them that there are many other invasive species. Give examples such as the Africanized honeybee, the Asian tiger mosquito, the wild boar, and the giant tiger shrimp.

• Have small groups choose one invasive species to research. Ask them to find out how and when the species was introduced and what harm the species might cause.

• Have groups present their research to the class.

Citing Evidence to Make Inferences

LESSON OBJECTIVES

- Use textual evidence, along with background knowledge, to make reasonable inferences about an informational text.

- Cite two or more pieces of text evidence to support an inference drawn from the text.

THE LEARNING PROGRESSION

- **Grade 6:** CCSS RI.6.1 requires students to cite textual evidence to support an analysis of what the text says and when drawing inferences from the text.

- **Grade 7: CCSS RI.7.1 builds on the Grade 6 standard by requiring students to deepen their textual connections to include citing several pieces of evidence to support their analysis of and inferences drawn from a text.**

- **Grade 8:** CCSS RI.8.1 builds on the Grade 7 standard by having students analyze the purpose and function of evidence by evaluating which evidence most strongly supports a given statement or inference.

PREREQUISITE SKILLS

- Understand that some information in a text is not explicitly stated.

- Understand that readers often have to add up clues to make an inference from a text.

- Cite textual evidence to support inferences drawn from a text.

TAP STUDENTS' PRIOR KNOWLEDGE

- Tell students that they will be working on a lesson about citing evidence to make inferences. Ask students what an inference is. (*a logical guess*) Remind them that when readers make an inference, they combine what they know with evidence in the text to figure out what is not said explicitly.

- Have students think about a girl who comes home and finds that her parents and the dog are not there, but the car is parked out front. The girl notices that the dog's leash is missing. Ask students to make an inference based on the evidence and their own knowledge. (*The parents took the dog for a walk.*) Discuss how this is a logical guess because all the information suggests this idea. The inference that the parents are still at work, for example, would not be supported by the evidence that their car is parked out front.

- Explain to students that as they develop their ability to use text evidence to make inferences, they will be able to better understand what they read in informational texts.

■ **Ready** *Teacher Toolbox*		*teacher-toolbox.com*
	Prerequisite Skills	*RI.7.1*
Ready Lessons	✓	✓
Tools for Instruction		✓ ✓
Interactive Tutorials		✓

CCSS Focus

RI.7.1 Cite several pieces of textual evidence to support analysis of what the text says explicitly as well as inferences drawn from the text.

ADDITIONAL STANDARDS: **RI.7.2, RI.7.3, RI.7.4, RI.7.6; L.7.1c, L.7.4a, L.7.4d, L.7.5; W.7.2, W.7.3, W.7.4, W.7.8; SL.7.1, SL.7.4, SL.7.6**
(See page A39 for full text.)

AT A GLANCE

By studying an illustration, students find evidence to support an inference about a character's feelings. They recognize that inferences are based on facts from a text and a reader's own background knowledge.

STEP BY STEP

- Read aloud the paragraphs that include the definitions of *analyze*, *explicitly*, and *inference*.

- Ask students to study the illustration and circle details that support the stated inference about the runner's feelings.

- Explain that the chart represents the process of combining text evidence with background knowledge to support an inference.

- Tell students that *text evidence* means facts and details from a text.

- Read the first column, and ask students to use the details they circled in the drawing to help them fill in the blanks.

- Then read the second column. Discuss how the background knowledge about sports and athletes, combined with the text evidence, supports the inference in the third column.

- Provide students with an inference about an informational text they have read recently in class. Then have volunteers cite evidence from the text to support the inference.

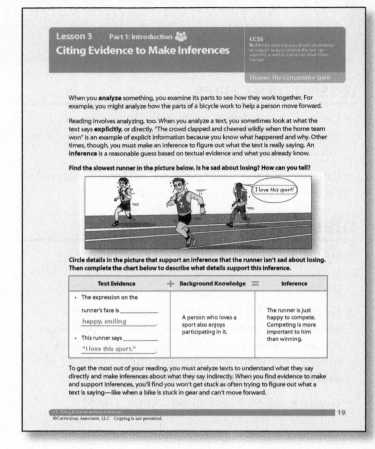

- Reiterate the value of making inferences by sharing an inference you made while reading and the evidence you found to support it. Describe how this inference helped you find deeper meaning in the text.

Genre Focus

Informational Texts: Speeches

Tell students that in this lesson they will read a speech. Explain that a speech is written remarks, spoken and delivered to an audience.

Speeches have an introduction, a body, and a conclusion. In the body, facts and details are usually included to support the opinions or ideas of the speaker. In the conclusion, the speaker's opinions may be repeated to reinforce the ideas to the listener.

Speeches can have different purposes. They might be delivered in order to persuade the audience of an opinion, inform about a topic, or simply entertain. Some speeches are very influential.

Have students share any speeches that they have read or heard. You may also wish to share how or why a speech you once heard had an impact on you.

Explain that the excerpt from "The President's Speech to Students" is a speech that was given by President Barack Obama to students as they headed back to school. This speech was witnessed by millions of television viewers with the purpose of motivating students to succeed and not wait to make a difference. President Obama used real examples to make his point, and he repeated his call to action from the beginning as he began to wrap up the speech.

Mention that the other passages students will read in this lesson include an article and a historical account.

AT A GLANCE

Students make inferences about a magazine article and cite text evidence to support their inferences.

STEP BY STEP

- Invite volunteers to tell what they learned on the previous page about using evidence to make inferences.

- Tell students that in this lesson they will make inferences about what they read based on text evidence and their own knowledge.

- Read aloud "The Flu Game."

- Then read the questions: "What is Michael Jordan's attitude toward competition? What text evidence supports your idea?"

- Tell students you will use a Think Aloud to demonstrate a way of answering the questions.

Think Aloud: The article doesn't say directly what Jordan's attitude toward competition is, but I will look for evidence in the text that can help me make an inference. In paragraph 1, I read that Jordan was diagnosed with the stomach flu before Game 5.

- Direct students to the chart and ask where they've seen a similar chart before. Review that it shows how textual evidence combined with background knowledge can be used to make an inference. Point out the first clue in column 1.

Think Aloud: In paragraph 2, I read that Jordan suited up and appeared on the court three hours before the start of Game 5.

- Have students write this clue from the text in column 1 of the chart.

Think Aloud: I know that the Bulls were relying on Jordan greatly, because he was the team's star player. I also know that playing sports while sick requires determination because it is not easy. Based on this knowledge and the text evidence, I can make an inference about Jordan's attitude toward competition.

- Have students complete the inference in column 3. Have volunteers share their answers with the class.

- Finally, ask students to work in pairs to find text evidence that supports the inference that Michael Jordan is a fierce competitor. Ask volunteers to share their answers with the class.

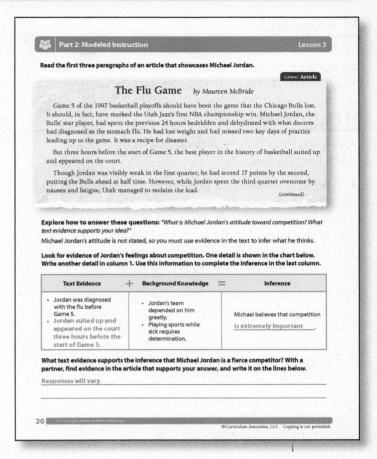

ELL Support: Idioms

- Ask students to reread the last sentence in paragraph 1. Tell them that the phrase *recipe for disaster* is an idiom, or a common expression whose meaning cannot be literally or directly translated.

- Explain that people often say that a series of events or circumstances that are expected to bring about a bad ending is a *recipe for disaster*. In this example, the game was important. The star player was very sick, had lost weight, and had missed the last two practices. These are all factors that should have brought about a terrible game for the Bulls, or they were a *recipe for disaster*.

- Have students use this idiom in their own complete sentences to demonstrate understanding. **(L.7.5a)**

AT A GLANCE

Students continue reading about Michael Jordan. They answer a multiple-choice question and analyze the evidence that helped them make an inference.

STEP BY STEP

- Tell students they will continue reading about Michael Jordan.

- Remind students that good readers notice important details that can serve as evidence when making an inference or supporting a point. Close Reading will help students identify evidence of Jordan's feelings. The Hint will help them connect the article to Jordan's attitude toward playing basketball.

- Have students read the rest of the passage and underline two sentences that show what Michael Jordan thinks about losing, as directed by Close Reading. Point out the connection between underlining these sentences and using them as evidence for making an inference.

- Ask volunteers to share the sentences they underlined and describe why they are the best descriptions of Jordan's attitude.

- Have students answer the question, using the Hint to help them. Then have them respond to the question in Show Your Thinking.

ANSWER ANALYSIS

Choice A is incorrect. This sentence shows that he is tired and determined but not necessarily talented.

Choice B is correct. Jordan scored many points in one quarter, closing the gap between his team and the Jazz.

Choice C is incorrect. This sentence shows that Jordan scored the winning point. This could mean that he is a good player, but it could also mean he was lucky. It is therefore not the best evidence; scoring 18 points shows more talent than scoring 3.

Choice D is incorrect. This sentence shows that Jordan is dedicated but not necessarily talented.

ERROR ALERT: Students who didn't choose B may not have understood the inference to be about how well Jordan plays basketball. The incorrect choices show his dedication and luck but not his skill.

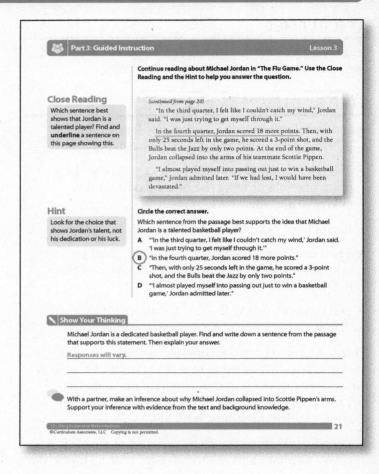

Continue reading about Michael Jordan in "The Flu Game." Use the Close Reading and the Hint to help you answer the question.

Close Reading
Which sentence best shows that Jordan is a talented player? Find and **underline** a sentence on this page showing this.

(continued from page 20)
"In the third quarter, I felt like I couldn't catch my wind," Jordan said. "I was just trying to get myself through it."

In the fourth quarter, Jordan scored 18 more points. Then, with only 25 seconds left in the game, he scored a 3-point shot, and the Bulls beat the Jazz by only two points. At the end of the game, Jordan collapsed into the arms of his teammate Scottie Pippen.

"I almost played myself into passing out just to win a basketball game," Jordan admitted later. "If we had lost, I would have been devastated."

Hint
Look for the choice that shows Jordan's talent, not his dedication or his luck.

Circle the correct answer.
Which sentence from the passage best supports the idea that Michael Jordan is a talented basketball player?

A "In the third quarter, I felt like I couldn't catch my wind,' Jordan said. 'I was just trying to get myself through it.'"

B "In the fourth quarter, Jordan scored 18 more points."

C "Then, with only 25 seconds left in the game, he scored a 3-point shot, and the Bulls beat the Jazz by only two points."

D "I almost played myself into passing out just to win a basketball game,' Jordan admitted later."

Show Your Thinking
Michael Jordan is a dedicated basketball player. Find and write down a sentence from the passage that supports this statement. Then explain your answer.
Responses will vary.

With a partner, make an inference about why Michael Jordan collapsed into Scottie Pippen's arms. Support your inference with evidence from the text and background knowledge.

L3: Citing Evidence to Make Inferences
©Curriculum Associates, LLC Copying is not permitted.
21

Tier Two Vocabulary: *Devastated*

- Direct students to the last paragraph on page 21. Ask students how they would feel if they had played an important game really well while feeling so sick—and then lost the game anyway.

- After collecting students' thoughts about feeling disappointed, ask students what kind of player Jordan is. *(serious, committed)*

- Now read aloud the last sentence of the article, and ask students what they think *devastated* means. Guide them to use context clues related to the events of the game and what they know about Jordan's commitment to the game. *("shocked, stunned, or crushed")* **(RI.7.4; L.7.4a)**

AT A GLANCE

Students read a historical account about the race to the South Pole twice. After the first reading, you will ask three questions to check your students' comprehension of the passage.

STEP BY STEP

- Have students read the historical account silently without referring to the Study Buddy or Close Reading text.

- Ask the following questions to ensure students' comprehension of the text:

  Which explorer reached the South Pole first? (*Amundsen*)

  Contrast the different ways the explorers planned to travel once in Antarctica. (*Scott planned to use motor sleds, while Amundsen used sled dogs.*)

  How did Scott learn that Amundsen was on his way to the South Pole? (*Amundsen sent Scott a telegram.*)

- Ask students to reread paragraph 1 and look at the Study Buddy think aloud. What does the Study Buddy help them think about?

Tip: The Study Buddy tells students to look for evidence relating to each of the two explorers so they can make inferences about them. Tell students that noticing facts and details about people in a text will help them make inferences.

- Have students read the rest of the historical account. Tell them to follow the directions in the Close Reading.

Tip: Explain to students that, when contrasting two people or characters in a text, it is helpful to underline or highlight information about one of them and circle information about the other. This will help them organize the information so they can use it later to analyze the text.

- Finally, have students answer the questions on page 23. Use the Answer Analysis to discuss correct and incorrect responses.

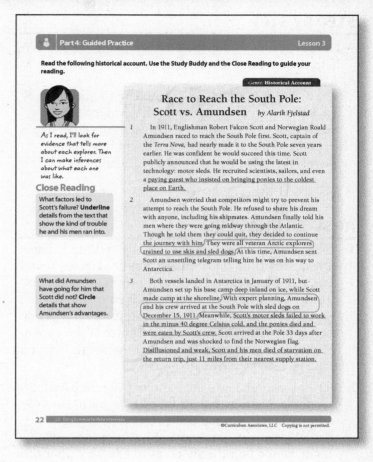

Part 4: Guided Practice   Lesson 3

Read the following historical account. Use the Study Buddy and the Close Reading to guide your reading.

Genre: Historical Account

Race to Reach the South Pole: Scott vs. Amundsen   *by Alarik Fjelstad*

As I read, I'll look for evidence that tells more about each explorer. Then I can make inferences about what each one was like.

Close Reading

What factors led to Scott's failure? **Underline** details from the text that show the kind of trouble he and his men ran into.

What did Amundsen have going for him that Scott did not? **Circle** details that show Amundsen's advantages.

1   In 1911, Englishman Robert Falcon Scott and Norwegian Roald Amundsen raced to reach the South Pole first. Scott, captain of the *Terra Nova*, had nearly made it to the South Pole seven years earlier. He was confident he would succeed this time. Scott publicly announced that he would be using the latest in technology: motor sleds. He recruited scientists, sailors, and even a paying guest who insisted on bringing ponies to the coldest place on Earth.

2   Amundsen worried that competitors might try to prevent his attempt to reach the South Pole. He refused to share his dream with anyone, including his shipmates. Amundsen finally told his men where they were going midway through the Atlantic. Though he told them they could quit, they decided to continue the journey with him. They were all veteran Arctic explorers trained to use skis and sled dogs. At this time, Amundsen sent Scott an unsettling telegram telling him he was on his way to Antarctica.

3   Both vessels landed in Antarctica in January of 1911, but Amundsen set up his base camp deep inland on ice, while Scott made camp at the shoreline. With expert planning, Amundsen and his crew arrived at the South Pole with sled dogs on December 15, 1911. Meanwhile, Scott's motor sleds failed to work in the minus 40 degree Celsius cold, and the ponies died and were eaten by Scott's crew. Scott arrived at the Pole 33 days after Amundsen and was shocked to find the Norwegian flag. Disillusioned and weak, Scott and his men died of starvation on the return trip, just 11 miles from their nearest supply station.

22   L3: Citing Evidence to Make Inferences   ©Curriculum Associates, LLC   Copying is not permitted.

Tier Two Vocabulary: *Vessel*

- Direct students to the word *vessels* in paragraph 3. Work with students to identify context clues that help them determine the meaning of this word. (*Clues may include "landed in Antarctica," "captain of the* Terra Nova," *"sailors," and "shipmates."*)

- Then ask students to define this term. (*"a boat or ship"*) Point out that they can check their meaning in the context to see if it makes sense. They can also use a dictionary to help them verify the meaning of a word. (*RI.7.4; L.7.4a, L.7.4d*)

STEP BY STEP

- Have students read questions 1–3, using the Hints to help them answer those questions.

Tip: If students are having trouble with questions 2 and 3, direct them to return to the evidence they circled and underlined about Amundsen's advantages and Scott's failure. This evidence will help them eliminate distractors and make an inference.

- Discuss with students the Answer Analysis below.

ANSWER ANALYSIS

1 The correct choice is B. By "finally" telling his men the destination, it is implied that he secretively did not tell them earlier. Choice A proves Amundsen's ability to travel on ice; he did not go inland to be secretive. Choice C shows that Amundsen was not secretive with his competitor. Choice D shows that Amundsen successfully reached the South Pole, not that he was secretive about it.

2 The correct choice is A. Scott was not prepared. For example, his motor sleds failed to work in the cold. Choice B is incorrect. Scott's technology was actually too new, not outdated. It is true Scott's team camped on the shore, as in Choice C, but this did not cause him to be unsuccessful. Choice D is incorrect. Scott had nearly made it to the South Pole before, so he was not unfamiliar with the challenge.

3 Sample response: Amundsen succeeded because he was well prepared. His men were all veteran Arctic explorers who knew what they were doing, and they used sled dogs, which were much more reliable and better suited to the environment than Scott's motor sleds.

RETEACHING

Use a chart to verify the correct answer to question 1. Draw the chart below and work with students to fill in the boxes. Sample responses are provided.

Evidence	Prior Knowledge	Inference
"Amundsen finally told his men where they were going mid-way through the Atlantic."	A secretive person doesn't tell others the whole truth.	Amundsen is secretive.

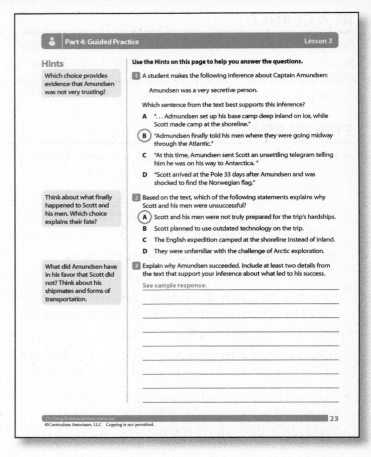

Integrating Standards

Use these questions to further students' understanding of "Race to Reach the South Pole: Scott vs. Amundsen."

1 Find a central idea in this historical account and explain how it is developed in the text. **(RI.7.2)**

Sample response: One central idea is that Amundsen's expert planning enabled him to make it to the South Pole first. Amundsen kept a low profile when setting out, which was part of his strategy. He brought skilled and experienced men with him, used a proven method of transportation, and brought ample supplies. He ended up proudly placing his country's flag in the ground first.

2 How did Scott and Amundsen influence how their teams made it to the South Pole? **(RI.7.3)**

Sample response: Amundsen and Scott were in a race to the South Pole. This competition influenced how they hurried to get to the South Pole, with Scott's team making some mistakes.

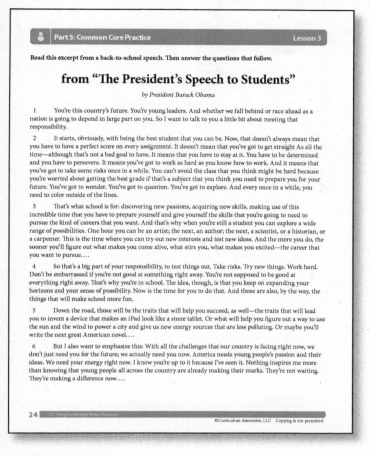

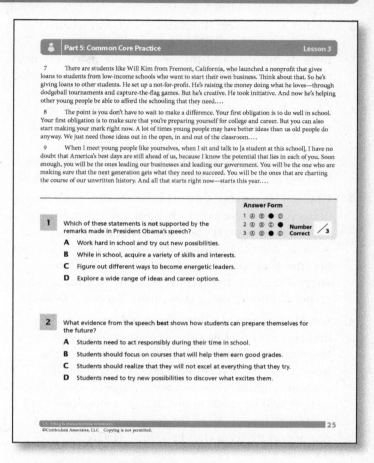

AT A GLANCE

Students independently read a longer speech and answer questions in a format that provides test practice.

STEP BY STEP

- Tell students to use what they have learned about reading carefully and citing evidence to make inferences to read the speech on pages 24 and 25.

- Remind students to underline or circle important points.

- Tell students to answer the questions on pages 25 and 26. For questions 1–3, they should fill in the correct circle on the Answer Form.

- When students have finished, use the Answer Analysis to discuss correct responses and the reasons for them. Have students fill in the Number Correct on the Answer Form.

ANSWER ANALYSIS

1   Choice C is correct. Though President Obama does encourage students to become leaders, he does not specifically mention that they "figure out different ways to be energetic leaders." Choice A is supported by his remarks in paragraph 2: "It means you've got to work as hard as you know how to work." Choice B is supported by paragraph 3: "That's what school is for: discovering new passions, acquiring new skills…" Choice D is also supported by paragraph 3: "This is the time where you can try out new interests and test new ideas." **(DOK 2)**

Theme Connection

- How do all the passages in this lesson relate to the theme of the competitive spirit?

- Without the spirit of competition, what do you think would motivate the world's athletes, explorers, and leaders?

2   Choice D is correct. It relates directly to when Obama says, "So that's a big part of your responsibility, to test things out. Take risks. Try new things." Choice A is incorrect. The speech focuses more on taking risks than acting responsibly. Choice B is incorrect. Obama says the opposite: students shouldn't always choose courses that will guarantee good grades. Choice C is incorrect. Realizing you will not excel at everything does not best support how to prepare for the future. **(DOK 2)**

3   Choice C is correct. Obama believes that students are obliged to prepare themselves for college and career. Choice A is incorrect because it discusses the present, not the future. Choices B and D are incorrect because they discuss students' future roles but suggest nothing about those students taking personal responsibility to make that future happen. **(DOK 2)**

4   Sample response: In this speech, Obama demonstrates that he values creativity. Not only does he recommend that students "color outside of the lines" and "try new things," he also suggests that students should "explore a wide range of possibilities" so they will be ready to invent new technologies or write new books. All of the careers he highlights require creativity, a trait he values. **(DOK 3)**

Part 5: Common Core Practice   Lesson 3

3   Which sentence from the passage **best** supports the idea that President Obama thinks students must take responsibility for their own futures?

  A   "Now, that doesn't always mean that you have to have a perfect score on every assignment."

  B   "Down the road, those will be the traits that will help you succeed, as well—the traits that will lead you to invent a device that makes an iPad look like a stone tablet."

  C   "Your first obligation is to make sure that you're preparing yourself for college and career."

  D   "Soon enough, you will be the ones leading our businesses and leading our government."

4   Read the statement below, and then answer the question that follows it.

  President Obama believes that creativity is a valuable trait for people to have.

  Explain how you can tell that the above statement is true. Write a paragraph responding to this question. Use at least **two** details from the passage to support your response.

  See sample response.

_____

_____

_____

_____

_____

_____

_____

_____

_____

_____

✓ **Self Check**   Go back and see what you can check off on the Self Check on page 2.

26   L3: Citing Evidence to Make Inferences   ©Curriculum Associates, LLC   Copying is not permitted.

Integrating Standards

Use these questions and tasks as opportunities to interact with "The President's Speech to Students."

1   What do you think President Obama's point of view toward young people is? Support your response with at least one piece of evidence from the speech. **(RI.7.6)**

Sample response: Obama views young people as the key to the future success of the United States and values their ideas. In his speech, he says, "I have no doubt that America's best days are still ahead of us, because I know the potential that lies in each of you."

2   Read this sentence from the speech: "You will be the ones that are charting the course of our unwritten history." Find the example of figurative language and explain its meaning in this context. **(RI.7.4; L.7.5)**

"Charting the course" in this instance means that the youth of today will be deciding what direction the future will go in and making important decisions that will shape history.

3   Imagine that President Obama met a student who had a bad report card. Based on what you have read in his speech, write out the conversation you think he is likely to have with the student. **(RI.7.1; W.7.3)**

Responses will vary. Encourage students to consider the tone of the President's speech and think about what similarities or differences he would adopt with one of his own children.

4   Discuss with a partner whether you think Obama's speech was timeless or would need to be changed for today's students or for future students. Support your ideas with evidence from the passage. **(SL.7.1)**

Discussions will vary. Encourage students to consider what it means for a speech to be timeless and how the points Obama makes would or would not apply to students attending school in the past or in the future.

Writing Activities

Speech Conclusion *(W.7.2, W.7.4)*

- Challenge students to write a conclusion paragraph for President Obama's speech. Encourage them to follow the style and content of what they already read.

- Allow time for students to share their paragraphs with the class.

Misplaced Modifiers *(L.7.1c)*

- Read aloud this phrase from page 20: *Though Jordan was visibly weak in the first quarter.* Point out to students that the word *visibly* describes the verb *weak.* Discuss that this means people could see that Jordan was not at his full strength.

- Then restate the phrase by saying: *Though Jordan was weak in the first quarter visibly.* Have students explain why this phrase is difficult to understand. (*It is not clear what the word* visibly *describes.*) Tell students that this is an example of a misplaced modifier.

- Have students write several sentences that include misplaced modifiers. Encourage them to exchange sentences with a partner and rewrite the sentences with the modifiers placed correctly.

LISTENING ACTIVITY *(SL.7.1, SL.7.6)*

Listen Closely/Audience Adjustment

- Discuss with students the importance of adapting their speech when addressing a specific audience. Review President Obama's speech, and discuss the intended audience.

- Have students consider how the speech would be different if it were delivered to another audience, such as young children or graduating seniors.

- Challenge students to deliver President Obama's points for a different audience. Listeners then infer the audience that the speech is intended for.

DISCUSSION ACTIVITY *(SL.7.1)*

Talk in a Group/Discuss the Theme

- Have groups of students discuss the theme of competitive spirit based on this lesson's passages.

- Encourage groups to consider what they learned about the competitive spirit from each passage. *How is the spirit of competition in sports similar to and different from competitiveness at school or reaching the South Pole?*

- Have groups share the results of their discussions with the class.

MEDIA ACTIVITY *(RI.7.1)*

Be Creative/Draw a Cartoon

- Have students review the illustration on page 19. Remind them that they examined it to make an inference about the runner's feelings.

- Invite students to create illustrations or cartoons of their own that require the reader to make an inference about the spirit of competition, using one of the real people from this lesson's texts.

- Have students exchange drawings and explain how they inferred meaning from the pictures.

RESEARCH ACTIVITY *(W.7.8; SL.7.4)*

Research and Present/Present a Time Line

- Review with students that "Race to Reach the South Pole: Scott vs. Amundsen" features two men competing to reach the South Pole first. Have students use details from the historical account to create a time line with one explorer's activities on the top and the other's on the bottom.

- Encourage students to use print or digital sources to find more information about each explorer's expedition.

- Have students present their time lines to the class.

Analyzing Interactions in a Text

LESSON OBJECTIVES

- Identify relationships between individuals, events, and ideas in informational text.

- Analyze how interactions between individuals, events, and ideas influence other events and ideas.

THE LEARNING PROGRESSION

- **Grade 6:** CCSS RI.6.3 requires students to analyze how an author develops and elaborates upon a key individual, event, or idea.

- **Grade 7: CCSS RI.7.3 requires students to combine what they have learned in prior grades to analyze how different factors in informational text interact with one another and influence other individuals, events, and ideas.**

- **Grade 8:** CCSS RI.8.3 asks students to continue to study the relationships between and among key elements, analyzing how an author makes connections and distinctions between them.

PREREQUISITE SKILLS

- Identify ideas, individuals, and events in an informational text.

- Explain how two or more individuals, events, or ideas within a text are connected.

- Determine how an author introduces, illustrates, and elaborates upon a key individual, event, or idea in an informational text.

TAP STUDENTS' PRIOR KNOWLEDGE

- Tell students they will work on a lesson about analyzing the interactions between individuals, events, and ideas to figure out how they influence one other. Ask students what *influence* means. (*"to have an effect on a person or the course of events"*)

- Review cause-and-effect relationships. (*A cause makes something happen. An effect is what happens as a result.*) Then present students with a simple example: "Jake failed the test because he didn't study." Discuss how the two events are related: What happened? (*Jake failed the test.*) What caused Jake to fail? (*He didn't study.*) Point out that the word *because* helps to signal this relationship.

- Remind students that one factor or set of factors may cause one or more effects. Share an example from your own life, such as, "I forgot to charge my cell phone, so it wouldn't work. Then, when I got a flat tire, I couldn't call a service station or let the principal know I'd be late." Discuss the relationship between the single cause and the many effects. Have volunteers share instances from their own lives.

- Point out that paying attention to relationships among factors in informational texts can help students figure out how different individuals, events, and ideas influence and interact with one another.

Ready *Teacher Toolbox*		*teacher-toolbox.com*
	Prerequisite Skills	*RI.7.3*
Ready Lessons	✓	✓
Tools for Instruction	✓	
Interactive Tutorials		✓

CCSS Focus

RI.7.3 Analyze the interactions between individuals, events, and ideas in a text (e.g., how ideas influence individuals or events, or how individuals influence ideas or events).

ADDITIONAL STANDARDS: RI.7.1, RI.7.2, RI.7.4, RI.7.7; L.7.2a, L.7.4a, L.7.4b; W.7.1, W.7.1b, W.7.7; SL.7.1, SL.7.4, SL.7.6
(*See page A39 for full text.*)

AT A GLANCE

Through a cartoon, students are introduced to the concept of interactions between individuals, ideas, and events. Students learn that paying attention to relationships between the different factors presented in a text can help them figure out complex interactions.

STEP BY STEP

- Together, read the paragraph about how a combination of factors often influence an inventor. Then direct students to study the cartoon to identify factors that influenced Urg, the inventor.

- Point out that the chart shows how the factors influence one another. Have students complete the chart by adding Urg's response. Then discuss how Ogg's wish for a comfy place to sit influenced Urg. It gave her an idea that inspired her to invent the chair. Explain that, unlike Urg, most inventors have been influenced by many factors over time.

- Then read and discuss the next paragraph about factors influencing the Wright brothers. Have students brainstorm some factors that might have interacted to produce the airplane. (*Examples might include earlier ideas and experiments related to hot-air balloons and gliders; observations about birds in flight; inventions such as gas-powered engines; the brothers' experiences at their bike shop.*)

- Note that, most likely, the Wright brothers were inspired by the interactions of a combination of factors at different points in their lives. Stress that such interactions can often be quite complex.

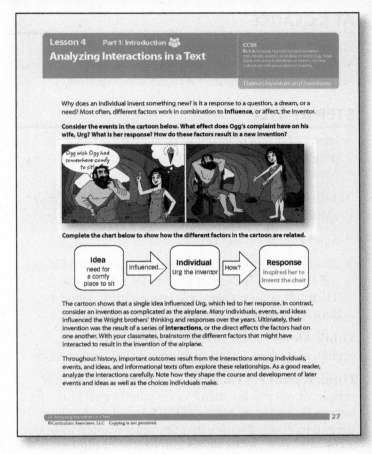

- Ask students to share real-life situations when ideas or events influenced their responses. Then discuss how analyzing interactions in a text can help students understand why people respond as they do and what happens as a result.

Genre Focus

Informational Texts: Biography

Tell students that in this lesson they will read a biography. Explain that a biography is an account of events in the life of a real person that has been written by someone else. Biographies usually share the following characteristics:

- They include facts, anecdotes, and details about all or part of the person's life story.

- They may tell about the life of an ordinary person or a famous person who achieved great things.

- They may focus on important experiences in a person's life to reveal more about his or her personality, thoughts, opinions, and motivations.

Based on these characteristics, ask students to describe biographies they have read, including the name of the person being featured and what might be learned from his or her experiences. Students may mention books about famous people in history, science, the arts, or sports.

Explain that "Extraordinary People: Tim Berners-Lee," the last text in this lesson, is a biography about the inventor of the World Wide Web.

AT A GLANCE

Students read a historical account about Eadweard Muybridge. They identify an idea that caused Muybridge to photograph a racehorse in action.

STEP BY STEP

- Invite volunteers to tell what they learned on the previous page about identifying the interactions between individuals, events, and ideas.

- Tell students that in this lesson they will continue identifying such interactions in informational texts.

- Read aloud "Flying Horses."

- Read the question: "What people, events, and ideas led to Muybridge's plan to photograph a horse?" Then tell students you will use a Think Aloud to demonstrate a way of answering the question.

Think Aloud: While reading, I looked for people, events, and ideas and thought about their interactions.

Think Aloud: For example, paragraph 1 states that people wondered for many years whether all four of a horse's hooves ever came off the ground at the same time. Paragraph 2 states that Stanford wanted to know if this was true, so he hired Muybridge to photograph the movements of his horse.

Think Aloud: So, here are the interactions I'm seeing. The idea of whether horses can "fly" led to Stanford hiring Muybridge. Muybridge, in turn, planned to use his knowledge of cameras to investigate this idea.

- Direct students to the chart. Review that visualizing interactions between factors can help students make connections. Have students write the idea in the chart. Then discuss how the factors are related.

Think Aloud: The chart helps me see how individuals, events, and ideas interact with one another. The question of whether horses can fly drives events. Stanford asks Muybridge to photograph his horse because he wants to answer this question.

- Have students respond to the question at the bottom of the page. Invite volunteers to share their answers. (*Sample response: The question of whether horses "fly" is what leads to subsequent events. Stanford asks Muybridge to photograph his horse because he wants to answer the question. This event causes Muybridge to figure out a plan to capture a horse's movements.*)

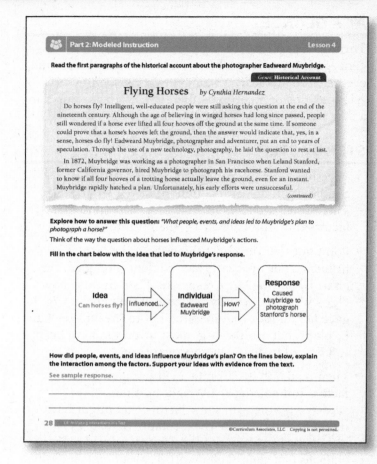

Tier Two Vocabulary: *Indicate*

- Point out the word *indicate* in paragraph 1, line 4. Ask students to tell what *indicate* means in this sentence. (*to show, to point to*) Guide them to identify context clues that helped them figure out this meaning. (*"If someone could prove" and "the answer . . . yes, in a sense"*)

- Ask how the word *indicate* functions as a part of speech in this sentence. (*as a verb*) Write *indication*, and point out the suffix *-ion*. Have students describe how the suffix affects the meaning of the base word. (*-ion means "act or process," so it changes* indicate *from a verb to a noun meaning "the act of showing or pointing to."*)

- As time permits, explain that *indicate* comes from a Latin root meaning "to show, to point the way." Discuss other words related to this root: *index* (forefinger), *indicative, indicator.* (**RI.7.4; L.7.4a, L.7.4b**)

AT A GLANCE

Students continue reading about Eadweard Muybridge. They answer a multiple-choice question and analyze how his actions influenced the public's thinking.

STEP BY STEP

- Tell students they will continue reading the account of Eadweard Muybridge.

- Close Reading helps students find a sentence that describes the images in Muybridge's photographs. The Hint will help them recognize how Muybridge's images offered proof about a horse's movements.

- Have students read the account and underline the sentence that explains what the photographs showed, as directed by the Close Reading. Then discuss how the high-speed photographs captured different images as the horse trotted, including proof that all its hooves left the ground. If necessary, ask: "How would high-speed photos of a horse be almost as useful as the slow-motion replays shown on TV?"

- Ask students to complete the page. Then discuss the Answer Analysis below and students' written responses. Also discuss how Muybridge's knowledge of photography influenced other events and ideas.

ANSWER ANALYSIS

Choice A is incorrect. It states what Muybridge set out to explore.

Choice B is incorrect. It describes Muybridge's plan, not the results of his efforts.

Choice C is correct. It describes the proof Muybridge got from his high-speed photographs of the horse. These results then influenced how the world thought about horses, motion, and photography.

Choice D is incorrect. It describes what happened as a result of Muybridge's success with his photographs.

ERROR ALERT: Students who did not choose C may have misunderstood the question. Point out that all choices are sentences from the text. The question asks which one *best* describes how Muybridge's photos provided proof about how a horse lifts its hooves as it trots. Have students eliminate choices that do not describe how a horse moves.

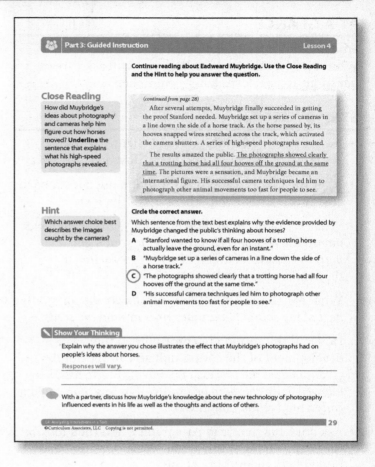

Tier Two Vocabulary: *Activated*

- Direct students to the word *activated* in the fourth line. Work with them to determine that in this context it means "to set into motion."

- Ask students to think of other words that are synonyms for *activated*. (*started, set off, triggered*)

- Have students suggest sentences in which *activated* is used in a similar context. (*The outdoor lights are activated by a motion sensor. The television is activated by remote control. My cell phone is activated by pressing a button.*) **(RI.7.4; L.7.4a)**

AT A GLANCE

Students twice read a historical account about Eli Whitney. After the first reading, you will ask three questions to check students' comprehension.

STEP BY STEP

- Have students read the account silently without referring to the Study Buddy or Close Reading text.

- After the first reading, ask the following questions to ensure students' comprehension of the text:

  What is this account mostly about? *(It is about a man named Eli Whitney. He invented the cotton gin, a machine that revolutionized cotton production in the South in the late 1700s.)*

  What are cotton bolls? *(Cotton bolls are the soft, fluffy part of the cotton plant that grows around the seeds.)*

  How did the cotton gin contribute to the development of the cotton industry in the South? *(It automated the process of removing the seeds. This allowed more cotton to be processed in less time, making cotton production profitable.)*

- Ask students to reread paragraph 1 and then look at the Study Buddy think aloud. What does the Study Buddy help them think about?

Tip: The Study Buddy reminds students to figure out how the mechanization of spinning and weaving in England affected Eli Whitney.

- Have students read the rest of the account. Tell them to follow the directions in the Close Reading.

Tip: Point out that the details identified in the Close Reading focus on the interactions among important events and ideas in the text. Students should recognize the connection between a greater demand for cotton and the way the cotton gin made it easier to supply. This invention was largely responsible for the growth of the cotton industry in the South.

- Finally, have students answer the questions on page 31. Use the Answer Analysis to discuss correct and incorrect responses.

Read the historical account. Use the Study Buddy and the Close Reading to guide your reading.

Genre: Historical Account

Eli Whitney and the Cotton Gin
by Timothy Morris

I wonder how changes in England affected Eli Whitney in America. I'll have to read carefully to figure out how the interactions between events and ideas resulted in his response.

Close Reading

Why couldn't Southern states make money by growing cotton in 1792? **Underline** the sentence explaining the problem Whitney hoped to solve.

Underline clues in the text that show how Whitney's invention changed life in the South.

1 In the late 1700s, England was hungry for cotton. Until this time, women and girls of the family generally did the spinning and weaving. Then improvements were made to the spinning wheel and loom, making them faster and more efficient. As a result, the process became mechanized, and new textile mills opened to meet the growing demand for cotton cloth.

2 In America in 1792, Eli Whitney recognized that the mechanization of the cloth-making process meant a greater demand for cotton. Cotton grew easily in the Southern states, but the cotton bolls contained numerous small seeds that were difficult and time-consuming to remove by hand. Unless a more efficient way could be found to separate the seeds from the bolls, there was little money to be made in growing cotton.

3 As a young man, Eli Whitney liked figuring out things. He studied machines and often found ways to improve them. Whitney began to think about the problem of removing seeds from cotton and decided that a machine could be built to do the job efficiently.

4 The machine Whitney designed was simple, but it worked like a charm. Cotton was fed into a machine with short wire teeth on a revolving cylinder. The thin cotton fibers were pulled through, leaving the seeds behind. Now, a single machine was capable of cleaning and processing up to fifty pounds of raw cotton daily.

5 The invention of the cotton gin brought about many changes. The most significant effect was that, at long last, growing cotton could be profitable. Cotton plantations sprang up in the South where once empty fields stood, and textile mills opened to make cloth. Thanks to Whitney's invention, the world was never the same again. Just as mechanization revolutionized life in England, the cotton gin gave the American South a new industry to call its own.

ELL Support: Multiple-Meaning Words

- Explain that some words have more than one meaning. These are called multiple-meaning words. As an example, work with students to come up with a common meaning for the word *hungry*. *(needing food)*

- Next, point out the word *hungry* in the first sentence. Have students tell what England is *hungry* for. *(cotton)* What is cotton? *(a fluffy material used to produce thread and fabric)* Ask students to use these context clues to help them determine the meaning of *hungry* in this sentence. *("having a strong desire or need for")*

- Help students develop sentences using each meaning of the word *hungry*.

- Repeat with the multiple-meaning word *teeth* in paragraph 4. **(RI.7.4; L.7.4a)**

STEP BY STEP

- Have students read questions 1–3, using the Hints to help them answer those questions.

Tip: If students have trouble answering question 3, have them reread paragraph 5 and refer to the text they underlined in the Close Reading. Ask students to identify changes that resulted from the invention of the cotton gin.

- Discuss with students the Answer Analysis below.

ANSWER ANALYSIS

1 The correct choice is C. It explains why growing cotton was not profitable. Choices A and B are incorrect. Each refers to a different aspect of cloth-making, not to growing cotton. Choice D is incorrect. It describes how the cotton gin provided a solution, which allowed growers to make a profit.

2 The correct answer is D. It tells what happened as a result of Whitney's invention. Choice A tells something readers might infer, but the text says nothing about profits Whitney made. Choice B is incorrect; the account does not address the effect of the cotton gin on the lives of the workers. Choice C is incorrect. The increase in cotton production resulting from Whitney's invention had no direct impact on the use of the spinning wheel.

3 Sample response: The mechanization of cloth-making in England led to a growing demand for cotton. After Whitney's invention overcame the problem of separating seeds from the fiber, growers could meet the demand for raw cotton and make a profit. These new opportunities for profit influenced others to get into the business of growing cotton and producing textiles. As a result, cotton plantations grew and textile mills were built, which changed life in the South.

RETEACHING

Use a chart to verify the answer to question 1. Draw the chart below and work with students to fill in the boxes. Sample responses are provided.

Idea	Individual	Response
Removing seeds from cotton bolls was a problem.	Eli Whitney	Whitney was inspired to invent the cotton gin.

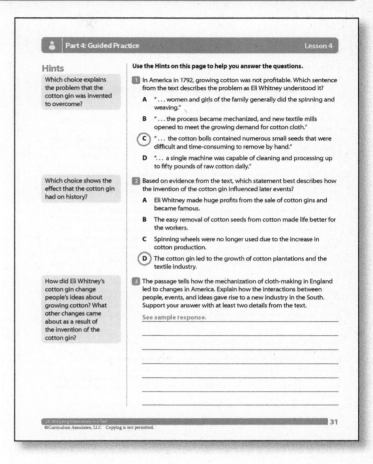

 Part 4: Guided Practice   Lesson 4

Hints

Which choice explains the problem that the cotton gin was invented to overcome?

Which choice shows the effect that the cotton gin had on history?

How did Eli Whitney's cotton gin change people's ideas about growing cotton? What other changes came about as a result of the invention of the cotton gin?

Use the Hints on this page to help you answer the questions.

1 In America in 1792, growing cotton was not profitable. Which sentence from the text describes the problem as Eli Whitney understood it?

A "... women and girls of the family generally did the spinning and weaving."

B "... the process became mechanized, and new textile mills opened to meet the growing demand for cotton cloth."

C "... the cotton bolls contained numerous small seeds that were difficult and time-consuming to remove by hand."

D "... a single machine was capable of cleaning and processing up to fifty pounds of raw cotton daily."

2 Based on evidence from the text, which statement best describes how the invention of the cotton gin influenced later events?

A Eli Whitney made huge profits from the sale of cotton gins and became famous.

B The easy removal of cotton seeds from cotton made life better for the workers.

C Spinning wheels were no longer used due to the increase in cotton production.

D The cotton gin led to the growth of cotton plantations and the textile industry.

3 The passage tells how the mechanization of cloth-making in England led to changes in America. Explain how the interactions between people, events, and ideas gave rise to a new industry in the South. Support your answer with at least two details from the text.

See sample response.

L4: Analyzing Interactions in a Text   31
©Curriculum Associates, LLC   Copying is not permitted.

Integrating Standards

Use these questions to further students' understanding of "Eli Whitney and the Cotton Gin."

1 Explain why the new textile mills created a demand for cotton. Cite text evidence. **(RI.7.1)**

The text states that "... mechanization of the cloth-making process meant a greater demand for cotton." This means that the machines in textile mills spun cotton thread and wove cloth at a much faster rate. As a result, the mills needed more and more raw cotton to feed the process.

2 Summarize why Whitney's cotton gin made growing cotton profitable. **(RI.7.2; W.7.4)**

Sample response: Cotton grew well in the South, but it was not a good cash crop because removing seeds by hand took large amounts of time and effort. Whitney's cotton gin gave growers the means to process raw cotton much faster so they could sell more cotton and make a profit.

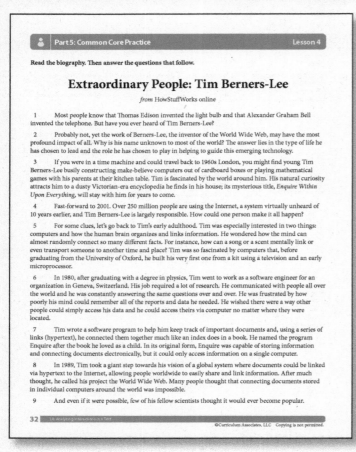

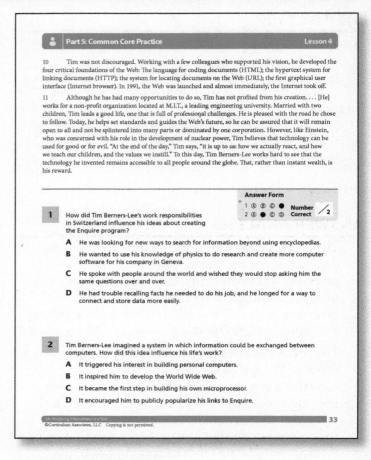

AT A GLANCE

Students independently read a longer biography and answer questions in a format that provides test practice.

STEP BY STEP

• Tell students to use what they have learned about reading carefully and analyzing interactions between individuals, events, and ideas in a text to read the biography on pages 32 and 33.

• Remind students to underline or circle important points in the text.

• Tell students to answer the questions on pages 33 and 34. For questions 1 and 2, they should fill in the correct circle on the Answer Form.

• When students have finished, use the Answer Analysis to discuss correct responses and the reasons for them. Have students fill in the Number Correct on the Answer Form.

ANSWER ANALYSIS

1 Choice D is correct. Tim was frustrated when he couldn't remember all the information. Choice A is incorrect. Tim looked for ways to remember information. Choice B is incorrect. He did use his knowledge of physics, but this didn't motivate him. Choice C is incorrect. There is no evidence that he wished people wouldn't ask the same questions. **(DOK 2)**

2 Choice B is correct. Tim's idea of a system in which information could be exchanged inspired him to develop the Web. Choice A is incorrect because the opposite is true. Choice C is incorrect. Tim did not build a microprocessor; he used one to build his first computer. The text does not support choice D. **(DOK 2)**

Theme Connection

• How do all the texts in this lesson relate to the theme of inventors and inventions?

• Tell how one of the inventions you read about influences your life.

3 Sample response: As a child, Tim Berners-Lee loved math, made make-believe computers, and had a "natural curiosity" about the world around him. He found a Victorian encyclopedia with the title *Enquire Within Upon Everything*, which became his motto for the rest of his life. These childhood interests led him to the field of physics and into a career in computer programming. His love of computers and his tireless quest for knowledge led him to invent the World Wide Web. *(DOK 3)*

4 Sample response: The sentences reflect Tim Berners-Lee's fascination with creating a program that organizes and connects different bits of information in a way similar to how the brain functions. This led him to write the Enquire software program in which hypertext connects documents together "much like an index does in a book." But his curiosity about how the mind connects random facts and has the ability to "transport someone to another time or place" led him to write computer programming that recreated his ideas about the workings of the human mind. *(DOK 3)*

(Reproduction of student worksheet page 34)

Part 5: Common Core Practice   Lesson 4

3 Based on the biography, explain how Tim Berners-Lee's early childhood interests influenced the path he chose as an adult. Use at least **two** details from the text to support your answer.

See sample response.

4 Read these sentences from paragraph 5 of the biography.

> He wondered how the mind can almost randomly connect so many different facts. For instance, how can a song or a scent mentally link or even transport someone to another time and place?

Describe what influence this idea had on Tim Berners-Lee's approach to writing new programs that operate computers. Use at least **two** details from the biography to support your answer.

See sample response.

✓ Self Check   *Go back and see what you can check off on the Self Check on page 2.*

34   L4: Analyzing Interactions in a Text   ©Curriculum Associates, LLC   Copying is not permitted.

Integrating Standards

Use these questions and tasks as opportunities to interact with "Extraordinary People: Tim Berners-Lee."

1 How did people react to Tim's idea of the World Wide Web at first? Cite text evidence. *(RI.7.1)*

Many people originally thought that "connecting documents stored in individual computers around the world was impossible."

2 Cite two details supporting the idea that Tim is more interested in how his invention can help people than he is in fame or wealth. *(RI.7.2)*

"Although he has had many opportunities to do so, Tim has not profited from his creation. . . ." "Today, he helps set standards and guides the Web's future, so he can be assured that it will remain open to all. . . ."

3 Paragraph 11 says Tim wants to make sure the Web will "not be splintered into many parts." What does *splintered* mean here? *(RI.7.4; L.7.4a)*

Used as a verb, splinter *means, "to split or break," so* splintered *means "broken." Tim does not want the Web to be broken apart into many pieces.*

4 The author compares the work of Tim Berners-Lee with that of Thomas Edison and Alexander Graham Bell, claiming that the work of Berners-Lee may have the most profound impact of all. Write a paragraph to agree or disagree with this claim. *(W.7.1)*

Student paragraphs will vary. Remind them to support their claims with logical reasoning and to include text evidence.

5 Discuss in small groups: Based on what you've read, what inferences can you draw about the kind of person Tim Berners-Lee is? *(RI.7.1; SL.7.1)*

Discussions will vary. Students might mention characteristics such as brilliant, creative, hard-working, and unassuming.

Writing Activities

Argumentative Essay (W.7.1, W.7.1b)

- Have students review "Flying Horses," "Eli Whitney and the Cotton Gin," and "Extraordinary People: Tim Berners-Lee." Then discuss how each of the inventions described influenced people, events, and ideas. Finally, ask students to decide which invention has altered lives and changed history the most.

- Challenge students to write an argument that states their opinion. Remind them to explain their claims clearly and to provide reasons and relevant evidence as support. Allow time for students to share their work.

Separate Coordinate Adjectives (L.7.2a)

- Direct students to this sentence on page 28: "Intelligent, well-educated people were still asking this question at the end of the nineteenth century."

- Write the sentence on the board, and underline the adjectives *intelligent* and *well-educated*. Explain that these are coordinate adjectives—they modify a noun equally and separately. That means their order can be reversed and the word *and* can be inserted between them. Circle the comma, and tell students that coordinate adjectives are separated with a comma.

- Have students write a sentence that includes two coordinate adjectives and uses appropriate punctuation.

LISTENING ACTIVITY (SL.7.4, SL.7.6)

Listen Closely/Conduct an Interview

- Have partners use the information in "Extraordinary People: Tim Berners-Lee" to conduct an interview for a television broadcast.

- Have partners take turns being the interviewer and the interviewee, Tim Berners-Lee.

- Students must listen carefully to each other as they ask and answer questions. Encourage them to be creative while basing their discussion on information in the biography they read.

DISCUSSION ACTIVITY (SL.7.1)

Talk in a Group/Compare Biographies

- Review characteristics of biographies.

- Have students form small groups to discuss the biographical aspects of the accounts they read in this lesson as well as others they've read. Use these prompts: How are the biographical aspects alike and different? What can you learn by reading biographies? Which ones inspire you?

- Appoint one member of each group to take notes. Allow 10 to 15 minutes for the discussion. Then have each group share its results with the class.

MEDIA ACTIVITY (RI.7.7)

Be Creative/Make a Flipbook

- Review "Flying Horses," and remind students how Muybridge's succession of high-speed photos captured the movements of a trotting horse.

- Then invite students to create flipbooks to demonstrate motion using a similar principle. If needed, students can find videos online providing instructions and tips to create a flipbook.

- Allow time for students to exchange their flipbooks with classmates.

RESEARCH ACTIVITY (W.7.7; SL.7.4)

Research and Present/Give a Presentation

- Have students use the information in this lesson as a springboard to plan an oral presentation about the Wright brothers or another inventor.

- Ask students to use print and digital sources to research details to include, such as biographical facts, information about the invention and factors that influenced its creation, and the changes that resulted from its existence.

- Suggest that students make their presentations by speaking as if they themselves were the inventor.

SCORING GUIDE AND ANSWER ANALYSIS

Informational Passage Answer Analysis

1A ⒶⒷ●Ⓓ	4 ⒶⒷ●Ⓓ
1B ⒶⒷⒸ●	5 ⒶⒷⒸ●
2 ●ⒷⒸⒹ	6 Ⓐ●ⒸⒹ
3 Ⓐ●ⒸⒹ	7 ⒶⒷⒸ●

1 **Part A:** Choice C is correct. Edward Cope accidentally placed an animal's skull on its tail, and both Cope and Othniel Marsh "made many mistakes" in their rush to outdo each other. There is no information about scientists from other nations or in other fields, so choices A and D are incorrect. Choice B is incorrect because the other scientist quickly found Cope's error. **(RI.7.2; DOK 3)**

Part B: Choice D is correct. This statement shows that American paleontologists were not knowledgeable enough to notice when earlier scientists had made mistakes. Choice A seems to contradict this idea by showing one scientist correcting another's error. Choice B does not reflect on this claim, but on Marsh's petty rivalry with Cope. Likewise, choice C shows more about Marsh and Cope than paleontologists generally. **(RI.7.1; DOK 3)**

2 Choice A is correct. This event occurred at the beginning and started the feud, making it the most important influence on the relationship.

Choice B is incorrect. Marsh's claim didn't ease the rivalry, but it was not the most influential event. Choice C is incorrect. The workers' behavior reflected their employer's attitude. Choice D is incorrect. The attacks in the newspaper occurred well into the rivalry. It showed how the feud played out but was not the most influential event. **(RI.7.3; DOK 2)**

3 Choice B is correct. The first paragraph states that the feud "brought to light some of the most spectacular creatures that ever walked the earth." The men discovered 136 new dinosaur species because they were trying to outdo each other.

Choice A is incorrect. Cope and Marsh became celebrities, but nothing suggests that this was their

main goal. Choice C is incorrect. Cope and Marsh made mistakes, but they still seemed to be well-respected. Choice D is incorrect. It was the rivalry between the men that caused them to discover so many dinosaur bones. It's unlikely a partnership would have led to more discoveries. **(RI.7.3; DOK 2)**

4 Choice C is correct. In Cope's time, scientists believed that a large brain indicated intelligence. The fact that Cope wanted his brain compared to Marsh's suggests that he believed he had the larger brain and was thus smarter than his rival.

Choice A is incorrect. Cope telling newspaper about Marsh's actions shows he believed Marsh was wrong, not that he thought he was smarter than Marsh. Choice B is incorrect. While Cope might have thought himself smart to find *Elasmosaurus*, this does not show he thought he was smarter than Marsh. Choice D is incorrect. The fact that Cope published scientific articles attacking Marsh indicates that he believed Marsh's ideas to be faulty, not that he believed he was smarter. **(RI.7.1; DOK 3)**

5 Choice D is correct. While interesting, this is not an important detail to include in a summary.

Choice A is incorrect. Cope and Marsh's desire to outdo each other is an important idea. Choice B is incorrect. An important part of the feud's legacy is how productive they were in digging up bones. Choice C is incorrect. The passage gives a balanced view of Cope and Marsh. They made important finds, but they also made mistakes, an idea that would be important in a summary. **(RI.7.2; DOK 2)**

6 Choice B is correct. The term "mixed legacy" shows positives and negatives to the rivalry. The author develops this idea in the last paragraph.

Choice A is incorrect. The author does not concentrate on mistakes as this would not indicate a "mixed legacy." Choice C is incorrect. The causes and effects of the rivalry would not support the idea of a "mixed legacy." Choice D is incorrect. The author gives events in sequence, but this does not support the idea of a "mixed legacy." **(RI.7.2; DOK 3)**

SAMPLE RESPONSES

7 Choice D is correct. These are the main topics in order and without extraneous details.

Choice A is incorrect. It is an accurate time line, but it leaves out main topics such as the feud's lasting effects on paleontology. Choice B is incorrect. It lists some key details, meaning it is not a list of topics. Choice C is incorrect. The first topic is out of order. Paragraph 1 broaches the idea of celebrity, but its true topic is the introduction to the Bone Wars. *(RI.7.2; DOK 2)*

Short Response

8 The competition between the men was more important to them than accuracy with their work. Their teams used dynamite to bury fossils so they would not fall into the other team's hands. This left many discoveries buried beneath the rubble. In addition, the men worked quickly in order to publish their findings first, which led to many mistakes being made. *(RI.7.1; DOK 3)*

9 The rivalry between Cope and Marsh had a positive influence on the field of paleontology at the time. Because the rivalry drove them to work harder, the men were able to discover 136 new dinosaur species. Their teams dug up a remarkable number of dinosaur bones. The discovery of this raw material allows scientists to still learn new things about the fossils today. Because of this, the rivalry has had a positive influence on the field of paleontology today. *(RI.7.3; DOK 3)*

Performance Task

10 One central idea that the author presents is that the rivalry between Cope and Marsh heated up soon after it began. The author presents important events about the beginning of the rivalry in sequence. The reader first learns that the pair started out on friendly terms when they met in 1864. Then, in 1868, Marsh bribed Cope's foreman to send new fossils to him. This started the feud, which grew when Marsh told others about a mistake Cope had made in his illustration of *Elasmosaurus*. Each man was soon publishing scientific articles attacking the other's ideas.

Another central idea is that Cope and Marsh's rivalry kept growing. The author describes acts of sabotage committed by both teams. This included bribing workers to quit, sending spies to steal bones from the opposing camp, and using dynamite to bury fossils to keep them from the other team. The author also indicates how fieldwork was rushed so that each man could more quickly claim credit for discoveries.

A third central idea is that Cope and Marsh made many mistakes but also made important discoveries. The author develops this idea by first stating how the rush to publish led to mistakes. Cope mistakenly stuck the skull of *Elasmosaurus* on its tail in an illustration. Marsh accidentally stuck the head of one dinosaur onto the body of another. To present a balanced view, the author gives details about the men's amazing discoveries in the last paragraph. They discovered 136 new dinosaur species. Their teams dug up so many fossils that scientists are still learning new things about them today. Also, the author mentions specific dinosaur species found by Cope and Marsh that are displayed in museums today throughout the United States. *(RI.7.2; DOK 3)*

SCORING RUBRICS

Short-Response Rubric

2 points   The response is accurate, complete, and fulfills all requirements of the task. Text-based support and examples are included. Any information that goes beyond the text is relevant to the task.

1 point   The response is partially accurate and fulfills some requirements of the task. Some information may be inaccurate, too general, or confused. Support and examples may be insufficient or not text-based.

0 points   The response is inaccurate, poorly organized, or does not respond to the task.

Performance Task Rubric

4 points   The response
- Fulfills all requirements of the task
- Uses varied sentence types and some sophisticated vocabulary
- Includes relevant and accurate details from the texts as well as text-based inferences
- Demonstrates a thorough understanding of the texts
- Maintains a clear focus and organization
- Is fluent and demonstrates a clear voice
- Uses correct spelling, grammar, capitalization, and punctuation

3 points   The response
- Fulfills all requirements of the task
- Uses simple sentences and grade-level vocabulary
- Includes relevant and accurate details from the texts
- Demonstrates a mainly literal understanding of the texts
- Maintains a mostly clear focus and organization
- Is fluent and demonstrates some sense of voice
- Uses mostly correct spelling, grammar, capitalization, and punctuation

2 points   The response
- Fulfills some requirements of the task
- Uses simple sentences, some fragments, and grade-level vocabulary
- Includes some relevant and accurate details from the texts
- Demonstrates some misunderstandings or gaps in understanding of the texts
- Attempts to maintain a clear focus and organization
- Is difficult to read, includes some inaccuracies, and demonstrates little or no sense of voice
- Contains some inaccurate spelling, grammar, capitalization, and punctuation that may hinder understanding

1 point   The response
- Fulfills few requirements of the task
- Uses sentence fragments and below-grade-level vocabulary
- Includes no details or irrelevant details to support the response
- Demonstrates very little understanding of the texts
- Does not establish a clear focus or organization
- Is difficult to read, contains many inaccuracies, and demonstrates no sense of voice
- Uses incorrect spelling, grammar, capitalization, and punctuation to an extent that impedes understanding

0 points   The response is irrelevant, poorly organized, or illegible.

Citing Evidence to Support Inferences

Theme: *The Element of Surprise*

LESSON OBJECTIVES

- Use textual evidence, along with background knowledge, to make reasonable inferences about the characters, setting, and plot of a literary text.

- Cite two or more pieces of textual evidence to support inferences drawn from the text.

THE LEARNING PROGRESSION

- **Grade 6:** CCSS RL.6.1 emphasizes analysis and requires students to use details and quotations from the text to support their statements and inferences about a story.

- **Grade 7 CCSS RL.7.1 builds on the Grade 6 standard by requiring students to provide greater depth in their analyses by citing several pieces of textual evidence to support their statements and inferences about a story, poem, or drama.**

- **Grade 8:** CCSS RL.8.1 requires students to investigate further how textual evidence functions to convince readers and to make writing more vivid. It also requires students to evaluate evidence to identify which details most directly support explicit and implicit information.

PREREQUISITE SKILLS

- Understand that some information in a text is not directly stated.

- Understand how to use clues from a story and personal experiences to make inferences.

- Cite details and examples from a text used to make inferences.

TAP STUDENTS' PRIOR KNOWLEDGE

- Tell students they will be working on a lesson about citing text evidence to support inferences. Ask students what an inference is. (*an informed guess*)

- Ask students what they would think if they saw someone crying quietly. (*The person is sad or upset about something.*) Point out that no one directly told them this. Students used clues and their own experience to figure it out.

- Next, ask what students can do when they need to figure something out in a text that the author does not directly state. (*Use text clues and consider what they already know from their life experiences.*) Discuss how students can use their own experiences to help them understand what they read. For example, if students are reading about a situation with children, they might use their knowledge about a younger sibling to help them understand the feelings expressed in the text. Encourage students to give other examples.

- Then ask students what text evidence is. (*facts, examples, and other information from the text*) Review that quoting from a text is a powerful way to offer evidence, or proof, to support an inference.

- Point out that making inferences and citing evidence to support inferences will help students better understand fictional text.

Ready *Teacher Toolbox*   teacher-toolbox.com

	Prerequisite Skills	RL.7.1
Ready Lessons	✓	✓
Tools for Instruction		✓ ✓
Interactive Tutorials		✓

CCSS Focus

RL.7.1 Cite several pieces of textual evidence to support analysis of what the text says explicitly as well as inferences drawn from the text.

ADDITIONAL STANDARDS: **RL.7.2, RL.7.3, RL.7.4, RL.7.6, RL.7.7; L.7.2b, L.7.4a, L.7.4b, L.7.4d; W.7.3, W.7.4, W.7.7; SL.7.1, SL.7.2, SL.7.4, SL.7.6** (*See page A39 for full text.*)

AT A GLANCE

Through a short passage, students practice finding evidence to support an inference about a character. They learn that inferences are not blind guesses but informed conclusions based on evidence and reasoning.

STEP BY STEP

• Read aloud the paragraphs that include the definitions of *analysis*, *explicit*, and *inference*.

• Ask students to read the passage and underline any details that tell them how the main character in the passage is feeling.

• Explain that the chart shows the process of supporting an inference.

• Read the first and second columns, and ask students to use the details they underlined in the passage and their own background knowledge to help them fill in the blanks.

• Have students complete the inference in the third column by filling in the blank. Then discuss why the inference is reasonable, based on the text evidence and background knowledge in the chart.

• Provide students with an inference about a story they have read recently in class. Then have volunteers cite evidence from the story to support the inference.

• To reinforce how making and supporting inferences is a valuable reading strategy, share an inference you made about a novel or short story. Explain how the inference helped you better understand the characters or plot.

Genre Focus

Literary Texts: Short Stories

Tell students that in this lesson they will read short stories. Explain that short stories are short works of fiction that can be read in one sitting. They usually include the following characteristics:

• focus on only a few characters

• concentrate on one major event or conflict

• set an immediate mood or tone

• have a unity of theme, character, setting, and plot

• are written to entertain the reader

Based on these characteristics, ask students to name some places where they have read short stories, such as in magazines or in collections of short stories. What was appealing about the stories, and what did students notice about the genre? How did any illustrations help them better understand the characters or plot? If students read short stories in a collection, what was the unifying feature of the book?

Explain that "The Ransom of Red Chief" is a short story that takes place in the 1800s and tells about a kidnapping that goes wrong. The short story "Dusk" describes a surprising error in judgment.

Lesson 5   Part 1: Introduction
Citing Evidence to Support Inferences

CCSS
RL.7.1 Cite several pieces of textual evidence to support analysis of what the text says explicitly as well as inferences drawn from the text.

Theme: *The Element of Surprise*

Have you ever looked at something that interested you, such as a hot air balloon or a telescope, and tried to figure out how it works? An **analysis** is an examination of how the different parts of something work together. When you read a story, you analyze how its parts—its characters, settings, and events—work together to create meaning.

Some story details are **explicit**, or clearly stated. "Jesse was excited about going to the museum" is an example of an explicit detail: You know that Jesse is excited and why. But story information can also be less direct. You might have to make an **inference**, or an educated guess based on details in the story and your own knowledge, to figure out what's going on.

> After his dad had gone upstairs, Pete clenched his fists and stomped out of the room to go get a bucket and fill it with soapy water. His dad had just told him they were having company that evening and that Pete had to help out by doing some extra chores. Pete had finished all of his homework in study hall that day and had planned on spending the afternoon reading his new comic book, not mopping floors and dusting shelves.

Using details from the text and your own knowledge, fill in the blanks in the chart below.

Evidence	+	Background Knowledge	=	Inference
• Pete "clenched his fists and stomped out of the <u>room</u>."		When people clench their fists and stomp out of a room, these are signs that they <u>feel angry</u>		Pete is angry about <u>having to do</u> <u>extra chores</u> _____
• Pete had "planned on spending the afternoon <u>reading his new comic book</u>, not <u>mopping floors and dusting shelves</u>."				

When you're analyzing a story to make an inference, pay close attention to details in the text. Read closely to find evidence that you can cite, or give as proof, that the inference is reasonable. By making and supporting inferences, you'll be like an engineer looking at a machine you've never seen before, piecing together clues to figure out how it works.

AT A GLANCE

Students make an inference about a short story and use text evidence to support their inference.

STEP BY STEP

- Invite volunteers to tell what they learned on the previous page about making inferences.

- Tell students that in this lesson they will practice making inferences when they read.

- Read aloud "The Ransom of Red Chief."

- Then read the prompt: "Use details from the passage to predict whether Sam and Bill's plot will succeed."

- Now tell students you will perform a Think Aloud to demonstrate a way of answering the question.

Think Aloud: It's too early to be certain whether Sam and Bill's plot will succeed, but I can make a prediction about their chances.

Think Aloud: A prediction is a type of educated guess. In other words, a prediction is based on both my prior knowledge and specific evidence. This means that a prediction is a type of inference. And just like an inference, I need evidence to support a prediction.

Think Aloud: In the second paragraph, I read that the boy is "throwing rocks at a kitten on the opposite fence." In the fourth paragraph, I read that "the boy catches Bill neatly in the eye with a piece of brick." This is evidence that meshes well with background knowledge that I have—that people who throw rocks at cats and people are mean and can be hard to deal with.

- Direct students to the chart and ask where they've seen a similar chart before. Remind them that it shows the process of making an inference, and point out the first piece of text evidence.

- Tell students to add text evidence to the chart.

Think Aloud: Based on this knowledge and evidence from the text, I can make a prediction about whether Sam and Bill's plot will succeed.

- Ask students to fill in the blank in the third column and complete the chart. Have volunteers share their answers.

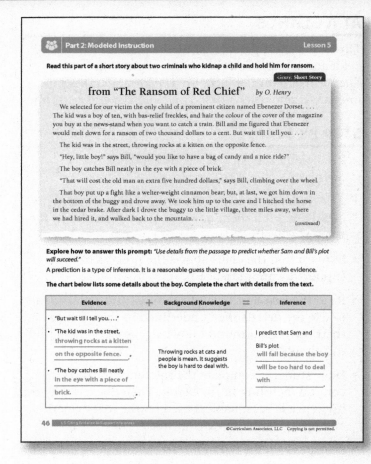

ELL Support: Multiple-Meaning Words

- Explain to students that words that have more than one meaning are called multiple-meaning words. Tell students they can use other words or phrases in a sentence to help them know which meaning of a multiple-meaning word is being used.

- Point out the word *catches* in paragraph 4. Work with students to come up with different meanings for the word. *("takes hold of," "captures," "hits")* Then work with students to figure out which meaning of *catches* is used in this context. *("hits")* Guide students to see which words in the text helped them figure out this meaning. *("in the eye with a brick," "put up a fight")* **(RL.7.4; L.7.4a)**

AT A GLANCE

Students continue reading about the kidnapping. They answer a multiple-choice question and analyze the evidence that helped them select the correct answer.

STEP BY STEP

- Tell students that they will continue reading about Sam and Bill's plan to get a ransom for "Red Chief." Close Reading helps students identify and remember important evidence. The Hint will help them look for specific evidence in each answer choice.

- Have students read the text and underline two details that are clues to Bill's feelings about the boy, as directed by the Close Reading. Ask volunteers to share the details they underlined. Discuss why those details show evidence of Bill's feelings. If necessary, ask: Why is Bill tearful? How does he describe the boy? Why does he say, "I'm willing to take a chance at fifteen hundred dollars"?

- Have students answer the question and complete the activities. Sample response for Show Your Thinking: I chose C because Bill suggests "it ain't human" for someone to pay so much money to get a "freckled wildcat" back. He implies that the boy's parents must recognize how difficult he can be.

- Sample response for Pair/Share question: "Forty-pound chunk" implies the boy is still small and young but solid. "Freckled wildcat" implies that the boy is cute ("freckled"), but "wildcat" implies that he acts like a wild animal and is uncontrollable.

ANSWER ANALYSIS

Choice A is incorrect. The text doesn't say anything about the boy's father not being able to pay the ransom.

Choice B is incorrect. Bill has no problem with charging fifteen hundred dollars for ransom.

Choice C is correct. Bill thinks that even the boy's parents recognize how difficult living with the boy is.

Choice D is incorrect. Sam has not expressed any reservations about the plan or the ransom amount.

ERROR ALERT: Students who did not choose C may have misunderstood Bill's reasoning. Have them determine the meanings of unfamiliar words and restate Bill's thoughts in their own words.

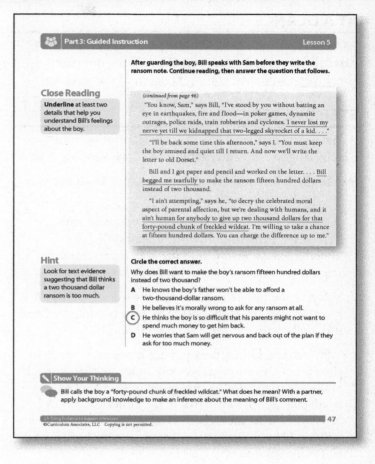

Part 3: Guided Instruction Lesson 5

After guarding the boy, Bill speaks with Sam before they write the ransom note. Continue reading, then answer the question that follows.

Close Reading
Underline at least two details that help you understand Bill's feelings about the boy.

(continued from page 46)

"You know, Sam," says Bill, "I've stood by you without batting an eye in earthquakes, fire and flood—in poker games, dynamite outrages, police raids, train robberies and cyclones. <u>I never lost my nerve yet till we kidnapped that two-legged skyrocket of a kid. . . .</u>"

"I'll be back some time this afternoon," says I. "You must keep the boy amused and quiet till I return. And now we'll write the letter to old Dorset."

Bill and I got paper and pencil and worked on the letter. . . . <u>Bill begged me tearfully to make the ransom fifteen hundred dollars instead of two thousand.</u>

"I ain't attempting," says he, "to decry the celebrated moral aspect of parental affection, but we're dealing with humans, and it ain't human for anybody to give up two thousand dollars for that forty-pound chunk of freckled wildcat. I'm willing to take a chance at fifteen hundred dollars. You can charge the difference up to me."

Hint
Look for text evidence suggesting that Bill thinks a two thousand dollar ransom is too much.

Circle the correct answer.

Why does Bill want to make the boy's ransom fifteen hundred dollars instead of two thousand?

A He knows the boy's father won't be able to afford a two-thousand-dollar ransom.

B He believes it's morally wrong to ask for any ransom at all.

C He thinks the boy is so difficult that his parents might not want to spend much money to get him back.

D He worries that Sam will get nervous and back out of the plan if they ask for too much money.

Show Your Thinking

Bill calls the boy a "forty-pound chunk of freckled wildcat." What does he mean? With a partner, apply background knowledge to make an inference about the meaning of Bill's comment.

Tier Two Vocabulary: *Decry*

- Direct students to the word *decry* in the last paragraph of the story. Encourage students to look for context clues that help them understand the meaning of this word as it is used in the story. Remind them that they can use a dictionary to help them verify the meaning of the term.

- Ask students what *decry* means in this context. (*"criticize," "belittle"*) Ask about other characteristics of a person, such as a public figure, that others might *decry*. **(RL.7.4; L.7.4a, L.7.4d)**

AT A GLANCE

Students continue to read "The Ransom of Red Chief." After the first reading, you will ask three questions to check your students' comprehension of the passage.

STEP BY STEP

- Have students read the passage silently without referring to the Study Buddy or Close Reading text.

- Ask the following questions to ensure students' comprehension of the text:

  What does the boy's father mean when he says, "You are a little high in your demands"? (*His understatement means that the kidnappers' ransom request is ridiculous, given the boy's behavior.*)

  What is the father's counter-proposition? (*The father proposes that the kidnappers pay him two hundred and fifty dollars to take the boy off their hands.*)

  Why are the kidnappers paying money to Dorset at the end of the story? How do you know this, since it is not clearly stated? (*They want to get rid of the troublemaker, so they agree to the father's terms. It can be inferred from their comments. Bill claims that the boy will send him to Bedlam, and Sam says the boy is getting on his nerves, too.*)

- Then ask students to reread the title and look at the Study Buddy think aloud. What does the Study Buddy help them think about?

> **Tip:** Point out to students that short stories sometimes include a surprise or a plot twist. Students need to infer the plot twist based on text evidence. Have them consider who actually winds up paying the ransom in this story.

- Have students read the rest of the story. Tell them to follow the directions in the Close Reading.

> **Tip:** Close Reading helps students identify explanations and examples that can be used as text evidence. Learning to analyze text evidence will help students infer the author's meaning and understand the characters and plot events as they read.

- Finally, have students answer the questions on page 49. When students have finished, use the Answer Analysis to discuss correct and incorrect responses.

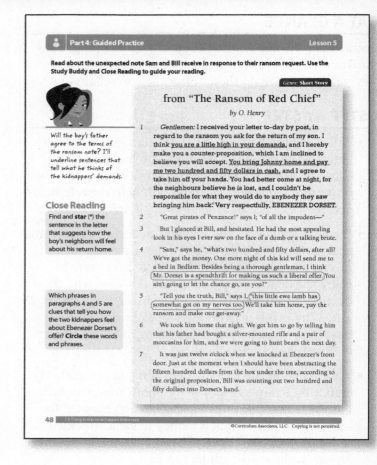

Read about the unexpected note Sam and Bill receive in response to their ransom request. Use the Study Buddy and Close Reading to guide your reading.

Genre: Short Story

from "The Ransom of Red Chief"
by O. Henry

Will the boy's father agree to the terms of the ransom note? I'll underline sentences that tell what he thinks of the kidnappers' demands.

Close Reading

Find and star (*) the sentence in the letter that suggests how the boy's neighbors will feel about his return home.

Which phrases in paragraphs 4 and 5 are clues that tell you how the two kidnappers feel about Ebenezer Dorset's offer? Circle these words and phrases.

1   *Gentlemen:* I received your letter to-day by post, in regard to the ransom you ask for the return of my son. I think you are a little high in your demands, and I hereby make you a counter-proposition, which I am inclined to believe you will accept. You bring Johnny home and pay me two hundred and fifty dollars in cash, and I agree to take him off your hands. You had better come at night, for the neighbours believe he is lost, and I couldn't be responsible for what they would do to anybody they saw bringing him back. Very respectfully, EBENEZER DORSET.

2   "Great pirates of Penzance!" says I; "of all the impudent—"

3   But I glanced at Bill, and hesitated. He had the most appealing look in his eyes I ever saw on the face of a dumb or a talking brute.

4   "Sam," says he, "what's two hundred and fifty dollars, after all? We've got the money. One more night of this kid will send me to a bed in Bedlam. Besides being a thorough gentleman, I think Mr. Dorset is a spendthrift for making us such a liberal offer. You ain't going to let the chance go, are you?"

5   "Tell you the truth, Bill," says I, "this little ewe lamb has somewhat got on my nerves too. We'll take him home, pay the ransom and make our get-away."

6   We took him home that night. We got him to go by telling him that his father had bought a silver-mounted rifle and a pair of moccasins for him, and we were going to hunt bears the next day.

7   It was just twelve o'clock when we knocked at Ebenezer's front door. Just at the moment when I should have been abstracting the fifteen hundred dollars from the box under the tree, according to the original proposition, Bill was counting out two hundred and fifty dollars into Dorset's hand.

48   L5: Citing Evidence to Support Inferences   ©Curriculum Associates, LLC   Copying is not permitted.

Tier Two Vocabulary: *Abstracting*

- Direct students to the word *abstracting* in paragraph 7. Ask them what *abstracting* means in this sentence. (*"taking away," "removing"*) Have them identify the context clues that helped them determine this meaning. (*"from the box under the tree"*)

- Have students identify related words that would make sense in place of *abstracting*. (*removing, extracting*) **(RL.7.4; L.7.4a)**

STEP BY STEP

• Have students read questions 1–3, using the Hints to help them answer those questions.

Tip: If students have trouble answering question 1, direct them to paragraphs 2 and 3, and have them think about their background knowledge. What does *impudent* mean? What does it mean when someone has an "appealing look" in his eye?

• Discuss with students the Answer Analysis below.

ANSWER ANALYSIS

1   The correct choice is D. The word *impudent* shows that Sam is initially angry. Then he sees Bill's face silently pleading with him to accept Dorset's counter-proposition. Choice A is incorrect. It tells what Sam's initial reaction was but not his response upon reflection. Choice B does not describe Sam's initial reaction nor his decision to accept Dorset's counter-proposition. Choice C is incorrect. The text evidence does not support that answer.

2   The correct choice is B. It gives the father's demands and shows that it is Dorset who sets the final terms of the ransom. Choice A doesn't give Dorset's counter-proposition. Choices C and D are details that show why Sam and Bill accept the demands.

3   Sample response: Ebenezer Dorset says, "You had better come at night, for the neighbors believe he is lost, and I couldn't be responsible for what they would do to anybody they saw bringing him back." This phrase from Dorset's counter-proposition supports the idea that no one would willingly pay to take back such a troublemaker.

RETEACHING

Use a chart to verify the correct answer to question 1. Draw the chart below, leaving the boxes blank. Work with students to fill in the boxes, using information from the passage. Sample responses are provided.

Text Evidence	What I Know	Inference
"'of all the impudent—'" "But I glanced at Bill, and hesitated."	*Impudent* means "lack of respect." *Hesitated* means "paused." An *appealing look* is a request.	Sam was insulted and angry but then saw Bill's face and changed his mind.

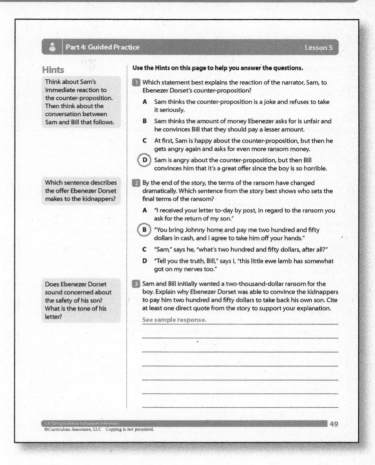

 Part 4: Guided Practice Lesson 5

Hints

Think about Sam's immediate reaction to the counter-proposition. Then think about the conversation between Sam and Bill that follows.

Which sentence describes the offer Ebenezer Dorset makes to the kidnappers?

Does Ebenezer Dorset sound concerned about the safety of his son? What is the tone of his letter?

Use the Hints on this page to help you answer the questions.

1   Which statement best explains the reaction of the narrator, Sam, to Ebenezer Dorset's counter-proposition?

A   Sam thinks the counter-proposition is a joke and refuses to take it seriously.

B   Sam thinks the amount of money Ebenezer asks for is unfair and he convinces Bill that they should pay a lesser amount.

C   At first, Sam is happy about the counter-proposition, but then he gets angry again and asks for even more ransom money.

D   Sam is angry about the counter-proposition, but then Bill convinces him that it's a great offer since the boy is so horrible.

2   By the end of the story, the terms of the ransom have changed dramatically. Which sentence from the story best shows who sets the final terms of the ransom?

A   "I received your letter to-day by post, in regard to the ransom you ask for the return of my son."

B   "You bring Johnny home and pay me two hundred and fifty dollars in cash, and I agree to take him off your hands."

C   "Sam," says he, "what's two hundred and fifty dollars, after all?"

D   "Tell you the truth, Bill," says I, "this little ewe lamb has somewhat got on my nerves too."

3   Sam and Bill initially wanted a two-thousand-dollar ransom for the boy. Explain why Ebenezer Dorset was able to convince the kidnappers to pay him two hundred and fifty dollars to take back his own son. Cite at least one direct quote from the story to support your explanation.

See sample response.

L5: Citing Evidence to Support Inferences
©Curriculum Associates, LLC   Copying is not permitted.   49

Integrating Standards

Use these questions to further students' understanding of "The Ransom of Red Chief."

1   What are some phrases used to describe the boy? How do these help you infer more about the character? *(RL.7.4)*

Descriptive phrases such as "welter-weight cinnamon bear" and "forty-pound chunk of freckled wildcat" help readers infer that the boy's behavior is uncontrollable from the kidnappers' point of view.

2   Write a brief summary of the plot of "The Ransom of Red Chief." *(RL.7.2)*

Sample response: Sam and Bill kidnap a little boy, "Red Chief," who turns out to be too much for them to handle. By the end of the story, the kidnappers pay ransom to the father so he will take the boy back.

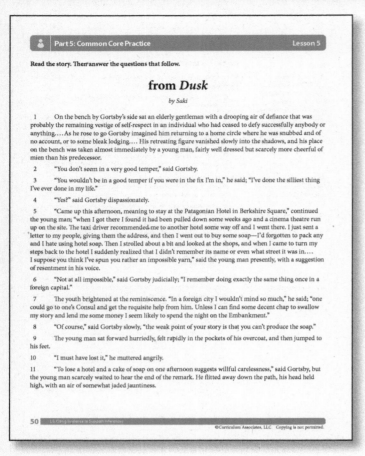

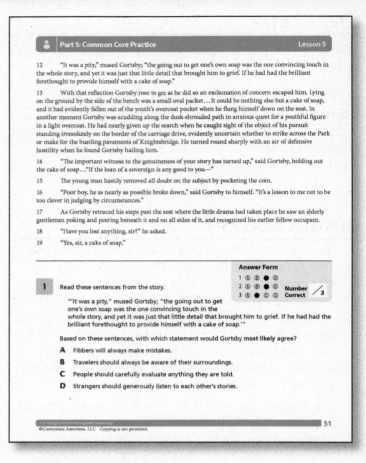

AT A GLANCE

Students independently read another short story and answer questions in a format that provides test practice.

STEP BY STEP

- Tell students to use what they have learned about reading closely and making inferences that are supported by text evidence to read the story on pages 50 and 51.

- Remind students to underline or circle important text evidence.

- Tell students to answer the questions on pages 51 and 52. For questions 1–3, they should fill in the correct circle on the Answer Form.

- When students have finished, use the Answer Analysis to discuss correct responses and the reasons for them. Have students fill in the Number Correct on the Answer Form.

ANSWER ANALYSIS

1 Choice C is correct. The sentences show that Gortsby is proud that he carefully evaluated the young man's story. Choice A is incorrect. Gortsby doesn't suggest that all liars make the mistake that the young man made. Choice B is incorrect because he claims he also made a similar mistake. Choice D is incorrect. The details in the sentences do not describe the need to listen to strangers' stories. **(DOK 2)**

Theme Connection

- How do the short stories in this lesson relate to the theme of the element of surprise?

- Which story surprised you the most? Why?

2 Choice C is correct. It shows that Gortsby makes a judgment that the young man's actions prove he is careless. Choice A is incorrect. It does not describe Gortsby. Choice B is incorrect. It shows that Gortsby uses his own experiences to relate to the man's problem, not to judge him. Choice D shows that Gortsby thinks he was too quick to use circumstantial evidence to judge the man; it does not reflect his interest in judging people. *(DOK 2)*

3 Choice B is correct. It shows that Gortsby questions the young man's honesty, since he points out the weakness in the man's story. Choice A is incorrect. It gives details from the young man's story. Choice C is incorrect. It tells about the bar of soap that may support the young man's honesty. Choice D is incorrect. It shows Gortsby's opinion about the young man's attitude. *(DOK 2)*

4 Sample response: Gortsby is concerned because he finds the bar of soap and feels guilty. It makes him think that he should not have doubted the young man's story. Gortsby thinks, "It could be nothing else but a cake of soap, and it had evidently fallen out of the youth's overcoat pocket … ." Now he feels he should help the young man with a loan of money because the man was being truthful. *(DOK 3)*

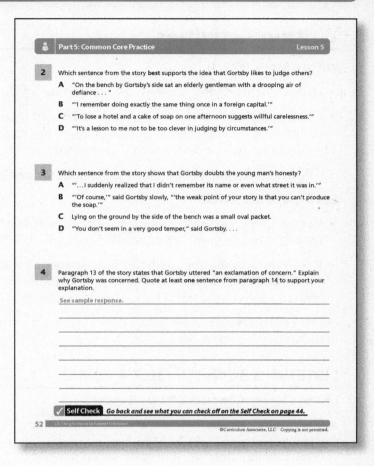

Integrating Standards

Use these questions and tasks as opportunities to interact with "Dusk."

1 How do Gortsby's character traits affect the way the story events unfold? *(RL.7.3)*

Sample response: Gortsby confidently believes he's a good judge of character until he doubts a young man's hard-luck story and refuses him a loan. When Gortsby finds the bar of soap, he is honest enough to admit he is mistaken. Only later does he learn that he has been conned by the young man.

2 Write a brief summary of "Dusk." *(RL.7.2; W.7.4)*

Gortsby judges other people while seated on a bench in a park. He listens to a young man's tale of how he cannot find his hotel. Gortsby does not believe him because the fellow does not have the bar of soap he says he purchased. Later, Gortsby finds a bar of soap next to the bench and thinks he has misjudged the young man. He rushes to give the young man money for a hotel room. Afterwards, Gortsby discovers that the soap belonged to another man.

3 What does *vestige* mean in paragraph 1? How does the word from the Latin meaning "footprint" relate to the text? *(RL.7.4; L.7.4b)*

Vestige means "a mark or trace evidence of a thing no longer present." It relates to this meaning because a footprint is a trace of someone's former presence.

4 What is Gortsby's point of view of the old man on the bench? How do you think the bar of soap might change his initial judgment? *(RL.7.6)*

Sample response: Gortsby sees the old man as a hopeless, defeated person who has all but given up on life. The soap, however, shows that the man is proud enough to still care about his appearance.

5 Discuss in small groups: What is the theme of this story? Cite evidence from the text to support your answer. *(SL.7.1)*

Discussions will vary. To help students determine the theme, remind them to think about what the characters in this story learn.

Writing Activities

Write a Story *(W.7.3)*

• Have students review the surprises that cause a plot twist in each of this lesson's passages.

• Challenge students to write a short narrative of their own that ends with a surprising twist. Tell them to include relevant descriptive details and sensory language to convey the setting and characters. Also ask students to include dialogue in their narratives.

• Allow time for students to share their stories with the class.

Spell Correctly *(L.7.2b)*

• Review potentially troublesome spellings, such as *while, Chief, wrapped, mountain, weight, received,* and *piece.* Include words commonly misspelled by your students.

• Review how to use the spell-checking feature on a computer. Also review how to use a dictionary to check spellings. Point out common letter combinations used to represent sound-spellings, and note that there are limited choices that stand for a particular sound.

• Have partners review their narratives to correct the spelling of any words as needed. Encourage them to use a dictionary for reference.

LISTENING ACTIVITY *(SL.7.4, SL.7.6)*

Listen Closely/Conduct a News Report

• Have pairs of students use the information from "The Ransom of Red Chief" to create a news report announcing the return of the kidnapped boy and the neighbors' reactions.

• One student is the interviewer from a news station while the other student is an eyewitness to some aspect of the kidnapping.

• Students listen carefully to each other as they ask and answer questions. Encourage them to be creative while basing their discussion on the story.

DISCUSSION ACTIVITY *(RL.7.6; SL.7.1)*

Talk in a Group/Compare and Contrast

• Have students form small groups to compare and contrast two of the characters they read about.

• Provide the following prompts: How are the characters similar? How are they different? What points of view about people do the characters share?

• Appoint one member of each group to take notes. Allow 10 to 15 minutes for discussion. Then have each group share its results with the class.

MEDIA ACTIVITY *(RL.7.7; SL.7.2)*

Be Creative/Draw a Cartoon

• Have students review the scene on page 45. Remind students that they made an inference.

• Invite students to create cartoons or comic book scenes that require the reader to make an inference about one of the characters' feelings.

• Have students exchange cartoons and scenes and take turns explaining how they inferred the meaning of their partner's work.

RESEARCH ACTIVITY *(W.7.7; SL.7.4)*

Research and Present/Give a Presentation

• Have students use "Dusk" and "The Ransom of Red Chief" to plan an oral biographical presentation on the authors of the short stories.

• Students should produce a visual display, such as a time line of important happenings at the turn of the twentieth century when both authors wrote.

• Ask students to research additional information to include. Students should take notes and write a brief report for their oral presentations.

Analyzing the Interaction of Story Elements

LESSON OBJECTIVES

- Analyze the ways in which a story's setting, characters, and plot affect one another, including how the main character develops or changes in response to the conflict.

- Analyze the ways in which a story's setting affects the way characters think and behave.

- Analyze the ways in which a story's setting affects the plot.

THE LEARNING PROGRESSION

- **Grade 6:** CCSS RL.6.3 requires students to analyze the development of the plot in a story or drama, and how characters respond.

- **Grade 7: CCSS RL.7.3 asks students to build on what they've learned in Grade 6 about plot to analyze and explore the relationship between two major ideas, such as character and setting, within a text.**

- **Grade 8:** CCSS RL.8.3 asks students to focus on dialogue and plot incidents and connect these to greater plot or character revelations.

PREREQUISITE SKILLS

- Identify setting, character, and plot.

- Recognize that story and drama elements are dependent upon each other.

- Identify causes and effects in a literary text.

- Explain how each element affects the others.

LESSON OBJECTIVES

- Tell students that they will work on a lesson about analyzing story elements and how they influence each other. Ask students to name story elements. (*setting, characters, dialogue, plot*) Explain that students will learn to analyze connections among these story elements.

- Present students with this text: "The day dawned gray and cold, and snow covered the ground. Harry shivered. He had to find some place to stay—and fast." Ask students to describe the setting. (*dawn on a gray, cold morning in winter*) Then discuss with them how the setting affects the character's actions and the plot events. (*Harry has to find someplace warm quickly.*)

- Finally, ask students to identify the setting in this description: "She was surrounded by fragile objects. She turned suddenly and her long skirt caught the edge of a cut-glass vase. The vase shattered. Ariel's nerve broke as well, and she began to cry." (*fragile objects, cut-glass vase*) Invite students to tell how the objects around a character are part of the setting that the character can manipulate.

- Tell students that analyzing the interactions between a story's setting, characters, and plot events will help students better understand and appreciate the stories they read.

Ready *Teacher Toolbox*   *teacher-toolbox.com*

	Prerequisite Skills	RL.7.3
Ready Lessons	✓ ✓	✓
Tools for Instruction	✓	✓
Interactive Tutorials	✓	✓

CCSS Focus

RL.7.3 Analyze how particular elements of a story or drama interact (e.g., how setting shapes the characters or plot).

ADDITIONAL STANDARDS: **RL.7.1, RL.7.2, RL.7.4; L.7.1, L.7.3a, L.7.4a, L.7.4d; W.7.2, W.7.3, W.7.4, W.7.8; SL.7.1, SL.7.4, SL.7.5**
(See page A39 for full text.)

AT A GLANCE

Through an illustration, students analyze a scene's story elements. They learn to recognize how the setting, characters, and plot interact to shape a story.

STEP BY STEP

- Read the paragraphs with the definitions of *story elements*, *analyzing*, *conflict*, and *resolution*.

- Have students look at the illustration. Tell them to think about the setting and how it creates a problem for the characters.

- Read the first question and answer under the illustration. Ask students to confirm the description of the setting by looking back at the picture.

- Read the second question and ask students to write down their answers. Guide students by asking them to think about the characters' problem and the role the setting plays in that problem.

- Finally, read the third question. Prompt students by having them think about what actions the characters might take to bring themselves to safety.

- Ask students to think about other stories they have read that include memorable settings, characters, and plots. Invite students to describe how the setting affected the characters or how the characters' actions and feelings affected the events.

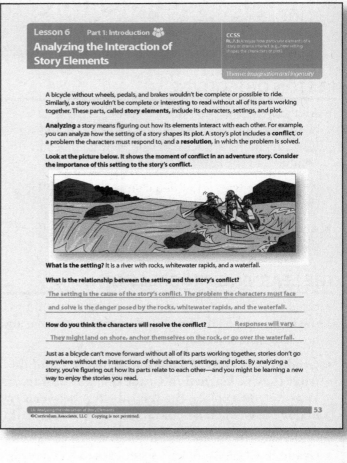

Genre Focus

Literary Texts: Historical Fiction

Tell students that in this lesson they will read a type of literature called historical fiction. Historical fiction is fiction that is set in the past. It may be about real people who lived in the past, real events that happened in the past, or both. The details are realistic for the time period. Parts of the story, such as dialogue and some characters, are usually made up. The author's purpose is most likely to entertain readers as well as inform them about the time period.

Based on these characteristics, ask students to name other works of historical fiction that they have read. What time and place were the stories set in? What cultural biases or historical anecdotes were included? Students may mention books about the American Revolution or American pioneer stories.

Discuss that students should identify a book's time period and setting when they read historical fiction. They should look for dates, places, and other details that tell more about the setting. Finally, they should recognize anecdotes from the time period that enhance the story's reality.

Explain that "Black Sunday" tells about a memorable day in history when a powerful dust storm hit the southern midwest. *The Prince and the Pauper* will take readers back in time to sixteenth-century London.

AT A GLANCE

Students read a piece of historical fiction. They examine the relationship between the story's setting and conflict.

STEP BY STEP

- Invite volunteers to tell what they learned on the previous page about identifying how story elements interact.

- Tell students that now they will read a historical fiction story and analyze how the story elements help to shape the story.

- Read aloud "Black Sunday."

- Read the question: "What is the relationship between the setting and the conflict in this story?"

- Tell students you will use a Think Aloud to demonstrate a way of answering the question.

Think Aloud: First, I'm going to reread the story and identify the setting. The second sentence says, "The sky darkened over the Oklahoma plains," so I know that the story takes place in Oklahoma on the plains. Later, in the third paragraph, Cora rides across the fields and helps her dad and brothers bring their livestock to safety in the barn. Based on these details, I can also guess that the story takes place on a farm.

- Have students answer the question, "What is the setting of this story?" As needed, encourage them to underline details in the text that tell about the setting before they write their answers.

Think Aloud: Now I'll look for the story's conflict. I know that a conflict is a major problem that one or more characters struggle with. I see that Cora's main concern right away is the safety of her mother and younger siblings as the dust storm approaches.

- Have students answer the question, "What is the conflict in this story"? As needed, encourage them to underline details in the text that tell about the conflict before they write their answers.

- Finally, have students describe the relationship between the story's setting and conflict. Invite volunteers to share their answers with the class. (*Sample response: The approaching storm creates conflict for the family by putting them and their animals in danger. Cora's mother and siblings find safety by*

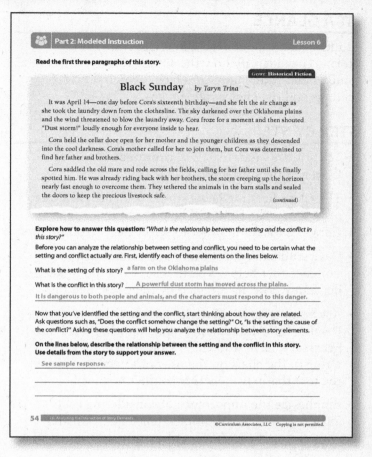

taking shelter in the cellar. Cora and her dad and brothers then bring the livestock to safety in the barn.)

ELL Support: Homophones

- Explain to students that homophones are two words that sound alike but have different meanings and spellings.

- Point out the word *mare* in paragraph 3 and say it aloud. Some students may hear *mayor*. Work with students to come up with a definition for the word they heard. (mare: *"a female horse;"* mayor: *"an elected city leader"*) Guide students to see that they can understand which homophone is used here based on the context.

- Point out the additional homophones *air* (heir) and *plains* (planes) in paragraph 1. Pronounce the words and discuss their meanings. **(L.7.1)**

AT A GLANCE

Students continue to read about Cora and the dust storm. They identify how the setting directly affects the conflict and challenges Cora faces, which impact her feelings and the choices she makes.

STEP BY STEP

- Tell students that they will continue reading about Cora and the dust storm.

- The Close Reading helps students identify the story's resolution. The Hint will help them understand Cora's character in order to select the correct answer.

- Have students read the text and underline the sentence that helps explain what Cora did to keep her family safe, as directed by the Close Reading.

- Ask volunteers to share the sentence they underlined. Discuss how the sentence sums up what Cora did. If necessary, have students review the conflict they wrote in the chart on the previous page and identify the text that tells how this conflict is solved.

- Emphasize the importance of considering each answer choice to a multiple-choice question and eliminating those that are obviously incorrect.

- Sample response for Show Your Thinking: Clue words in the answer, such as *calm* and *while under pressure*, show how Cora solved her conflict and moved all of her family to safety.

ANSWER ANALYSIS

Choice A is incorrect. This sentence shows Cora is taking charge but doesn't suggest a happy resolution.

Choice B is incorrect. This sentence shows Cora holding a door, but it doesn't necessarily suggest that she is taking charge or that the resolution will be happy.

Choice C is correct. It shows Cora taking charge and indicates that there will be a happy resolution.

Choice D is incorrect. This sentence suggests neither Cora's taking charge nor a happy resolution.

ERROR ALERT: Students who didn't choose C may not have understood that they need to find a sentence that both shows Cora taking charge and suggests a happy resolution. The incorrect answer choices show either one or the other but not both.

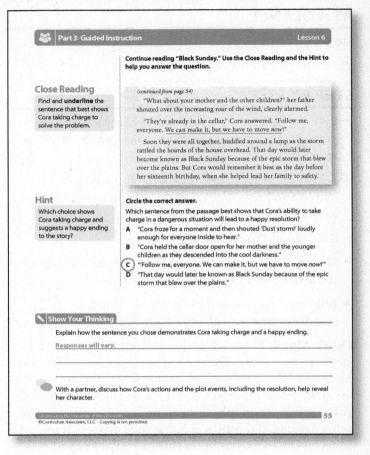

Tier Two Vocabulary: *Epic*

- Direct students to the word *epic* in the last paragraph of the story. Have them identify context clues that help them understand the meaning of *epic*. (*"later become known as"*) Then have students define *epic* in their own words. (*"unusual or extraordinary"*)

- Have students use a dictionary to verify the meaning of the term as it is used in this context. **(RL.7.4; L.7.4a, L.7.4d)**

AT A GLANCE

Students read a scene from a historical fiction story. After the first reading, you will ask four questions to check your students' comprehension of the passage.

STEP BY STEP

- Have students read the passage silently without referring to the Study Buddy or Close Reading text.

- Ask the following questions to ensure student comprehension of the text:

  What sets the chain of events in motion? *("Before he knew what he was about, he had his face against the gate-bars.")*

  Why did Tom peer through the gate? *(He had an overwhelming desire to get a look at the prince.)*

  What did the soldiers do to Tom that made the prince angry? *(They grabbed him and roughly "sent him spinning among the gaping crowd.")*

  How do you know the prince is angry? *(The young prince springs to the gate "with his face flushed, and his eyes flashing.")*

- Then ask students to reread the first four paragraphs and look at the Study Buddy think aloud. What does the Study Buddy help them think about?

Tip: The Study Buddy helps students identify how characters' actions help move the plot forward. This helps students better understand the key idea that the setting, characters, and plot events interact to shape the characters' lives and the story.

- Have students read the rest of the scene. Tell them to follow the directions in the Close Reading.

Tip: The Close Reading helps students identify the plot event that stirs a strong reaction in the prince. Help students to see the chain of events that led up to his command to the soldiers to "open the gates, and let him [Tom] in!"

- Finally, have students answer the questions on page 57. Use the Answer Analysis to discuss correct and incorrect responses.

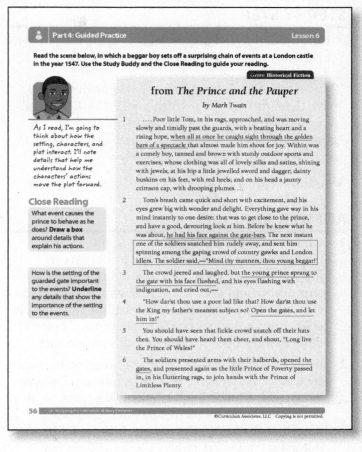

Tier Two Vocabulary: *Fickle*

- Point out the word *fickle* in the first sentence of paragraph 5. Given the context and what they know, ask students what *fickle* means. *("changeable or unstable")* **(RL.7.4; L.7.4a)**

- Then have students identify related words that would make sense in place of *fickle*. *(inconsistent, unpredictable, unsettled)*

STEP BY STEP

- Have students read questions 1–3, using the Hints to help them answer the questions.

Tip: If students have trouble answering question 1, have them refer to the text they boxed. Ask students how Tom's emotions and his desire to catch a glimpse of the prince affected what happened and in turn triggered the prince's response.

- Discuss with students the Answer Analysis below.

ANSWER ANALYSIS

1   Choice B is correct. It tells how Tom's overwhelming desire to see the prince sets in motion a chain of events. Choice A describes Tom's appearance and does not reveal why he is excited. Choice C tells what the soldier said to Tom, but the soldier did not start the chain of events. Choice D describes details about the prince's appearance.

2   Choice A is correct. The prince is angered by Tom's treatment. As a result, he commands that the gates be opened. Choice B tells the crowd's reaction. It does not describe a main character. Choice C describes the soldiers' attempts, but the soldiers are not main characters either. Choice D does not correctly tell the prince's motives in helping Tom.

3   Sample response: The guarded gate is an important cause of conflict because it prevents Tom from seeing the Prince; that is the problem (the conflict) that must be resolved. The relationship between the setting and the conflict is made clear when Tom presses "his face against the gate-bars" and is then thrown back by the guards. The conflict is resolved when the Prince sticks up for Tom and the guards open the gates, leading to a change of setting as Tom passes in.

RETEACHING

Use a chart to verify the answer to question 2. Draw the chart below, and work with students to fill in the boxes. Sample responses are provided.

Events	Character's Actions
Tom looks through the gate. Tom is tossed aside by the soldiers.	The prince is angered and orders the gates to be opened.

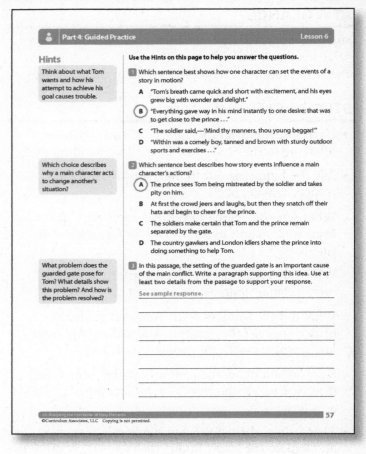

Part 4: Guided Practice Lesson 6

Hints

Think about what Tom wants and how his attempt to achieve his goal causes trouble.

Which choice describes why a main character acts to change another's situation?

What problem does the guarded gate pose for Tom? What details show this problem? And how is the problem resolved?

Use the Hints on this page to help you answer the questions.

1 Which sentence best shows how one character can set the events of a story in motion?

A "Tom's breath came quick and short with excitement, and his eyes grew big with wonder and delight."

B "Everything gave way in his mind instantly to one desire: that was to get close to the prince ..."

C "The soldier said,—'Mind thy manners, thou young beggar!'"

D "Within was a comely boy, tanned and brown with sturdy outdoor sports and exercises ..."

2 Which sentence best describes how story events influence a main character's actions?

A The prince sees Tom being mistreated by the soldier and takes pity on him.

B At first the crowd jeers and laughs, but then they snatch off their hats and begin to cheer for the prince.

C The soldiers make certain that Tom and the prince remain separated by the gate.

D The country gawkers and London idlers shame the prince into doing something to help Tom.

3 In this passage, the setting of the guarded gate is an important cause of the main conflict. Write a paragraph supporting this idea. Use at least two details from the passage to support your response.

See sample response.

L6: Analyzing the Interaction of Story Elements
©Curriculum Associates, LLC Copying is not permitted.

57

Integrating Standards

Use these questions to further students' understanding of "The Prince and the Pauper."

1   What sentence expresses the resolution of the conflict in the story? Cite evidence from the text in your response. **(RL.7.1)**

The conflict is resolved when Tom is allowed through the gates. The text states, "The soldiers presented arms with their halberds, opened the gates, and presented again as the little Prince of Poverty passed in, in his fluttering rags, to join hands with the Prince of Limitless Plenty."

2   What is the central idea of this text? How is it explained through specific details? **(RL.7.2)**

The central idea is the contrast between the two boys and their situations. It is shown through details of dress, appearance, and actions. Tom is slow and timid, beaten down. The prince is confident and decisive: "The young prince sprang to the gate … his eyes flashing with indignation."

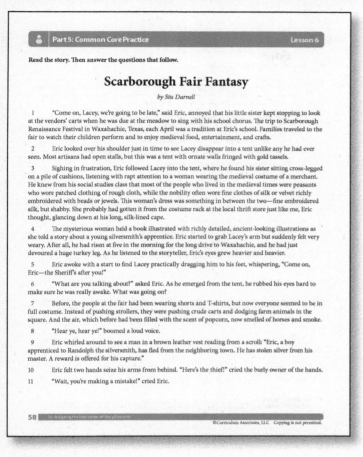

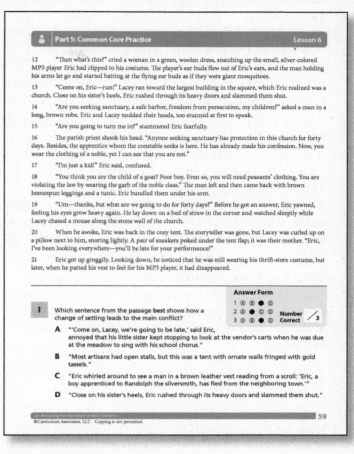

The reproduced student pages contain:

Part 5: Common Core Practice　　Lesson 6

Read the story. Then answer the questions that follow.

Scarborough Fair Fantasy

by Stu Darnell

1　"Come on, Lacey, we're going to be late," said Eric, annoyed that his little sister kept stopping to look at the vendors' carts when he was due at the meadow to sing with his school chorus. The trip to Scarborough Renaissance Festival in Waxahachie, Texas, each April was a tradition at Eric's school. Families traveled to the fair to watch their children perform and to enjoy medieval food, entertainment, and crafts.

2　Eric looked over his shoulder just in time to see Lacey disappear into a tent unlike any he had ever seen. Most artisans had open stalls, but this was a tent with ornate walls fringed with gold tassels.

3　Sighing in frustration, Eric followed Lacey into the tent, where he found his sister sitting cross-legged on a pile of cushions, listening with rapt attention to a woman wearing the medieval costume of a merchant. He knew from his social studies class that most of the people who lived in the medieval times were peasants who wore patched clothing of rough cloth, while the nobility often wore fine clothes of silk or velvet richly embroidered with beads or jewels. This woman's dress was something in between the two—fine embroidered silk, but shabby. She probably had gotten it from the costume rack at the local thrift store just like me, Eric thought, glancing down at his long, silk-lined cape.

4　The mysterious woman held a book illustrated with richly detailed, ancient-looking illustrations as she told a story about a young silversmith's apprentice. Eric started to grab Lacey's arm but suddenly felt very weary. After all, he had risen at five in the morning for the long drive to Waxahachie, and he had just devoured a huge turkey leg. As he listened to the storyteller, Eric's eyes grew heavy and heavier.

5　Eric awoke with a start to find Lacey practically dragging him to his feet, whispering, "Come on, Eric—the Sheriff's after you!"

6　"What are you talking about?" asked Eric. As he emerged from the tent, he rubbed his eyes hard to make sure he was really awake. What was going on?

7　Before, the people at the fair had been wearing shorts and T-shirts, but now everyone seemed to be in full costume. Instead of pushing strollers, they were pushing crude carts and dodging farm animals in the square. And the air, which before had been filled with the scent of popcorn, now smelled of horses and smoke.

8　"Hear ye, hear ye!" boomed a loud voice.

9　Eric whirled around to see a man in a brown leather vest reading from a scroll: "Eric, a boy apprenticed to Randolph the silversmith, has fled from the neighboring town. He has stolen silver from his master. A reward is offered for his capture."

10　Eric felt two hands seize his arms from behind. "Here's the thief!" cried the burly owner of the hands.

11　"Wait, you're making a mistake!" cried Eric.

58　L6: Analyzing the Interaction of Story Elements　©Curriculum Associates, LLC　Copying is not permitted.

Part 5: Common Core Practice　　Lesson 6

12　"Then what's this?" cried a woman in a green, woolen dress, snatching up the small, silver-colored MP3 player Eric had clipped to his costume. The player's ear buds flew out of Eric's ears, and the man holding his arms let go and started batting at the flying ear buds as if they were giant mosquitoes.

13　"Come on, Eric—run!" Lacey ran toward the largest building in the square, which Eric realized was a church. Close on his sister's heels, Eric rushed through its heavy doors and slammed them shut.

14　"Are you seeking sanctuary, a safe harbor, freedom from persecution, my children?" asked a man in a long, brown robe. Eric and Lacey nodded their heads, too stunned at first to speak.

15　"Are you going to turn me in?" stammered Eric fearfully.

16　The parish priest shook his head. "Anyone seeking sanctuary has protection in this church for forty days. Besides, the apprentice whom the constable seeks is here. He has already made his confession. Now, you wear the clothing of a noble, yet I can see that you are not."

17　"I'm just a kid!" Eric said, confused.

18　"You think you are the child of a goat? Poor boy. Even so, you will need peasants' clothing. You are violating the law by wearing the garb of the noble class." The man left and then came back with brown homespun leggings and a tunic. Eric bundled them under his arm.

19　"Um—thanks, but what are we going to do for forty days?" Before he got an answer, Eric yawned, feeling his eyes grow heavy again. He lay down on a bed of straw in the corner and watched sleepily while Lacey chased a mouse along the stone wall of the church.

20　When he awoke, Eric was back in the cozy tent. The storyteller was gone, but Lacey was curled up on a pillow next to him, snoring lightly. A pair of sneakers poked under the tent flap; it was their mother. "Eric, I've been looking everywhere—you'll be late for your performance!"

21　Eric got up groggily. Looking down, he noticed that he was still wearing his thrift-store costume, but later, when he patted his vest to feel for his MP3 player, it had disappeared.

Answer Form
1　Ⓐ Ⓑ ● Ⓓ
2　Ⓐ ● Ⓒ Ⓓ　Number
3　Ⓐ Ⓑ ● Ⓓ　Correct　／3

1　Which sentence from the passage best shows how a change of setting leads to the main conflict?

A　"'Come on, Lacey, we're going to be late,' said Eric, annoyed that his little sister kept stopping to look at the vendor's carts when he was due at the meadow to sing with his school chorus."

B　"Most artisans had open stalls, but this was a tent with ornate walls fringed with gold tassels."

C　"Eric whirled around to see a man in a brown leather vest reading from a scroll: 'Eric, a boy apprenticed to Randolph the silversmith, has fled from the neighboring town.'"

D　"Close on his sister's heels, Eric rushed through its heavy doors and slammed them shut."

L6: Analyzing the Interaction of Story Elements　59
©Curriculum Associates, LLC　Copying is not permitted.

AT A GLANCE

Students independently read a longer story and answer questions in a format that provides test practice.

STEP BY STEP

- Tell students to use what they have learned about reading closely and analyzing how story elements interact as they read the passage on pages 58 and 59.

- Remind students to underline or circle important points.

- Tell students to answer the questions on pages 59 and 60. For questions 1–3, they should fill in the correct circle on the Answer Form.

- When students have finished, use the Answer Analysis to discuss correct responses and the reasons for them. Have students fill in the Number Correct on the Answer Form.

ANSWER ANALYSIS

1　Choice C is correct. This sentence shows that the change in setting has inserted Eric into the main conflict: He has passed from a familiar setting into an unfamiliar place where he is sought by the law. Choice A is incorrect. There is no evidence the priest understands Eric is a time traveler. Choice B is incorrect. The sentence compares a stall to a tent, but it does not introduce a conflict. Choice D is incorrect. The sentence shows a change of setting, but it helps resolve the main conflict. **(DOK 2)**

Theme Connection

- How do all the stories in this lesson relate to the theme of imagination and ingenuity?

- Of the authors who wrote stories for this lesson, which one do you think has used the most ingenuity? Explain.

2   Choice B is correct. The priest misinterprets Eric's modern use of the word *kid*. Choice A is incorrect. It describes the priest's actions, not the impact of the setting. Choices C and D are incorrect. The priest informs Eric that the thief, the apprentice, is seeking sanctuary in the church as well. **(DOK 2)**

3   Choice C is correct. A woman in the crowd sees the MP3 player and thinks it is the stolen silver. Choice A is incorrect. It is the Sheriff and a bystander who try to take Eric into custody. Randolph the silversmith is not present. Choice B is incorrect. The cape is a detail that does not emerge until later in the story. Choice D is incorrect. Eric did not steal any silver and therefore does not have any. **(DOK 2)**

4   Sample response: When Eric falls asleep the first time, the setting changes from modern times to Renaissance times. The change in setting influences how people react in the story. Eric must deal with shifts in the way medieval people think and act. **(DOK 3)**

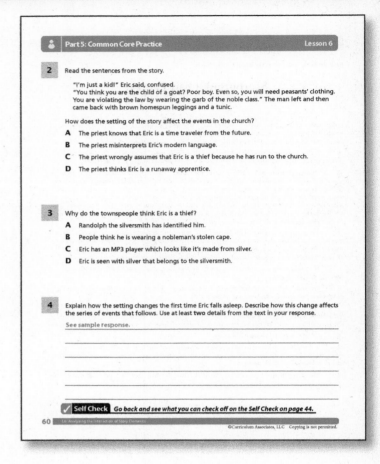

Integrating Standards

Use these questions and tasks as opportunities to interact with "Scarborough Fair Fantasy."

1   Cite two details from the text that support the idea that Eric and Lacey are unprepared for the differences between modern and medieval culture. **(RL.7.2)**

"Anyone seeking sanctuary has protection in this church for forty days." "You are violating the law by wearing the garb of the noble class."

2   In paragraph 14, the priest asks, "Are you seeking sanctuary … ?" What does *sanctuary* mean? What context clues help you to determine this meaning? **(RL.7.4; L.7.4a)**

The sentence provides context clues to help me understand that the meaning of sanctuary is "a safe harbor and freedom from persecution."

3   Explain who is most likely referred to in the text that describes a "man in a leather vest reading from a scroll." **(RL.7.1)**

The text is referring to the sheriff, because Lacey mentions that he is the official looking for Eric.

4   What important plot twist do you discover in paragraph 20? Cite evidence from the text. **(RL.7.1)**

Eric has been dreaming since he sat down in the tent. In paragraph 4, "Eric's eyes grew heavier and heavier." He wakes up in medieval times. Later, he falls asleep in the church, but paragraph 20 states, "When he awoke, Eric was back in the cozy tent."

5   In small groups, have students take turns reading a few paragraphs of the story and summarizing the key events and important details. **(RL.7.2; SL.7.1)**

Discussions will vary. Encourage students to use their own words in their summaries. Have listeners pay attention as speakers summarize the text to be sure the summaries are free of personal opinions or judgments about the story events and characters.

Writing Activities

Reader's Theater (W.7.3)

- Have students consider what they learned about Cora in "Black Sunday."

- Challenge students to write a reader's theater script based on other events that might happen in Cora's life on a farm in the 1930s. Explain that a reader's theater is like a play. Tell students to use details from other dust bowl events in their scripts and to include how Cora might react and speak in these situations. Remind students to use narrative techniques in their scripts, such as dialogue, description, and pacing.

- Allow time for students to share their scripts with the class.

Precise and Concise Language (L.7.3a)

- Point out the author's use of precise and concise language in sentence 2 of "Black Sunday." Then display this revision: "The sky grew much darker over the plains that were located in Arkansas. A strong wind in the area seemed ready to blow the different clothes out over the plains." Discuss the differences, and have students identify redundancies and wordiness.

- Have students revise the scripts they wrote to reduce wordiness by using precise and concise language, or words and phrases that are clear, accurate, and specific.

LISTENING ACTIVITY (SL.7.1)

Listen Closely/Pose a Question

- Have one student read aloud "Scarborough Fair Fantasy" while the other students listen closely.

- Then have each student pose a question about the setting, characters, or events in the story.

- Encourage students to pose basic questions and more complex questions, such as "What were some differences in customs that Eric and Lacey experienced when they went back in time?"

DISCUSSION ACTIVITY (SL.7.1)

Talk in a Group/What's Your Perspective?

- Have students review how each of this lesson's passages relates to the theme of imagination and ingenuity.

- Have students form small groups to discuss which character they think best portrays this theme. Encourage students to cite passage details to support their opinions. How do all the characters represent this theme? In what ways does one character represent the theme best?

- Have students appoint one group member to report to the class their group's perspective.

MEDIA ACTIVITY (RL.7.2; W.7.2, W.7.4)

Be Creative/Make a Book Cover and Flap

- Invite students to create a book cover and flap for The Prince and the Pauper. Have them create their own drawings or collages for the cover. Tell them to incorporate details that illustrate the main idea of the book.

- Tell students to write copy for the cover flap that includes a brief summary of the book and a brief author biography.

RESEARCH ACTIVITY (W.7.8; SL.7.4, SL.7.5)

Write a Report/Create a Display

- Have students research the actual event that is the setting for "Black Sunday."

- Ask students to write a report on the Dust Bowl and the storm that occurred on April 14, 1935.

- Have students create a visual display, such as a map or time line with photographs, and a bibliography to accompany the report.

- Students should share their reports with the class. Allow time for students to ask each other questions about the information they found.

Determining Theme

LESSON OBJECTIVES

- Recognize broad messages in works of literature as themes.

- Identify how characters' thoughts, feelings, and actions point to a story's theme.

- Analyze how the changes and growth experienced by a character develop the theme.

THE LEARNING PROGRESSION

- **Grade 6:** CCSS RL.6.2 requires students to determine a theme or central idea of a text and how it is conveyed through particular story details.

- **Grade 7: CCSS RL.7.2 builds on the Grade 6 standard by having students analyze how the theme develops over the course of the text.**

- **Grade 8:** CCSS RL.8.2 requires students to expand on this analysis by identifying the theme's relationship to the characters, setting, and plot.

PREREQUISITE SKILLS

- Recognize literary elements such as characters, setting, and plot.

- Make inferences based on story details.

- Explain how details about literary elements serve to develop the theme or central ides of a text.

TAP STUDENTS' PRIOR KNOWLEDGE

- Tell students they will be working on a lesson about theme. First, ask students what themes are. (*A theme is a message or lesson that an author wants to convey.*) Ask for examples of common themes. (*Stealing is wrong; Stand up for your beliefs; Hard work pays off.*)

- Explain that most stories have some kind of theme and that theme is an important element of fiction. Without some kind of theme, readers might have a hard time connecting a story to their own lives. When that happens, readers often lose interest.

- Point out that the story plot often reveals its theme. Discuss the main plot events in a familiar folk tale or myth. (*Sample response: King Midas wishes that everything he touches would turn to gold. His wish is granted, but he is no longer able to eat food or touch people.*) Ask students to use the main events to determine a theme; emphasize that there might be more than one theme. (*One theme from the story of King Midas is be careful what you wish for.*)

- Tell students that through theme, readers can identify with characters and situations in a story. By identifying a story's theme, they will be able to understand the message about life the author wants them to learn.

Ready *Teacher Toolbox*		*teacher-toolbox.com*
	Prerequisite Skills	**RL.7.2**
Ready Lessons	✓	✓
Tools for Instruction	✓	✓
Interactive Tutorials		✓

CCSS Focus

RL.7.2 Determine a theme or central idea of a text and analyze its development over the course of the text ….

ADDITIONAL STANDARDS: **RL.7.1, RL.7.3, RL.7.4, RL.7.7; L.7.1, L.7.4a, L.7.4b, L.7.5c; W.7.2, W.7.3, W.7.8; SL.7.1, SL.7.3, SL.7.4**
(See page A39 for full text.)

AT A GLANCE

By studying a newspaper image and headline, students practice determining a theme, or a lesson about life.

STEP BY STEP

- Read the first paragraph and the definition of *theme*. Explain that careful readers are mindful of theme development, since it helps them understand story events and characters' motivations. Alternatively, the specific story details can help students make a broad generalization about a life lesson.

- Have students study the newspaper image and headline. Then have them circle the most important words in the headline.

- Explain to students that the chart helps them organize the details in the illustration that will help them determine its theme, or message.

- Read each event in the chart, and have students explain how these events relate to the words they circled. Discuss how students are able to formulate a story about the team based on the information in the headline. Then read the theme listed in the chart, and discuss how the words in the newspaper headline relate to it.

- Have students share a real-life story of a time when they learned a life lesson through an experience. Discuss how students might convey this theme through details if they wrote a story about the lesson they learned.

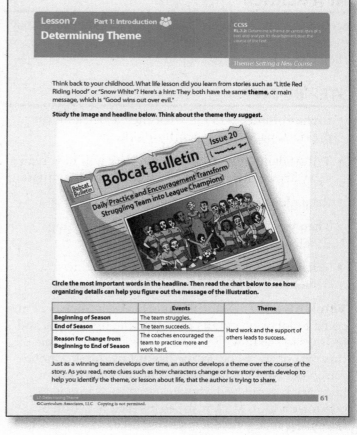

Genre Focus

Literary Texts: Realistic Fiction

A realistic fiction story is a story with characters who take part in activities that could really happen. The characters, setting, and situations are believable and realistic, but the story is invented by the author.

- Realistic fiction stories usually take place in the present or recent past.

- The characters are the types of people who might exist in real life. For instance, they might act very much like students or adults who are alive today.

- The situations described are also realistic and believable. Characters deal with the same problems and issues that people might face in real life.

Based on these characteristics, have students share realistic fiction stories they have read. Familiar examples may include *Hatchet*, *Because of Winn-Dixie*, and *Where the Red Fern Grows*.

The three stories in this lesson are examples of realistic fiction. Both "A Different Day" and "The Substitute" include characters, settings, and events familiar to students. The excerpt from the novel *Little Women* describes a problem faced by a family during the Civil War era, but the characters and situation are realistic and the theme is timeless.

AT A GLANCE

Students read the beginning of a story about how a boy deals with a difficult situation and then identify the theme that is being developed.

STEP BY STEP

- Invite volunteers to tell what they learned on the previous page about identifying theme.

- Tell students that in this lesson they will now read a story about how a boy deals with a difficult situation.

- Read aloud the story "A Different Day."

- Then read the question: "What theme is being developed in this part of the story?"

- Tell students you will use a Think Aloud to demonstrate a way of answering the question.

Think Aloud: This story is mostly about Mick, so I'm going to focus on details that describe his actions and feelings to see how these details develop the theme of this part of the story. At the beginning, Mick watches Aaron demand lunch money from another student, Jake. Mick is relieved, though, because Aaron isn't picking on him. Mick justifies his lack of action by reasoning that everyone picks on Jake.

- Direct students to the chart and ask where they've seen a similar chart before. Review that it helps them determine the story's theme based on the events.

- Point out the important event at the beginning of the story in the first row of the chart, as well as Mick's actions and feelings about what's happening.

Think Aloud: In the middle of the story, which is the last paragraph on this page, Jake stands up to Aaron. Mick watches as Aaron jabs Jake in the chest, but Mick still doesn't do anything.

- Have students record Mick's words, actions, and feelings in the second row of the chart. (*Sample response: Mick watches Aaron jab Jake in the chest.*)

Think Aloud: Based on the events of the story and the character's words, actions, and feelings, I can determine the theme of this part of the story.

- Have students suggest a possible theme for this part of the story and complete the chart. (*Sample response: "It's usually safer to avoid conflict."*)

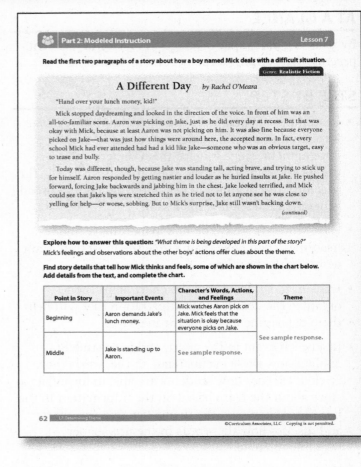

Tier Two Vocabulary: *Norm*

- Direct students to the word *norm* on this page. Write the word *normal* on the board, and have students explain its meaning. Then have them suggest some examples of things they consider normal.

- Explain that *normal* is most often used as an adjective, and *norm* is the noun form. With this in mind, have students suggest meanings for the noun. (*"something that is usual, typical, expected, or standard"*) **(RL.7.4; L.7.4a)**

- Encourage students to use the word *norm* in sentences that describe their classroom and school. Then have them use the word in a sentence to describe something that is out of the norm.

AT A GLANCE

Students continue reading the story about Mick. They answer a multiple-choice question and use clues from the story to determine a theme of the story.

STEP BY STEP

- Tell students they will continue reading the story about Mick watching a bully at school.

- The Close Reading helps students identify the point in the story at which Mick's feelings change and he moves into action. The Hint helps students recognize how one character's actions relate to the theme.

- Have students read the story and underline the sentence that describes when Mick takes action, as directed by the Close Reading.

- Ask volunteers to share the sentence they underlined. Discuss why they chose this sentence. If necessary, ask, "When does Mick move toward Aaron and Jake? What does Mick shout to Aaron?"

- Have students complete the page, and discuss their responses. Sample response to Show Your Thinking: The detail "he forced his feet toward the conflict" helped me choose this theme because it shows Mick decides to take a stand against the bully. Mick also calls attention to himself by shouting at Aaron, taking the pressure off Jake.

ANSWER ANALYSIS

Choice A is incorrect. There is no evidence that Mick had been bullied, but he still knew bullying was wrong.

Choice B is incorrect. It sums up the theme of the beginning of the story.

Choice C is correct. Mick arrives at the decision to stand up to bullies at the end of the story.

Choice D is incorrect. It may be true that bullying will always be a problem, but this idea is not supported by details in the text. Instead, it supports why teenagers can connect to this story.

ERROR ALERT: Students who did not choose *C* might have confused the theme at the beginning of the story with the theme of the entire story. Have students review Mick's thoughts and feelings throughout the entire story.

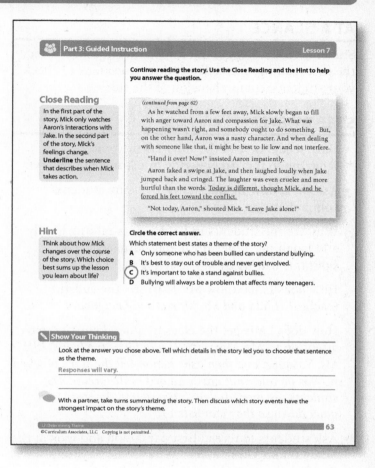

Continue reading the story. Use the Close Reading and the Hint to help you answer the question.

Close Reading

In the first part of the story, Mick only watches Aaron's interactions with Jake. In the second part of the story, Mick's feelings change. **Underline** the sentence that describes when Mick takes action.

(continued from page 62)

As he watched from a few feet away, Mick slowly began to fill with anger toward Aaron and compassion for Jake. What was happening wasn't right, and somebody ought to do something. But, on the other hand, Aaron was a nasty character. And when dealing with someone like that, it might be best to lie low and not interfere.

"Hand it over! Now!" insisted Aaron impatiently.

Aaron faked a swipe at Jake, and then laughed loudly when Jake jumped back and cringed. The laughter was even crueler and more hurtful than the words. <u>Today is different, thought Mick, and he forced his feet toward the conflict.</u>

"Not today, Aaron," shouted Mick. "Leave Jake alone!"

Hint

Think about how Mick changes over the course of the story. Which choice best sums up the lesson you learn about life?

Circle the correct answer.

Which statement best states a theme of the story?

A Only someone who has been bullied can understand bullying.

B It's best to stay out of trouble and never get involved.

C It's important to take a stand against bullies.

D Bullying will always be a problem that affects many teenagers.

✎ **Show Your Thinking**

Look at the answer you chose above. Tell which details in the story led you to choose that sentence as the theme.

Responses will vary.

With a partner, take turns summarizing the story. Then discuss which story events have the strongest impact on the story's theme.

ELL Support: Regular Past-Tense Verbs

- Explain to students that verbs are action words. The past tense of a verb tells that the action has already happened in the past. The past tense of a regular verb ends in *-ed.*

- Direct students to the words *watched* and *insisted* in the story. Write the words on the board. Work with students to identify the present tense of each verb. (*watch, insist*) Tell students these are both regular verbs since the past tense of each ends in *-ed.*

- Have students find other regular past-tense verbs in this story. (*forced, shouted*) **(L.7.1)**

AT A GLANCE

Students read a story about a substitute teacher. After the first reading, you will ask three questions to check your students' comprehension of the story.

STEP BY STEP

- Have students read the story silently without referring to the Study Buddy or Close Reading text.

- Ask the following questions to ensure students' comprehension of the text:

  Why are the students in Laila's class talking loudly and laughing? (*They are taking advantage of a substitute teacher by not behaving well.*)

  How does Laila know Mr. Marrero, the substitute teacher? (*Laila and Mr. Marrero are neighbors.*)

  How does Laila get the class to quiet down and pay attention to Mr. Marrero? (*Laila flicks the lights, like Ms. Vasquez, and then asks him to tell the story of when he was on a jet that crash-landed in the ocean. The students are immediately interested in the story and quiet down so they can listen.*)

- Ask students to reread first paragraph and look at the Study Buddy think aloud. What does the Study Buddy help them think about?

Tip: The Study Buddy guides students to look for clues about the main character. Explain that understanding his or her thoughts and feelings may help students understand the story's theme. Point out that the lesson the main character learns is often similar to the lesson the author wants readers to learn.

- Have students read the rest of the story. Tell them to follow the directions in the Close Reading.

Tip: In both this and the previous story, the theme is evident in the ways that the main character changes throughout the story. Remind students to pay attention to character development, as it often has a significant impact on the story as a whole.

- Finally, have students answer the questions on page 65. When they have finished, use the Answer Analysis to discuss correct and incorrect responses.

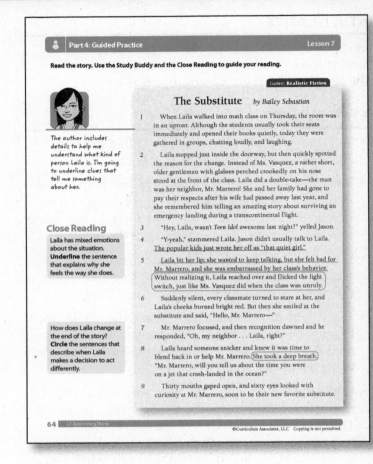

Tier Two Vocabulary: *Unruly*

- Direct students to the word *unruly* in paragraph 5. Ask students to explain what the prefix *un-* means (*"not"*) and have them identify the base word (*ruly*). Explain that *ruly* means "neat and tidy" or "obedient; following the rules." Based on these word parts and the context, have students define *unruly* as it is used in this story. (*"disorderly, disruptive"*)

- Have students describe things that are or can be unruly. Challenge students to think of synonyms for *unruly*. (*disruptive, disorderly, disobedient, rowdy*) **(RL.7.4; L.7.4a, L.7.4b)**

STEP BY STEP

- Have students read questions 1–3, using the Hints to help them answer those questions.

Tip: Question 3 requires students to find details to support their answer to question 2. Remind students to look for details at the beginning, middle, and end of the story.

- Discuss with students the Answer Analysis below.

ANSWER ANALYSIS

1   The correct choice is A. Laila is "embarrassed by her class's behavior" since they are all talking and not paying attention. The story also mentions that the popular students call her "that quiet girl." Choice B is incorrect. The story doesn't mention Laila talking with her friends before class. Choice C is incorrect. Laila's cheeks turn red when she flicks the light on and off, showing she doesn't like to be the center of attention. Choice D is incorrect. There is no evidence that Laila dislikes the popular kids.

2   The correct choice is A. Laila is nervous about helping Mr. Marrero, but she shows courage by quieting the kids and asking him to tell a story. Choice B, C, and D are incorrect because they aren't themes demonstrated by this story.

3   The correct choices are 6 and 7. These phrases show Laila realizing she needs courage and then mustering it to show Mr. Marrero kindness. Choices 1 and 8 are incorrect. These phrases show some support for choice D of item 2, but Mr. Marrero tells a story of adventure, not of wisdom. Choices 2 and 5 are incorrect. These phrases show some support for choice B of item 2, but popularity versus kindness is not the theme developed in the story. Choices 3 and 4 are incorrect. These phrases support choice C of item 2, but quiet versus shy is not the theme developed in this story.

RETEACHING

For question 2, draw the chart below. Help students fill in the boxes. Sample responses are given.

Important Events	Words, Actions, and Feelings	Theme
Laila's class is misbehaving.	Laila is uncomfortable.	Taking action requires courage.

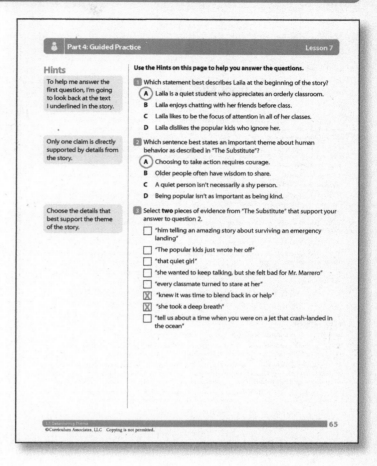

Integrating Standards

Use these questions to further students' understanding of "The Substitute."

1   How does Laila's class normally behave with Ms. Vasquez? How do you know? **(RL.7.1)**

The class normally behaves well for Ms. Vasquez because the story says, "the students usually took their seats immediately and opened their books quietly."

2   What is the meaning of *double-take*, and why is it used in Paragraph 2? **(RL.7.4; L.7.4a)**

A double-take is a delayed reaction to something unexpected. It shows surprise. When someone quickly looks at something twice in disbelief, he or she does a double-take. Laila does a double-take when she sees the substitute teacher. She is surprised to see that he is her neighbor. This is an unexpected turn of events.

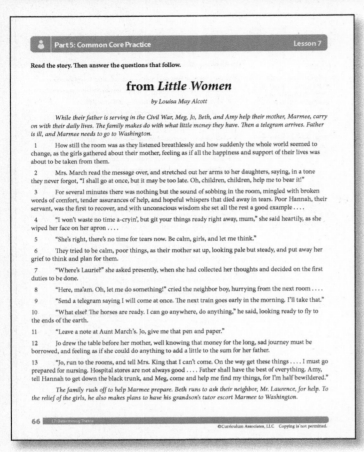

Part 5: Common Core Practice
Lesson 7

Read the story. Then answer the questions that follow.

from *Little Women*

by Louisa May Alcott

While their father is serving in the Civil War, Meg, Jo, Beth, and Amy help their mother, Marmee, carry on with their daily lives. The family makes do with what little money they have. Then a telegram arrives. Father is ill, and Marmee needs to go to Washington.

1   How still the room was as they listened breathlessly and how suddenly the whole world seemed to change, as the girls gathered about their mother, feeling as if all the happiness and support of their lives was about to be taken from them.

2   Mrs. March read the message over, and stretched out her arms to her daughters, saying, in a tone they never forgot, "I shall go at once, but it may be too late. Oh, children, children, help me to bear it!"

3   For several minutes there was nothing but the sound of sobbing in the room, mingled with broken words of comfort, tender assurances of help, and hopeful whispers that died away in tears. Poor Hannah, their servant, was the first to recover, and with unconscious wisdom she set all the rest a good example . . . .

4   "I won't waste no time a-cryin', but git your things ready right away, mum," she said heartily, as she wiped her face on her apron . . . .

5   "She's right, there's no time for tears now. Be calm, girls, and let me think."

6   They tried to be calm, poor things, as their mother sat up, looking pale but steady, and put away her grief to think and plan for them.

7   "Where's Laurie?" she asked presently, when she had collected her thoughts and decided on the first duties to be done.

8   "Here, ma'am. Oh, let me do something!" cried the neighbor boy, hurrying from the next room . . . .

9   "Send a telegram saying I will come at once. The next train goes early in the morning. I'll take that."

10   "What else? The horses are ready. I can go anywhere, do anything," he said, looking ready to fly to the ends of the earth.

11   "Leave a note at Aunt March's. Jo, give me that pen and paper."

12   Jo drew the table before her mother, well knowing that money for the long, sad journey must be borrowed, and feeling as if she could do anything to add a little to the sum for her father.

13   "Jo, run to the rooms, and tell Mrs. King that I can't come. On the way get these things . . . . I must go prepared for nursing. Hospital stores are not always good . . . . Father shall have the best of everything. Amy, tell Hannah to get down the black trunk, and Meg, come and help me find my things, for I'm half bewildered."

The family rush off to help Marmee prepare. Beth runs to ask their neighbor, Mr. Laurence, for help. To the relief of the girls, he also makes plans to have his grandson's tutor escort Marmee to Washington.

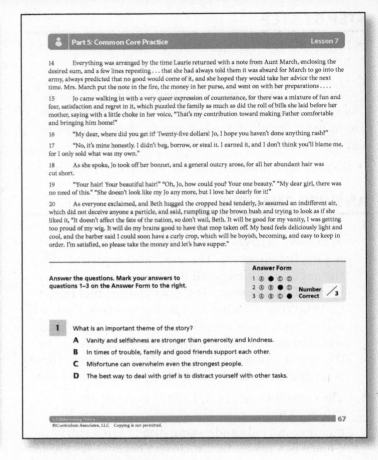

Part 5: Common Core Practice
Lesson 7

14   Everything was arranged by the time Laurie returned with a note from Aunt March, enclosing the desired sum, and a few lines repeating . . . that she had always told them it was absurd for March to go into the army, always predicted that no good would come of it, and she hoped they would take her advice the next time. Mrs. March put the note in the fire, the money in her purse, and went on with her preparations . . . .

15   Jo came walking in with a very queer expression of countenance, for there was a mixture of fun and fear, satisfaction and regret in it, which puzzled the family as much as did the roll of bills she laid before her mother, saying with a little choke in her voice, "That's my contribution toward making Father comfortable and bringing him home!"

16   "My dear, where did you get it? Twenty-five dollars! Jo, I hope you haven't done anything rash?"

17   "No, it's mine honestly. I didn't beg, borrow, or steal it. I earned it, and I don't think you'll blame me, for I only sold what was my own."

18   As she spoke, Jo took off her bonnet, and a general outcry arose, for all her abundant hair was cut short.

19   "Your hair! Your beautiful hair!" "Oh, Jo, how could you? Your one beauty." "My dear girl, there was no need of this." "She doesn't look like my Jo any more, but I love her dearly for it!"

20   As everyone exclaimed, and Beth hugged the cropped head tenderly, Jo assumed an indifferent air, which did not deceive anyone a particle, and said, rumpling up the brown bush and trying to look as if she liked it, "It doesn't affect the fate of the nation, so don't wail, Beth. It will be good for my vanity, I was getting too proud of my wig. It will do my brains good to have that mop taken off. My head feels deliciously light and cool, and the barber said I could soon have a curly crop, which will be boyish, becoming, and easy to keep in order. I'm satisfied, so please take the money and let's have supper."

Answer the questions. Mark your answers to questions 1–3 on the Answer Form to the right.

Answer Form

1 Ⓐ ● Ⓒ Ⓓ
2 Ⓐ Ⓑ ● Ⓓ   **Number Correct** /3
3 Ⓐ Ⓑ Ⓒ ●

1   What is an important theme of the story?

A   Vanity and selfishness are stronger than generosity and kindness.

B   In times of trouble, family and good friends support each other.

C   Misfortune can overwhelm even the strongest people.

D   The best way to deal with grief is to distract yourself with other tasks.

AT A GLANCE

Students independently read a longer story and answer questions in a format that provides test practice.

STEP BY STEP

• Tell students to use what they have learned about reading closely and determining theme to read the story on pages 66 and 67.

• Remind students to underline or circle important details.

• Tell students to answer the questions on pages 67 and 68. For questions 1–3, they should fill in the correct circle on the Answer Form.

• When students have finished, use the Answer Analysis to discuss correct responses and the reasons for them. Have students fill in the Number Correct on the Answer Form.

ANSWER ANALYSIS

1   Choice B is correct. During a critical time for her family, Jo sold her hair and earned a large sum of money, which she selflessly gave to help her father. This supports the theme that family and friends help one another during times of trouble. Choice A is the opposite of the actual theme. Characters' actions in this story show selflessness, not selfishness. Choice C is not the best answer since the characters seem worried about their father's well-being, but they are not overwhelmed by it. They find a way to solve the problem. Choice D is incorrect since none of the characters distract themselves with other tasks. **(DOK 2)**

Theme Connection

• How do all the passages in this lesson relate to the theme of setting a new course?

• Which theme from the lesson passages seems to be the most relevant to real-life situations? Explain.

2 Choice C is correct. Aunt March's note says "she had always told them it was absurd for March to go into the army," but she still sent along money to help. Choice A is not the best choice since, even though Aunt March reminds everyone she was right, she doesn't express the need to prove it. Also, it does not support the theme of the story. Choice B is incorrect. Aunt March doesn't indicate she feels obligated to give the money. Choice D is incorrect since Aunt March does not apologize. *(DOK 2)*

3 Choice D is correct. Jo's line supports the theme since no one asked her to sell her hair, yet she did it anyway and didn't want to make a big fuss about it. Choices A, B, and C do not support the story's theme since they are not about the family supporting one another during times of trouble. *(DOK 2)*

4 Sample response: The family and neighbors all work together to help Marmee when they hear the news about Father. The daughters help their mother prepare for the trip. Aunt March sends money. A neighbor sends someone to escort Marmee to Washington. Jo sells her hair to raise money. All these actions show how the family helps one another to make it through a difficult time. *(DOK 3)*

Part 5: Common Core Practice   Lesson 7

2 How does Aunt March's response to Marmee's note help to develop the theme?

A Despite the situation, Aunt March still wants to prove she was right.

B Aunt March gives only the amount of money she feels she is obligated to give.

C Even though she expressed her disapproval, Aunt March is still willing to help.

D Aunt March realizes that her early warnings were inappropriate and apologizes.

3 Which quote from the story **best** supports the story's theme?

A "'I won't waste no time a-cryin', but git your things ready right away, mum.'"

B "'I earned it, and I don't think you'll blame me, for I only sold what was my own.'"

C "'She's right, there's no time for tears now. Be calm, girls, and let me think.'"

D "'That's my contribution toward making Father comfortable and bringing him home.'"

4 Describe how the author uses the characters' actions to develop the theme over the course of this story. Cite at least **two** details from the text to support your response.

See sample response.

_____

_____

_____

_____

_____

_____

_____

_____

_____

☑ **Self Check** *Go back and see what you can check off on the Self Check on page 44.*

68   L7: Determining Theme   ©Curriculum Associates, LLC   Copying is not permitted.

Integrating Standards

Use these questions and tasks as opportunities to interact with the excerpt from *Little Women*.

1 What details from the story help you infer Marmee's feelings? *(RL.7.1)*

After Marmee reads the message about Father, she says, "Oh, children, children, help me to bear it!" Then there is much sobbing. Marmee is also described as "pale" as she has to "put away her grief." From these details, I can infer that Marmee is worried, scared, and needs the support of her family, but she is also willing and able to set aside her feelings in order to go to her husband and nurse him.

2 How does the setting of this story affect the characters and plot? *(RL.7.3)*

This story is set during the Civil War era, and Father has become ill near the fighting. Having little money to spare, the family finds it hard to address the problems of traveling and nursing him properly, which was necessary in those days when hospital care was far less advanced.

3 Why are the words in Hannah's dialogue spelled differently? Why does the author do this? *(RL.7.4)*

Hannah's lines are written as they are pronounced. The author does this to show how Hannah speaks and to differentiate her from the other characters. This detail helps develop the characters and show the time period.

4 Suppose you are Jo. Write a diary entry for the day described in this story. What are your thoughts? How do you feel about the day's events? *(W.7.3)*

Diary entries will vary. Encourage students to use details from the story dialogue in their entries.

5 Discuss in small groups: What do you learn about daily life during the Civil War era, based on story details? Cite evidence from the text. *(SL.7.1)*

Discussions will vary. Have students think about why the time period is significant in this story and how it is conveyed through specific details. Remind students to follow discussion rules.

Writing Activities

Write an Informative Essay (W.7.2)

• Have students review the themes of the stories in this lesson. Ask students to identify ways in which these themes were evident in the stories themselves. What details did the authors use to support the themes?

• Ask students to choose one of the themes from this lesson and write an informative essay about this theme. How is it conveyed through the text? Why is this theme important for people to read about?

• Encourage students to share their essays with the class.

Denotations and Connotations (L.7.5c)

• Review the definitions of and distinctions between the denotation and connotation of a word. (*Its denotation is its literal meaning, while its connotation is an idea and emotion associated with it.*)

• Direct students to "A Different Day" on student book page 63. Point out various words, such as *cringed, crueler,* and *hurtful.* Have students discuss or look up the meaning of each.

• Have students reread the story to determine the word connotations. How do the connotations differ from the denotations? Then discuss other words in the stories with strong connotations.

LISTENING ACTIVITY (SL.7.3, SL.7.4)

Listen Closely/Delineate a Speaker's Claims

• Have small groups of students reread one of the stories from this lesson. Then have them describe its theme and point out details in the story that support their responses.

• Have students listen closely to each group's claims and the supporting evidence. Students should evaluate the soundness of the group's reasoning and the relevance and sufficiency of the evidence.

DISCUSSION ACTIVITY (SL.7.1)

Talk in a Group/Compare Stories

• Ask students to compare and contrast two or more of this lesson's stories.

• Have students form small groups to compare and contrast aspects of realistic fiction that the authors chose to include in each story. What elements of each story make it part of the realistic fiction genre? Which story is the most realistic? Which is the least realistic? Why?

• Appoint one member of each group to take notes. Allow 10 to 15 minutes for discussion, and then have each group share its results with the class.

MEDIA ACTIVITY (RL.7.7)

Be Creative/Watch a Film Version of a Story

• Direct students to one (or more) of the many film versions of *Little Women.* Have students watch the scene represented in this lesson's final story.

• Students should compare and contrast the different versions. How does the visual presentation in the movie contribute to their understanding? How does it differ from what they "see" and "hear" in their minds' eye as they read?

RESEARCH ACTIVITY (W.7.8; SL.7.4)

Research and Present/Give a Presentation

• Ask students to research what life was like for many families during the Civil War. Are the experiences of the March family in *Little Women* typical? Why or why not?

• Have students present their findings to the class. Remind them to use appropriate eye contact, adequate volume, and clear pronunciation.

• Encourage students to include a multimedia component in their presentations, if possible. They should use these components to clarify their findings and emphasize important points.

Summarizing Literary Texts

LESSON OBJECTIVES

- Summarize a literary text by restating in one's own words the main characters, setting, and key events in sequence.

- Provide an objective summary free of personal opinions or judgments.

THE LEARNING PROGRESSION

- **Grade 6:** CCSS RL.6.2 requires students to use important story details to create an accurate summary that is free of bias and personal opinions.

- **Grade 7: CCSS RL.7.2 builds on the Grade 6 standard by requiring students to summarize important story details and elements briefly and objectively.**

- **Grade 8:** CCSS RL.8.2 requires students to provide an unbiased, accurate summary based on the relationships among various story elements.

PREREQUISITE SKILLS

- Identify main characters and setting.

- Identify key story events and plot development, including the conflict and its resolution.

- Organize events in sequential order.

- Summarize a text by identifying main characters, key events, and setting without offering bias or personal judgment.

TAP STUDENTS' PRIOR KNOWLEDGE

- Tell students that they will be working on a lesson about summarizing literary texts.

- First, ask students to define *plot*. (*a series of events in a story, including a conflict and its resolution*) Remind students that it is important to recognize the main plot events in a literary text.

- Next, ask students to define *character* and *setting*. (*the people, animals, or creatures who take part in the action; the time and place where the story is set*)

- Finally, review that a summary of a literary text is a brief retelling of a story that describes the main characters, setting, and important events, including the conflict and resolution. It should be told in the student's own words.

- Remind students that a good summary is accurate. It identifies the main characters and setting. It extracts the key plot events, presenting them in a sequential and concise way. Explain that good summaries do not include personal opinions or judgments about the text.

■ **Ready** *Teacher Toolbox*		teacher-toolbox.com
	Prerequisite Skills	*RL.7.2*
Ready Lessons	✓	✓
Tools for Instruction		✓
Interactive Tutorials		✓

CCSS Focus

RL.7.2 …provide an objective summary of the text.

ADDITIONAL STANDARDS: RL.7.1, RL.7.3, RL.7.4, RL.7.6, RL.7.7; L.7.1b, L.7.4a, L.7.4c, L.7.4d, L.7.5a; W.7.3, W.7.7, W.7.8, W.7.9a; SL.7.1, SL.7.2, SL.7.4, SL.7.5 (*See page A39 for full text.*)

AT A GLANCE

Through a cartoon, students practice summarizing literary content in an objective manner. They learn to identify the setting, characters, and main events to create a summary.

STEP BY STEP

- Read the first paragraph and the definitions of *summary* and *objective*. Then have students study the cartoon and make notes in the margin about the story's characters, setting, and events.

- Explain that the chart shows the important information needed to write a summary of a literary text. Read the setting and character boxes, and point out that this information is drawn from the text and the images. Have students compare this information to their notes about characters and setting.

- Then read the important event boxes. Point out the vertical arrows, which show the events are listed in chronological order. Discuss how the information in these boxes is drawn from the text and the images. Have students compare it to their notes about events.

- Before reading the summary, ask students how they would summarize the information. Then read the summary aloud. Explain that good readers summarize as they read to check their understanding of the plot and characters.

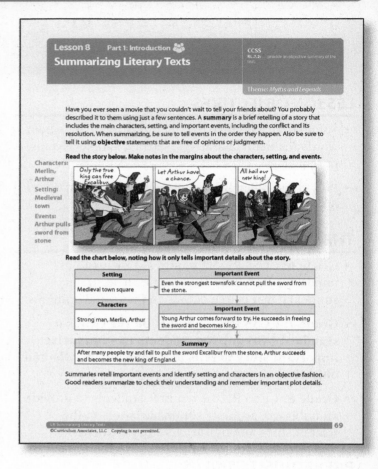

Genre Focus

Literary Texts: Myths and Legends

Tell students that in this lesson they will read myths and legends. Explain that a myth is a fictional story that often explains something about human behavior or the natural world. Myths usually have the following characteristics:

- beliefs and ideals from a particular culture

- characters that are gods, goddesses, or godlike beings with extraordinary powers

- heroes that possess traits valued by the culture

Based on these characteristics, ask students to name some myths. What are the myths about?

Next describe the characteristics of legends:

- tales passed down across generations and often told as if they were true stories

- human characters who perform brave deeds

- a main character who is usually ethical, moral, skillful, and honest

Ask students to name some familiar legends. What are the legends about?

Explain that students will read "Glooskap and the Wasis," a legend about a fierce Algonquin warrior. They will also read two myths about the defeat of a monster and how evil was loosed on the world.

AT A GLANCE

Students read a legend about Glooskap. They identify the characters, setting, and most important events to include in an objective summary.

STEP BY STEP

- Invite volunteers to tell what they learned on the previous page about writing objective summaries.

- Read aloud "Glooskap and Wasis."

- Then read the question: "What is the best way to summarize this part of the legend?"

- Tell students you will use a Think Aloud to demonstrate a way of answering the question.

Think Aloud: First, I'm going to identify the main characters and the setting. One of the main characters is Glooskap, a fierce Algonquin warrior. The other main character is the Wasis, a being who has never been defeated. The setting is Glooskap's village.

- Have students underline details about the characters, setting, and events in the story.

- If possible, display a chart similar to the chart on page 69. Work with students to fill in the information about the characters and setting.

Think Aloud: Next, I will note the main plot events. The first main event is Glooskap returning home, where he sees the Wasis. Then his wife warns him not to upset or interfere with the Wasis.

- Add these first two events to the chart. Have students describe the other main events in this part of the story. Remind them to list the events in order.

Think Aloud: Now I have the information I need to write a summary. When I write a summary, I need to make sure it is objective, or free from my judgments.

- Read aloud the summary on this page. Then read each bullet point and discuss why each word or phrase makes a summary that is not objective.

- Finally, read the summary with all the words crossed out. Ask students how the two are different.

- Have partners complete the activity at the bottom of the page. Invite volunteers to share their responses. *(Sample response: The Wasis' disobedience greatly angers Glooskap.)*

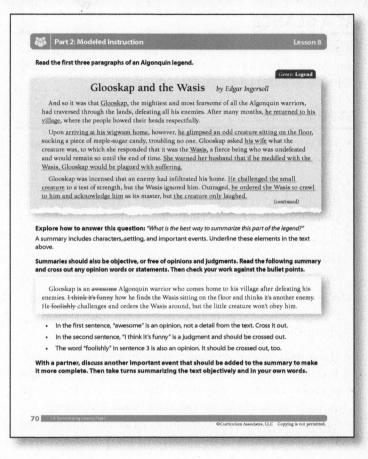

Tier Two Vocabulary: *Incensed*

- Direct students to the word *incensed* in paragraph 3. Help them use context clues to figure out its meaning. Ask what words in the text help them determine the meaning. (outraged) Then have them tell the meaning of the word. *("made very angry") (RL.7.4; L.7.4a)*

- Have students list some synonyms and antonyms for the word. *(synonyms: angry, furious; antonyms: happy, pleased)* Then encourage students to use a thesaurus to check their lists. *(L.7.4d)*

AT A GLANCE

Students continue reading the legend of Glooskap and the Wasis. They answer a multiple-choice question and objectively summarize the story.

STEP BY STEP

- Tell students that they will continue reading about Glooskap and the Wasis.

- The Close Reading helps students determine the important events and details. The Hint will help them identify choices that make judgments.

- Have students read the passage and underline details that describe the ways the Wasis responds to Glooskap's actions, as directed by the Close Reading.

- Ask volunteers to share the details they underlined. Discuss what these details help them understand about the characters and events.

- Have students answer the question and Show Your Thinking; then discuss their responses. Finally, have partners practice objectively summarizing the entire story. Sample response for Show Your Thinking: Choice A is not a good summary because the second sentence contains a judgment.

ANSWER ANALYSIS

Choice A is incorrect. The second sentence offers a judgment, which makes the summary biased.

Choice B is correct. The summary is objective and lists the most important events in chronological order.

Choice C is incorrect. The legend does not state that the wife's warning was wrong.

Choice D is incorrect. It leaves out important events. Glooskap picks up the Wasis, which soothes it, and after that, whenever a baby coos at his father, the Wasis remembers his victory.

ERROR ALERT: Students who did not choose B might not understand that a complete summary must include the main events and should not include personal judgments. Have students reread each choice and eliminate choices that are incomplete, inaccurate, or biased. They should recognize that only choice B gives a more complete, objective summary.

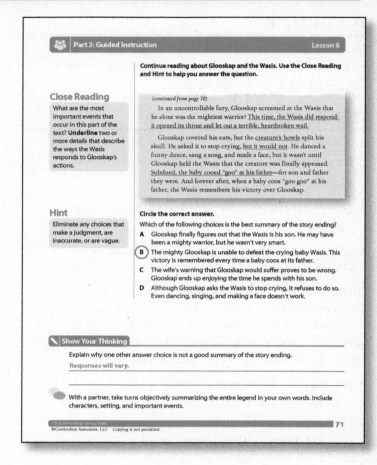

Part 3: Guided Instruction   Lesson 8

Continue reading about Glooskap and the Wasis. Use the Close Reading and Hint to help you answer the question.

Close Reading
What are the most important events that occur in this part of the text? **Underline** two or more details that describe the ways the Wasis responds to Glooskap's actions.

(continued from page 70)

In an uncontrollable fury, Glooskap screamed at the Wasis that he alone was the mightiest warrior! This time, the Wasis did respond: it opened its throat and let out a terrible, heartbroken wail.

Glooskap covered his ears, but the creature's howls split his skull. He asked it to stop crying, but it would not. He danced a funny dance, sang a song, and made a face, but it wasn't until Glooskap held the Wasis that the creature was finally appeased. Subdued, the baby cooed "goo" at his father—for son and father they were. And forever after, when a baby coos "goo goo" at his father, the Wasis remembers his victory over Glooskap.

Hint
Eliminate any choices that make a judgment, are inaccurate, or are vague.

Circle the correct answer.

Which of the following choices is the best summary of the story ending?

A Glooskap finally figures out that the Wasis is his son. He may have been a mighty warrior, but he wasn't very smart.

B The mighty Glooskap is unable to defeat the crying baby Wasis. This victory is remembered every time a baby coos at its father.

C The wife's warning that Glooskap would suffer proves to be wrong. Glooskap ends up enjoying the time he spends with his son.

D Although Glooskap asks the Wasis to stop crying, it refuses to do so. Even dancing, singing, and making a face doesn't work.

Show Your Thinking

Explain why one other answer choice is not a good summary of the story ending.
Responses will vary.

With a partner, take turns objectively summarizing the entire legend in your own words. Include characters, setting, and important events.

L8 Summarizing Literary Texts
©Curriculum Associates, LLC Copying is not permitted.   71

ELL Support: Comparatives and Superlatives

- Explain to students that superlatives are words that compare three or more things. To form the superlative, the ending *-est* is added to adjectives with one or two syllables. For longer words, the word *most* is used before the adjective.

- Read the first sentence. Point out that *mightiest* is the superlative form of the adjective *mighty*. Explain that *mightiest warrior* means "more mighty than any other warrior."

- Work with students to identify another superlative in the legend and explain its meaning. (most fearsome; *"more fearsome than any other warrior"*) **(L.7.1)**

AT A GLANCE

Students read a myth twice about a brave warrior named Beowulf. After the first reading, you will ask three questions to check your students' comprehension of the passage.

STEP BY STEP

- Have students read the passage silently without referring to the Study Buddy or Close Reading text.

- Ask the following questions to ensure students' comprehension of the text:

  What happens to make the music and laughter stop in Heorot Hall? (*A monster named Grendel kills thirty of Hrothgar's men. For twelve years, none of the soldiers could beat Grendel.*)

  Who is Beowulf, and what does he do? (*He is a young warrior who claims he will kill Grendel.*)

  What is the resolution of the story problem? (*Beowulf and Grendel fight, and Beowulf wins. Fatally wounded, Grendel runs back to the lake and dies.*)

- Ask students to reread paragraph 1 and look at the Study Buddy think aloud. What does the Study Buddy help them think about?

Tip: The Study Buddy tells students to think about how the elements of a myth might be included in a summary of the text. Remind students that the plot events are not the only important part of a summary. The setting is particularly important in a myth.

- Have students read the rest of the passage. Tell them to follow the directions in the Close Reading.

Tip: Close Reading guides students to underline details that reveal the central conflict and the characters who are most affected. Encourage students to use the strategy of rereading and taking notes when they encounter questions in other contexts, such as in standardized tests or when reading content-related texts in other subjects.

- Finally, have students answer the questions on page 73. Use the Answer Analysis to discuss correct and incorrect responses.

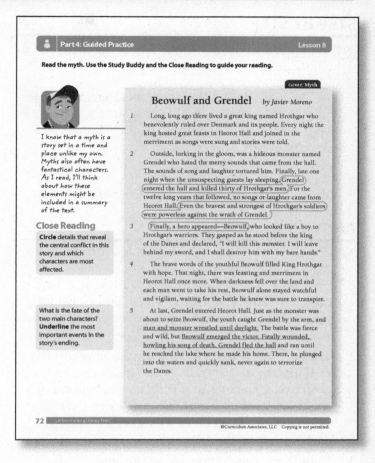

Read the myth. Use the Study Buddy and the Close Reading to guide your reading.

Genre: Myth

Beowulf and Grendel   *by Javier Moreno*

1   Long, long ago there lived a great king named Hrothgar who benevolently ruled over Denmark and its people. Every night the king hosted great feasts in Heorot Hall and joined in the merriment as songs were sung and stories were told.

2   Outside, lurking in the gloom, was a hideous monster named Grendel who hated the merry sounds that came from the hall. The sounds of song and laughter tortured him. Finally, late one night when the unsuspecting guests lay sleeping, Grendel entered the hall and killed thirty of Hrothgar's men. For the twelve long years that followed, no songs or laughter came from Heorot Hall. Even the bravest and strongest of Hrothgar's soldiers were powerless against the wrath of Grendel.

3   Finally, a hero appeared—Beowulf, who looked like a boy to Hrothgar's warriors. They gasped as he stood before the king of the Danes and declared, "I will kill this monster. I will leave behind my sword, and I shall destroy him with my bare hands."

4   The brave words of the youthful Beowulf filled King Hrothgar with hope. That night, there was feasting and merriment in Heorot Hall once more. When darkness fell over the land and each man went to take his rest, Beowulf alone stayed watchful and vigilant, waiting for the battle he knew was sure to transpire.

5   At last, Grendel entered Heorot Hall. Just as the monster was about to seize Beowulf, the youth caught Grendel by the arm, and man and monster wrestled until daylight. The battle was fierce and wild, but Beowulf emerged the victor. Fatally wounded, howling his song of death, Grendel fled the hall and ran until he reached the lake where he made his home. There, he plunged into the waters and quickly sank, never again to terrorize the Danes.

I know that a myth is a story set in a time and place unlike my own. Myths also often have fantastical characters. As I read, I'll think about how these elements might be included in a summary of the text.

Close Reading

Circle details that reveal the central conflict in this story and which characters are most affected.

What is the fate of the two main characters? **Underline** the most important events in the story's ending.

72   L8: Summarizing Literary Texts

©Curriculum Associates, LLC   Copying is not permitted.

Tier Two Vocabulary: *Benevolently*

- Point out the word *benevolently* in paragraph 1. Ask students what part of speech the word is and what it modifies. (*adverb*; ruled)

- Then help students use the context in the sentence and the paragraph to determine the meaning of *benevolently*. Have students list the words or phrases they used as clues to its meaning. (*"hosted great feasts," "joined in the merriment," "great king"*)

- Have students define *benevolently*. (*"kindly"*) Then have them use a dictionary to verify this meaning. **(RL.7.4; L.7.4a, L.7.4c, L.7.4d)**

STEP BY STEP

- Have students read questions 1–3, using the Hints to help them answer those questions.

Tip: The first Hint reminds students that summaries should be objective—free of bias or judgments—and include information about the main characters and important events. Have students cross out any choices that contain judgments or bias.

- Discuss with students the Answer Analysis below.

ANSWER ANALYSIS

1. The correct choice is D. This sentence includes the main character and one of the key events—Beowulf's promise to kill Grendel. It is also an objective statement. Choices A, B, and C include judgments, assumptions, or inaccurate details about King Hrothgar and Grendel.

2. The correct choice is B. This statement accurately explains the events in the story resolution and is objective. Choices A and C do not include enough about key events—Beowulf's victory or Grendel's death. Choice D includes a judgment about the defeat of Grendel.

3. Sample response: Long ago in the country of Denmark, a monster called Grendel attacked Heorot Hall and killed many of King Hrothgar's soldiers. A young warrior named Beowulf vowed to slay the monster. After a fierce battle, Beowulf managed to kill Grendel.

RETEACHING

Use a chart to verify the answer to question 2. Draw the chart below, and work with students to fill in the boxes. Sample responses are provided.

Setting: Heorot Hall	Event: Beowulf and Grendel have a fierce battle.
Characters: Beowulf, Grendel	Event: Beowulf defeats Grendel, who flees to the lake and dies.
Summary: Beowulf defeats Grendel, who returns to his lake and dies.	

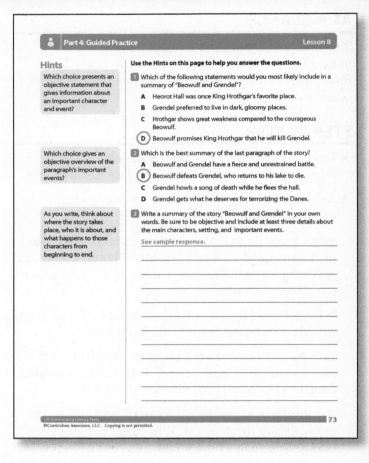

Hints

Which choice presents an objective statement that gives information about an important character and event?

Which choice gives an objective overview of the paragraph's important events?

As you write, think about where the story takes place, who it is about, and what happens to those characters from beginning to end.

Use the Hints on this page to help you answer the questions.

1. Which of the following statements would you most likely include in a summary of "Beowulf and Grendel"?
   - A Heorot Hall was once King Hrothgar's favorite place.
   - B Grendel preferred to live in dark, gloomy places.
   - C Hrothgar shows great weakness compared to the courageous Beowulf.
   - **D** Beowulf promises King Hrothgar that he will kill Grendel.

2. Which is the best summary of the last paragraph of the story?
   - A Beowulf and Grendel have a fierce and unrestrained battle.
   - **B** Beowulf defeats Grendel, who returns to his lake to die.
   - C Grendel howls a song of death while he flees the hall.
   - D Grendel gets what he deserves for terrorizing the Danes.

3. Write a summary of the story "Beowulf and Grendel" in your own words. Be sure to be objective and include at least three details about the main characters, setting, and important events.

   See sample response.
   _____
   _____
   _____
   _____
   _____
   _____
   _____
   _____
   _____
   _____
   _____
   _____

L8: Summarizing Literary Texts   73
©Curriculum Associates, LLC   Copying is not permitted.

Integrating Standards

Use these questions to further students' understanding of "Beowulf and Grendel."

1. How does the setting affect the characters and plot? **(RL.7.3)**

   The myth occurs long ago and is set in King Hrothgar's great hall where his people enjoy feasting, songs, and dancing. Because Grendel hates the noise, songs, and laughter, he kills many of the warriors. This slaughter sets in motion future events in which the hero, Beowulf, must fight the monster to the death.

2. What can you infer about Beowulf based on the details in the legend? **(RL.7.1)**

   Beowulf is strong, brave, and loyal even though he is young. I can infer this because Beowulf is not afraid to sit alone and wait for Grendel or to battle the huge monster.

Part 5: Common Core Practice   Lesson 8

Read the myth. Then answer the questions that follow.

Gift from the Heavens

by Flora Díaz

1   At one time, the gods lived in the heavens while the mortals toiled on the earth. Zeus, king of all gods, did not look kindly on the mortals. Zeus believed that all heavenly powers belonged only to the gods and goddesses. Prometheus believed that these powers should be shared with the mortals.

2   Prometheus and Zeus were constantly getting into disputes. Once, Prometheus was asked to solve a conflict between the gods and mortal men. The men were going to sacrifice a bull during a festival and they had to decide which parts of the bull should be offered to the gods and which parts should be reserved for the men. Prometheus saw this as an opportunity to play a trick on Zeus. He butchered the bull and put the lean, tasty parts of the meat into a small serving bowl and then placed the gristle, bones, and fat into a much larger serving bowl. When Prometheus asked Zeus to select his meal, naturally he chose the larger portion.

3   When Zeus realized how he had been deceived, he was furious and immediately sought revenge. To punish both Prometheus and the mortals he cared about, Zeus snatched fire away from the men of earth, and kept it only for the gods.

4   During one bitterly cold winter, Prometheus watched the mortals huddle together like a pack of animals to keep warm. "They need to have fire returned to earth," he thought. So he decided to ignore Zeus' decree, no matter the risk. Prometheus lit a torch with the fire from the wheels of the chariot that carried the sun across the sky. He brought the flaming torch to earth and delivered fire to the mortals. As a result, life on earth was transformed. Not only did fire keep people warm, it also enabled them to cook food for the first time, as well as smoke the food and preserve it for later use. With the heat of the fire, they could even smelt metals and turn them into tools to use for farming.

5   The king of the gods was furious when he learned what Prometheus had done. He wanted to punish Prometheus and return the mortals to a life of pain and hardship. So Zeus came up with a plan. He asked the other goddesses to help him create a beautiful, mortal woman. His daughter Athena offered her assistance, and when the lovely creature was fully formed, Athena breathed life into her. Zeus named the woman Pandora, and she possessed unequalled beauty and charm. Zeus gave Pandora an ornate lidded box and sent her to Prometheus as a gift. He told Prometheus that Pandora would make a perfect bride.

6   Prometheus was suspicious of any gift from Zeus, despite the woman's incredible beauty. He suggested to his brother Epimetheus that he marry Pandora instead, which he willingly did. After they were wed, Epimetheus asked his bride what was inside the sealed box.

7   "I don't know," she replied. "I only know that Zeus gave me strict instructions never to open it."

8   "That is most unusual, but I would not trust Zeus. Perhaps we should bury the box," her husband responded.

9   Pandora had never given a thought to what was inside the box until her husband asked her about it. Now she was consumed with curiosity and she could think of nothing else. She wondered what it could be and

74   L8: Summarizing Literary Texts

©Curriculum Associates, LLC   Copying is not permitted.

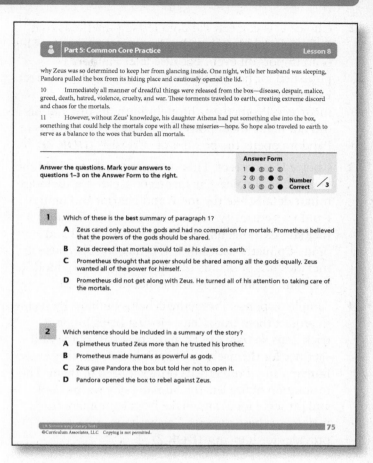

Part 5: Common Core Practice   Lesson 8

why Zeus was so determined to keep her from glancing inside. One night, while her husband was sleeping, Pandora pulled the box from its hiding place and cautiously opened the lid.

10   Immediately all manner of dreadful things were released from the box—disease, despair, malice, greed, death, hatred, violence, cruelty, and war. These torments traveled to earth, creating extreme discord and chaos for the mortals.

11   However, without Zeus' knowledge, his daughter Athena had put something else into the box, something that could help the mortals cope with all these miseries—hope. So hope also traveled to earth to serve as a balance to the woes that burden all mortals.

Answer the questions. Mark your answers to questions 1–3 on the Answer Form to the right.

Answer Form
1 ● Ⓑ Ⓒ Ⓓ
2 Ⓐ Ⓑ ● Ⓓ   **Number Correct**   /3
3 Ⓐ Ⓑ Ⓒ ●

1   Which of these is the **best** summary of paragraph 1?

A   Zeus cared only about the gods and had no compassion for mortals. Prometheus believed that the powers of the gods should be shared.

B   Zeus decreed that mortals would toil as his slaves on earth.

C   Prometheus thought that power should be shared among all the gods equally. Zeus wanted all of the power for himself.

D   Prometheus did not get along with Zeus. He turned all of his attention to taking care of the mortals.

2   Which sentence should be included in a summary of the story?

A   Epimetheus trusted Zeus more than he trusted his brother.

B   Prometheus made humans as powerful as gods.

C   Zeus gave Pandora the box but told her not to open it.

D   Pandora opened the box to rebel against Zeus.

L8: Summarizing Literary Texts   75
©Curriculum Associates, LLC   Copying is not permitted.

AT A GLANCE

Students independently read a longer myth and answer questions in a format that provides test practice.

STEP BY STEP

- Tell students to use what they have learned about reading closely and summarizing literary texts to read the passage on pages 74 and 75.

- Remind students to underline or circle important details about the characters, setting, and events.

- Tell students to answer the questions on pages 75 and 76. For questions 1–3, they should fill in the correct circle on the Answer Form.

- When students have finished, use the Answer Analysis to discuss correct responses and the reasons for them. Have students fill in the Number Correct on the Answer Form.

ANSWER ANALYSIS

1   Choice A is correct. It states the most important ideas in sequential order and names the two main characters, Zeus and Prometheus. Choices B, C, and D include ideas that are not in paragraph 1. They are inaccurate statements or judgments about Zeus's and Prometheus's beliefs and behavior. **(DOK 2)**

Theme Connection

- How do all the passages in this lesson relate to the theme of myths and legends?

- How are the main characters in the myths and legends similar in this lesson? How and why do they differ?

2 Choice C is correct. Pandora tells Epimetheus that Zeus only told her that she should never open it. This is an important event because later Pandora is punished for her disobedience. Choice A is incorrect. Epimetheus does not trust Zeus. Choice B is incorrect. Prometheus brought humans fire, but he did not make them powerful. Choice D is incorrect. Pandora opens the box out of curiosity. *(DOK 2)*

3 Choice D is correct. This summary includes only the key events. Choice A is incorrect because it includes minor details like the torch and chariot and omits Pandora's curiosity. Choice B is incorrect because it includes extraneous details such as the bull and omits Epimetheus. Choice C is incorrect because it includes minor details like humans smoking food and omits Epimetheus and Pandora. *(DOK 2)*

4 Sample response: Prometheus helps humans by trying to protect them from Zeus. He first helps humans trick Zeus so they can keep the best part of the bull sacrifice for themselves. Then, when Zeus takes away humans' fire, Prometheus brings it back to them. The restoration of fire lets the humans stay warm, cook and preserve food, and make farm equipment from metal. For these reasons, Prometheus protects and provides for humans. *(DOK 2)*

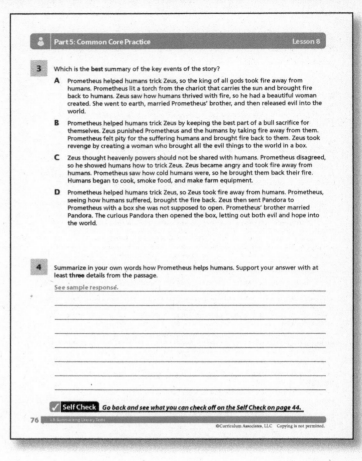

Integrating Standards

Use these questions and tasks as opportunities to interact with the myth of Pandora's box.

1 Contrast how Zeus and Prometheus feel about mortals. Cite evidence from the text to explain the differences. *(RL.7.1)*

Prometheus is kind to the mortals and believes they should share heavenly powers with gods and goddesses, while Zeus does not look kindly on them and does not believe they should share godly powers. The text states, "Zeus believed that all heavenly powers belonged only to the gods and goddesses. Prometheus believed that these powers should be shared with the mortals."

2 What does the phrase "consumed with curiosity" in paragraph 9 mean? How does this expression show Pandora feelings and foreshadow what will happen? *(RL.7.3, RL.7.4; L.7.5a)*

It means that Pandora desperately wants to know what is in the box. She is so curious that she can

think of nothing else. It foreshadows that she will certainly give in to her impulse and open it.

3 Write about the point of view in this myth. How does it help you understand the story? How might the story change if it were told from a different point of view? *(RL.7.6; W.7.9a)*

The point of view is third-person. The narrator is an objective observer who tells how each character feels and why they act in certain ways. If it were told in first-person from Pandora's point of view, the reader would not be given details about the conflict between Zeus and Prometheus nor Zeus' need for revenge .

4 Discuss in small groups: Why do you think people created myths like this one? Why do they help people explain or understand? How are myths important to cultures? *(SL.7.1)*

Discussions will vary. Encourage students to talk about what myths have meant to different cultures, and help them understand that myths were often created to explain things in nature.

Writing Activities

Another Point of View (W.7.3)

- Challenge students to think about how Beowulf might have described his battle with Grendel. How did he feel when he volunteered? How did he feel when he first saw Grendel? What was it like to battle the monster and defeat him?

- Have students rewrite the story of Beowulf and Grendel from Beowulf's point of view. Encourage students to use descriptive details and dialogue. Allow time for students to share their stories with the class.

Kinds of Sentences (L.7.1b)

- Have students reread the second and third sentence in paragraph 2 of "Gift from the Heavens." Ask students what kind of sentences these are. (*simple, complex*) Remind students that a complex sentence is made up of one independent clause and one or more dependent clauses.

- Explain that writers use a variety of sentence types when they write. Review compound and compound-complex sentences.

- Have students write a paragraph comparing and contrasting myths. Tell them to use all four kinds of sentences at least once.

LISTENING ACTIVITY (SL.7.2)

Listen Closely/Summarize

- Have students work in pairs to summarize "Gift from the Heavens." One student should read aloud the first paragraph and provide a summary that includes a non-objective statement. The other student must listen closely and revise the summary to exclude any bias or opinions.

- Have partners switch roles and repeat the activity until they have summarized the entire myth.

DISCUSSION ACTIVITY (SL.7.1)

Talk in a Group/Talk About Myths and Legends

- Ask students to review the heroes, gods, and goddesses they read about in this lesson's passages. Encourage students to describe other characters from myths or legends with which they are familiar.

- Have students form small groups to discuss the characteristics of heroes, gods, and goddesses in myths and legends. As a group, they should discuss the traits such supernatural characters have in common in these types of stories.

- Allow 10 to 15 minutes for discussion. Then have groups share their results with the class.

MEDIA ACTIVITY (RL.7.7)

Be Creative/Make a Script

- Have students review the story "Glooskap and the Wasis."

- Have students work in small groups to write a script for a play version of this story.

- Then ask groups to perform their scripts for the class. Have students compare and contrast watching and listening to the myth to reading it.

RESEARCH ACTIVITY (W.7.7, W.7.8; SL.7.4, SL.7.5)

Research and Present/Give a Presentation

- Remind students that "Gift from the Heavens" is an example of Greek mythology, which centers on Greek gods and mortal heroes.

- Have students research more information about Greek mythology and choose the god, goddess, or hero who most interests them. Then have them research that figure and write a presentation.

- Students should include a visual display and explain the attributes represented by that figure as well as summarize a myth featuring him or her.

SCORING GUIDE AND ANSWER ANALYSIS

Literature Passage Answer Analysis

1 Ⓐ ● Ⓒ Ⓓ   4 Ⓐ ● Ⓒ Ⓓ

2A ● Ⓑ Ⓒ Ⓓ   5 Ⓐ Ⓑ Ⓒ ●

3 Ⓐ Ⓑ ● Ⓓ

1 Choice B is correct. Nate wants very much to be a soldier, but after two years, he is "no closer to the fighting." This detail supports the statement that he is frustrated.

Choice A is incorrect. Nate's work in the potato fields is difficult, but this statement does not support the statement that he is frustrated. Choice C is incorrect. The detail about trudging to the house does not show his frustration. Choice D is also incorrect. Nate's gesture toward the house does not reveal frustration. **(RL.7.1; DOK 3)**

2 **Part A:** Choice A is correct. This is an important lesson that Nate learns at the end of the story, and it is the theme, or central idea, the author wants to convey.

Choice B is incorrect. This statement describes how wartime can affect people, but it does not explain what Nate learns at the end of the story. Choice C is incorrect. Even though family members have different duties, these duties did not influence Nate's decision at the end of the story. Choice D is also incorrect. Early in the story, Nate felt that life was unfair. But by the end, he has learned that there are many ways to serve a cause. This is the theme that the author wants to convey. **(RL.7.2; DOK 3)**

Part B: Students choose the first and last options. These are the only choices that provide details supporting the correct choice of theme described in Part A. **(RL.7.1; DOK 3)**

3 Choice C is correct. The setting, a New Hampshire farm far removed from the battlefields of the war, makes Nate feel that he has no real purpose.

Choice A is incorrect. The New Hampshire setting of the story does not make Nate feel alone; its distance from battle makes him feel that he is without purpose. Choice B is incorrect. The setting of a New Hampshire farm does not serve to make Nate feel that his family is safe, but to make him feel that he lacks a sense of purpose. Choice D is also incorrect. The setting of New Hampshire does not make Nate feel that his region is unpatriotic, but that he himself is without a real purpose. **(RL.7.3; DOK 2)**

4 Choice B is correct. The details about the commander's fatigue lines and silver hair imprsss on Nate how old and tired the man looks and how hard the fighting has been.

Choice A is incorrect. The halting of the troops by the commander's raised hand does not suggest the vivid impression the man makes on Nate. It is the physical details of fatigue lines and silver hair that make the impression. Choice C is incorrect. The commander's simple statement of need does not create the vivid impression. This is achieved by the details about fatigue lines and silver hair, which show the man's exhaustion. Choice D is also incorrect. The man's civility makes less of an impression on Nate than do the physical signs of exhaustion: fatigue lines and silver hair. **(RL.7.1, RL.7.3; DOK 3)**

5 Choice D is correct. Everyone can help out during the war by doing something in his or her own way.

Choice A is incorrect. Listening and never complaining is not really what Nate learns. Choice B is incorrect. Being jealous may be part of how Nate feels, but it is not the lesson of the story. Choice C is also incorrect. Soldiers may be just like ordinary people, but that is not a lesson learned in the story. **(RL.7.2; DOK 2)**

SAMPLE RESPONSES

Short Response

6 The story first shows that the family plays a role in the war when we learn that Nate's brother and cousin are serving in the militia. Later the family welcomes the soldiers, offering them a meal and a place to sleep. Nate realizes that he can play a role too, when he speaks up for the hungry troops and offers them food and water. **(RL.7.1; DOK 3)**

7 Nate keeps getting more and more frustrated as he thinks about his brother marching off to battle. Nate himself has to stay home and work in the stony New Hampshire potato fields. Then he hears that his cousin has been accepted into the militia, and that makes him even more frustrated. His attitude changes after he is able to help the commander and the troops. **(RL.7.2; DOK 2)**

8 The fact that Father has been injured and cannot be a soldier makes the meeting between him and the commander significant. The commander notices the other man's cane and silently acknowledges that Father has a good reason for not joining the army. In turn, Father respects the efforts of the commander in serving his country and wants to do what he can to help, even though he is not able to fight. This meeting helps support the theme that there are many ways to serve a cause. **(RL.7.3; DOK 2)**

Performance Task

9 Throughout the story, the author shows how Nate changes from an angry, frustrated farm boy to someone who knows he is playing an important part in the war. In the beginning of the story, Nate resents the fact that his older brother has had the chance to join the troops and defend his country. He considers the soldier's life "glorious," while he thinks of the potato fields as "stingy." Nate pictures himself as an experienced soldier with calloused hands, but then he remembers that the war has gone on for two years without him.

At dinner, Nate's frustration with his situation increases after his father tells the family that Nate's young cousin has joined the militia. Nate looks at his father with his mouth open because he is shocked by the news. Afterwards, he stomps out to the water pump to fill a bucket, another boring chore. More and more, we see the conflict Nate experiences between being a good son and helping at home, and leaving home with the army as his brother had done.

Then, Nate has an experience that causes a change in his attitude. A troop of tired soldiers arrives, clearly in need of rest and food. The commander is a tired-looking older man showing the wear and tear of army life. Now, Nate sees that there is a chance to assist and to show that he knows what to do. He helps to meet the soldiers' needs by offering water and by hurrying down to the root cellar to get the best potatoes for the men's meal. At the end of the story, Nate realizes that he will be a man soon enough. He feels more content with his situation and with the important job he has right now. **(RL.7.2, RL.7.3; DOK 3)**

SCORING RUBRICS

Short-Response Rubric

2 points   The response is accurate, complete, and fulfills all requirements of the task. Text-based support and examples are included. Any information that goes beyond the text is relevant to the task.

1 point   The response is partially accurate and fulfills some requirements of the task. Some information may be inaccurate, too general, or confused. Support and examples may be insufficient or not text-based.

0 points   The response is inaccurate, poorly organized, or does not respond to the task.

Performance Task Rubric

4 points   The response
- Fulfills all requirements of the task
- Uses varied sentence types and some sophisticated vocabulary
- Includes relevant and accurate details from the texts as well as text-based inferences
- Demonstrates a thorough understanding of the texts
- Maintains a clear focus and organization
- Is fluent and demonstrates a clear voice
- Uses correct spelling, grammar, capitalization, and punctuation

3 points   The response
- Fulfills all requirements of the task
- Uses simple sentences and grade-level vocabulary
- Includes relevant and accurate details from the texts
- Demonstrates a mainly literal understanding of the texts
- Maintains a mostly clear focus and organization
- Is fluent and demonstrates some sense of voice
- Uses mostly correct spelling, grammar, capitalization, and punctuation

2 points   The response
- Fulfills some requirements of the task
- Uses simple sentences, some fragments, and grade-level vocabulary
- Includes some relevant and accurate details from the texts
- Demonstrates some misunderstandings or gaps in understanding of the texts
- Attempts to maintain a clear focus and organization
- Is difficult to read, includes some inaccuracies, and demonstrates little or no sense of voice
- Contains some inaccurate spelling, grammar, capitalization, and punctuation that may hinder understanding

1 point   The response
- Fulfills few requirements of the task
- Uses sentence fragments and below-grade-level vocabulary
- Includes no details or irrelevant details to support the response
- Demonstrates very little understanding of the texts
- Does not establish a clear focus or organization
- Is difficult to read, contains many inaccuracies, and demonstrates no sense of voice
- Uses incorrect spelling, grammar, capitalization, and punctuation to an extent that impedes understanding

0 points   The response is irrelevant, poorly organized, or illegible.

Analyzing Word Meanings

LESSON OBJECTIVES

- Determine the figurative, connotative, and technical meanings of words and phrases as they are used in an informational text.

- Analyze the impact of specific word choice on meaning and tone.

THE LEARNING PROGRESSION

- **Grade 6:** CCSS RI.6.4 requires students to determine the meaning of words and phrases as used in a text.

- **Grade 7: CCSS RI.7.4 builds on the Grade 6 standard by requiring students not only to determine the meaning of words and phrases but also to analyze the impact of the author's word choice on meaning and tone.**

- **Grade 8:** CCSS RI.8.4 requires students to further their analysis of the impact of language by determining the figurative and connotative meanings of words and phrases in more complex texts.

PREREQUISITE SKILLS

- Use context to determine the meaning of unfamiliar words and phrases.

- Identify words having connotative as well as denotative meanings.

- Identify examples of figurative language and recognize the ways in which authors use words and phrases figuratively.

- Understand the relationship between an author's choice of words and the overall meaning or tone of a text.

TAP STUDENTS' PRIOR KNOWLEDGE

- Tell students that they will be learning more about the different meanings of words, including their technical, figurative, and connotative meanings.

- Display an excerpt from a textbook or other type of informational text. Tell students that they will have a scavenger hunt for words that are used figuratively or for words that have a strong connotation.

- Challenge students to find words and phrases that fit within various categories, such as figures of speech, words with strong connotations, and words specific to the topic. List the identified words and phrases on the board. Discuss with students why the author might have made the choices he or she did—that is, how these choices contribute to the readers' understanding of the text overall.

- Through word scavenger hunts, students can learn to differentiate among different types of word choices, and they can better understand the various ways words function to create meaning.

- Point out that by building their familiarity with different types of word meanings, students will become more aware of the impact of an author's language choices on the meaning and tone of the texts they read.

Ready *Teacher Toolbox*   teacher-toolbox.com

	Prerequisite Skills	RI.7.4
Ready Lessons	✓	✓
Tools for Instruction	✓ ✓	✓ ✓
Interactive Tutorials	✓	✓

CCSS Focus

RI.7.4 Determine the meaning of words and phrases as they are used in a text, including figurative, connotative, and technical meanings; analyze the impact of a specific word choice on meaning and tone.

ADDITIONAL STANDARDS: RI.7.1, RI.7.2, RI.7.3, RI.7.5, RI.7.6, RI.7.7, RI.7.9; L.7.1a, L.7.4a, L.7.4b, L.7.4d; W.7.1, W.7.6; SL.7.1, SL.7.5
(See page A39 for full text.)

AT A GLANCE

By studying callouts on a diagram, students identify words and phrases that have technical, connotative, and figurative meanings. They analyze why the author chose to use certain phrases and how these phrases impact the meaning of the text.

STEP BY STEP

- Read the first paragraph and the bullet points with the definitions of *technical*, *connotative*, and *figurative meaning*. Then direct students to the diagram of the wasp. Have them underline words with technical, figurative, or connotative meanings.

- Invite volunteers to share the words and phrases they marked. Ask volunteers to explain their choices.

- Explain that the chart organizes ideas to help students analyze different word meanings from the diagram and why the author chose to use them.

- Read the first row of the chart. To help clarify the connotative meaning, ask students how the phrase's meaning would change if the author had written "obtain its meal" instead.

- Then read the next two rows of the chart and have students fill in the blank cells. Refer to the definitions of the different kinds of meanings to help students fill in the second column. To help them complete the third column, ask what the author suggests by comparing the wasp's eyes to those of a space alien.

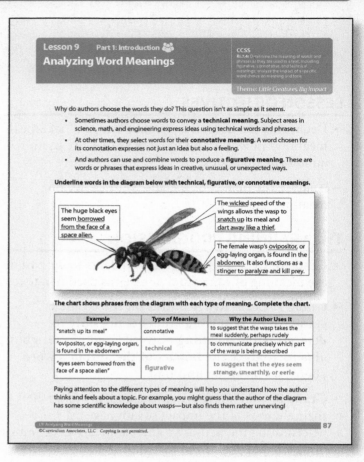

- Share an example of a word or phrase with a technical, connotative, or figurative meaning in a book you are reading. Explain how the word or phrase helps you understand the author's feelings toward the topic of the text or what kind of knowledge the author has about the topic.

Genre Focus

Informational Text: Scientific Account

Tell students that in this lesson they will read scientific accounts. Explain that a scientific account is a text that provides information about some aspect of the natural world. Share with students these characteristics of scientific accounts:

- Its purpose is to inform or explain, typically about life science, physical science, or earth and space science.

- The body of the account gives facts, examples, reasons, and descriptions. It may also contain subheadings, which help to organize information and ideas in a text.

- An account may include photographs, captions, and other text features to expand on or clarify ideas.

- The ending usually repeats or summarizes the main idea of the account.

Based on these characteristics, ask students about scientific accounts they have read. What was the topic and purpose? Did the author successfully answer the questions *who, what, when, where, why,* and *how*?

Tell students that in this lesson they will read scientific accounts about bedbugs, the Goliath beetle, and cicadas.

AT A GLANCE

Students read a text about bedbugs. Using context clues, they determine the technical, connotative, and figurative meanings of words and phrases.

STEP BY STEP

- Invite volunteers to tell what they learned on the previous page about the technical, connotative, and figurative meanings of words and phrases.

- Tell students they will read a text about bedbugs.

- Read aloud "Don't Let the Bedbugs Bite."

- Read the prompt: "The underlined words and phrases in the passage express technical, connotative, and figurative meanings. Determine the meaning of each word or phrase as it is used in the passage."

- Tell students that you will use a Think Aloud to demonstrate a way of answering the question.

Think Aloud: To help me figure out the meaning of each word or phrase, I'm going to look back at the passage and study the words and sentences around the underlined words. I know from experience that surrounding words and sentences can provide hints about the meaning of unfamiliar words.

- Direct students to the chart. Explain that it lists context clues to help students figure out the meaning of *proboscis*. Ask students to complete the chart based on the context clues in the second column, referring back to the passage as necessary.

Think Aloud: I know that a *victim* is someone who is harmed or injured. And I read in the passage that the bedbug's bite is painless, so the victim, or person bitten, doesn't wake up from the bite. Based on this information, I think the word *victim* suggests someone who is helplessly harmed by a bedbug.

- Have students complete the writing line to describe what the word *victim* suggests.

Think Aloud: In the last sentence, I read that the bedbug's saliva "can make you itch so badly you'll want to scratch your skin off." I know that you scratch to relieve an itch, and the phrase "scratch your skin off" suggests scratching so much you can't stop. This phrase helps me understand how itchy bedbug bites can be.

- Finally, have students answer the last question.

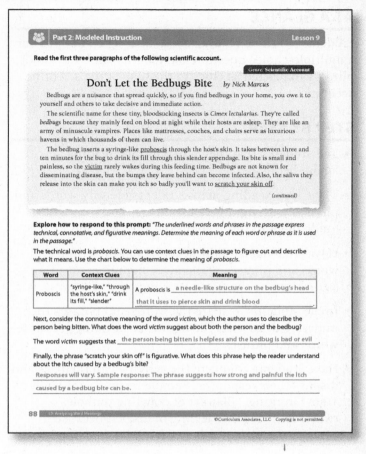

Tier Two Vocabulary: *Minuscule*

- Point out the word *minuscule* in paragraph 2. Remind students that figuring out the part of speech of an unfamiliar word can help reveal the meaning. Note that the word appears after the word *army*, which is a noun. Ask students what part of speech *minuscule* is. *(adjective)*

- Now have students review the previous sentence for additional context clues. Have students determine the meaning of *minuscule*. *("very small")*

- Then encourage students to use a thesaurus to identify synonyms for *minuscule*. Challenge them to tell which synonym is closest in meaning to how *minuscule* is used in the scientific account. **(RI.7.4; L.7.4a, L.7.4d)**

AT A GLANCE

Students continue reading about bedbugs. They answer a multiple-choice question and identify the words and phrases that acted as clues to the tone of the scientific account.

STEP BY STEP

• Tell students that they will continue reading about bedbugs.

• The Close Reading helps students identify words and phrases with figurative meanings. The Hint will guide them to think about the author's tone.

• Have students read the account and underline the words and phrases that convey figurative meanings, as directed by the Close Reading.

• Invite students to share the words and phrases they underlined. Discuss the figurative meanings of these words and phrases.

• Have students complete the activities on the page and discuss their responses. Sample response for Show Your Thinking: "Blanket of crawling pinholes" expresses a negative feeling of disgust because it conveys the idea of being covered by crawling bugs.

ANSWER ANALYSIS

Choice A is incorrect. The phrases are not intended to give the account a humorous tone.

Choice B is incorrect. These words relate to the idea of comfort, but other words give the account an opposite tone. Bedbugs invading a bed and feeding off someone like vampires do not reflect a comforting tone.

Choice C is incorrect. While some readers might feel the need to protect themselves from bedbugs, the tone of this account is more informative than threatening.

Choice D is correct. This sentence best describes the impact of word choice in creating an informative yet slightly negative and disgusted tone.

> **ERROR ALERT:** Students who did not choose D may have trouble determining the author's tone. Remind them that tone is the attitude toward a subject revealed by the author's word choice. How does the author feel about bedbugs? How do you know this?

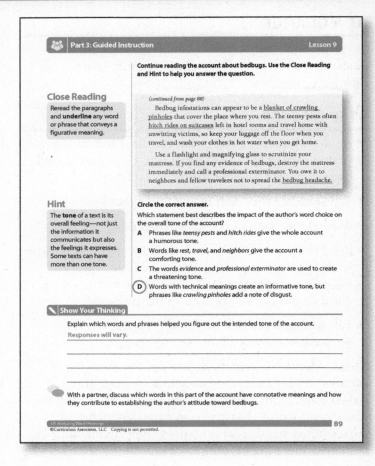

Continue reading the account about bedbugs. Use the Close Reading and Hint to help you answer the question.

Close Reading
Reread the paragraphs and **underline** any word or phrase that conveys a figurative meaning.

(continued from page 88)

Bedbug infestations can appear to be a <u>blanket of crawling pinholes</u> that cover the place where you rest. The teensy pests often <u>hitch rides on suitcases</u> left in hotel rooms and travel home with unwitting victims, so keep your luggage off the floor when you travel, and wash your clothes in hot water when you get home.

Use a flashlight and magnifying glass to scrutinize your mattress. If you find any evidence of bedbugs, destroy the mattress immediately and call a professional exterminator. You owe it to neighbors and fellow travelers not to spread the <u>bedbug headache</u>.

Hint
The **tone** of a text is its overall feeling—not just the information it communicates but also the feelings it expresses. Some texts can have more than one tone.

Circle the correct answer.

Which statement best describes the impact of the author's word choice on the overall tone of the account?

A Phrases like *teensy pests* and *hitch rides* give the whole account a humorous tone.

B Words like *rest*, *travel*, and *neighbors* give the account a comforting tone.

C The words *evidence* and *professional exterminator* are used to create a threatening tone.

(D) Words with technical meanings create an informative tone, but phrases like *crawling pinholes* add a note of disgust.

✎ Show Your Thinking

Explain which words and phrases helped you figure out the intended tone of the account.
Responses will vary.

💬 With a partner, discuss which words in this part of the account have connotative meanings and how they contribute to establishing the author's attitude toward bedbugs.

L9: Analyzing Word Meanings
©Curriculum Associates, LLC   Copying is not permitted.   89

Tier Two Vocabulary: *Scrutinize*

• Direct students to the word *scrutinize* in the last paragraph. Remind students that word parts can help them figure out the meaning of an unfamiliar word. Write *scrutinize* on the board, and ask students to identify the suffix. (*-ize*)

• Tell students that, in this case, the suffix *-ize* changes a noun to a verb. The root word is the noun *scrutiny*.

• Ask students to identify words and phrases in the sentence that are clues to the meaning of *scrutinize* ("*flashlight*," "*magnifying glass*") and to tell the meaning of the word. ("*study something carefully*") **(RI.7.4; L.7.4a, L.7.4b)**

AT A GLANCE

Students read a passage twice about the Goliath beetle. After the first reading, you will ask three questions to check your students' comprehension of the text.

STEP BY STEP

- Have students read the text silently without referring to the Study Buddy or Close Reading text.

- Ask the following questions to ensure students' comprehension of the text:

  What was the Goliath beetle named after? Why? *(The beetle is named after a biblical giant named Goliath because both are gigantic.)*

  Where is the Goliath beetle's habitat? *(The Goliath beetle lives in the tropical rainforests of Africa.)*

  What are the stages in the life cycle of a Goliath beetle? *(There are four stages to the life cycle of a Goliath beetle: egg stage, larva stage, pupa stage, and adult stage.)*

- Then ask students to reread Paragraph 1 and look at the Study Buddy think aloud. What does the Study Buddy help them think about?

Tip: The Study Buddy points out to students that the scientific nature of the text results in the author's use of many technical terms to name concepts related to the topic. Recognizing the characteristics of different genres helps students know what types of language they might encounter in a text.

- Have students read the rest of the scientific account. Tell them to follow the directions in the Close Reading.

Tip: Close Reading guides students to identify the connotative and figurative meanings of words. Reiterate to students that this skill helps them improve their ability to make inferences and draw conclusions about a text.

- Finally, have students answer the questions on page 91. Use the Answer Analysis to discuss correct and incorrect responses.

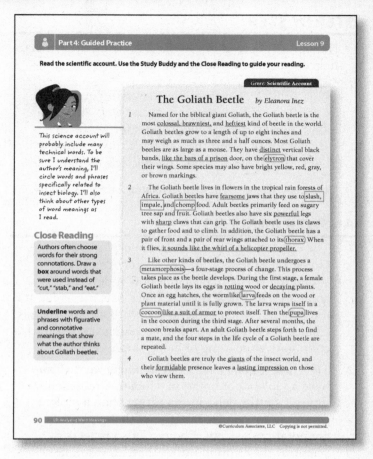

Part 4: Guided Practice Lesson 9

Read the scientific account. Use the Study Buddy and the Close Reading to guide your reading.

Genre: Scientific Account

The Goliath Beetle   by Eleanora Inez

1   Named for the biblical giant Goliath, the Goliath beetle is the most colossal, brawniest, and heftiest kind of beetle in the world. Goliath beetles grow to a length of up to eight inches and may weigh as much as three and a half ounces. Most Goliath beetles are as large as a mouse. They have distinct vertical black bands, like the bars of a prison door, on the elytron that cover their wings. Some species may also have bright yellow, red, gray, or brown markings.

2   The Goliath beetle lives in flowers in the tropical rain forests of Africa. Goliath beetles have fearsome jaws that they use to slash, impale, and chomp food. Adult beetles primarily feed on sugary tree sap and fruit. Goliath beetles also have six powerful legs with sharp claws that can grip. The Goliath beetle uses its claws to gather food and to climb. In addition, the Goliath beetle has a pair of front and a pair of rear wings attached to its thorax. When it flies, it sounds like the whirl of a helicopter propeller.

3   Like other kinds of beetles, the Goliath beetle undergoes a metamorphosis—a four-stage process of change. This process takes place as the beetle develops. During the first stage, a female Goliath beetle lays its eggs in rotting wood or decaying plants. Once an egg hatches, the wormlike larva feeds on the wood or plant material until it is fully grown. The larva wraps itself in a cocoon like a suit of armor to protect itself. Then the pupa lives in the cocoon during the third stage. After several months, the cocoon breaks apart. An adult Goliath beetle steps forth to find a mate, and the four steps in the life cycle of a Goliath beetle are repeated.

4   Goliath beetles are truly the giants of the insect world, and their formidable presence leaves a lasting impression on those who view them.

This science account will probably include many technical words. To be sure I understand the author's meaning, I'll circle words and phrases specifically related to insect biology. I'll also think about other types of word meanings as I read.

Close Reading

Authors often choose words for their strong connotations. Draw a **box** around words that were used instead of "cut," "stab," and "eat."

Underline words and phrases with figurative and connotative meanings that show what the author thinks about Goliath beetles.

90   L9: Analyzing Word Meanings   ©Curriculum Associates, LLC   Copying is not permitted.

ELL Support: Comparatives and Superlatives

- Explain that comparatives are words that compare two things, and superlatives are used to compare three or more things.

- Point out the word *brawniest*. Have students identify the base word (brawny, *meaning "strong"*) and the word ending (*-est*). Explain that this ending is added to an adjective to form the superlative. Then have students tell what the superlative compares. *(the Goliath beetle to all other kinds of beetles)*

- Have students compare the beetle to another creature using *brawny* and the comparative ending *-er*.

- Repeat the activity for the word *heftiest*. **(L.7.1)**

STEP BY STEP

• Have students read questions 1–3, using the Hints to help them answer the questions.

Tip: If students have trouble answering question 3, ask them to explain how the author feels about the Goliath beetle. Have students look for words that bring out feelings and then analyze those words to see what they reflect about the author's thoughts.

• Discuss with students the Answer Analysis below.

ANSWER ANALYSIS

1   The correct choice is B. A *metamorphosis* is a biological process. Choice A is incorrect. The sound the beetle makes, not how it develops, is compared to a helicopter. Choice C is incorrect. It is too general, not specific to the word *metamorphosis*. Choice D is incorrect. *Metamorphosis* doesn't have a connotative meaning of being impressed.

2   The correct choice is D. *Slash*, *impale*, and *chomp* have a violent connotation. Choice A represents a more scientific description rather than a violent connotation. Choice B suggests the opposite connotation—safety. Choice C also reflects a scientific description rather than an example of a violent connotation.

3   Sample response: The author's overall tone is one of awe and wonder. She uses words such as *colossal*, *brawniest*, and *heftiest* to describe the Goliath beetle, and these words have a mighty and powerful connotation. Her use of the simile *like a suit of armor* and *formidable presence* also suggest her admiration for this large creature.

RETEACHING

Use a graphic organizer to answer question 3. Draw the graphic organizer below, leaving the boxes blank. Work with students to fill in the boxes, using information from the passage. Sample responses are provided.

Word Choice colossal, brawniest, heftiest, giant	
Tone positive	**Meaning** The beetle is incredibly powerful and mighty.

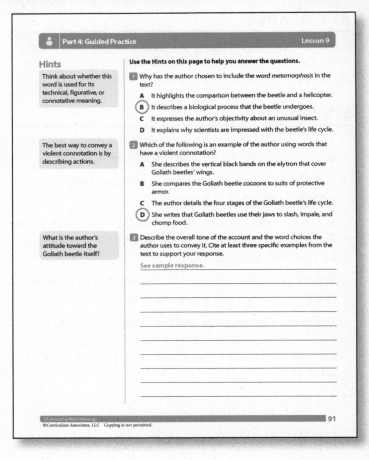

Hints

Think about whether this word is used for its technical, figurative, or connotative meaning.

The best way to convey a violent connotation is by describing actions.

What is the author's attitude toward the Goliath beetle itself?

Use the Hints on this page to help you answer the questions.

1   Why has the author chosen to include the word *metamorphosis* in the text?

   A   It highlights the comparison between the beetle and a helicopter.

   B   It describes a biological process that the beetle undergoes.

   C   It expresses the author's objectivity about an unusual insect.

   D   It explains why scientists are impressed with the beetle's life cycle.

2   Which of the following is an example of the author using words that have a violent connotation?

   A   She describes the vertical black bands on the elytron that cover Goliath beetles' wings.

   B   She compares the Goliath beetle cocoons to suits of protective armor.

   C   The author details the four stages of the Goliath beetle's life cycle.

   D   She writes that Goliath beetles use their jaws to slash, impale, and chomp food.

3   Describe the overall tone of the account and the word choices the author uses to convey it. Cite at least three specific examples from the text to support your response.

   See sample response.

   _____

   _____

   _____

   _____

   _____

   _____

   _____

   _____

L9: Analyzing Word Meanings
©Curriculum Associates, LLC   Copying is not permitted.   91

Integrating Standards

Use these questions to further students' understanding of "The Goliath Beetle."

1   Identify a sentence in the scientific account that supports the claim "the Goliath beetle is the most colossal, brawniest, and heftiest kind of beetle in the world." **(RI.7.1)**

   These sentences support the statement about the size of the Goliath beetle: "Goliath beetles grow to a length of up to eight inches long and may weigh as much as three and a half ounces. Most Goliath beetles are as large as a mouse."

2   Explain the life cycle of a Goliath beetle. Tell how this cycle is "circular." **(RI.7.3)**

   First, a female beetle lays eggs. Next, an egg hatches, and the larva feeds and grows. After that, the larva becomes a pupa that stays in a cocoon for several months. Once hatched, the adult mates, and the female lays eggs again. Because the life cycle begins once again, it is considered to be circular.

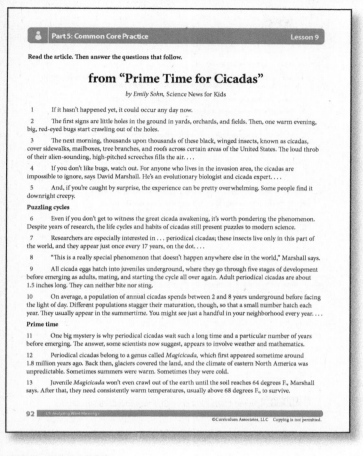

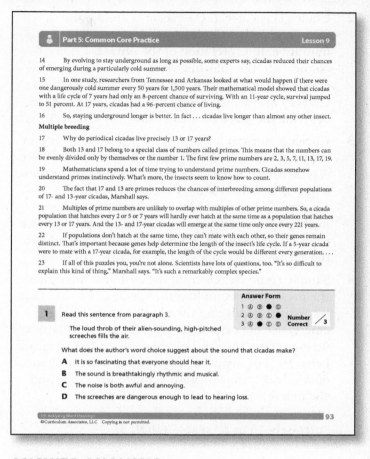

AT A GLANCE

Students independently read a longer scientific account and answer questions in a format that provides test practice.

STEP BY STEP

- Tell students to use what they have learned about reading closely and analyzing word meanings to read the text on pages 92 and 93.

- Remind students to underline or circle important points.

- Tell students to answer the questions on pages 93 and 94. For questions 1–3, they should fill in the correct circle on the Answer Form.

- When students have finished, use the Answer Analysis to discuss correct responses and the reasons for them. Have students fill in the Number Correct on the Answer Form.

ANSWER ANALYSIS

1 The correct choice is C. Phrases such as *loud throb, alien-sounding,* and *high-pitched screeches* reflect negative connotations in sound. Choice A and Choice B present a positive connotation of the sound, and that interpretation is not supported by the word choices. Choice D correctly reflects a negative connotation, but the claim of hearing loss is not supported by the sentence. **(DOK 3)**

Theme Connection

- How do all the scientific accounts in this lesson relate to the theme, Little Creatures, Big Impact?

- What is one fact or idea you learned about little creatures that have a big impact from each scientific account?

2 Choice D is correct. *On the dot* is an idiom that means "exactly." Choice A represents a literal, not figurative, interpretation of the phrase. Choice B connects to the information about the cicadas' life cycles, but *on the dot* is not used for this purpose. Choice C is incorrect. The phrase is not meant to describe the place where cicadas live. **(DOK 3)**

3 Choice B is correct. Timing and prime numbers play important roles in the life cycle of the cicada. Choice A is incorrect. It does not reflect the author's purpose, which is to inform about the cicadas' life cycle. Choice C is incorrect because scientists still have many unanswered questions about cicada life cycles. Choice D is incorrect. *Prime time* sometimes refers to the evening, but it does not in this title. **(DOK 3)**

4 Sample response: Overall, the author is amazed at the mystery surrounding the species. She says that it's "worth pondering the phenomenon" of the emergence of periodic cicadas. She also explains the ways that weather and mathematics relate to cicada behavior. For instance, she notes how their chance of survival "jumped" with a longer life cycle, and she marvels that they "understand primes instinctively," which keeps their life cycles at "precisely 13 or 17 years." **(DOK 3)**

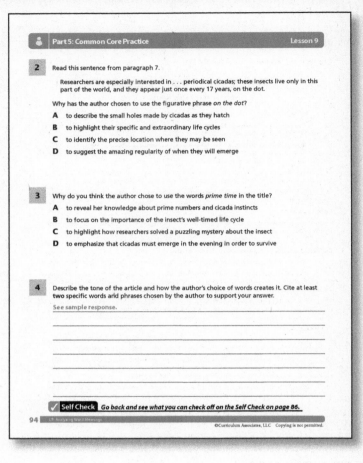

Integrating Standards

Use these questions and tasks as opportunities to interact with "Prime Time for Cicadas."

1 What is the author's purpose in writing this account? **(RI.7.6)**

The author wants to inform the audience about the interesting and somewhat mysterious characteristics of cicadas and their life cycle.

2 Identify two central ideas in the account. **(RI.7.2)**

Scientists do not completely understand cicada life cycles. They do know that weather cues and mathematics, specifically prime numbers, figure in the evolution of cicada life cycles. Also, the staggered emergence of adult cicadas reduces interbreeding.

3 To what is the author referring when she says, "the great cicada awakening" in paragraph 6? **(RI.7.1)**

The author is referring to the time when cicadas "awake" and come to the surface to finish their life cycle above ground—where humans are sometimes surprised by their presence.

4 Evaluate the structure of the account. How does the author present the information? How helpful is the inclusion of the section headings? **(RI.7.5)**

Sample response: First, the author introduces the sudden appearance of the cicadas. Then she explains which scientific facts about cicada life cycles still puzzle scientists. Next, she explains how evolution and mathematics factor into the cicada life cycle. The information is presented logically, but the section headings are slightly confusing. I think "Prime Time" would make a better heading for the section "Multiple breeding."

5 Discuss in small groups: What is your opinion of cicadas? Do you find them fascinating or creepy? Support your opinion with details from the account. **(SL.7.1)**

Discussions will vary. Point out that an opinion is neither correct nor incorrect. Encourage students to persuade others to believe their opinion through citing textual evidence.

Writing Activities

Newspaper Editorial *(W.7.1)*

- Have students discuss the information they learned about insects in this lesson. Review that an editorial is a piece of writing that tries to convince readers of an opinion, using persuasive language.

- Challenge students to write a persuasive newspaper editorial to express their opinion about an insect discussed in the lesson, using details from that scientific account to support their ideas. Alternatively, they might share their opinion about insects in general, using information from all accounts as support.

- Allow time for students to share their editorials with the class, and encourage other students to ask the presenters questions about their point of view.

Subordinate Clauses *(L.7.1a)*

- Direct students to the first sentence in "Prime Time for Cicadas." Point out that the sentence begins with an "if" clause. Explain that "if" clauses are called dependent, or subordinate, clauses because they have a subject and a predicate, but they cannot stand alone as a sentence. Ask students to identify other dependent clauses in the scientific account. Other words that might begin a dependent clause include *when, whether,* and *that.*

- Have students write a paragraph that uses at least three subordinate clauses.

LISTENING ACTIVITY *(SL.7.1)*

Listen Closely/Pose a Question

- Read aloud the account "Don't Let the Bedbugs Bite" again, and ask students to listen carefully as you do, paying attention to any information that confuses them or makes them wonder.

- After reading, have each students pose one question they have about the information in the account. Have students decide if the answer can be found within the text or if it is likely to be found in outside sources.

- Have students listen carefully to classmates' questions and take turns responding.

DISCUSSION ACTIVITY *(RI.7.9; SL.7.1)*

Talk in a Group/Compare and Contrast Creatures

- Have students form small groups to compare and contrast two insects that they read about.

- Provide the following prompts for the discussion: How are the insects alike? How are they different? How are the authors' tones, or attitudes, about the insects alike or different?

- Allow 10 to 15 minutes for discussion. Then have each group share their ideas with the class.

MEDIA ACTIVITY *(RI.7.7)*

Be Creative/Draw an Illustration

- Have students review the photograph of the wasp on page 87. Remind students that photographs and illustrations put information in a visual format to make that information easier to understand.

- Ask each student to choose one insect discussed in this lesson and create an illustration that describes the creature's main features and their functions. Encourage students to use details from the account in their descriptions.

- Have students present their illustrations and compare the ones featuring the same insect.

RESEARCH ACTIVITY *(W.7.6; SL.7.5)*

Research and Present/Multimedia Presentation

- Point out that the authors of "The Goliath Beetle" and "Prime Time for Cicadas" both include written descriptions of sounds the insects make.

- Challenge students to research audio or video recordings of these and other insects' sounds.

- Have students share and describe the media files they chose, and encourage audience members to ask the presenters any questions that arise.

Analyzing Text Structure

LESSON OBJECTIVES

- Analyze how major sections of an informational text fit into the overall structure and contribute to the development of the central ideas.

THE LEARNING PROGRESSION

- **Grade 6:** CCSS RI.6.5 requires students to analyze how paragraphs and chapters fit into the overall structure of a text.

- **Grade 7: CCSS RI.7.5 builds on the Grade 6 standard by having students analyze the organizational structure of major sections of a text and how they contribute to the development of ideas.**

- **Grade 8:** CCSS RI.8.5 requires students to analyze the structure of paragraphs and the role of each sentence in developing and clarifying a key concept.

PREREQUISITE SKILLS

- Identify organizational structures of texts, including compare-contrast, problem-solution, and cause-effect.

- Analyze how the organizational structure helps develop the main idea of a paragraph.

- Analyze how authors organize texts so that major sections contribute to the whole work.

TAP STUDENTS' PRIOR KNOWLEDGE

- Tell students that they will be working on a lesson about analyzing the text structures authors use to present information. Remind students that authors organize facts, examples, and ideas in their writing to make the concepts clear to their readers.

- To illustrate the point, discuss how a teen might try to persuade a parent that he or she needs a cell phone. (*First, the teen might explain the problems caused by not being able to contact parents during the day and then explain that the solution is to get a cell phone.*)

- Next, ask students how the same teen would present information about the different family cell phone plans offered. (*He or she might explain the different plans and point out their similarities and differences.*)

- Explain that in the first example, the teen organized ideas in a cause-effect structure, presenting a solution to the problem at the end. In the second, the teen used a compare-and-contrast structure. Tell students that writers also organize their ideas in different ways to achieve different goals.

- Point out that identifying how a text is structured will help students better understand the ideas an author wants to convey about a topic.

Ready *Teacher Toolbox*   teacher-toolbox.com

	Prerequisite Skills	RI.7.5
Ready Lessons	✓	✓
Tools for Instruction		✓
Interactive Tutorials		✓

CCSS Focus

RI.7.5 Analyze the structure an author uses to organize a text, including how the major sections contribute to the whole and to the development of ideas.

ADDITIONAL STANDARDS: **RI.7.1, RI.7.2, RI.7.4, RI.7.6, RI.7.8; L.7.1c, L.7.2a, L.7.4a, L.7.4b, L.7.4d; W.7.7, W.7.8, W.7.9b; SL.7.1, SL.7.4, SL.7.5** (*See page A39 for full text.*)

AT A GLANCE

By studying a table of contents from an informational text, students develop their understanding of how authors use different text structures to organize ideas. Students learn that identifying and analyzing text structures helps them understand the relationship between ideas and the central ideas in the text.

STEP BY STEP

- Read the first paragraph that includes an analogy of how authors build their texts and the definition of *text structure*.

- Then encourage students to study the graphic and read the callouts. Discuss the kind of text structure that is likely to appear in each chapter shown in the table of contents. Also have students consider how the chapters themselves are organized.

- Explain that the chart describes the purposes of common types of text structures. Read the first two rows, and ask students why those organizational patterns might be good ways to arrange the content of Chapters 2 and 3 in the graphic.

- Then read the last two rows. Ask students what topics might be arranged by cause-effect and compare-contrast.

- Reinforce the idea that identifying text structure will help students understand the relationships between ideas and how those ideas all help to develop the central ideas.

Lesson 10 Part 1: Introduction

Analyzing Text Structure

CCSS
RI.7.5: Analyze the structure an author uses to organize a text, including how the major sections contribute to the whole and to the development of the ideas.

Theme: *What Makes Us Us?*

Authors "build" their texts carefully, the way carpenters build a house. Like a carpenter, a writer first chooses his or her materials. In this case, though, the materials are the ideas that will be used to develop a topic.

The way the author decides to organize those ideas—the **text structure**—determines how each part supports and relates to others; it also brings meaning to the whole text. Sections, chapters, and even paragraphs in a book or magazine must all be arranged in a logical way.

Think about the kind of text structure that might be used in each chapter shown in the Table of Contents below. Also consider how the chapters themselves are organized.

What Makes Us US?
Chapter 1 ———— 6
What Is Genetics?
Chapter 2 ———— 33
Solving the Problems of Heredity
Chapter 3 ———— 25
How DNA Was Discovered
Chapter 4 ———— 31
What DNA Can Tell Us
Chapter 5 ———— 50
The Argument of Genes vs. Environment

The ideas might be arranged to explain a set of problems and their solutions.

This chapter might use a chronological text structure to describe the way "DNA" was discovered.

Study the chart below, and note the description of each text structure. Think about how each structure might be used to present the central idea in a piece of writing.

Structure	Purpose
Chronological	presents steps or events in time order
Problem-Solution	describes a problem along with solutions
Cause-Effect	shows how one event makes other events happen
Compare-Contrast	points out similarities and differences between two or more subjects

When you read a text, remember that the author has made choices about the organization of ideas. Use the text structure to help you understand the relationships between ideas, which all help develop the central idea. Each chapter, section, or paragraph has a role to play.

L10: Analyzing Text Structure
©Curriculum Associates, LLC Copying is not permitted.
95

Genre Focus

Informational Texts: Scientific Account

Tell students that in this lesson they will read informational texts. One type of informational text is a scientific account, or a piece of writing that provides information about scientific research or another science-related topic.

- Its purpose is to explain scientific findings or any event or discovery with ties to science.

- It can be written by professional scientists to relate findings to the scientific community or to contribute to knowledge in a particular field of study. It may also be written by someone with scientific expertise for the general public.

- It often opens with an explanation about the thesis or theory behind the scientific topic and then gives examples or further details to elaborate on it.

- Some may include charts, graphics, or photos. Others may have sidebars with additional facts or subheadings to show how the ideas are organized.

Explain that students will read "It's All in Our DNA" and "Nature Versus Nurture: The Great Debate," two scientific accounts describing the influence of DNA on our lives. "The Discovery of DNA's Structure" tells about the discovery of the structure of DNA.

AT A GLANCE

Students identify the text structure of an informational article. They explain why the structure is a good choice for the ideas in the text.

STEP BY STEP

- Ask volunteers to tell what they learned on the previous page about the kinds of text structures.

- Tell students that in this lesson they will read about the discovery of DNA's structure.

- Read aloud "The Discovery of DNA's Structure."

- Then read the questions: "What seems to be the main text structure in this article? Why has the author chosen it?"

- Now tell students you will use a Think Aloud to demonstrate a way of answering the questions.

Think Aloud: When I'm trying to figure out the text structure, I look for clue words and phrases that show the relationship between ideas or events. I notice that in the first sentence, the date 1953 is used. Then I see another date in the second paragraph—1943—and another date in the third paragraph, 1951. These dates might signal the type of structure.

- Direct students to the chart, and read the Central Idea box. Discuss how the details in the text support this central idea.

- Then ask students what type of organizational structure uses dates. Have them write the structure in the second box.

Think Aloud: Once I recognize the structure, I think about why the author chose it and how it helps me understand the relationship between ideas related to the topic. Because this article is about the history of the discovery of the structure of DNA, the author wants to show the order of events that led to the discovery.

- Have students write the purpose behind the use of the text structure to complete the chart.

- Then have students answer the question at the bottom of the page. Invite volunteers to share their answers with the class. Be sure students understand that the first paragraph serves to introduce the nature of the question that scientists wanted to answer through their research.

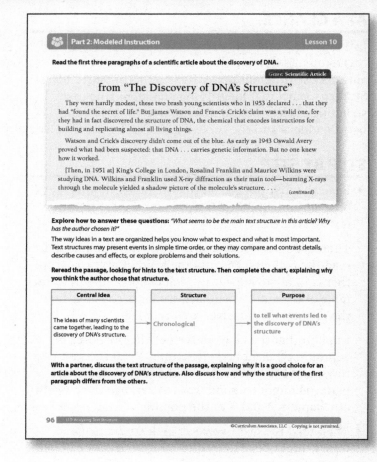

Tier Two Vocabulary: *Brash*

- Point out the word *brash* in paragraph 1. Tell students this word has multiple meanings. When words have more than one meaning, it's important to use the context to determine which meaning is being used.

- Remind students of the different types of context clues: restatement, synonym, antonym, example, and definition. Have students identify the context clues that helped them determine which meaning is being used. (*hardly modest*) Ask them what kind of clue it is. (*antonym*) Then have students give the meaning for *brash* as used in the text (*rude, self-confident*).

- Ask students what other meaning the word *brash* has (*hasty, foolish*). Have them use a dictionary to check their meaning. (**RI.7.4; L.7.4a, L.7.4d**)

AT A GLANCE

Students continue reading about the discovery of DNA's structure. They answer a multiple-choice question and analyze the text's structure.

STEP BY STEP

- Tell students that they will continue reading about the discovery of DNA's structure.

- The Close Reading helps students recognize how the overall structure helped them understand the importance of the ideas. The Hint will help them understand how ideas are related to each other.

- Have students read the text and underline the most important idea, as directed by the Close Reading.

- Ask volunteers to share the idea they found. Discuss why it is central to the article. If necessary, ask, "What clue words help you determine the overall text structure of this paragraph? How does this structure help you understand the central idea?"

- Have students circle the answer to the question, using the Hint to help. Then have them respond to the question in Show Your Thinking. (*Sample response: The author begins by presenting the solution to a problem and then uses sequence to tell how the work of different scientists led to the discovery of DNA's structure.*)

ANSWER ANALYSIS

Choice A is incorrect. The central idea is the discovery of DNA's structure, not that the X-ray image would inspire other scientists.

Choice B is incorrect. The article does not explain the actual makeup of DNA.

Choice C is incorrect. The author's claim that the scientists were brash is a detail, not the central idea.

Choice D is correct. These paragraphs support the idea that several scientists worked to discover the structure of DNA and that they built on each other's research.

ERROR ALERT: Students who did not choose D might not have read the question carefully. Point out that the question asks them to identify how the ideas in these paragraphs develop the text's central idea. Have students eliminate choices that are details.

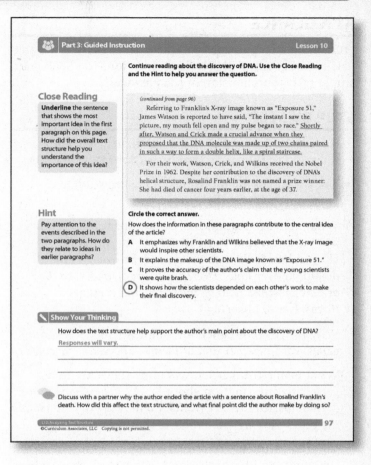

Tier Two Vocabulary: *Crucial*

- Point out the word *crucial* in paragraph 1. Help students use the context to figure out its meaning. Remind them that they may have to read the entire paragraph to find clues to the word's meaning. (*"critical;" "of great importance"*)

- Once they have determined the meaning, have students think of two synonyms for *crucial* (*key, vital, critical*). Remind students that synonyms can have slightly different meanings and connotations.

- Have students share their list with the class. Discuss why the author might have chosen the word *crucial* instead of a synonym, such as *important*. **(RI.7.4; L.7.4a, L.7.5b)**

AT A GLANCE

Students read a passage twice about our DNA. After the first reading, you will ask three questions to check your students' comprehension of the passage.

STEP BY STEP

- Have students read the passage silently without referring to the Study Buddy or Close Reading text.

- Ask the following questions to ensure students' comprehension of the text:

  What are two examples of dominant traits? What does it mean that these traits are "dominant"? (*Brown hair is dominant over red. Brown eyes are dominant over blue. These traits are stronger, so they are the most likely to be inherited and present themselves in offspring.*)

  Why is eye color called a "complex trait"? (*Several genes work together and influence a person's eye color.*)

  What is one thing scientists hope they can do by gathering information about DNA? (*They hope that certain diseases can be avoided if they are able to isolate the genes that are vulnerable to those diseases.*)

- Then ask students to reread paragraph 1 and look at the Study Buddy think aloud. What does the Study Buddy help them think about?

Tip: The Study Buddy tells students to think about the text structure the author uses to organize the ideas in each paragraph. This will help students figure out how each part helps develop the central idea about DNA.

- Have students read the rest of the passage. Tell them to follow the directions in the Close Reading.

Tip: The Close Reading guides students to underline clues that help them to determine the structure. Recognizing common clue words that signal a particular text structure will help students determine the structure the author chose to use.

- Finally, have students answer the questions on page 99. Use the Answer Analysis to discuss correct and incorrect responses.

ELL Support: Regular Plural Nouns

- Explain to students that nouns name people, places, or things. Students can look at the endings of nouns to know how many.

- Point out the plural noun *brothers* in paragraph 1 and discuss with students how the plural was formed. (*add* s) Then work with students to identify other regular plural nouns in this account. (*eyes, genes, traits*)

- Next, work with students to form the plural of some singular nouns in this account. Point out the singular nouns *mother, family,* and *illness.* Have students identify the plural forms and explain how they are formed. (*mothers: add* s; *families: change* y *to* i *and add* es; *illnesses: add* es) **(L.7.1)**

STEP BY STEP

- Have students read questions 1–3, using the Hints to help them answer the questions.

Tip: The first Hint reminds students to look for clues that signal four types of text structures. Remind students to also look back at the phrases they underlined in other paragraphs as they answer the questions.

- Discuss with students the Answer Analysis below.

ANSWER ANALYSIS

1 The correct choice is A. The words *caused* and the phrase *create the same result* signal a cause-and-effect relationship between genes and traits. Choices B, C, and D are incorrect. They list other types of text structures, none of which are used in the second paragraph. These structures would be signaled by key words such as *first*, *then*, *like*, and *different from*.

2 The correct choice is B. The phrase *solve complex problems* signals the problem and solution the author is presenting in the last paragraph. The problem is illnesses, and the solution is the study of DNA to determine how to take precautions against or cure those illnesses. Choices A, C, and D are incorrect. None of these choices describe the focus of the final paragraph.

3 Sample response: The first paragraph uses a compare/contrast structure. It contrasts Kate's physical features with those of her family to emphasize their difference. Ideas in the paragraph serve to introduce the central idea of the account, which is that DNA causes differences in people.

RETEACHING

Use a chart to verify the correct answer to question 1. Draw the chart below, and work with students to fill in the boxes. Sample responses are provided.

Structure	Signal Words	Purpose
Cause-Effect	*caused, create the same result*	explain why genes cause some family members to have different traits

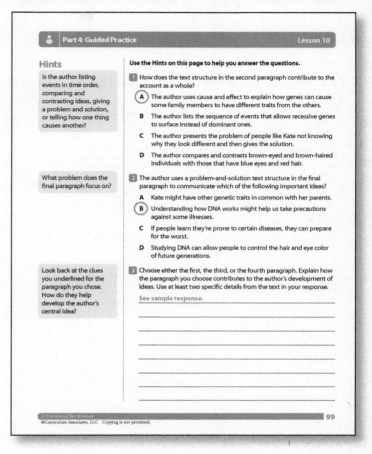

Integrating Standards

Use these questions to further students' understanding of "It's All in Our DNA."

1 What are the two central ideas of "It's All in Our DNA"? Provide details from the text that support these central ideas. **(RI.7.2)**

DNA determines our physical traits. Kate looks different from her brothers. The recessive genes she got from her parents surfaced instead of the dominant traits in her brothers.

Studying DNA can help scientist solve complex problems. Understanding DNA may help scientists isolate genes that make us vulnerable to certain diseases and help avoid those diseases.

2 What is the author's purpose and point of view in this account? **(RI.7.6)**

The author's purpose is to inform readers about how DNA determines our traits and to convince us that studying it is important.

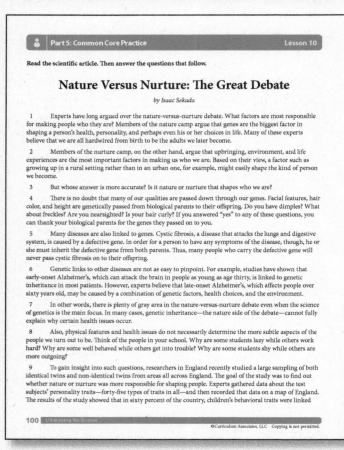

Part 5: Common Core Practice   Lesson 10

Read the scientific article. Then answer the questions that follow.

Nature Versus Nurture: The Great Debate

by Isaac Sekada

1   Experts have long argued over the nature-versus-nurture debate. What factors are most responsible for making people who they are? Members of the nature camp argue that genes are the biggest factor in shaping a person's health, personality, and perhaps even his or her choices in life. Many of these experts believe that we are all hardwired from birth to be the adults we later become.

2   Members of the nurture camp, on the other hand, argue that upbringing, environment, and life experiences are the most important factors in making us who we are. Based on their view, a factor such as growing up in a rural setting rather than in an urban one, for example, might easily shape the kind of person we become.

3   But whose answer is more accurate? Is it nature or nurture that shapes who we are?

4   There is no doubt that many of our qualities are passed down through our genes. Facial features, hair color, and height are genetically passed from biological parents to their offspring. Do you have dimples? What about freckles? Are you nearsighted? Is your hair curly? If you answered "yes" to any of these questions, you can thank your biological parents for the genes they passed on to you.

5   Many diseases are also linked to genes. Cystic fibrosis, a disease that attacks the lungs and digestive system, is caused by a defective gene. In order for a person to have any symptoms of the disease, though, he or she must inherit the defective gene from both parents. Thus, many people who carry the defective gene will never pass cystic fibrosis on to their offspring.

6   Genetic links to other diseases are not as easy to pinpoint. For example, studies have shown that early-onset Alzheimer's, which can attack the brain in people as young as age thirty, is linked to genetic inheritance in most patients. However, experts believe that late-onset Alzheimer's, which affects people over sixty years old, may be caused by a combination of genetic factors, health choices, and the environment.

7   In other words, there is plenty of gray area in the nature-versus-nurture debate even when the science of genetics is the main focus. In many cases, genetic inheritance—the nature side of the debate—cannot fully explain why certain health issues occur.

8   Also, physical features and health issues do not necessarily determine the more subtle aspects of the people we turn out to be. Think of the people in your school. Why are some students lazy while others work hard? Why are some well behaved while others get into trouble? Why are some students shy while others are more outgoing?

9   To gain insight into such questions, researchers in England recently studied a large sampling of both identical twins and non-identical twins from areas all across England. The goal of the study was to find out whether nature or nurture was more responsible for shaping people. Experts gathered data about the test subjects' personality traits—forty-five types of traits in all—and then recorded that data on a map of England. The results of the study showed that in sixty percent of the country, children's behavioral traits were linked

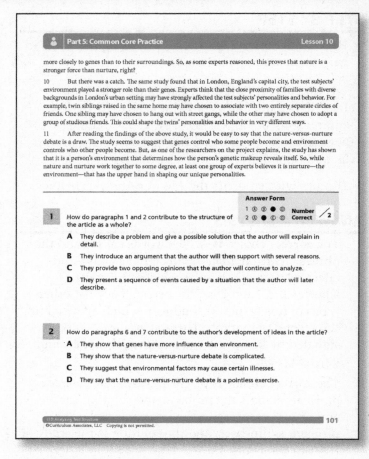

Part 5: Common Core Practice   Lesson 10

more closely to genes than to their surroundings. So, as some experts reasoned, this proves that nature is a stronger force than nurture, right?

10   But there was a catch. The same study found that in London, England's capital city, the test subjects' environment played a stronger role than their genes. Experts think that the close proximity of families with diverse backgrounds in London's urban setting may have strongly affected the test subjects' personalities and behavior. For example, twin siblings raised in the same home may have chosen to associate with two entirely separate circles of friends. One sibling may have chosen to hang out with street gangs, while the other may have chosen to adopt a group of studious friends. This could shape the twins' personalities and behavior in very different ways.

11   After reading the findings of the above study, it would be easy to say that the nature-versus-nurture debate is a draw. The study seems to suggest that genes control who some people become and environment controls who other people become. But, as one of the researchers on the project explains, the study has shown that it is a person's environment that determines how the person's genetic makeup reveals itself. So, while nature and nurture work together to some degree, at least one group of experts believes it is nurture—the environment—that has the upper hand in shaping our unique personalities.

---

1   How do paragraphs 1 and 2 contribute to the structure of the article as a whole?

Answer Form
1 Ⓐ Ⓑ ● Ⓓ
2 Ⓐ ● Ⓒ Ⓓ
Number Correct ⟋ 2

   A   They describe a problem and give a possible solution that the author will explain in detail.

   B   They introduce an argument that the author will then support with several reasons.

   C   They provide two opposing opinions that the author will continue to analyze.

   D   They present a sequence of events caused by a situation that the author will later describe.

2   How do paragraphs 6 and 7 contribute to the author's development of ideas in the article?

   A   They show that genes have more influence than environment.

   B   They show that the nature-versus-nurture debate is complicated.

   C   They suggest that environmental factors may cause certain illnesses.

   D   They say that the nature-versus-nurture debate is a pointless exercise.

AT A GLANCE

Students independently read a longer article and answer questions in a format that provides test practice.

STEP BY STEP

- Tell students to use what they have learned about reading closely and analyzing text structures to read the passage on pages 100 and 101.

- Remind students to underline or circle important points.

- Tell students to answer the questions on pages 101 and 102. For questions 1 and 2, they should fill in the correct circle on the Answer Form.

- When students have finished, use the Answer Analysis to discuss correct responses and the reasons for them. Have students fill in the Number Correct on the Answer Form.

ANSWER ANALYSIS

1   The correct choice is C. Phrases such as *on the other hand* and *rather than* signal that the author is comparing the two sides of the debate that he will analyze. Choice A is incorrect. The author is not presenting a problem. Choice B is incorrect. The author is presenting a debate, or argument, but he is not choosing one side and then supporting his argument with reasons. He is explaining the debate and presenting evidence that supports each side of the issue. Choice D is incorrect. The author does not present a sequence of events. **(DOK 2)**

Theme Connection

- How do all the passages in this lesson relate to the theme of what makes us who we are?

- What is one fact or idea you learned about DNA or heredity from each passage in this lesson?

2 The correct choice is B. The author says "not as easy to pinpoint" and "plenty of gray area," which shows that there is no clear evidence that proves one side is completely correct. Choice A is incorrect. These paragraphs do not show that genes have more influence than environment. Choice C provides one detail from these paragraphs but does not explain how this detail contributes to the author's development of ideas. Choice D is incorrect because the author never implies that the debate is pointless, merely that it is complicated. *(DOK 2)*

3 Sample response: The structure of the paragraph is compare and contrast. It contrasts the influence of nature on development by describing details that support the other side of the debate. It shows that environment also has a strong influence on people. *(DOK 3)*

4 Sample response: Paragraph 4 is structured around direct questions such as, Do you have dimples? and Are you nearsighted? The questions quickly convey the fact that genes produce common features such as dimples, freckles, nearsightedness, and curly hair. The author might have structured the paragraph around these questions to pull readers directly into a challenging topic that might seem distant from their everyday lives. At the very least, rapid-fire questions can be more interesting to read than a series of simple sentences. *(DOK 3)*

Inset image of student page:

Part 5: Common Core Practice   Lesson 10

3 Explain how paragraph 10 connects to the paragraph that comes before it and continues the analysis of nature versus nurture. Use at least **one** detail from the text in your response.

See sample response.

4 In paragraph 4, the author asks four questions, one right after the other. Explain why the author might have done this. Use at least **two** details from the passage to support your response.

See sample response.

Self Check *Go back and see what you can check off on the Self Check on page 86.*

102   L10: Analyzing Text Structure   ©Curriculum Associates, LLC   Copying is not permitted.

Integrating Standards

Use the questions and tasks as opportunities to interact with "Nature Versus Nurture: The Great Debate."

1 What is the effect of paragraph 3? How do these questions help you understand the author's purpose and point of view? *(RI.7.6)*

These questions are used to make the reader connect to the article and recognize the central idea by stating exactly what the author will discuss. The author's purpose is to explain claims and evidence used to support each side of the debate. The author is unbiased and finds the debate interesting.

2 What does the author mean by "…experts believe that we are hardwired from birth" in paragraph 1? What is the impact of this phrase? *(RI.7.4)*

The author means that the nature camp believes we are who we are because of genetics and nothing can change who we become. This phrase emphasizes that the nature camp firmly believes in their opinion.

3 What evidence does the author provide to support the claims of each side of the debate? Cite evidence from the text. *(RI.7.1, RI.7.8)*

The author cites several facts and a study that support each side's claims. The findings of the London study support both sides.

4 Discuss in small groups: What side of the debate do you agree with? Give reasons from the text to support your argument. *(SL.7.1)*

Discussions will vary. Encourage students to give reasons to support their response based on textual evidence. Remind students to be respectful of each other's opinions and to follow discussion rules.

Writing Activities

Evaluate an Argument *(W.7.9b)*

• Have students reread "Nature Versus Nurture: The Great Debate" and choose one side of the debate presented by the author. Have them underline the evidence the members of that side use to support their claim.

• Have students write a paragraph analyzing the evidence presented and determine whether or not it is sound and adequately supports the claim. Encourage students to consider what additional evidence could be used to support the claim. Allow time for students to share their analysis with the class.

Commas with Words and Phrases *(L.7.1c, L.7.2a)*

• Explain that commas are often used to separate clauses from the rest of the sentence.

• Read sentence 2 in paragraph 5 of "Nature Versus Nurture: The Great Debate." Point out the appositive phrase and explain that an appositive phrase identifies or renames a preceding noun. Nonessential appositives are set off with commas. Read the next two sentences. Point out the introductory phrases and the interrupter. Explain that these are also separated by commas.

• Have students write a paragraph that contains at least one of each type of phrase, using commas correctly.

LISTENING ACTIVITY *(SL.7.1)*

Listen Closely/Ask Questions

• Have students form small groups. One at a time, have each member explain why they think it is important to study DNA.

• Tell students to listen carefully and then respond to the speaker's opinion by asking him or her at least one question.

• Each speaker should listen closely to each question and respond to it.

DISCUSSION ACTIVITY *(SL.7.1)*

Talk in a Group/Talk About Traits

• Have students talk in small groups about the theme "What Makes Us *Us*?"

• Provide the following prompts to begin the discussion: How do people inherit their traits? What are environmental factors that some people think impact these traits?

• Appoint one member of each group to take notes. Allow 10 to 15 minutes for discussion. Then have each group share its results with the class.

MEDIA ACTIVITY *(RI.7.2, RI.7.5)*

Be Creative/Create a Time Line

• Have students reread the "The Discovery of DNA's Structure" and underline the main dates and events listed.

• Have them research the events and scientists involved to learn more about them and find images of the scientists or their discoveries.

• Finally, have students create an illustrated time line of the discovery. Have students display their time lines in the classroom.

RESEARCH ACTIVITY *(W.7.7, W.7.8; SL.7.4, SL.7.5)*

Research and Present/Give a Presentation

• Have students choose something they learned from one of the readings and conduct a research project to learn more about it. For example, they might research one of the scientists or the debate of nature versus nurture.

• Have students create a presentation about their topic. Remind them to use facts, details, and descriptions as well as visuals during their presentations.

Determining Point of View

Theme: *Catastrophes*

LESSON OBJECTIVES

- Determine an author's purpose and point of view about the topic in informational text.

- Cite evidence to explain how the author's point of view is conveyed in a text.

- Analyze the techniques an author uses to distinguish his or her position on an issue from that of others.

THE LEARNING PROGRESSION

- **Grade 6:** CCSS RI.6.6 focuses on using evidence to describe and determine the author's point of view.

- **Grade 7: CCSS RI.7.6 requires students to determine an author's point of view and analyze how the author "distinguishes his or her position from that of others."**

- **Grade 8:** CCSS RI.8.6 requires that students work to analyze how an author's overall position differs from others and how he or she specifically acknowledges or responds to different viewpoints.

PREREQUISITE SKILLS

- Identify the author's point of view or purpose in a text.

- Recognize statements and word choices signaling that the text is expressing the author's point of view (for example, *I think, I believe, I feel; fortunately, unfortunately*)

- Explain how word choice and tone help establish an author's perspective and biases.

TAP STUDENTS' PRIOR KNOWLEDGE

- Tell students that they will be working on a lesson about determining an author's point of view. Remind them that authors of informational texts often have a certain point of view about the topic they are explaining. It is revealed in their word choice, tone, and the details they leave out or emphasize.

- First ask students what they would think if a passage started with this sentence: *I love to spend my summer at camp.*

- Ask what students know about the author's point of view from this sentence. What information can be inferred? Does the author have a positive or negative attitude about the topic? (*The author's point of view is that summer camp is a great experience. The word* love *shows this strong positive attitude.*)

- Next ask students how the tone of the sentence influences their understanding of the meaning. How does the tone reflect the author's feelings? (*The tone is positive. This influences the meaning that the author loves to spend the summer at camp.*)

- Point out that several text elements work together to give the reader a picture of the author's point of view. Recognizing an author's point of view will help students understand the author's purpose for writing and the meaning and focus of the text.

Ready *Teacher Toolbox*   teacher-toolbox.com

	Prerequisite Skills	*RI.7.6*
Ready Lessons	✓	✓
Tools for Instruction	✓	
Interactive Tutorials		✓

CCSS Focus

RI.7.6 Determine an author's point of view or purpose in a text and analyze how the author distinguishes his or her position from that of others.

ADDITIONAL STANDARDS: *RI.7.1, RI.7.2, RI.7.3, RI.7.4, RI.7.5, RI.7.7; L.7.4a, L.7.4b, L.7.4c, L.7.4d, L.7.5c; W.7.3, W.7.4, W.7.7; SL.7.1, SL.7.4, SL.7.6* (*See page A39 for full text.*)

AT A GLANCE

Through an illustration, students explore the idea of point of view. They learn to recognize text clues that indicate an author's point of view.

STEP BY STEP

- Read the first paragraph that includes the definition of *point of view*. Encourage students to study the illustration and circle clues that help them figure out the points of view of the parade viewers.

- Explain that the chart details the point of view for each of the people watching the parade. Have students compare the information in the chart to the clues they circled. Discuss how a person's actions and body language reveal his or her point of view about what is happening.

- Have students give real-life examples of when they were able to determine someone else's perspective about a situation based on that person's actions and body language.

- Reinforce the idea that picking up clues indicating a positive or negative attitude while reading will help students infer the author's point of view about the topic being explained.

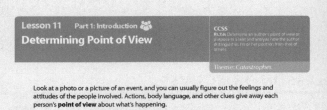

Lesson 11 Part 1: Introduction
Determining Point of View

CCSS
RI.7.6: Determine an author's point of view or purpose in a text and analyze how the author distinguishes his or her position from that of others.

Theme: *Catastrophes*

Look at a photo or a picture of an event, and you can usually figure out the feelings and attitudes of the people involved. Actions, body language, and other clues give away each person's **point of view** about what's happening.

Can you figure out the feelings of the people watching the parade in the picture below? Circle clues that help you figure out their points of view.

Read the chart below, which provides details that suggest different points of view about the parade scene.

Topic	Evidence	Positive (+) or Negative (–) Attitude	Point of View
Parade	The woman is smiling. The man in the baseball cap is waving a flag.	+	The man and woman are excited and happy to be watching the parade.
	The child is frowning and holding his ears.	–	The child dislikes the noise from the parade.

When you're reading a book or magazine, you must use different clues to help you determine the author's point of view. Notice the content and language choices; they'll help you infer an author's position on a topic. Also look for clues that reflect an author's **purpose**, or main reason for writing, and the tone being adopted. Analyze facts an author includes and leaves out, the opinions expressed, and word choices. All of these details help reveal the author's point of view—where he or she stands—on a particular topic.

L11: Determining Point of View
©Curriculum Associates, LLC   Copying is not permitted.
103

Genre Focus

Informational Texts: Scientific Accounts

Tell students that in this lesson they will read informational texts. One type of informational text is a scientific account, or a piece of writing that provides information about scientific research or another science-related topic.

- Its purpose is to explain scientific findings or any event or discovery with ties to science.

- It can be written by professional scientists to relate findings to the scientific community or to contribute to knowledge in a particular field of study. It may also be written by someone with scientific expertise for the general public.

- It often opens with an explanation about the thesis or theory behind the scientific topic and then gives examples or further details to elaborate on it.

- Some may include charts, graphics, or photos. Others may have sidebars with additional facts or subheadings to show how the ideas are organized.

Have students describe any scientific accounts they may have read about a topic of interest.

Explain that "Rising from the Ashes" tells about the eruption of Mount St. Helens. An editorial describes the author's opinion about the effects of the BP oil spill. Finally, "A Dire Shortage of Water" explains the causes of the water shortage and its effects.

AT A GLANCE

Students determine the author's point of view about a topic in an informational text.

STEP BY STEP

- Invite volunteers to tell what they learned on the previous page about identifying points of view in an illustration or a text.

- Read aloud "Rising from the Ashes." Then read the question: "What is the author's point of view about the eruption?"

- Tell students you will use a Think Aloud to demonstrate a way of answering the question.

Think Aloud: I can look for clues to help me figure out how the author feels about the eruption. In the first sentence, the author writes, "It was a disaster, the stuff of nightmares." The words *disaster* and *nightmares* suggest his feeling of horror about the event.

- Direct students to the chart and remind them that it shows the process of determining point of view. Point out the first piece of evidence.

Think Aloud: In the second sentence, the author uses the phrase "a horrendous blast." This phrase is also a clue as to how the author feels about the eruption.

- Tell students to complete the second row of the chart by identifying whether this text evidence implies a positive or negative attitude about the event.

Think Aloud: In paragraph 2, the text "thought it was the end of the world" also suggests a negative attitude. Based on the evidence I've found, I can determine the author's point of view.

- Ask students to write a third piece of evidence in the chart and to note if it is positive or negative.

- Then have students describe the author's point of view to complete the chart. (*Sample response: The author believes that the eruption of Mount St. Helens is a remarkable but terrible event because of the widespread damage it caused.*)

- Finally, have students answer the question at the bottom of the page. Invite volunteers to share their answers with the class.

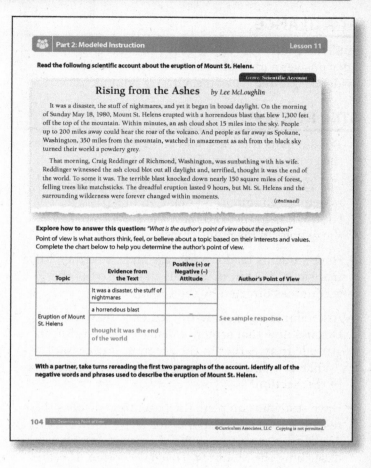

ELL Support: Compound Words

- Explain that compound words are made up of two smaller words. Tell students that they can often use the meaning of the two smaller words to figure out the meaning of the compound word.

- Direct students to the word *daylight* in paragraph 1. Ask them what two words make up this compound word. (*day* and *light*) Have students use the meanings of the smaller words to define *daylight*. (*"time when it is light out during the day"*) Have students check this meaning by using the context.

- Mention that some compound words mean something different from the two smaller words. *Ladybug*, for example, does not mean "a lady who is a bug."

- Work with students to identify and define other compound words in the account. (*nightmares, sunbathing, matchsticks*) **(RI.7.4; L.7.4b)**

AT A GLANCE

Students continue reading about Mount St. Helens. They answer a multiple-choice question and cite evidence that indicates the author's point of view.

STEP BY STEP

- Tell students that they will continue reading about the eruption of Mount St. Helens.

- The Close Reading helps students identify and remember an important detail in this passage. The Hint will help them connect the author's purpose to the change in his point of view.

- Have students read the passage and circle the phrase that signals a shift in attitude in this part of the account, as directed by the Close Reading.

- Ask volunteers to share the sentence they circled. Discuss how that sentence demonstrates a shift in attitude from earlier in the account. If necessary, ask: "What new point of view does the author introduce in this section?"

- Have students complete the page; then discuss their responses. Sample response for Show Your Thinking: The author conveys a sense of amazement when describing the Mount St. Helens eruption. He calls the blast "spectacular" and describes the terrible devastation it caused. He is even more awed by the ability of the ecosystem to recover from the disaster.

ANSWER ANALYSIS

Choice A is incorrect. The author's purpose is to inform, not to persuade readers of an opinion.

Choice B is incorrect. The description about the eruption may be frightening yet exciting, but that is not the author's purpose for writing about the event.

Choice C is correct. The author informs readers about the disaster and some of its positive aftereffects.

Choice D is incorrect. There is no text evidence to suggest the author wants readers to research this topic.

ERROR ALERT: Students who did not chose C might not have understood the question. Point out that it asks which sentence most accurately describes the author's purpose. Some choices include points the author made, but only C sums up the account.

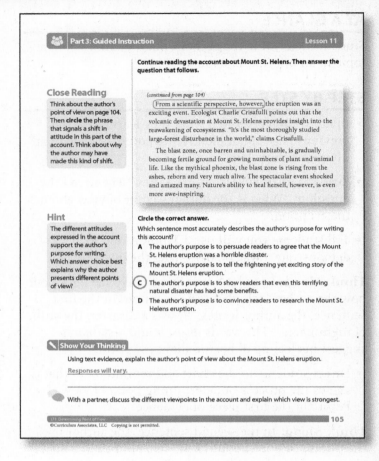

Tier Two Vocabulary: *Uninhabitable*

- Direct students to the word *uninhabitable* in paragraph 2. Have students identify the base word (*inhabit*), the prefix (*un-*) and the suffix (*-able*). Review that the prefix *un-* means "not." Have students identify the meaning of the suffix *-able*. ("*capable of*") Point out that this suffix changes a noun to an adjective.

- Have students use this information as well as the context to figure out the meaning. ("*not able to support life*") Encourage them to verify this definition in a dictionary. (**RI.7.4; L.7.4a, L.7.4c, L.7.4d**)

AT A GLANCE

Students read an editorial twice about the Gulf oil spill. After the first reading, you will ask three questions to check your students' comprehension of the passage.

STEP BY STEP

- Have students read the editorial silently without referring to the Study Buddy or Close Reading text.

- Ask the following questions to ensure students' comprehension of the text:

  According to the author, why was the "Disaster in the Gulf" a tragic event? *(It killed workers and innocent wildlife. It assaulted the environment.)*

  What did BP's David Rainey assure the U.S. Senate of? *(He assured the Senate that oil drilling was safe.)*

  What warnings did BP ignore, and what was the outcome? *(BP ignored warnings about the difficulty of capping a deep water spill. It took five months for them to seal the underwater well properly.)*

- Ask students to reread the passage and look at the Study Buddy think aloud. What does the Study Buddy help them think about?

Tip: The Study Buddy guides students to look for words that show how the author feels. Ask: What clues do the word choices provide? Do they suggest the author has a strong opinion? How does the tone influence your understanding of the author's view?

- Have students answer the questions and follow the directions in the Close Reading.

Tip: Have students analyze how the author portrays the point of view of the BP executives. Point out words the author uses to describe the aftermath of the oil spill. Does the evidence the author includes support or counter the executives' point of view?

- Finally, have students answer the questions on page 107. Use the Answer Analysis to discuss correct and incorrect responses.

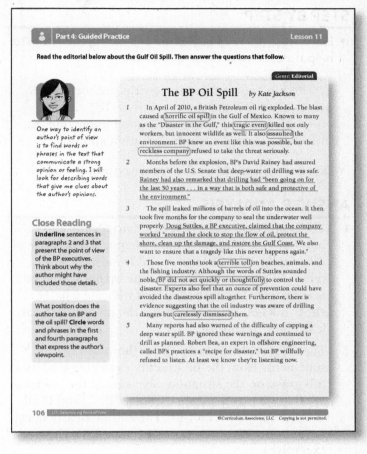

Tier Two Vocabulary: *Assaulted*

- Direct students to the word *assaulted* in paragraph 1. Work with students to identify context clues in this paragraph that help them understand the word *assaulted*. *("blast," "tragic event," "killed")* Then ask students to define *assaulted* in their own words. *("made an attack on")* **(RI.7.4; L.7.4a)**

- Ask students what they think the author meant when she used the word *assaulted* relative to the environment. What does an *assault* on the environment involve?

STEP BY STEP

- Have students read questions 1–3, using the Hints to help them answer those questions.

Tip: Remind students to review the author's word choices about BP and the executives. The connotations of the words are a good indication of her feelings toward both the situation and BP.

- Discuss with students the Answer Analysis below.

ANSWER ANALYSIS

1 The correct choice is B. It summarizes the author's point of view that the disaster happened because of BP's negligence. Choices A and D more closely reflect BP's point of view, not the author's. Choice C is incorrect. The author doesn't indicate whether she thinks oil spills are events the oil industry can learn how to control.

2 The correct choice is A. The author used the statements from the BP executives to give readers a full grasp on the situation. She wanted the reader to see that BP was negligent. Choices B, C, and D all show some support for BP. The author clearly does not support BP or the statements made by the executives.

3 Sample response: The author's purpose for writing this editorial is to persuade readers that the oil company BP neglected to establish and follow safe procedures for deep-sea drilling in the Gulf of Mexico. The author wants to convince readers that BP's procedures were a "recipe for disaster," and that the company did not act quickly enough to repair the oil spill damage.

RETEACHING

Use a chart to answer question 3. Draw the chart below, and work with students to fill in the boxes. Sample responses are provided.

Topic: BP Oil Spill		
Evidence	Attitude	Point of View
"recipe for disaster"	negative	BP neglected to establish safe procedures.
oil industry "carelessly dismissed" dangers	negative	

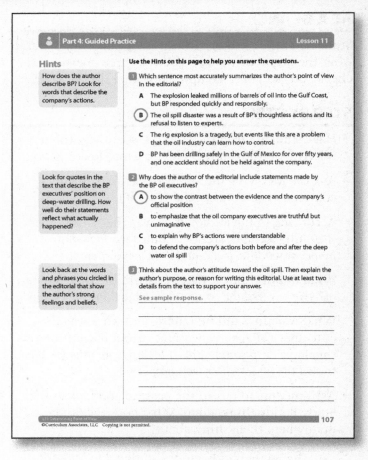

Integrating Standards

Use these questions to further students' understanding of "The BP Oil Spill."

1 Give examples of the evidence the author used to oppose BP's claims. *(RI.7.1)*

She referred to expert opinions and reports that countered their claims: "Experts also feel that an ounce of prevention could have avoided the disastrous spill altogether." Reports "had also warned of the difficulty of capping a deep water spill."

2 Name two central ideas that the author tries to convey to readers in her editorial. *(RI.7.2)*

The author wants readers to know that the BP oil spill was devastating for the environment, as well to humans. She also wants readers to agree that BP is to blame for the spill because it didn't listen to warnings or expert opinion, nor did it clean up the spill quickly and efficiently.

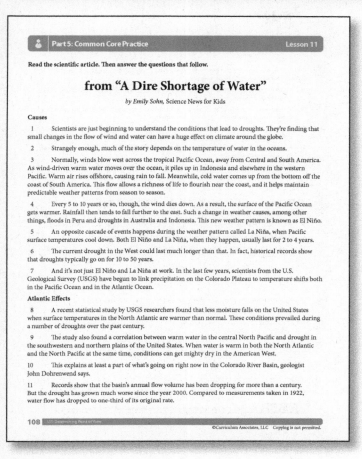

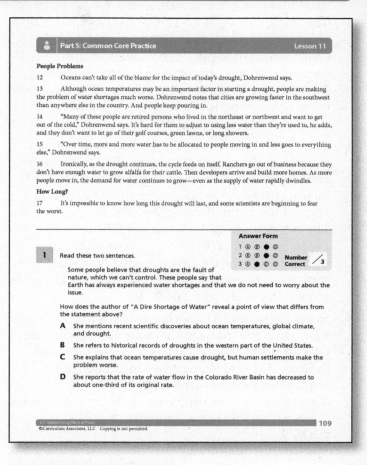

AT A GLANCE

Students independently read a longer article and answer questions in a format that provides test practice.

STEP BY STEP

• Tell students to use what they have learned about reading closely and determining point of view to read the passage on pages 108 and 109.

• Remind students to circle or underline important word choices that convey a point of view.

• Tell students to answer the questions on pages 109 and 110. For questions 1–3, they should fill in the correct circle on the Answer Form.

• When students have finished, use the Answer Analysis to discuss correct responses and the reasons for them. Have students fill in the Number Correct on the Answer Form.

ANSWER ANALYSIS

1 The correct choice is C. The author explains how humans make the issue worse, which differs from the opinion that water shortages are only caused by nature. Choices A, B, and D are incorrect because they all point to the forces of nature that impact the drought issue. They do not differ from the point of view in the given statement. **(DOK 3)**

Theme Connection

• How do all the texts in this lesson relate to the theme of catastrophes?

• What is one fact or idea that surprised you about a catastrophe described in this lesson?

2 The correct choice is C. This sentence shows how environmental factors and human activity both contribute to drought. Choices A and B are incorrect because they mention environmental factors but no human factors. Choice D is incorrect because it mentions a human factor but no environmental factors. **(DOK 3)**

3 The correct choice is B. The author's point of view focuses on the growing problem of water shortages and the variety of contributing factors. Choice A is incorrect. The author uses scientific research to support her point of view. Choice C is incorrect. The author's words do not suggest she feels hopeless. Choice D is incorrect. The author may dislike that cities are growing quickly in the southwest, but this does not reflect her overall point of view in the passage. **(DOK 3)**

4 Sample response: The author believes that the water shortage is caused by both nature and people. She cites scientific studies that explain the causes of drought. She also shows that human decisions impact the drought's length and severity. She disapproves of how people use water, but she knows that some people won't change their habits. **(DOK 3)**

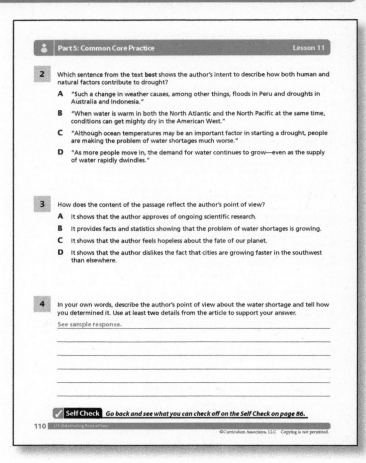

Integrating Standards

Use these questions and tasks as opportunities to interact with "A Dire Shortage of Water."

1 What is the effect of the winds over the ocean dying down every 5 to 10 years? **(RI.7.1)**

The effect of the winds dying down is that the surface of the Pacific Ocean increases in temperature. This then results in rainfall that tends to fall farther to the east, resulting in flooding as well as droughts.

2 Name three factors that the author includes to explain the cause of water shortages. **(RI.7.3)**

Answers will vary but may include water temperature, changes in the flow of wind and water, change in human settlements, warm weather and droughts, and El Niño and La Niña.

3 How does paragraph 9 help to develop the author's central idea in this article? **(RI.7.5)**

This paragraph provides an example of scientific research that explains one factor that contributes to water shortages.

4 Summarize: Write a brief summary of the passage, including key points that support the author's purpose. **(RI.7.2; W.7.4)**

Summaries will vary. Sample response: The central idea of this passage is that various factors contribute to the growing problem of water shortages. The author explores the conditions that lead to droughts, including natural causes and the impact of humans.

5 Discuss in small groups. What do you think should be done about the water shortage problem? Should people be given water rations? Should the problem be ignored and left in nature's hands? Use evidence from the article to convince others of your opinion. **(SL.7.1)**

Discussions will vary. Encourage students to talk about the water shortage problem and its similarity to other environmental issues.

Writing Activities

Narrative Writing (W.7.3)

- Have students write a short, firsthand account using "A Dire Shortage of Water" as a background resource for the different story details.

- Students should write from the perspective of a person who is in the midst of a drought in the southwestern United States. Encourage students to write in a personal narrative style and include the details of day-to-day life during a drought. Remind them to include descriptive details and present events in a logical order.

- Allow time for students to share their stories with the class.

Connotations (L.7.5c)

- Have students reread the first paragraph of "Rising from the Ashes." Ask them to focus on the phrases "stuff of nightmares" or "horrendous blast." What connotations do the words convey?

- Have students suggest other catastrophes that could create such a spectacle. Then have them provide additional words and phrases that use strong word connotations to describe the event.

- Have students write sentences that use word connotations to vividly describe a catastrophic scene.

LISTENING ACTIVITY (SL.7.4)

Listen Closely/Point of View

- Have students review the theme of catastrophes in texts in this lesson. Then have students take turns making a statement about a catastrophe from which a certain point of view can be inferred.

- Listeners must pay attention to the speaker's statement and then identify the point of view and the word choices they used to determine it.

DISCUSSION ACTIVITY (SL.7.1)

Talk in a Group/Discuss an Action Plan

- Have students form small groups and assign each group a catastrophe they read about: oil spill, drought, volcanic eruption.

- Have students in each group discuss and write an action plan for their assigned catastrophe. What should people do to prepare for this catastrophe? What action would people need to take if this catastrophe happened near them? Point out that being prepared will help people stay safe.

- Have groups share their plans with the class. Discuss the different needs and emergencies specific to each type of catastrophe.

MEDIA ACTIVITY (RI.7.7)

Be Creative/Draw a Cartoon

- Have students review the illustration on page 103. Remind them that the illustration portrays many points of view through the characters' actions, body language, and other clues.

- Have students draw their own cartoons to show two opposing points of view as characters react differently to the same situation. For example, students might draw a teenage boy and his grandmother at a rock concert.

RESEARCH ACTIVITY (W.7.7; SL.7.4, SL.7.6)

Research and Present/Hold a Debate

- Have students form small groups. Assign each group one side of the BP Oil Spill debate: those in favor of the BP executives and those against.

- Students should conduct research to find out more information about their side of the topic and reasons and evidence that discredit the opposing side's arguments.

- Have students conduct a formal debate in which each panel presents its arguments and rebuts the opposing side's claims.

SCORING GUIDE AND ANSWER ANALYSIS

Informational Passage Answer Analysis

1 Ⓐ Ⓑ Ⓒ ●   5 ● Ⓑ Ⓒ Ⓓ

2 Ⓐ ● Ⓒ Ⓓ   6 ● Ⓑ Ⓒ Ⓓ

3 Ⓐ ● Ⓒ Ⓓ   7A Ⓐ Ⓑ Ⓒ ●

4 Ⓐ Ⓑ ● Ⓓ   7B ● Ⓑ Ⓒ Ⓓ

1 Choice D is correct. The word "unblinking" in the preceding sentence suggests that the word "fixed" means "not moving" or "stationary."

Choice A is incorrect. Although "fixed" can mean "influenced," "unblinking" suggests that it means "not moving" or "stationary." Choice B is incorrect. Although "fixed" can mean "mended," the word "unblinking" suggests that it means "not moving" or "stationary." Choice C is also incorrect. Although "fixed" can mean "ready" or "prepared," the word "unblinking" suggests that it means "not moving" or "stationary." *(RI.7.4; DOK 2)*

2 Choice B is correct. This sentence shows the type of information the Kepler mission is gathering.

Choice A is incorrect. This sentence describes what the telescope does, not the information it gathers. Choice C is incorrect. This sentence points out the limits of the information being gathered, not the type of information gathered. Choice D is incorrect. It shows the type of information the mission is currently not gathering. *(RI.7.6; DOK 3)*

3 Choice B is correct. The fourth paragraph compares Kepler-22b to Earth and describes similarities, such as the length of their years, their close temperatures, and their "twin" stars.

Choice A is incorrect. The fourth paragraph explains what scientists already know about Kepler-22b. It describes similarities between Kepler-22b and Earth. Choice C is incorrect. The fourth paragraph explains what scientists have learned since they discovered Kepler-22b, not the events that led to its discovery. It describes how Kepler-22b and Earth are alike. Choice D is incorrect. The fourth paragraph provides a comparison between Kepler-22b and Earth. *(RI.7.5; DOK 2)*

4 Choice C is correct. This sentence brings to mind a common picture that people have when they consider what life on other planets may be like. It was most likely included to describe how many people think of life on other planets.

Choice A is incorrect. This sentence paints a common picture of what people think of when they consider life on other planets. It does not challenge that common opinion. Choice B is incorrect. This sentence asks readers to assume that there could be life on others planets. It does not suggest that finding life on other planets is impossible. Choice D is also incorrect. The sentence mentions the human curiosity about life on other planets, but it was likely included to focus reader attention on a common view that many people share about what life on other planets may be like. *(RI.7.5; DOK 3)*

5 Choice A is correct. The author argues that theorizing about life on other planets should be left to writers of science fiction, and that researchers should focus on scientific fact. Therefore, the author's point of view is that NASA scientists should focus on interpreting the data.

Choice B is incorrect. The author states that NASA scientists should be concerned with scientific facts. Therefore, the author is unlikely to have the point of view that scientists should spend time developing technology to find life on other planets. Choice C is incorrect. The author states that NASA scientists should be concerned with scientific facts. Therefore, the author is most likely to believe that these scientists should focus on interpreting the data they have collected. Choice D is also incorrect. The article is about habitable zones beyond the solar system, so the point of view in this choice is unrelated to the topic of the article. *(RI.7.6; DOK 3)*

6 Choice A is correct. The illustration clarifies what a habitable zone is.

Choice B is incorrect. The illustration shows some of the Kepler mission's purpose, but it doesn't show how the spacecraft works. Choice C is incorrect. The illustration shows that Kepler-22b is in a habitable zone, but mapping is not the primary purpose. Choice D is incorrect. The illustration shows data the Kepler mission has produced, but this is not the primary purpose. *(RI.7.5; DOK 2)*

SAMPLE RESPONSES

7 **Part A:** Choice D is correct; in this case, the connotation of particular is fussy. The other choices are possible meanings of particular, but none of them are synonyms for particular as it is used in the passage. *(RI.7.4; DOK 2)*

Part B: Choice A is correct. The phrase "neither too hot nor too cold" shows that the girl mentioned in the sentence for Part A is choosy about her porridge. Choices B, C, and D do not provide the support needed to select the correct connotation of "particular" in this context. *(RI.7.4; DOK 2)*

Short Response

8 In the sentence, the phrase "with a grain of salt" means "with doubt." The author uses it to indicate that it is best to view the excitement about the possibility of life on other planets with doubt. The author makes this statement before introducing the scientific definition of "life" and concluding that life on other planets could be "nothing more than some bacteria." The author seems to think that microscopic organisms are not worth much excitement and views the excitement over the possibility of life on other planets with doubt. *(RI.7.4; DOK 3)*

9 The NASA scientists mentioned in the article think that finding any form of life on another planet, no matter how small, is exciting. The author, however, thinks that excitement is necessary only if scientists identify a planet capable of supporting human life. The author says, "Some think that the idea of discovering life on other planets is thrilling," but later notes, "I think it is vital to consider the scientific definition of life." The author then goes on to identify "life" in scientific terms as "nothing more than some bacteria." The author does this to show the difference between what many people think of when they consider life on other planets and what scientists have in mind. The "life" scientists may or may not discover could be a disappointment. *(RI.7.6; DOK 3)*

Performance Task

10 The author compares a few different people and places to Goldilocks throughout the article. The author begins by explaining that Goldilocks will not settle for porridge that is too hot or too cold; she will eat only porridge that is just right. The author goes on to compare NASA scientists to Goldilocks, because they too are looking for something that is "just right." For NASA scientists, the goal is to find habitable zones in space rather than the perfect bowl of porridge. The NASA scientists believe that life could exist in these habitable zones.

Next, the author mentions that NASA scientists have nicknamed the habitable zones "Goldilocks zones" because they are regions in space around a star where the temperature is just right for water to exist on the planet's surface. Such zones are not too hot and not too cold for water to exist, just as Goldilocks's porridge was neither too hot nor too cold.

The author compares herself to Goldilocks because she is waiting until the time is "just right" to celebrate the idea of life on other planets. The author thinks that all the excitement over the possibility of life on other planets right now is, as the title states, "a lot of hype." If and when scientists discover a planet that could support human life, the author will feel "just right" about celebrating life on other planets. The comparison of the various people and places to Goldilocks helps to bring the whole article together. Each new idea in the article relates back to the idea of Goldilocks' search for what is "just right." *(RI.7.5; DOK 3)*

SCORING RUBRICS

Short-Response Rubric

2 points	The response is accurate, complete, and fulfills all requirements of the task. Text-based support and examples are included. Any information that goes beyond the text is relevant to the task.
1 point	The response is partially accurate and fulfills some requirements of the task. Some information may be inaccurate, too general, or confused. Support and examples may be insufficient or not text-based.
0 points	The response is inaccurate, poorly organized, or does not respond to the task.

Performance Task Rubric

4 points   The response
- Fulfills all requirements of the task
- Uses varied sentence types and some sophisticated vocabulary
- Includes relevant and accurate details from the texts as well as text-based inferences
- Demonstrates a thorough understanding of the texts
- Maintains a clear focus and organization
- Is fluent and demonstrates a clear voice
- Uses correct spelling, grammar, capitalization, and punctuation

3 points   The response
- Fulfills all requirements of the task
- Uses simple sentences and grade-level vocabulary
- Includes relevant and accurate details from the texts
- Demonstrates a mainly literal understanding of the texts
- Maintains a mostly clear focus and organization
- Is fluent and demonstrates some sense of voice
- Uses mostly correct spelling, grammar, capitalization, and punctuation

2 points   The response
- Fulfills some requirements of the task
- Uses simple sentences, some fragments, and grade-level vocabulary
- Includes some relevant and accurate details from the texts
- Demonstrates some misunderstandings or gaps in understanding of the texts
- Attempts to maintain a clear focus and organization
- Is difficult to read, includes some inaccuracies, and demonstrates little or no sense of voice
- Contains some inaccurate spelling, grammar, capitalization, and punctuation that may hinder understanding

1 point   The response
- Fulfills few requirements of the task
- Uses sentence fragments and below-grade-level vocabulary
- Includes no details or irrelevant details to support the response
- Demonstrates very little understanding of the texts
- Does not establish a clear focus or organization
- Is difficult to read, contains many inaccuracies, and demonstrates no sense of voice
- Uses incorrect spelling, grammar, capitalization, and punctuation to an extent that impedes understanding

0 points   The response is irrelevant, poorly organized, or illegible.

Lesson 12 (Student Book pages 121–128)

Determining Word Meanings

LESSON OBJECTIVES

- Determine the meanings of words and phrases used in a text.

- Analyze the meaning of connotative and figurative language.

- Analyze the impact of figurative and connotative language on the overall tone and meaning of a text.

THE LEARNING PROGRESSION

- **Grade 6:** CCSS RL.6.4 requires students to determine the meaning of words and phrases as they are used in a text, including figurative and connotative meanings.

- **Grade 7: CCSS RL.7.4 builds on the Grade 6 standard by having students determine the intended meaning of figurative and connotative language and how it develops the tone of the writing.**

- **Grade 8:** CCSS RL.8.4 requires students to expand on this analysis by studying analogies or allusions to other texts.

PREREQUISITE SKILLS

- Determine the meaning of an unfamiliar word using context clues.

- Identify figurative language and words that have strong connotations.

TAP STUDENTS' PRIOR KNOWLEDGE

- Tell students they will be working on a lesson about determining word meanings, including words that are used as figurative language and words with strong connotations.

- Ask students what context clues are. *(words or phrases near an unfamiliar word that help you understand the meaning of that word)* Review that context clues may be synonyms and antonyms.

- Then review figurative language with students. Ask what figurative language is. *(words or phrases that help readers create a vivid mental picture)*

- Display the following sentences: *The lunch line wound around the tables. The lunch line snaked around the tables.* Have students identify which sentence is more interesting and explain why. (*The second sentence; it accurately describes the way the lunch line moves.*)

- Then discuss with students that words with strong connotations have positive, neutral, or negative feelings associated with them. Display the word *tired.* Have students list synonyms of this word. (*worn out, exhausted, weary, drained*) Challenge them to describe the connotation of each synonym.

- Explain to students that determining the meaning of the words in a text, including their figurative and connotative meanings, will help them better understand what they read.

Ready *Teacher Toolbox*

teacher-toolbox.com

	Prerequisite Skills	RL.7.4
Ready Lessons	✓	✓
Tools for Instruction	✓ ✓	✓ ✓
Interactive Tutorials		✓

CCSS Focus

RL.7.4 Determine the meaning of words and phrases as they are used in a text, including figurative and connotative meanings ….

ADDITIONAL STANDARDS: RL.7.1, RL.7.2, RL.7.5, RL.7.6, RL.7.7; L.7.2b, L.7.4a, L.7.4b, L.7.4d, L.7.5b; W.7.3, W.7.4, W.7.8; SL.7.1, SL.7.2, SL.7.3, SL.7.4 *(See page A39 for full text.)*

AT A GLANCE

By reading a short passage, students practice interpreting figurative language.

STEP BY STEP

- Read the first three paragraphs and review the definitions of *connotative meaning* and *figurative language*. Explain that careful readers are mindful of word connotations and figurative language because this helps them understand what an author means.

- Discuss the connotations of words with similar meanings—for example, *confident*, *proud*, and *arrogant* or *young*, *youthful*, and *childish*. Ask volunteers to suggest the different feelings such words evoke.

- Have students read the passage and look for examples of figurative language.

- Explain that the chart organizes ideas to help students interpret examples of figurative language.

- Read the first row of the chart, making sure students understand the comparison. Ask: How is the breeze like a person's arms? How does the author make the breeze seem calming?

- Read the next two rows and have students fill in the cells.

- Regarding the second row, guide students by first asking them how toy cars compare to real cars.

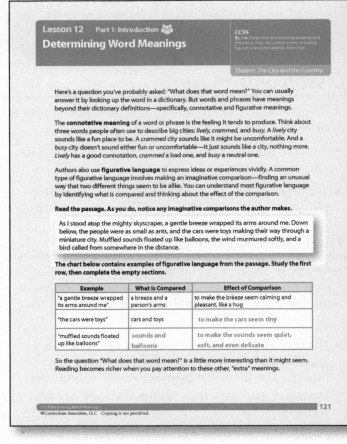

- Regarding the third row, ask students what is floating up like a balloon. Help students understand the comparison by having them list adjectives that describe a floating balloon—for example, *quiet*, *light*, *gentle*, and *fragile*.

Genre Focus

Literary Texts: Lyric Poetry

Remind students that a poem is a piece of writing that uses language in unusual and vivid ways to express emotions, ideas, or experiences. Many poems have stanzas, or groups of lines that form a pattern.

Two common features of poems are rhyme and rhythm. Rhyme is the use of repeated sounds at the ends of words. Rhythm is the pattern of beats, or stressed syllables.

The language used in most poems is descriptive and speaks to the senses. Similes, metaphors, and personification are common forms of figurative language often found in poems.

One type of poem is a lyric poem. In lyric poems, a speaker expresses his or her personal thoughts or feelings. A lyric poem often has a strong rhythmic pattern, and it may deal with broad topics such as love, death, or loyalty. Alternatively, it may deal with more everyday topics.

Point out that, in this lesson, students will read lyric poems that express the speakers' feelings about cities and their personal relationships with nature.

Explain that lyric poetry may be written in many different forms. Haiku, sonnet, limerick, and cinquain are all examples of lyric poems.

AT A GLANCE

Students read a poem and then interpret figurative language that is used to make comparisons.

STEP BY STEP

- Invite volunteers to tell what they learned on the previous page about analyzing figurative language.

- Tell students that they will now analyze the figurative language used in a poem.

- Read aloud "Composed Upon Westminster Bridge."

- Read the question: "How does the speaker use figurative language to make comparisons, and what is the effect?" Then use a Think Aloud to demonstrate a way of answering it.

Think Aloud: First, I'll look for comparisons the poet makes. I'm going to look for words or phrases that are usually used when comparing two things. In the fourth line, I see the phrase "like a garment." I know that authors often use the word *like* to compare things in figurative phrases.

- Direct students to the chart. Point out that the first column gives an example of figurative language from the poem.

Think Aloud: To make the comparison clearer, I'm going to try reorganizing the lines: "This City now doth wear the beauty of the morning like a garment." Now I can see that the speaker is comparing the beauty of morning in the city to a garment, or piece of clothing.

- Have students fill in the second column of the chart.

Think Aloud: How can a garment be like the beauty of the morning? I'll think about the qualities these two things might have in common. I know the speaker says the city wears the beauty of the morning. I also know that a garment is something a person wears. I think the speaker is saying the city wears the morning's beauty like a person wears a piece of beautiful clothing.

- Have students explain the effect of the comparison and complete the chart.

- Finally, have students respond to the prompt. Invite volunteers to share their answers with the class. (*Sample response: The speaker uses bright, glittering, and other words to show his positive feelings about the beautiful city.*)

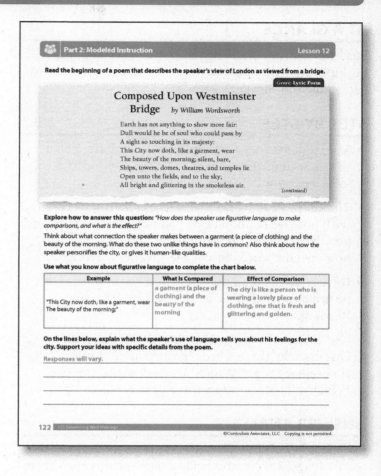

ELL Support: Suffixes

- Explain to students that many English words have suffixes. A suffix is a group of letters that is added to the end of a word to change the word's meaning.

- Direct students to the word *smokeless* in the last line of the poem. Write the word on the board and circle the suffix. (*-less*) Underline the base word. (*smoke*)

- Explain that the suffix *-less* means "without." Encourage students to figure out the meaning of *smokeless* ("*without smoke*"). Then have students name other words with the same suffix and explain their meanings (*windowless, aimless, bottomless*). **(RL.7.4; L.7.4b)**

AT A GLANCE

Students continue reading the poem. They answer a multiple-choice question and use word connotations to determine the speaker's feelings.

STEP BY STEP

- Tell students they will continue reading the poem that describes the speaker's view of London and identify connotations of specific words.

- The Close Reading helps students identify words with positive connotations and note how they create positive feelings. The Hint helps students recognize how specific words reveal the speaker's feelings.

- Have students read the poem and circle words with positive connotations, as directed by the Close Reading.

- Ask volunteers to share the words they circled. Discuss why these words have positive connotations. If necessary, ask, "Which words describe the sun? Which adjectives help paint a positive picture?"

ANSWER ANALYSIS

Choice A is correct. The connotations of the three words suggest peace and beauty. The speaker uses them to describe London, so he must have the same attitude about the city.

Choice B is incorrect. This poem tells about the speaker's feelings toward the city, not the valleys and hills of the country. There is no evidence to show how he feels about the country.

Choice C is incorrect. The river is just one aspect of the city in the morning. The connotations of the three words point to feelings about the entire city.

Choice D is incorrect. The speaker is describing the city scene and the feelings it evokes in him. He doesn't say what he hopes or wants to happen.

ERROR ALERT: Students who did not choose A might have made inferences about what the speaker thinks or wants. Point out that the question asks for a conclusion about the speaker's attitude based on the words he uses and their connotations.

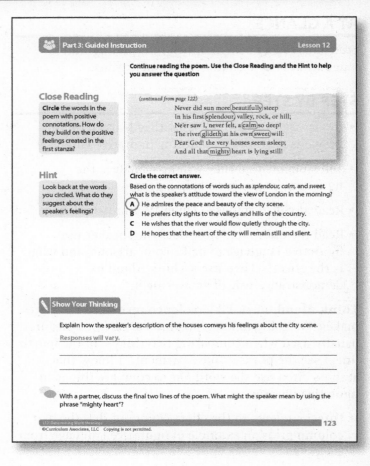

Tier Two Vocabulary: *Splendour*

- Direct students to the word *splendour* in the second line. Explain that the spelling of this word follows British spelling rules. The accurate spelling in the United States is *splendor*. **(L.7.2b)**

- Encourage students to think of another word that is similar to *splendor*. (*splendid*) Then have them use this relationship and context clues to figure out a possible meaning of *splendor*. ("*magnificent or impressive*")

- Have students look up the word in a dictionary to compare the actual meaning with the one they determined from context clues. **(RL.7.4; L.7.4a, L.7.4d)**

AT A GLANCE

Students read a poem excerpt comparing city and country life. After the first reading, you will ask three questions to check your students' comprehension of the poem.

STEP BY STEP

- Have students read the poem silently without referring to the Study Buddy or Close Reading text.

- Ask the following questions to ensure students' comprehension of the text:

  What does the speaker describe in this poem? (*He describes his feelings about life in the city and country.*)

  Where is the speaker as he composes this poem? Explain. (*He is in the country. He use the phrases "Since I left the city's heat" and "I have lost the urban ways."*)

  What is the speaker trying to convince the reader to do? How do you know? (*He wants the reader to join him in the country. He says, "Leave the city . . . Come with me, ah, come away."*)

- Ask students to reread the poem and look at the Study Buddy think aloud. What does the Study Buddy help them think about?

Tip: The Study Buddy directs students to think about figurative language and words that have connotations. If students have trouble, have them work in pairs to discuss their ideas about the meanings of the figurative language and the connotations suggested by certain words.

- Have students answer the questions and follow the directions in the Close Reading.

Tip: While figurative language and the use of word connotations figure prominently in poetry, being able to recognize and understand the authors' intended meanings in descriptive language will help students become better readers across genres.

- Finally, have students answer the questions on page 125. When students have finished, use the Answer Analysis to discuss correct and incorrect responses.

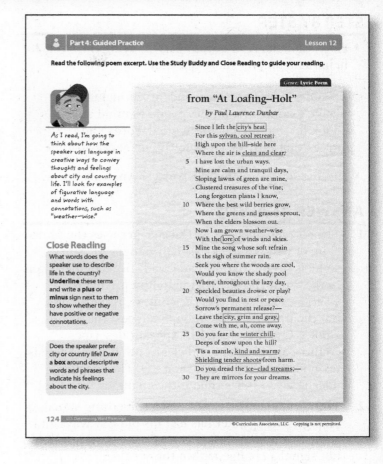

Part 4: Guided Practice   Lesson 12

Read the following poem excerpt. Use the Study Buddy and Close Reading to guide your reading.

Genre: Lyric Poem

from "At Loafing–Holt"
by Paul Laurence Dunbar

As I read, I'm going to think about how the speaker uses language in creative ways to convey thoughts and feelings about city and country life. I'll look for examples of figurative language and words with connotations, such as "weather–wise."

Since I left the city's heat
For this sylvan, cool retreat;
High upon the hill–side here
Where the air is clean and clear;
5 I have lost the urban ways.
Mine are calm and tranquil days,
Sloping lawns of green are mine,
Clustered treasures of the vine;
Long forgotten plants I know,
10 Where the best wild berries grow,
Where the greens and grasses sprout,
When the elders blossom out.
Now I am grown weather–wise
With the lore of winds and skies.
15 Mine the song whose soft refrain
Is the sigh of summer rain.
Seek you where the woods are cool,
Would you know the shady pool
Where, throughout the lazy day,
20 Speckled beauties drowse or play?
Would you find in rest or peace
Sorrow's permanent release?—
Leave the city, grim and gray.
Come with me, ah, come away.
25 Do you fear the winter chill;
Deeps of snow upon the hill?
'Tis a mantle, kind and warm;
Shielding tender shoots from harm.
Do you dread the ice–clad streams,—
30 They are mirrors for your dreams.

Close Reading

What words does the speaker use to describe life in the country? **Underline** these terms and write a **plus** or **minus** sign next to them to show whether they have positive or negative connotations.

Does the speaker prefer city or country life? Draw a **box** around descriptive words and phrases that indicate his feelings about the city.

124   L12: Determining Word Meanings   ©Curriculum Associates, LLC   Copying is not permitted.

Tier Two Vocabulary: *Clustered*

- Direct students to the word *clustered* in line 8. What surrounding words in the poem give clues about the meaning of this word? (*"treasures of the vine," "plants," "wild berries"*) What is the poet describing? (*fruits on a vine, such as grapes*) Then have students use these clues to determine the meaning of *clustered*. (*"grouped together in bunches"*) (**RL.7.4; L.7.4a**)

- Ask students to brainstorm a list of things that can be clustered together.

STEP BY STEP

- Have students read questions 1–3, using the Hints to help them answer those questions.

Tip: Question 3 requires students to include specific examples from the poem. Remind students to look for and include individual words and phrases that provide clues to the speaker's attitude.

- Discuss with students the Answer Analysis below.

ANSWER ANALYSIS

1   The correct choice is B. The speaker uses the phrase "lore of winds and skies." *Lore* can mean "stories," so he is saying that he can "read" or recognize signs in the wind and sky that help him predict the weather. Choice A sets the context in the woods, but the lines don't mention or suggest the woods. Choice C is incorrect. The speaker describes country air as "clean and clear," not harsh. There is no evidence to support Choice D. The speaker doesn't write stories about the changing weather.

2   The correct choice is A. Losing something signals a change. The speaker has lost his old city ways and gained calm and tranquility. Choices B, C, and D do not signal a change within the speaker.

3   Sample response: The speaker uses connotative and figurative language to contrast the city with the country. For example, the city is "grim and gray." In contrast, the country has "calm and tranquil days." Moreover, the speaker uses figurative language to emphasize the beauty of the country over that of the city. For example, the poet describes grapes as "clustered treasures of the vine."

RETEACHING

Use a chart to organize details from the poem to answer question 3. Draw the chart below, and have students fill in the columns. Sample responses are provided.

Figurative Language	Connotations	Speaker's Meaning
"Leave the city, grim and gray"	negative feeling about the city	He is relieved to leave the city.
"calm and tranquil days"	positive feeling about country	He celebrates the country.

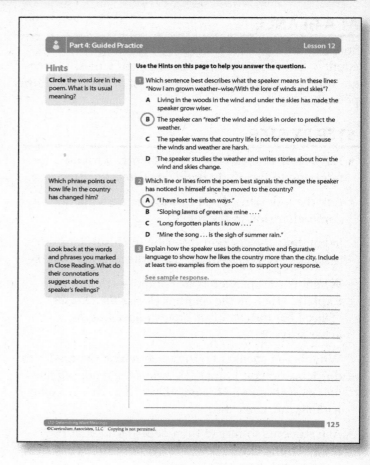

Integrating Standards

Use these questions to further students' understanding of the excerpt from "At Loafing-Holt."

1   How do the pairs of rhyming lines in this poem contribute to its meaning? *(RL.7.5)*

The pairs of short rhyming lines create a steady, soothing rhythm, which conveys a sense of calm. The speaker includes many descriptions, almost one per line, so the rhyming lines help the reader understand and interpret the many ideas and images.

2   How does the speaker develop his point of view about country life? *(RL.7.6)*

The speaker contrasts city life and country life. He uses descriptive words and makes comparisons to help the reader understand his feelings. The connotations of the words and phrases he uses help the reader see that he favors country life over city life. By the end of the poem, the speaker tries to convince the reader to join him in the country.

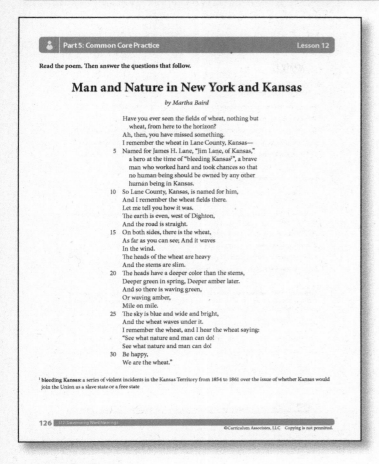

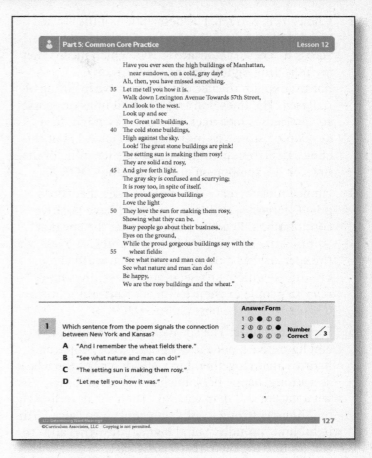

AT A GLANCE

Students independently read a longer poem and answer questions in a format that provides test practice.

STEP BY STEP

- Tell students to use what they have learned about reading closely and connotations and figurative language to read the poem on pages 126 and 127.

- Remind students to pay attention to the positive or negative connotations that certain words evoke.

- Tell students to answer the questions on pages 127 and 128. For questions 1–3, they should fill in the correct circle on the Answer Form.

- When students have finished, use the Answer Analysis to discuss correct responses and the reasons for them. Have students fill in the Number Correct on the Answer Form.

ANSWER ANALYSIS

1   Choice B is correct. The first half of the poem is about Kansas, and the second half is about New York. The poem ends with the repeated phrase "See what nature and man can do!" This phrase ties the two sections together. Choice A is about the wheat fields in Kansas. It does not connect to New York. Choice C describes buildings in New York. It does not connect to Kansas. Choice D is a phrase that is used in both halves, but it is the speaker talking to the reader. It does not explicitly signal a connection between New York and Kansas. (DOK 2)

Theme Connection

- How do all the poems in this lesson relate to the theme of city and country?

- What feelings about the settings are shared by the speakers of the poems in this lesson?

2 Choice D is correct. The description of the sky as "confused and scurrying" refers to clouds moving across it. These clouds are "rosy," which means they are reflecting light from the setting sun. Choice A doesn't explain the use of the figurative meaning of *confused*. The lines don't refer to buildings or people, so Choice B is incorrect. The gray sky might be a developing storm, as indicated in Choice C, but this choice doesn't explain the figurative meaning of the lines or the symbolism of the sunlight. **(DOK 3)**

3 Choice A is correct. The speaker uses the words *proud*, *gorgeous*, and *love*, which all have positive connotations. Readers can infer that the speaker admires the buildings. Choices B and C suggest that the speaker has a negative attitude toward the buildings, which isn't accurate. These lines don't refer to people or their feelings about sunlight, so Choice D isn't the best choice. **(DOK 3)**

4 Sample response: The speaker's use of connotative and figurative language celebrates what people and nature can do together. First, she describes the wheat as a strong, happy person who "waves" and says, "See what nature and man can do!" Then she describes the buildings as strong, confident people who "give forth light" and "proudly" stand loving "the light" and "the sun for making them rosy." **(DOK 3)**

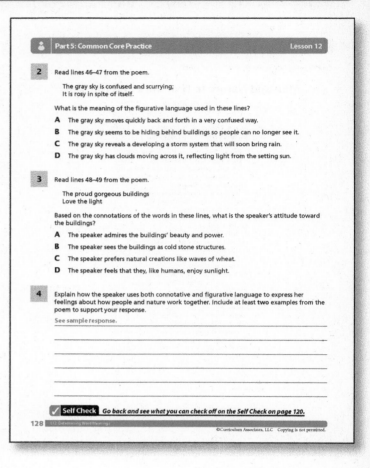

Integrating Standards

Use these questions and tasks as opportunities to interact with "Man and Nature in New York and Kansas."

1 Which lines from the poem directly connect the speaker's attitudes about New York and Kansas? **(RL.7.1)**

Lines 54–56 express the speaker's feelings about both places. "While the proud gorgeous buildings say with the / wheat fields: / "See what nature and man can do!" Based on these lines, readers can infer that the speaker admires and has respect for both the Kansas wheat fields and the New York buildings.

2 How does the poem's structure contribute to its meaning and your understanding of the poem? **(RL.7.5)**

The lines in this poem do not rhyme. Each line of the poem is a sentence or phrase, which makes it easy to understand and read. The speaker's ideas are organized like a poem, but it reads like a narrative.

3 What is the theme or central idea of this poem? Which line from the poem best captures the central idea? **(RL.7.2)**

The theme is that both man-made and natural places are beautiful and connected and should be celebrated. The last two lines of the poem best summarize this idea: "Be happy, / We are the rosy buildings and the wheat."

4 Write a narrative version of this poem. Be sure to introduce the narrator, establish a context, and include relevant details and figurative language from the poem. **(W.7.3)**

Narratives will vary.

5 In small groups, compare and contrast the form and structure of a lyric poem and a fiction story. How do the differences contribute to your understanding of each form? **(SL.7.1)**

Discussions will vary. Remind students to refer to their experiences to support their ideas.

Writing Activities

Lyric Poem (W.7.4)

- Have students discuss the attributes of lyric poems they learned about during this lesson. Also discuss the use of figurative language and word connotations. Tell students they will write a lyric poem of their own.

- Ask students to think about a personal experience that could be described in a poem. Have each student write a lyric poem to describe it. Poems should be at least 10 lines long and should feature the use of word connotations and figurative language. Have volunteers share their poems with the class.

Word Relationships (L.7.5b)

- Review the definitions of *synonym* and *antonym*. Point out that, based on word connotations, poets often choose synonyms to convey particular feelings or emotions and to add interesting variations in word use.

- Direct students to line 6 in "At Loafing-Holt." Point out the synonyms *calm* and *tranquil*. Have them suggest reasons why the speaker used those two words.

- Have students choose one of this lesson's poems and find pairs of synonyms or antonyms in it. Then have them explain why the author chose those words and how those word relationships contribute to their understanding and enjoyment of the poem.

LISTENING ACTIVITY (SL.7.2)

Listen Closely/Identify Descriptive Details

- Assign small groups of students a short poem to be read aloud. The poems should be unfamiliar but be about familiar topics.

- Students must listen closely to identify word connotations and figurative language in the poem. Then have students interpret the poet's intended meanings and describe the poem's central idea.

DISCUSSION ACTIVITY (SL.7.3)

Talk in a Group/Compare Poems

- Ask students to review each of this lesson's poems. Then have them compare and contrast two or more of this lesson's poems.

- Have students form small groups to compare and contrast the subjects of the poems and the speakers' feelings and claims as conveyed through figurative language and word connotations in the poems.

- Appoint one member of each group to take notes. Allow 10–15 minutes for discussion, and then have each group share its results with the class.

MEDIA ACTIVITY (RL.7.7)

Be Creative/Listen to a Poetry Reading

- Direct students to a reading of "Composed Upon the Westminster Bridge" by William Wordsworth.

- After students have listened to the reading, ask them to compare and contrast the experience of reading a poem with listening to it. How does what they hear contribute to their understanding and enjoyment? How does it differ from what they "see" and "hear" in their minds' eye as they read?

RESEARCH ACTIVITY (W.7.8; SL.7.4)

Research and Present/Give a Presentation

- Ask students to identify and research a specific poet who wrote one of this lesson's poems. When and where did he or she live? What kind of poetry is he or she famous for? What did the poet write about? How did his or her life contribute to his or her poems?

- Remind students to assess the credibility of each source they find and paraphrase the information.

- Students should present a brief biography to the class. Have them also read aloud one or two other poems from the poet.

Analyzing Rhyme and Repetition

LESSON OBJECTIVES

- Determine the impact of rhymes, repetitions, and alliteration on a text.
- Analyze how sound devices makes text more vivid and imaginative.
- Analyze the impact of sound devices on the overall tone and meaning of a poem, play, and story.

THE LEARNING PROGRESSION

- **Grade 6:** CCSS RL.6.4 requires students to determine the meaning of words and phrases as they are used in a text, including figurative and connotative meanings. Students also analyze the impact of specific word choice on meaning and tone.

- **Grade 7: CCSS RL.7.4 builds on the Grade 6 standard by having students analyze the impact of rhymes and other repetitions of sounds (such as alliteration) on a specific verse or stanza of a poem or section of a story or drama.**

- **Grade 8:** CCSS RL.8.4 requires students to expand on this analysis by studying analogies or allusions to other texts.

PREREQUISITE SKILLS

- Understand the characteristics of poetry and how those characteristics create meaning.
- Identify common sound devices, such as rhyming words, repeated words and phrases, and alliteration.
- Explain how details and sound devices contribute to the theme of a text.

TAP STUDENTS' PRIOR KNOWLEDGE

- Tell students they will be working on a lesson about sound devices, such as rhyme, repetition, and alliteration. Ask students how these devices differ from other literary elements they have learned about. (*Sound devices focus on individual sounds or words. Other literary elements, such as plot and theme, focus on entire sentences or broad ideas.*)

- Display and read aloud a stanza from a poem or a verse from a song that students are familiar with. It should include rhyme and repetition. Remind students that the rhythm is the beat created by the pattern of stressed and unstressed syllables. Ask students to identify words that rhyme and any words, phrases, or lines that are repeated.

- Ask students to suggest reasons why an author might repeat words or phrases. (*Repeated phrases are easy for readers to remember.*) Then ask students to explain why poems or songs use rhyming words. (*Rhymes create a musical rhythm that is pleasant to read aloud.*) Then guide students to understand what impact this language has on them as a reader.

- Point out that tongue twisters are examples of alliteration. Have students suggest favorites, and challenge them to say the tongue twisters aloud.

- Tell students that analyzing an author's word choices will help them better understand a text.

Ready *Teacher Toolbox*   teacher-toolbox.com

	Prerequisite Skills	RL.7.4
Ready Lessons	✓	✓
Tools for Instruction		✓
Interactive Tutorials		✓

CCSS Focus

RL.7.4 … analyze the impact of rhymes and other repetitions of sounds (e.g., alliteration) on a specific verse or stanza of a poem or section of a story or drama.

ADDITIONAL STANDARDS: RL.7.1, RL.7.2, RL.7.5, RL.7.6, RL.7.7; L.7.1, L.7.4a, L.7.4d; W.7.3, W.7.4, W.7.5, W.7.8; SL.7.1, SL.7.3, SL.7.4, SL.7.6 (*See page A39 for full text.*)

AT A GLANCE

By reading a poem, students practice identifying rhyme, repetition, and alliteration.

STEP BY STEP

- Explain to students that many poems and some prose use the musical qualities of language in creative ways. Rhyme, repetition, and alliteration are common characteristics of poems.

- Read the first paragraph aloud. Review the meanings of *repetition*, *alliteration*, and *rhyme*. Explain that careful readers are mindful of these sounds since poets often use them to draw readers into a poem and convey feelings and emotions on top of meaning.

- Have students study the poem and then draw arrows to connect pairs of rhyming words. Then have them circle the alliterative sounds. Encourage students to think of how the poet's word choice affects the poem.

- Explain to students that the chart helps them organize their ideas about how rhyming words and alliteration affect the poem's meaning. Read aloud the examples in the chart, and have students compare them to the examples they marked. Then discuss the information in the third column and have students compare it to their thoughts about how the poet's word choice impacts the poem's meaning.

- Discuss with students that in order to understand poetry and other literary texts, it is important to recognize and interpret choices the author makes.

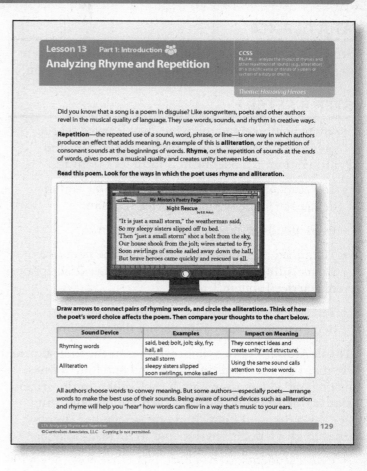

Genre Focus

Literary Texts: Drama

Tell students that they will read a type of literature called drama. Plays are works of fiction intended to be performed on stage. They include dialogue, or the words that each character says. Dialogue helps reveal information about the plot and characters' traits, attitudes, and motivations. A character's words also help a reader understand other characters. Because a play is performed on stage, the dialogue is the main element that moves the plot of the story forward.

Based on these characteristics, have students name some plays that they have read or seen performed on stage. Ask them to describe the characters, setting, and plot events. What did the characters say? How did the way the characters talked influence the plot? If students saw the play performed, have them describe the experience. Students may be familiar with plays such as *Oliver!*

Tell students that in this lesson they will read a play called "To Honor," which quotes from famous poems. This play is about a group of students discussing their group project. Have students predict why a play is a good format to choose for this topic.

Explain that students will also read a poem called "Harriet Tubman," which honors this famous African American woman. "Welcome Home" is a story about a girl and her brother, who is in the Air Force and is deployed to the Middle East.

AT A GLANCE

Students read a poem about Harriet Tubman and then analyze the poem's rhyme, alliteration, and repetition.

STEP BY STEP

- Invite volunteers to tell what they learned on the previous page about how rhyme, repetition, and alliteration in a poem can inform its meaning.

- Tell students that they will now examine sound devices in a poem about Harriet Tubman.

- Read aloud the poem "Harriet Tubman."

- Then read the question: "How does the poet use rhyme, alliteration, and repetition in her description of Harriet Tubman?"

- Tell students you will use a Think Aloud to demonstrate a way of answering the question.

Think Aloud: I notice that two lines in the first stanza rhyme. The last words of the second and fourth lines, *neither* and *either*, rhyme with each other. In the second stanza, the lines ending with "behind her" and "find her" also rhyme. I know that poets often use rhyming lines to give a poem rhythm and to tie ideas together.

- Direct students to the chart. Note that now they will analyze the use of repetition in addition to rhyme and alliteration.

- Point out the examples of rhyme in the first row. Have students fill in the chart to tell what impact on the poem's meaning they think the rhymes have.

Think Aloud: I notice an example of alliteration in the first stanza. Alliteration is repetition of the same sound. It could be only twice, or it could be many times. In the second line, the poet repeats the initial sound /n/ twice in "nothing neither." When I read the poem aloud, I notice that this alliteration gives the poem a sort of musical quality. It sounds interesting and draws me in.

- Have students find other examples of alliteration and add them to the chart. Then have them fill in the chart to explain how the alliteration affects the meaning.

- Ask students to identify an example of repetition in the poem. Guide them to determine its impact on the poem's meaning.

- Have pairs respond to the question at the bottom of the page. Invite volunteers to share their answers.

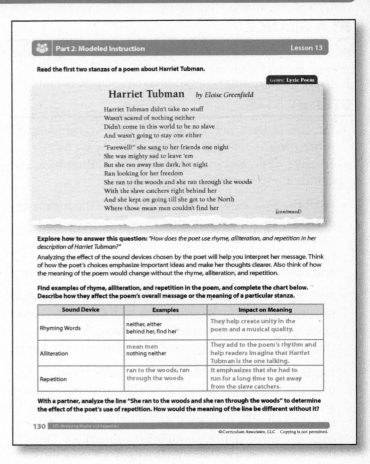

ELL Support: Compound Words

- Explain that a compound word is made up of two smaller words. Tell them that they may be able to use the meaning of the two smaller words to figure out the meaning of the compound word.

- Direct students to the word *farewell* at the beginning of the second stanza. Write the word on the board and have a volunteer draw a line between the two smaller words. *(fare/well)*

- Talk about the meaning of the words *fare* ("travel") and *well* ("good, safe"). Then ask students what they think the word *farewell* means. ("*good-bye, best wishes before travel*") **(RL.7.4; L.7.4a)**

AT A GLANCE

Students continue reading the poem about Harriet Tubman. They answer a multiple-choice question and analyze how repetition affects the poet's message.

STEP BY STEP

- Tell students they will continue reading the poem about Harriet Tubman and analyze how the poet uses repetition.

- The Close Reading helps students recognize and identify sound devices common to many poems. The Hint helps students analyze their own feelings as they read a repeated phrase in the poem.

- Have students read the poem, circle examples of rhyming words, and underline words or phrases that are repeated, as directed by the Close Reading.

- Ask volunteers to share the examples they marked. Discuss the effect of these examples. If necessary, ask, "Did you notice the rhymes or repetition as you read? How did they make you feel?"

ANSWER ANALYSIS

Choice A is incorrect. The phrase is used in the first few lines of the stanza, but it doesn't create a musical rhythm. It is used at the beginning of the first line and at the end of the third line.

Choice B is incorrect. Although the repetition does emphasize how many times Tubman traveled South, that is not the poet's main purpose in using the repetition. Therefore, this is not the best choice.

Choice C is incorrect. "Nineteen times" is an important detail the poet is highlighting in this stanza, but it is not the most important idea.

Choice D is correct. Other context clues suggest that returning to the South was very dangerous for Tubman. Repeating the phrase "nineteen times" reinforces the courage and determination it required to make the trip.

ERROR ALERT: Students who did not choose D might have been confused about other answer choices that are factually correct but are not the best answer. Have students consider the message the author wanted to get across through repetition.

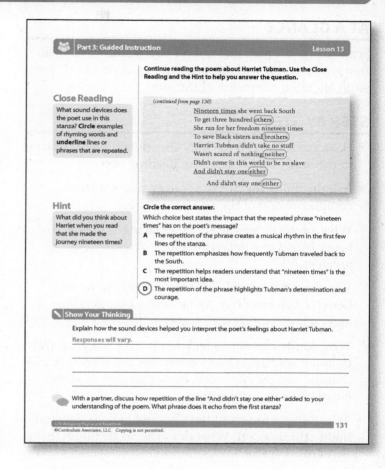

ELL Support: Contractions

- Explain to students that a contraction is a word made up of two words that have been joined together and shortened. When the words are joined, letters are dropped. An apostrophe is then added to take the place of any dropped letters.

- Direct students to the word *didn't* in the fifth line. Write the word on the board. Work with students to identify the two words in the contraction. (*did not*) Tell students the letter *o* in *not* has been dropped, and an apostrophe has been put in its place. **(L.7.1)**

- Have students point out other contractions in this lesson's passages.

AT A GLANCE

Students read a play that quotes two poems. After the first reading, you will ask three questions to check your students' comprehension of the play.

STEP BY STEP

- Have students read the play silently without referring to the Study Buddy or Close Reading text.

- Ask the following questions to ensure students' comprehension of the text:

  What problem are the students facing? (*They must honor heroes in a unique way for a Veteran's Day program.*)

  The characters decide on a unique way to honor a hero for Veteran's Day. What is it? (*They decide to make a presentation with poems and music.*)

  Why do the characters feel that poetry is a good way to honor soldiers? (*Many poems are about bravery and courage, and the characters know that a lot of soldiers have proven they are brave.*)

- Ask students to reread the play and look at the Study Buddy think aloud. What does the Study Buddy help them think about?

Tip: The Study Buddy points out that, so far, students have been analyzing sound devices used in poetry. Now they will think about sound devices used in plays. Check that students are able to transfer what they've learned so far to this genre.

- Have students answer the questions and follow the directions in the Close Reading.

Tip: Rhyme and repetition are common in poems, but some writers also use them in prose to create a specific effect or emphasize a particular point. Students should be mindful of these devices not only in the poems in the play, but also in the dialogue.

- Finally, have students answer the questions on page 133. After students have finished, use the Answer Analysis to discuss correct and incorrect responses.

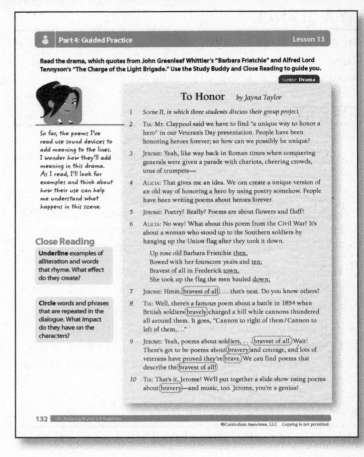

Tier Two Vocabulary: *Veteran*

- Direct students to the word *veteran* in paragraph 2. Ask students to use the context and their knowledge of Veteran's Day to determine what *veteran* means. (*"a hero who fought in a war for our country"*) Have them identify the clues they used to help them determine this meaning. (*"heroes," "conquering generals," "Civil War," "soldiers"*)

- Have students use a dictionary to verify the inferred meaning of the word. Note that anyone who has served in the military is considered a veteran. (**RL.7.4; L.7.4a, L.7.4d**)

STEP BY STEP

- Have students read questions 1–3, using the Hints to help them answer those questions.

Tip: Question 3 requires students to analyze the effect of repetition on the scene. This requires them to not only identify examples of repetition in the poem but also analyze the characters' reactions and emotions that are revealed by repetition in the play.

- Discuss with students the Answer Analysis below.

ANSWER ANALYSIS

1   The correct choice is B. The first and second lines of the poem rhyme, as do the third and fourth lines. These rhymes tie the lines together and create a musical quality when read aloud. Poets use repetition of sounds at the beginning of words or repetition of entire words. Choice A identifies an incorrect use of repetition. The word *up* is repeated but used two different ways, neither of which is the one identified in Choice C. Choice D is incorrect since the poet does not emphasize the initial /f/ sound.

2   The correct choice is C. Jerome kept saying this phrase aloud, and he eventually changed his mind about poetry. The other choices include phrases that are not repeated in the poem.

3   Sample response: The author repeats "bravest of all" to emphasize how the students build on each other's ideas as they plan their presentation. Alicia introduces the phrase in a Civil War poem about a woman who is the "bravest of all" in her town. Jerome picks up the phrase, repeating it as he thinks aloud. Tia then hears the phrase, and it helps her focus on an approach for their presentation poems about bravery. The repetition of "bravest of all" shows how one idea can lead to other ideas.

RETEACHING

Use a chart to organize details from the play to answer question 3. Draw the chart below, and have students fill in the columns. Sample responses are provided.

	Examples	Impact on Meaning
Repetition	"bravest of all"; "bravery"; "brave"	It sparks new ideas and inspires the characters.

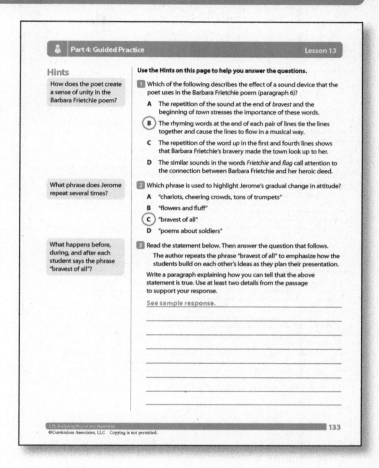

Integrating Standards

Use these questions to further students' understanding of "To Honor."

1   What is the structure of this play? How does it contribute to the meaning? **(RL.7.5)**

The play is a dialogue among three students, trying to decide how to complete a school project. Two students quote poems. The play's dialogue then repeats a line from one of the poems, "bravest of all," to emphasize that idea and how it affects all three characters.

2   How does the author develop Jerome's point of view about using poetry? **(RL.7.6)**

Jerome originally thinks "poems are about flowers and fluff." After he listens to Alicia and Tia recite two examples that are about the bravery of soldiers, Jerome begins to repeat one of the lines. He eventually decides to use poems about bravery and courage in the school project. His point of view about poetry completely changes during this scene.

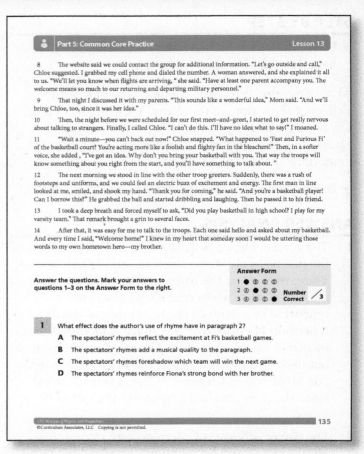

AT A GLANCE

Students independently read a long story and answer questions in a format that provides test practice.

STEP BY STEP

- Tell students to use what they have learned about reading closely and rhyme, repetition, and alliteration to read the story on pages 134 and 135.

- Remind students to pay attention to the feelings and emotions that the rhyming words and repeated words and phrases evoke.

- Tell students to answer the questions on pages 135 and 136. For questions 1–3, they should fill in the correct circle on the Answer Form.

- When students have finished, use the Answer Analysis to discuss correct responses and the reasons for them. Have students fill in the Number Correct on the Answer Form.

ANSWER ANALYSIS

1   Choice A is correct. The rhymes are used in chants, which have a musical quality. The chants are catchy, quick, and easy to say. They reflect the excitement spectators feel at the basketball games. Choice B is incorrect because the musical quality of the rhymes is not added to the paragraph. It is used in the paragraph as an example of rhythm that is added to the basketball games. Choice C is incorrect because the rhymes are not an example of foreshadowing. They reflect the spectators' excitement. Choice D is not the best choice because the rhymes encourage Fiona during the game, but they don't reinforce the bond with her brother. **(DOK 3)**

Theme Connection

- How do all the texts in this lesson relate to theme of honoring heroes?

- What is one fact or idea you learned about honoring heroes from each text in this lesson?

2   Choice B is correct. The alliteration highlights that these phrases create a sense of stillness and sadness in the scene. Choice A is incorrect. These phrases do not highlight similarities between Fi and her brother. Fi, not her brother, felt lost and lonely. These phrases do not create suspense, so Choice C is incorrect. The close relationship between Fi and her brother is emphasized elsewhere rather than in these phrases, so Choice D is incorrect. **(DOK 3)**

3   Choice D is correct. The alliterative phrase reminds Fi of the chants during games and the confidence she has on the basketball court. It helps her find the courage she needs off the court as well. Choices A, B, and C are not supported by evidence in the story. **(DOK 3)**

4   Sample response: The author uses repetition and alliteration to emphasize Fiona's feelings at different points. For example, when Fiona's brother repeats his nickname for her ("fast and furious"), Fiona thinks that she feels more "lost and lonely" instead. These alliterative phrases highlight the contrast between how Fiona feels while playing basketball with how she feels when her brother leaves. Later on, Fiona's friend contrasts "fast and furious" with a "foolish and flighty fan" when Fiona admits how she's feeling about greeting the returning soldiers. **(DOK 3)**

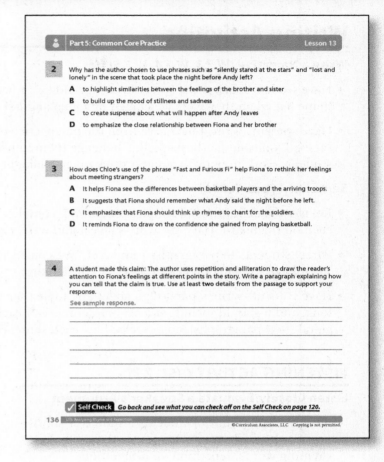

Integrating Standards

Use these questions and tasks as opportunities to interact with "Welcome Home."

1   Which lines from the story directly describe Fiona's feelings when her brother leaves? **(RL.7.1)**

Paragraphs 3–6 include textual evidence to support Fiona's feelings. Fiona says, "'I don't know what I'll do without you' … despite my feeble attempt to put on a brave face." The story also says that Fiona "couldn't stop crying," she "felt lost and lonely," and she "worried about him."

2   How does Fiona's point of view change from the beginning to the end of the story? **(RL.7.6)**

In the beginning of the story, Fiona describes herself as "shy and timid," except when she's on the basketball court. Because of her brother's support and encouragement, she is able to be like a different person on the court. She says, "My life just wasn't the same after Andy left." By the end of the story, her friend helps her find courage and bravery inside of herself and off the basketball court.

3   What is the theme or central idea of this story? **(RL.7.2)**

The theme of this story can be summed up as "believe in yourself." Fiona believes in herself on the basketball court, but she has difficulty believing in herself off the court. Finally, thanks to her brother's and her friend's encouragement, she is able to believe in herself and find the courage to greet the troops.

4   Write a brief poem about the events of this story. Be sure to include rhyming words, repetition, and alliteration to support the meaning. **(W.7.3)**

Poems will vary.

5   Discuss in small groups: What does Fiona learn about believing in herself? Why is it important to believe in yourself? What things have people told you that help you find the courage to do certain things? **(SL.7.1)**

Discussions will vary. Remind students to refer to the text and their experiences to support their ideas.

Writing Activities

Write a Narrative *(W.7.3, W.7.4, W.7.5)*

- Have students review the story "Welcome Home." Encourage them to think about how the soldiers coming home felt when they were welcomed by Fiona and her classmates. What would they have said and thought?

- Have students write a narrative from the perspective of one of the soldiers. Have them include details about seeing Fiona and her basketball. Challenge them to use narrative techniques in their stories. Then have students work in pairs to suggest ways to use dialogue and add sensory language to convey events.

Sentence Types *(L.7.1b)*

- Review the definitions of simple, compound, complex, and compound-complex sentences. Write examples of each on the board. Have students suggest and write examples of their own.

- Direct students to paragraphs 1 and 2 of "Welcome Home." Help students identify the sentence types used. Then have students find examples of each sentence type in this lesson's passages.

- Have students write a paragraph about any topic they choose. The paragraph should be at least four sentences long, and it should include at least one sentence of each of the four sentence types. Ask volunteers to read aloud their paragraphs and describe how each sentence type relates to the ideas the sentence presents.

LISTENING ACTIVITY *(SL.7.3)*

Listen Closely/Evaluate a Speaker's Argument

- Assign small groups of students a stanza or short poem to be read aloud. The poems should include rhyming words, repetition, or alliteration.

- Each group should make an argument that explains how and why sound devices contribute to the meaning of the poem.

- Students must listen closely to each group's argument and then evaluate the soundness and relevance of the argument.

DISCUSSION ACTIVITY *(SL.7.6)*

Talk in a Group/Adapt Speech

- Have three students perform "To Honor." Make sure students adapt their speech and perform the play's dialogue distinct from the poetry excerpts.

- Based on this performance, have students form groups to compare and contrast how plays are performed with how poems are read aloud.

- Appoint one member of each group to take notes. Allow 10–15 minutes for discussion, and then have each group share its results with the class.

MEDIA ACTIVITY *(RL.7.7)*

Be Creative/Watch a Performance

- Direct students to video recordings of plays or musicals. Encourage students to watch brief scenes from a number of different shows.

- Students should identify how rhyme, repetition, and alliteration are used in the performances, especially in musicals. Have students compare and contrast how the sound devices are used in these shows with how they are used in poems.

RESEARCH ACTIVITY *(W.7.8; SL.7.4)*

Research and Present/Write a Report

- Have students use this lesson's passages to inform an essay about how sound devices impact the meaning of a literary text.

- Tell students that the audience of their essay is a younger group of students, so they need to define terms clearly and present information logically.

- Have students research relevant examples of poetry or prose to include to support their points.

- Students should present their essays to the class. They may use technology, such as slideshow software, to present their work.

Analyzing the Structure of a Poem

Theme: *A Family Scrapbook*

LESSON OBJECTIVES

- Recognize and identify forms, patterns, and structures in poetry.

- Analyze how the poet's choice of sound devices, stanzas, and patterns function in a poem.

- Analyze how the poet's choice of form and structure contributes to meaning and theme.

THE LEARNING PROGRESSION

- **Grade 6:** CCSS RL.6.5 requires students to understand how a particular part of a poem fits into the poem's overall structure.

- **Grade 7: CCSS RL.7.5 builds on the Grade 6 standard by requiring students to not only identify a poem's structure but also to analyze how the poetic structure contributes to the poem's meaning.**

- **Grade 8:** CCSS RL.8.5 requires students to compare the structures of various poems, analyzing how different structures contribute to meaning and style.

PREREQUISITE SKILLS

- Understand the characteristics of and language used in poetry and how those characteristics create meaning.

- Recognize the general nature and purpose of rhyme, repetition, and rhythm in a poem.

- Explain how a particular choice of sound devices, stanzas, and patterns function in a poem.

TAP STUDENTS' PRIOR KNOWLEDGE

- Tell students that in this lesson they will learn about how the structure of a poem affects the poem's meaning. Ask how poems differ from other kinds of writing. (*Poems are usually written in groups of lines called stanzas rather than in paragraphs; they often feature rhyme, repetition, and rhythm as well as figurative language and imagery; they may tell a story or express the speaker's feelings and thoughts.*)

- Explain that poems, like stories, have patterns that help readers interpret the poet's message. The way a poem is organized is called poetic structure.

- Build on what students know by comparing stanzas to paragraphs. Point out that, like ideas grouped into a paragraph, related ideas grouped into a set of lines in a poem is called a stanza. Stanzas work together to build an image, thought, or feeling.

- Ask students to name and describe types of poem structures they know, such as limericks, haiku, and ballads.

- Explain to students that determining a poem's structure and figuring out how it reveals more about a poem's meaning will help them to better understand poems they read.

Ready *Teacher Toolbox*

teacher-toolbox.com

	Prerequisite Skills	RL.7.5
Ready Lessons	✓	✓
Tools for Instruction		✓
Interactive Tutorials		✓

CCSS Focus

RL.7.5 Analyze how a … poem's form or structure (e.g. … sonnet) contributes to its meaning.

ADDITIONAL STANDARDS: RL.7.1, RL.7.2, RL.7.4, RL.7.7; L.7.1, L.7.4a, L.7.4c, L.7.5a; W.7.4, W.7.9a; SL.7.1, SL.7.4, SL.7.6 (*See page A39 for full text.*)

AT A GLANCE

Students analyze the internal structure of a poem and consider what that structure adds to the meaning. They learn that recognizing the connection between structure and meaning enhances a reader's experience.

STEP BY STEP

- Read aloud the definitions of *stanzas, free verse,* and *rhyme scheme.* Ask students to study the excerpt from "Song of the Old Mother." Discuss how the poem's regular patterns of rhythm and rhyme mean that it is not a free verse poem.

- Ask students to underline the two words that rhyme in lines 1 and 2 and draw a box around the two words that rhyme in lines 3 and 4. Then have them circle the verbs at the end of each line.

- Lead students through a discussion of the chart. Point out how the rhyme scheme groups the lines in pairs. Ask volunteers to explain how lines 1 and 2 center around one idea (*starting the fire*) and how lines 3 and 4 center around another idea (*chores that follow*). Also discuss how the repeated pattern of verb use adds to the meaning.

- Suggest that, when students read a poem, the first step is simply to read and experience it. Sometimes analyzing the poem's structure reinforces what they first thought about it. Other times, identifying a poem's structure can help them interpret the lines to gain a clearer understanding of their meanings.

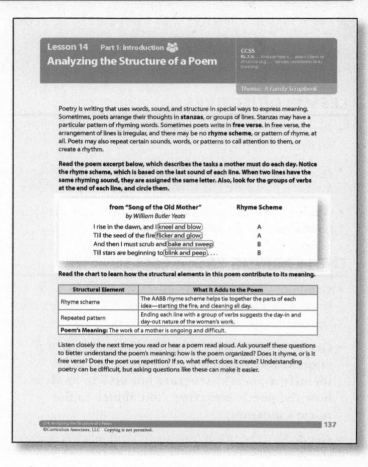

Genre Focus

Literary Texts: Sonnets

Tell students that in this lesson they will read lyric poems. Remind them that a lyric poem expresses the feelings of the speaker.

One type of lyric poem is called a sonnet. A sonnet is a lyric poem of 14 lines, written in iambic pentameter, a pattern of units of unstressed and stressed syllables.

Most sonnet forms follow a strict rhyme scheme. One of the most famous sonnet writers was William Shakespeare. The rhyme scheme of a Shakespearean sonnet is ABAB, CDCD, EFEF, GG. The final pair of rhyming lines in this type of sonnet is called a couplet. Perhaps Shakespeare's most famous sonnet is

"Shall I Compare Thee to a Summer's Day?" This sonnet ends with the following couplet:

> So long as men can breathe, or eyes can see,
> So long lives this, and this gives life to thee.

Tell students that another famous sonnet is Elizabeth Barrett Browning's "How Do I Love Thee?" Students will read this sonnet in this lesson.

At some point, if desired, discuss how the rhyme scheme of "How Do I Love Thee?" (ABBA, ABBA, CDC, DCD) differs from the typical Shakespearean sonnet (ABAB, CDCD, EFEF, GG).

Point out to students that all sonnets they read are lyric poems but not all lyric poems are sonnets.

AT A GLANCE

Students read a lyric poem, and then identify and analyze its structural elements.

STEP BY STEP

- Invite volunteers to tell what they learned on the previous page about identifying the rhyme scheme and repeated elements of a poem.

- Tell students that in this lesson they will practice identifying some structural elements of poems.

- Read aloud "A Barred Owl." Explain the meaning of the word *barred* if it is unfamiliar to students.

- Then read the question: "How does the structure of the poem contribute to its meaning?" Tell students that you will use a Think Aloud to demonstrate a way of answering the question.

Think Aloud: To answer the question, I'll focus on the stanzas, rhyme scheme, and repetition to determine how the structure reveals the poem's meaning. First, I'll number the stanzas and think about the meaning of each one. The first stanza tells what the parents say to their child. What is the central idea of the second stanza? How do the ideas differ?

- Direct students to the chart, and review how it helps them think about the poem's structural elements. Have students fill in the chart to describe what the stanzas add to the poem's meaning.

Think Aloud: The poem includes end rhymes: *boom* in line 1 and *room* in line 2 is the first pair. I know the poet chose a particular rhyme scheme for a reason, so I'll mark the rhyme scheme of the poem to help me think about how it affects the poem's meaning.

- Point out to students that, as stated in the chart, the AABB rhyme scheme is similar to a lullaby.

Think Aloud: Now I will look for words that are repeated in the poem. I remember that a poet might choose to repeat words to add emphasis to them.

- Have students underline examples of repetition. Then ask them to describe how this structural element adds to the poem's meaning. Have students write their ideas in the chart.

- Finally, have students complete their charts and discuss their answers with partners.

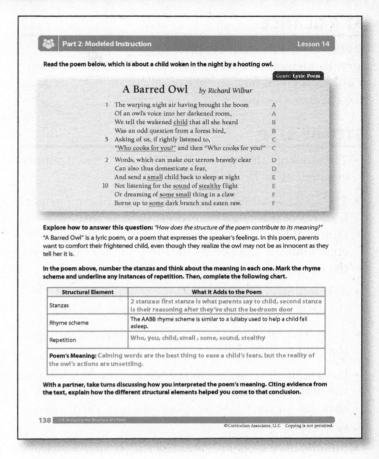

Tier Two Vocabulary: *Domesticate*

- Ask students to look at the word *domesticate* in line 8. Remind students that figuring out the part of speech of an unfamiliar word can help reveal its meaning. Sometimes a word's ending shows its function, but in this case the ending *-ate* appears in different parts of speech.

- Explain that when context clues and word parts do not reveal the meaning of an unfamiliar word, a dictionary or thesaurus can help. This strategy is particularly helpful when reading an unfamiliar word in a poem.

- Have partners use a thesaurus to identify a synonym for *domesticate*. (*tame, trained, cultivated*) Then have students name the synonym closest in meaning to *domesticate* as it is used in the poem. (*tame*) Discuss how a fear can be "tamed." **(RL.7.4; L.7.4c)**

AT A GLANCE

Students read the sonnet "How Do I Love Thee?" and identify elements of poetic structure. Then they answer a question about how the use of repetition helps express the speaker's feelings.

STEP BY STEP

- Tell students that they will read a well-known sonnet entitled "How Do I Love Thee?"

- The Close Reading helps students identify important features of the poem that reveal its structure. The Hint will help them analyze what that structure contributes to the poem's meaning in order to answer the question.

- Ask volunteers to share the repeated phrase and rhyme scheme, as directed by the Close Reading.

- Then have students respond to the question, using the Hint to help them.

- Have students respond to the Show Your Thinking at the bottom of the page. Remind them that the work they did for the Close Reading will help them answer this question.

- Finally, have students complete the partner activity. If they have trouble identifying the separate ideas in the poem, encourage pairs to "translate" each line into modern language.

ANSWER ANALYSIS

Sample response: The poet uses repetition to emphasize the ways in which the speaker expresses his or her love.

Sample response for Show Your Thinking: The poet repeats the phrase "I Love Thee" a total of nine times in the poem. By repeating this phrase so often and then describing specific ways, the poet helps readers understand the nature and extent of the speaker's love.

ERROR ALERT: Students who had difficulty explaining how the speaker's feelings are represented by the poem's repetition might be struggling with the abstract nature of poetry. Guide these students in forming a concrete understanding of the content and message of the poem first. Then discuss how the poet's choices in presenting the ideas also serve that content or message.

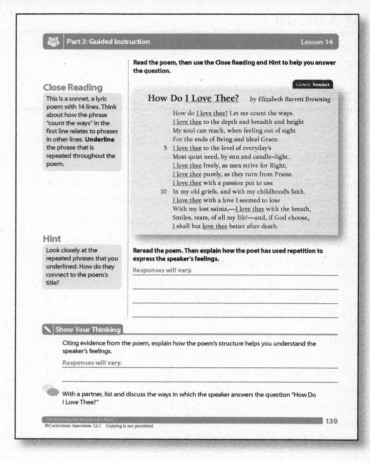

Tier Two Vocabulary: *Strive*

- Have students look at the word *strive* in line 7. Point out that line 7 has the same structure as line 8 below it. Suggest that the lines have the same parts of speech in the same places, only the words are different.

- Lead students in identifying some clues in line 8 that can help reveal the meaning of *strive* in line 7. Ask students how the prepositions *for* and *from* help suggest the meaning of *strive*. (*They suggest that men strive for something positive but turn from something negative.*)

- Have students determine the meaning of the word *strive* ("*reach for or make an effort to achieve*") and confirm it by using a dictionary. (***RL.7.4; L.7.4a***)

AT A GLANCE

Students read a poem twice about family photographs. After the first reading, you will ask three questions to check your students' comprehension of the poem.

STEP BY STEP

- Have students read the poem silently without referring to the Study Buddy or the Close Reading text.

- Ask the following questions to ensure students' comprehension of the text:

  Why does the speaker mention so many family members in this poem? (*The speaker sees these family members in the old family photos that he or she is viewing.*)

  Who was responsible for taking most of the "family photographs" and how do you know? (*The speaker's mother, or Mama, took the pictures. This detail is suggested by line 3, lines 14–15, and line 17.*)

  What does the speaker seem to like best about the family photographs? (*The speaker enjoys remembering the fun the family was having when each picture was snapped; he also sees the humor in his mother's inability to take good photos.*)

- Ask students to reread the poem and look at the Study Buddy think aloud. How does the Study Buddy help them think about the poem's meaning?

- Tell students to follow the directions in the Close Reading.

> **Tip:** Remind students that not all poems include rhyme. Point out that "Ode to Family Photographs" is a free-verse poem. (If necessary, reread the first paragraph on page 1 of this lesson, which explains free verse.) Point out its conversational nature, its lack of end rhyme, and the varying stanza lengths as elements of free verse.

- Ask students to think about other choices the poet made, such as the repetition of *This is...*, and to explain how the structural choices reveal more about the speaker's feelings and attitude toward his mother.

- Finally, have students answer the questions on page 141. Use the Answer Analysis to discuss correct and incorrect responses.

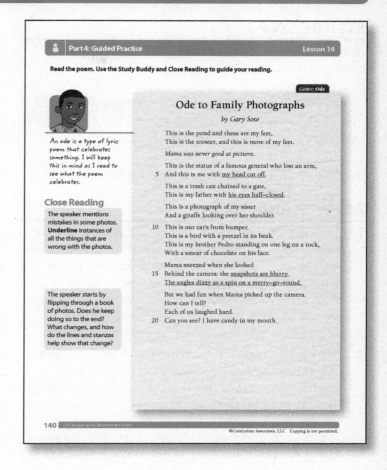

Read the poem. Use the Study Buddy and Close Reading to guide your reading.

Genre: Ode

Ode to Family Photographs
by Gary Soto

An ode is a type of lyric poem that celebrates something. I will keep this in mind as I read to see what the poem celebrates.

Close Reading

The speaker mentions mistakes in some photos. **Underline** instances of all the things that are wrong with the photos.

The speaker starts by flipping through a book of photos. Does he keep doing so to the end? What changes, and how do the lines and stanzas help show that change?

This is the pond and these are my feet,
This is the rooster, and this is more of my feet.

Mama was never good at pictures.

This is the statue of a famous general who lost an arm,
5   And this is me with my head cut off.

This is a trash can chained to a gate,
This is my father with his eyes half-closed.

This is a photograph of my sister
And a giraffe looking over her shoulder.

10 This is our car's front bumper.
This is a bird with a pretzel in its beak.
This is my brother Pedro standing on one leg on a rock,
With a smear of chocolate on his face.

Mama sneezed when she looked
15 Behind the camera: the snapshots are blurry,
The angles dizzy as a spin on a merry–go–round.

But we had fun when Mama picked up the camera.
How can I tell?
Each of us laughed hard.
20 Can you see? I have candy in my mouth.

140   L14: Analyzing the Structure of a Poem   ©Curriculum Associates, LLC   Copying is not permitted.

ELL Support: Possessives

- Tell students that possessives are words that show who or what owns something. Explain that adding an apostrophe and an -s makes most nouns possessive.

- Suggest that possessive pronouns are different because they are not formed by adding an apostrophe and an -s. Instead, the possessive forms of pronouns must be memorized: *my, your, our, his, her, its,* and *their*.

- Point out the possessive pronoun *my* in line 1. Ask students who *owns* the feet. (the speaker) **(L.7.1)**

- Challenge students to identify two more possessive pronouns in "Ode to Family Photographs." (*his, her*)

STEP BY STEP

- Have students read questions 1–3, using the Hints to help them answer those questions.

Tip: If students have trouble answering question 2, guide them to reread the final stanza. Have them describe the central idea of this stanza is.

- Discuss with students the Answer Analysis below.

ANSWER ANALYSIS

1 The correct choice is B. The lack of rhyme scheme helps show the fun, conversational tone. Choice A is incorrect. It is a detail in the poem that is not related to the overall structure. Choice C is incorrect. The speaker does not express anger toward Mama's photos. Choice D is incorrect because the poem does not have a rhyme scheme.

2 The correct choice is C. Words such as "fun" and "laughed" show the speaker likes his mother's photos. Choice A is incorrect. The speaker recalls Mama's poor picture-taking as part of the fun times. Choice B is incorrect. The last stanza doesn't suggest regret. Choice D is incorrect. The speaker's tone is positive; he is not upset in the last stanza.

3 Sample response: Repetition contributes to this poem's meaning. The poet repeats "This is" at the beginning most lines, suggesting what a person might say while flipping through photos. But then the speaker stops looking at photos and begins thinking about the person who took them—his mother. Suddenly he seems less hurried and more thoughtful. This switch from action to thought are reflected by the stanzas. Initially the stanzas are short, but they lengthen, as if the speaker, after a hurried beginning, ends up taking the time to linger over the memories those photos evoke.

RETEACHING

With students, fill in the chart to answer question 3.

Structural Element	What It Adds to the Poem
Repetition	sense of excitedly flipping through pictures
Stanzas	length going from short to long
Poem's Meaning: From excitement at seeing to thought.	

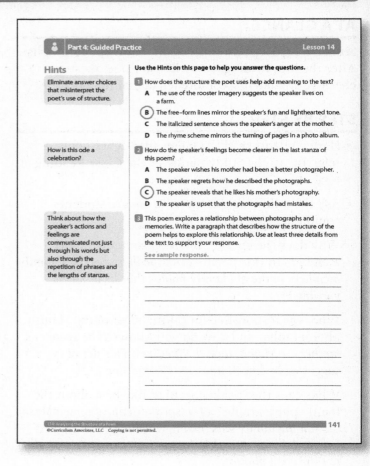

Integrating Standards

Use these questions to further students' understanding of "Ode to Family Photographs."

1 What does the speaker probably mean when he says that the photographs' angles are as "dizzy as a spin on a merry-go-round"? **(RL.7.4; L.7.5a)**

The speaker suggests that, unlike in normal photos, the angles from which the photos are shot make them difficult to identify and follow. The speaker wants readers to recall the feeling they have after a ride on a merry-go-round so they can understand what the photos look like.

2 How does the poet's choice of free verse reflect the theme or central idea of the poem? **(RL.7.2)**

By choosing a structure with few rules and expectations, the poet uses a style much like Mama's style of taking photographs. The poem collects the speaker's ideas freely and imperfectly, just as Mama's photos collect happy memories randomly and imperfectly.

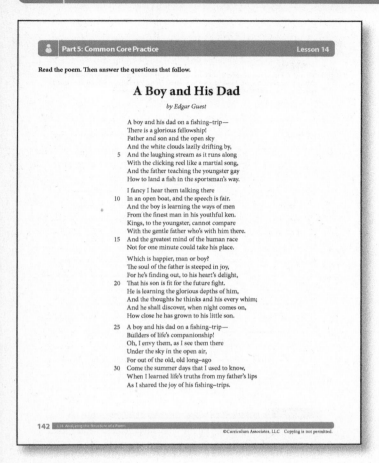

Read the poem. Then answer the questions that follow.

A Boy and His Dad

by Edgar Guest

A boy and his dad on a fishing–trip—
There is a glorious fellowship!
Father and son and the open sky
And the white clouds lazily drifting by,
5 And the laughing stream as it runs along
With the clicking reel like a martial song,
And the father teaching the youngster gay
How to land a fish in the sportsman's way.

I fancy I hear them talking there
10 In an open boat, and the speech is fair.
And the boy is learning the ways of men
From the finest man in his youthful ken.
Kings, to the youngster, cannot compare
With the gentle father who's with him there.
15 And the greatest mind of the human race
Not for one minute could take his place.

Which is happier, man or boy?
The soul of the father is steeped in joy,
For he's finding out, to his heart's delight,
20 That his son is fit for the future fight.
He is learning the glorious depths of him,
And the thoughts he thinks and his every whim;
And he shall discover, when night comes on,
How close he has grown to his little son.

25 A boy and his dad on a fishing–trip—
Builders of life's companionship!
Oh, I envy them, as I see them there
Under the sky in the open air,
For out of the old, old long–ago
30 Come the summer days that I used to know,
When I learned life's truths from my father's lips
As I shared the joy of his fishing–trips.

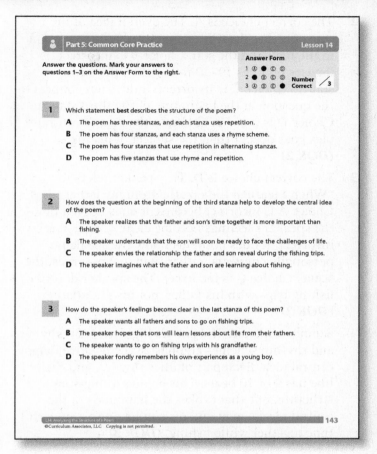

Answer the questions. Mark your answers to questions 1–3 on the Answer Form to the right.

Answer Form
1 Ⓐ ● Ⓒ Ⓓ
2 ● Ⓑ Ⓒ Ⓓ   Number Correct /3
3 Ⓐ Ⓑ Ⓒ ●

1 Which statement **best** describes the structure of the poem?

A The poem has three stanzas, and each stanza uses repetition.

B The poem has four stanzas, and each stanza uses a rhyme scheme.

C The poem has four stanzas that use repetition in alternating stanzas.

D The poem has five stanzas that use rhyme and repetition.

2 How does the question at the beginning of the third stanza help to develop the central idea of the poem?

A The speaker realizes that the father and son's time together is more important than fishing.

B The speaker understands that the son will soon be ready to face the challenges of life.

C The speaker envies the relationship the father and son reveal during the fishing trips.

D The speaker imagines what the father and son are learning about fishing.

3 How do the speaker's feelings become clear in the last stanza of this poem?

A The speaker wants all fathers and sons to go on fishing trips.

B The speaker hopes that sons will learn lessons about life from their fathers.

C The speaker wants to go on fishing trips with his grandfather.

D The speaker fondly remembers his own experiences as a young boy.

AT A GLANCE

Students independently read a longer poem and answer questions in a format that provides test practice.

STEP BY STEP

- Tell students to use what they have learned about reading closely and analyzing poetic structure to read the poem on page 142.

- Remind students to underline or circle important points, including those that reveal poetic structure, such as rhyme scheme and repetition.

- Tell students to answer the questions on pages 143 and 144. For questions 1–3, they should fill in the correct circle on the Answer Form.

- When students have finished, use the Answer Analysis to discuss correct responses and the reasons for them. Have students fill in the Number Correct on the Answer Form.

ANSWER ANALYSIS

1 The correct choice is B. The poem has four stanzas, and each stanza uses a rhyme scheme. Choice A is incorrect because the poem has four stanzas. Choice C is incorrect because all stanzas use repetition. Choice D is incorrect because the poem has four stanzas. **(DOK 2)**

Theme Connection

- How do all the poems in this lesson relate to the theme, *A Family Scrapbook*?

- Which poem do you connect with most? Why?

2 The correct choice is A. The overall idea of the stanza is that the time spent together is important to the man and the son. Choice B is incorrect. It focuses on lines 19–20 rather than the entire stanza. Choice C is incorrect. It does not connect to the question at the beginning of the third stanza. Choice D is incorrect because the poem's central idea goes deeper than the subject of fishing. **(DOK 2)**

3 The correct choice is D. The speaker refers to "When I learned life's truths from my father's lips." Choice A is incorrect because it does not tell how the speaker's feelings become clear. Choice B is incorrect. It does not reflect how the speaker personally connects, rather than just observes, the scene. Choice C is incorrect. The speaker describes fishing trips with his father, not his grandfather. **(DOK 2)**

4 Sample response: The poem's highly regular rhyme and rhythm schemes emphasize the positive, happy central idea. Each pair of lines rhymes, and each line has 9 or 10 beats. This creates a sing-song structure, one that evokes the happiness of the central idea: a man and his son having a wonderful time together while fishing. **(DOK 3)**

---

4 The central idea of this poem is that a man and his son happily bond while on a fishing trip. Write a paragraph that describes how the structure of the poem helps to express this central idea. Use at least **three** details from the text to support your response.

See sample response.

✓ **Self Check**   *Go back and see what you can check off on the Self Check on page 120.*

144   L14: Analyzing the Structure of a Poem   ©Curriculum Associates, LLC Copying is not permitted.

Integrating Standards

Use these questions and tasks as opportunities to interact with "A Boy and His Dad."

1 How would you describe the theme of "A Boy and His Dad"? **(RL.7.2)**

The theme of "A Boy and His Dad" might be described as "Both father and son discover new truths about life and each other through time spent together."

2 How would you describe the speaker of "A Boy and His Dad"? Use details from the poem to support your ideas. **(RL.7.1)**

The speaker of the poem is a keen observer of the world, as shown by the details included about the clouds and the stream in the first stanza. The speaker thinks very highly of his own father, as shown by the descriptions of what the young son thought about his father (lines 13–16). Because the speaker could not possibly know what the far-off boy thought about the father, readers can infer that those feelings reflect the speaker's feelings for his own father.

3 Write a paragraph to describe the similarities between the rhyming words in stanza 1 and those in stanza 4. What is the most likely reason for this similarity? **(W.7.9a)**

The rhyming pair fishing-trip *and* fellowship *are the first two rhymes in lines 1 and 2. The same word begins line 25, which is the first line of stanza 4. The same word,* fishing-trip, *also ends the final line of the poem, line 32. The poet repeats* fishing-trip *often to emphasize the importance of the father-son bonding that, in the poet's mind, has resulted.*

4 Discuss in small groups the question the speaker presents in line 17 of the poem: "Which is happier, man or boy?" What does this line mean? How do you think the poet would answer it? **(SL.7.1)**

Discussions will vary. Remind students that their interpretations should be supported by details from the text and that their opinions can be formed from details and their prior knowledge.

Writing Activities

Write a Sonnet (W.7.4)

- Have students reread the sonnet "How Do I Love Thee?" and remind them of the main features of a sonnet from the Genre Focus on page 128.

- Challenge students to write a sonnet to express their feelings about an important person in their lives. Students do not need to write in strict iambic pentameter, but encourage them to keep to the fourteen-line structure and to use a rhyme scheme of their choice.

- Tell students that their poems need not deal with serious ideas as some sonnets do. Remind them of the playful way the speaker of "Ode to Family Photographs" shares memories and a message about his mother.

Multiple-Meaning Words (L.7.4a)

- Write *fancy* on the board, and ask students to give a common meaning for it. (*"not plain"*) Direct students to line 9 of "A Boy and His Dad." Discuss how the familiar meaning of *fancy* does not match the way *fancy* is being used in this poem. Have students suggest the meaning of *fancy* in line 9. (*"imagine; daydream"*)

- Challenge students to find three other multiple-meaning words in "A Boy and His Dad" and to use each word in two sentences that show its different meanings. (*Examples:* open, fair, close)

LISTENING ACTIVITY (SL.7.1, SL.7.6)

Listen Closely/Make a Rhyme

- Have one student read aloud a line from one of the poems in the lesson while other students listen.

- When the student finishes reading, he or she chooses one student to make up a new line that rhymes with the line that was read aloud. Encourage playful creativity in the new lines, as long as they end with a rhyming word.

- Have students discuss how rhyme adds to the poem even if it creates nonsensical lines.

MEDIA ACTIVITY (RL.7.7)

Be Creative/Make a Digital Collage

- Challenge students to use the poems in this lesson as a starting point for making a collage that reflects their ideas about friends and family.

- If available, invite students to use photo-editing or presentation-creating programs to make their collages digitally.

- Have students discuss how ideas presented in multimedia are similar to and different from ideas presented in a poem.

DISCUSSION ACTIVITY (SL.7.1)

Talk in a Group/Discuss Poetry

- Have students think about the representation of family created by the poems in this lesson.

- Ask them to discuss the following questions: Which family relationships were discussed in the poems in this lesson? Which family relationships were not mentioned in these poems? Which poem made you think of your own family? Why?

- Allow 10 to 15 minutes for discussion. Then have groups share their results with the class.

RESEARCH ACTIVITY (W.7.7; SL.7.4)

Research and Present/Research a Poet

- Tell students that the author of the poem "A Barred Owl," Richard Wilbur, was once a Poet Laureate of the United States.

- Have students choose one U.S. Poet Laureate to research and prepare a report about.

- Ask them to include in their reports a brief explanation of what a Poet Laureate does in the United States, information about the poet's life, and at least one favorite poem to read aloud.

- Allow time for students to present to the class.

Analyzing the Structure of Drama

LESSON OBJECTIVES

- Develop an understanding of the structure and elements of drama, including acts, scenes, characterization, dialogue, and stage directions.

- Analyze the ways in which a drama's structure helps an author organize ideas and convey meaning.

THE LEARNING PROGRESSION

- **Grade 6:** CCSS RL.6.5 has students consider form as it pertains to prose texts as well as poetry or drama, allowing students to focus on how chapters, scenes, and so on contribute to theme, setting, and plot.

- **Grade 7: CCSS RL.7.5 emphasizes drama and poetry, having students consider how form impacts meaning in genres that use forms with which they might be less familiar.**

- **Grade 8:** CCSS RL.8.5 has students deepen their understanding of form and its impact by comparing texts and considering how form contributes to the meaning of each.

PREREQUISITE SKILLS

- Identify a text's setting, characters, plot, and theme.

- Recognize the general structure of a text.

- Explain how a particular act, scene, set of stage directions, or line of dialogue functions within a larger text.

- Describe how a particular act, scene, set of stage directions, or line of dialogue contributes to a text's setting, characters, plot, or theme.

TAP STUDENTS' PRIOR KNOWLEDGE

- Tell students that they will work on a lesson about analyzing the structure of drama. Explain that a drama, or play, has other story elements as well as characters, setting, and plot. Drama contains dialogue, or characters' spoken words, and stage directions, information about how characters speak or move and descriptions of setting. Dramas are divided into acts that are further divided into scenes.

- Display this sentence: *Mr. Davidson spoke out loudly at the meeting, voicing his concerns about the proposed sports stadium.*

- Ask students what character traits might describe Mr. Davidson. (*outspoken, confident, community-minded*)

- Display this dialogue: *Mr. Davidson (fervently): A stadium of this size will bring increased traffic to our neighborhood, negatively affecting our quality of life! Moderator: Your comments will be included in our community response, Mr. Davidson.*

- Have students identify the tone of voice used by Mr. Davidson (*fervently*) and words that show his level of concern (*negatively affecting our quality of life*).

- Discuss how stage directions, dialogue, and setting contribute to an understanding of events. Analyzing these elements of a play will help students picture the events being described.

Ready *Teacher Toolbox*	*teacher-toolbox.com*	
	Prerequisite Skills	*RL.7.5*
Ready Lessons	✓	✓
Tools for Instruction	✓	
Interactive Tutorials		✓

CCSS Focus

RL.7.5 Analyze how a drama's ... form or structure (e.g., soliloquy ...) contributes to its meaning.

ADDITIONAL STANDARDS: **RL.7.1, RL.7.2, RL.7.3, RL.7.4, RL.7.7, RL.7.9; L.7.1, L.7.1c, L.7.4a, L.7.4d; W.7.2, W.7.5, W.7.8, W.7.9a; SL.7.1, SL.7.5, SL.7.6** *(See page A39 for full text.)*

AT A GLANCE

By reading a scene in a play, students learn how stage directions and dialogue contribute to their understanding of characters, setting, and plot.

STEP BY STEP

- Read aloud the description of a drama's elements. Have students read the first scene from *The Diary of Anne Frank*, underlining details about setting and characters. Remind them that details can be found in both the stage directions and the dialogue.

- Explain that the chart shows details about the setting, characters, and plot in this scene.

- Read the first detail in the Setting column. Ask students to find this detail in the text. Discuss how the second detail is not stated directly but can be inferred from stage directions: *The rooms are dusty, the curtains in rags. Chairs and tables are overturned.*

- Read the details in the Characters column. Have students identify text they underlined that tells about these details. Then read the Plot details and have students identify "finding the glove makes Mr. Frank cry" as a stated detail, while "something tragic happened" is an inference. Have students share other details they underlined.

- Discuss how stage directions and dialogue help students understand the play as though they were watching it performed on stage.

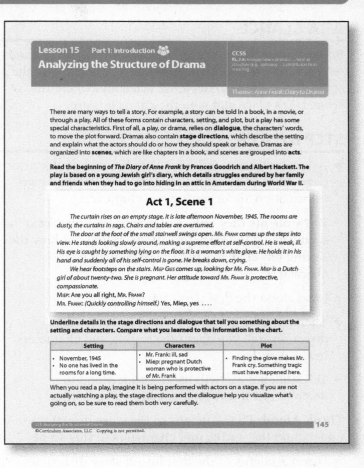

Genre Focus

Literary Texts: Drama

Tell students that in this lesson they will read a type of literature called drama. A drama, or play, is a story to be acted out on a stage. A drama has a script with dialogue and stage directions.

A drama's script tells each character, or actor, what to say. The dialogue is presented with the character's name followed by a colon. The text after the colon contains the words that the character speaks. A script may include a monologue, or a speech that one character says to other characters. Or it may include a soliloquy, which is a speech that a character directs to the audience that reveals the character's feelings.

Stage directions are often shown in a separate format, such as in an italicized font. The stage directions describe the setting and tell the actors how to speak, move, or behave on the stage.

Ask students to name dramas they have read. What were the plays about? What did they learn about the settings and characters from the dialogue and stage directions? Students may mention plays such as *Annie*.

Explain that in this lesson, students will read scenes from *The Diary of Anne Frank*, a drama based on real-life twentieth century events, which has multiple acts and scenes. The script provides the dialogue between the characters and stage directions, which describe setting, actions, and emotions.

AT A GLANCE

Students read Act 1, Scene 2 in *The Diary of Anne Frank,* which contains only stage directions. Students use the stage directions to understand when and where the scene takes place and who the characters are.

STEP BY STEP

- Ask volunteers to tell what they learned on the prior page about how stage directions and dialogue give information about setting and characters.

- Tell students they will read part of the play's next scene, using the stage directions to find out how the setting has changed and to learn about new characters.

- Read aloud the first part of Act 1, Scene 2.

- Then read the question: "What do these stage directions tell you about the setting and characters in the play?"

- Tell students you will use a Think Aloud to demonstrate a way of answering the question.

Think Aloud: I'll use details in the stage directions to understand the setting and characters in this scene.

- Direct students to the first line of stage directions.

Think Aloud: I see the date, July, 1942, in the first sentence of the stage directions. I know that World War II took place during that time period. I also see that the stage directions describe the rooms looking different than they did in the earlier scene. This is a clue that this scene took place after the first scene.

- Tell students to find details about the rooms in the stage directions. Have them add their descriptions to the chart.

Think Aloud: The characters in this scene are Mr. and Mrs. Van Daan and their son, Peter. The stage directions tell me that Mr. Van Daan is tall, portly, and nervous. I will reread the stage directions to look for descriptions of the other two characters.

- Have students find details about Mrs. Van Daan and Peter and write the descriptions in the chart.

- Finally, have partners compare and contrast their descriptions of setting and characters and explain any different interpretations they made. Invite volunteers to share their answers with the class.

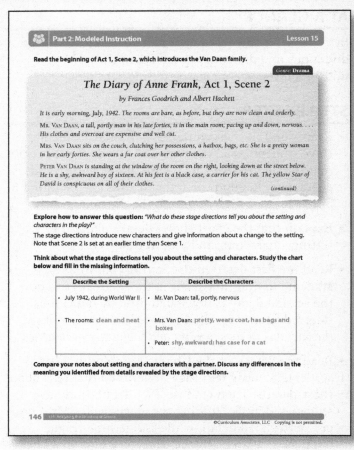

👥 Part 2: Modeled Instruction   Lesson 15

Read the beginning of Act 1, Scene 2, which introduces the Van Daan family.

Genre: Drama

The Diary of Anne Frank, Act 1, Scene 2
by Frances Goodrich and Albert Hackett

It is early morning, July, 1942. The rooms are bare, as before, but they are now clean and orderly.

Mr. Van Daan, a tall, portly man in his late forties, is in the main room, pacing up and down, nervous. . . . His clothes and overcoat are expensive and well cut.

Mrs. Van Daan sits on the couch, clutching her possessions, a hatbox, bags, etc. She is a pretty woman in her early forties. She wears a fur coat over her other clothes.

Peter Van Daan is standing at the window of the room on the right, looking down at the street below. He is a shy, awkward boy of sixteen. At his feet is a black case, a carrier for his cat. The yellow Star of David is conspicuous on all of their clothes.

(continued)

Explore how to answer this question: *"What do these stage directions tell you about the setting and characters in the play?"*

The stage directions introduce new characters and give information about a change to the setting. Note that Scene 2 is set at an earlier time than Scene 1.

Think about what the stage directions tell you about the setting and characters. Study the chart below and fill in the missing information.

Describe the Setting	Describe the Characters
• July 1942, during World War II	• Mr. Van Daan: tall, portly, nervous
• The rooms: clean and neat	• Mrs. Van Daan: pretty, wears coat, has bags and boxes
	• Peter: shy, awkward; has case for a cat

Compare your notes about setting and characters with a partner. Discuss any differences in the meaning you identified from details revealed by the stage directions.

146   L15: Analyzing the Structure of Drama   ©Curriculum Associates, LLC Copying is not permitted.

Tier Two
Vocabulary: *Conspicuous*

- Read the last sentence of the stage directions. Tell students that there may be context clues in nearby words and phrases that can help them figure out the meaning of *conspicuous.*

- Point out the phrases *yellow Star of David* and *on all of their clothes.* Ask what these phrases tell about the characters' clothing. (*Each person's clothing has a bright, obvious marking on it.*)

- Ask students what they think *conspicuous* means. (*prominent and easily seen*) Then have students confirm the meaning of *conspicuous* in a dictionary. **(RL.7.4; L.7.4a, L.7.4d)**

AT A GLANCE

Students continue reading Act 1, Scene 2. They answer a multiple-choice question and analyze the details that helped them select the correct answer.

STEP BY STEP

- Tell students they will continue reading Act 1, Scene 2 in *The Diary of Anne Frank.*

- The Close Reading focuses students' attention on plot details in the dialogue and stage directions. Point out that the stage directions reveal details about the characters' emotions. The Hint helps students identify details that indicate events might be out of the ordinary.

- Have students read the text and underline details that tell about events that are occurring, as directed by the Close Reading. Ask volunteers to share the details they underlined. If necessary, ask: "How do the stage directions help you know that the Van Daans are anxious or worried?"

- Have students respond to and discuss the Show Your Thinking. Choices C and D do not fit the details in the passage. Choice B tells about a character instead of a plot event.

ANSWER ANALYSIS

Choice A is correct. The scene describes Mrs. Van Daan's concern for Mr. Frank's family and Mr. Van Daan's reassurances to her. An accurate summary of this plot event is that people the Van Daans know may not be safe.

Choice B is incorrect. It describes Mrs. Van Daan's character but does not describe the plot.

Choice C is incorrect. The Van Daans are waiting for friends to arrive, but there is no mention of dinner.

Choice D is incorrect. No details in the text support the assertion that Mr. Frank called to say he would be late.

ERROR ALERT: Students who did not choose A might not have connected the stage directions to the characters' behavior. Tell students that they can ask themselves what the characters' problem is in this scene and how it is or is not resolved. This will help students identify the plot event.

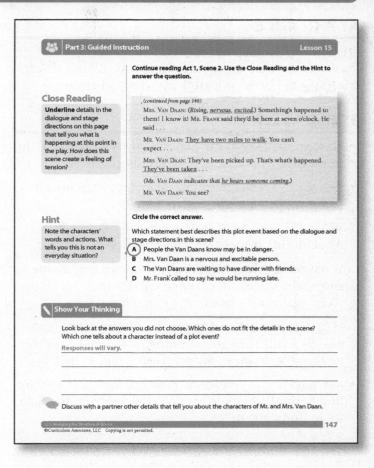

👥 Part 3: Guided Instruction   Lesson 15

Continue reading Act 1, Scene 2. Use the Close Reading and the Hint to answer the question.

Close Reading

Underline details in the dialogue and stage directions on this page that tell you what is happening at this point in the play. How does this scene create a feeling of tension?

(continued from page 146)

Mrs. Van Daan: (*Rising, nervous, excited.*) Something's happened to them! I know it! Mr. Frank said they'd be here at seven o'clock. He said . . .

Mr. Van Daan: They have two miles to walk. You can't expect . . .

Mrs. Van Daan: They've been picked up. That's what's happened. They've been taken . . .

(*Mr. Van Daan indicates that he hears someone coming.*)

Mr. Van Daan: You see?

Hint

Note the characters' words and actions. What tells you this is not an everyday situation?

Circle the correct answer.

Which statement best describes this plot event based on the dialogue and stage directions in this scene?

(A) People the Van Daans know may be in danger.

B Mrs. Van Daan is a nervous and excitable person.

C The Van Daans are waiting to have dinner with friends.

D Mr. Frank called to say he would be running late.

✏️ **Show Your Thinking**

Look back at the answers you did not choose. Which ones do not fit the details in the scene? Which one tells about a character instead of a plot event?

Responses will vary.

💬 Discuss with a partner other details that tell you about the characters of Mr. and Mrs. Van Daan.

L15: Analyzing the Structure of Drama
©Curriculum Associates, LLC Copying is not permitted.   147

ELL Support: Contractions

- Display the contraction *they'd.* Explain that this contraction is two words that have been joined together and shortened. Letters have been dropped, and an apostrophe has been put in place of the dropped letters.

- Identify the two words in the contraction *they'd* as the pronoun *they* and the helping verb *would.* Tell students the letters *w-o-u-l* in *would* have been dropped and an apostrophe has been inserted. Substitute *they would* in the sentence from the play: *Mr. Frank said they'd be here at seven o'clock.* Explain that the meaning remains the same.

- Repeat with other contractions that appear in the text: *something's, can't, they've, that's, what's.* **(L.7.1)**

AT A GLANCE

Students read another scene from *The Diary of Anne Frank* twice. After the first reading, you will ask three questions to check your students' comprehension.

STEP BY STEP

- Have students read the play silently without referring to the Study Buddy or Close Reading text.

- Ask the following questions to ensure students' comprehension of the text:

  What gift does Mr. Frank present to his daughter Anne in this scene? (*Mr. Frank gives Anne a diary.*)

  What reason does Mr. Frank give when explaining to Anne why she cannot ever go outside the door of the room again? (*Mr. Frank says that it is not safe.*)

  What activities does Mr. Frank tell Anne the family will do while they are in hiding? (*Mr. Frank says they will read books about history, poetry, and mythology.*)

- Ask students to reread the play and look at the Study Buddy think aloud. What does the Study Buddy help them think about?

> **Tip:** The Study Buddy reminds students that a character's actions are often a clue about that character. Review with students that they can learn more about a character through what he or she says and does and what others say about him or her.

- Have students answer the questions and follow the directions in the Close Reading.

> **Tip:** The Close Reading helps students connect the play's structure, including a character's spoken words in a monologue and stage directions about a character's actions and reactions, to the unfolding events in the plot. It guides students to recognize how the structure of a drama contributes to its meaning.

- Finally, have students answer the questions on page 149. Use the Answer Analysis to discuss correct and incorrect responses.

Tier Two
Vocabulary: *Advantages*

- Direct students to the word *advantages* in Mr. Frank's monologue. Have students read the sentence in which the word appears. Tell them that context clues in nearby words and phrases can help them figure out the meaning of *advantages*.

- Explain that sometimes they will need to read on to find helpful context clues. Ask students to consider the overall meaning of Mr. Frank's monologue that describes how being in hiding will affect Anne's activities. (*"never have to wear overshoes! Isn't that good? … You won't have to practice on the piano … this is going to be a fine life for you!"*)

- Ask students what *advantages* means. (*benefits, pluses*) (**RL.7.4; L.7.4a**)

STEP BY STEP

- Have students read questions 1–3, using the Hints to help them answer the questions.

Tip: If students have trouble answering question 3, remind them that they can look back at the stage directions describing how Mr. Frank behaves before his monologue and during his monologue.

- Discuss with students the Answer Analysis below.

ANSWER ANALYSIS

1   The correct choice is D. This stage direction shows Anne is no longer alarmed. Choices A, B, and C are incorrect. These stage directions come before Mr. Frank's speech, so they don't show Anne's reaction.

2   The correct choice is B. The stage directions tell that Anne throws her arms around her father, indicating their close relationship. Choice A inaccurately characterizes Anne's reaction to her father grabbing her arm as anger. Choice C is incorrect. Anne shows respect for her father when she replies, "I see." The text doesn't support Choice D, that Anne wishes to be treated as an adult.

3.   Sample response: Mr. Frank tries to comfort Anne by telling her that no one can lock up her mind and listing out the benefits of going into hiding, such as not having to practice the piano. He also puts his arm around her to help ease her panic. However, his earlier words and actions show that he is afraid for her, as seen in the stage direction "*(He goes after her, catching her by the arm and pulling her back).*" It is not safe for her ever to go beyond the door.

RETEACHING

Use a chart to answer question 3. Draw the chart below. Work with students to fill in the boxes. Sample responses are provided.

Character: Mr. Frank	Plot
Words: "no bolts, no locks that anyone can put on your mind"	Mr. Frank comforts his daughter.
Actions: pulls Anne back as she heads to the stairs Words: tells Anne she must never go beyond the door	Mr. Frank is afraid for his daughter.

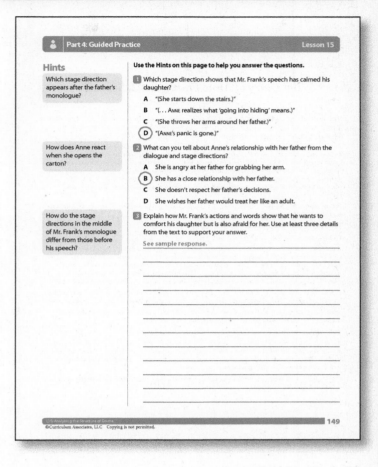

Hints

Which stage direction appears after the father's monologue?

How does Anne react when she opens the carton?

How do the stage directions in the middle of Mr. Frank's monologue differ from those before his speech?

Use the Hints on this page to help you answer the questions.

1. Which stage direction shows that Mr. Frank's speech has calmed his daughter?

   A   "(She starts down the stairs.)"

   B   "(. . . Anne realizes what 'going into hiding' means.)"

   C   "(She throws her arms around her father.)"

   D   "(Anne's panic is gone.)"

2. What can you tell about Anne's relationship with her father from the dialogue and stage directions?

   A   She is angry at her father for grabbing her arm.

   B   She has a close relationship with her father.

   C   She doesn't respect her father's decisions.

   D   She wishes her father would treat her like an adult.

3. Explain how Mr. Frank's actions and words show that he wants to comfort his daughter but is also afraid for her. Use at least three details from the text to support your answer.

See sample response.

Integrating Standards

Use these questions to further students' understanding of Act 1, Scene 2 from *The Diary of Anne Frank*.

1   What stage directions and dialogue show Anne's disbelief when her father tells her she can never go beyond the room's door? **(RL.7.1)**

"Anne: (Sobered.) "Never … ? Not even at nighttime, when everyone is gone? Or on Sundays? Can't I go down to listen to the radio?"

2   After Anne receives the diary from her father, why do you think her dialogue includes four repetitions of the word "pencil"? **(RL.7.4)**

Anne is excited about the diary. Repeating the word "pencil" over and over shows that she intends to write in the diary right away.

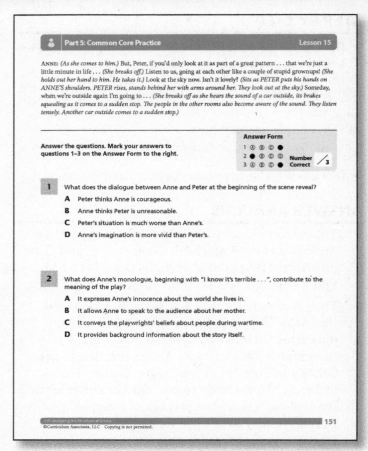

AT A GLANCE

Students independently read a longer scene from *The Diary of Anne Frank* and answer questions in a format that provides test practice.

STEP BY STEP

- Tell students to use what they have learned about analyzing how a drama's structure contributes to its meaning to read the play on pages 150 and 151.

- Remind students to underline or circle important points.

- Tell students to answer the questions on pages 151 and 152. For questions 1–3, they should fill in the correct circle on the Answer Form.

- When students have finished, use the Answer Analysis to discuss correct responses and the reasons for them. Have students fill in the Number Correct on the Answer Form.

ANSWER ANALYSIS

1 The correct answer is D. Anne "thinks herself out" when she can't stand being cooped up, showing she has a vivid imagination. Peter says he only gets madder when he thinks of being cooped up. Choice A is incorrect. Peter's dialogue doesn't suggest he thinks Anne is courageous. Choice B is incorrect. Anne tries to encourage Peter to feel as she does, but she does not think Peter is unreasonable. Choice C is incorrect. Peter's statement "if we don't get out of here" indicates that he and Anne are in the same situation. Peter's situation is not worse than Anne's. **(DOK 1)**

Theme Connection

- How do all the scenes in this lesson contribute to the theme of people enduring hardship?

- What is one fact or idea about enduring hardship that you learned from each of this lesson's scenes?

2 The correct answer is A. Anne's words show that she believes in the goodness of people. Choice B is incorrect. Anne mentions her relationship with her mother to show a parallel to phases that the world may be going through. Choice C is incorrect. Anne's monologue shows her beliefs, not the playwright's. Choice D is incorrect. The monologue does not provide background information about the story. **(DOK 2)**

3 The correct answer is D. The final stage directions tell that cars driving outside quickly stop, so the location of the hiding place may have been found out. Choice A is incorrect. If the war had ended, there would likely have been people celebrating in the streets, not just two cars stopping. Choice B is incorrect. The people in the attic listen tensely, not with relief. There are no indications of a bombing, so choice C is also incorrect. **(DOK 2)**

4 Sample response: Anne's statement that "people are really good at heart" shows the great difference between the girl's beliefs and the violence going on around her. This contrast creates irony. Anne is focusing on positive things like the beauty of nature, and she is trying to see the good in people. Yet all around her, people are being tortured and killed. **(DOK 3)**

>
> **3** What do the final stage directions **most likely** indicate about the setting of the play?
> A The war in Europe has suddenly ended.
> B The people in the attic have been rescued.
> C The house in Amsterdam has been bombed.
> D The hiding place in the attic has been discovered.
>
> **4** Write a paragraph explaining how Anne's statement that "people are really good at heart" creates irony in the scene. Use at least two details from the text to support your response.
> See sample response.
>
> _____
> _____
> _____
> _____
> _____
> _____
> _____
> _____
> _____
> _____
> _____
> _____
> _____
> _____
> _____
> _____
>
> ✓ **Self Check** *Go back and see what you can check off on the Self Check on page 120.*
> 152 L15: Analyzing the Structure of Drama
> ©Curriculum Associates, LLC Copying is not permitted.

Integrating Standards

Use these questions and tasks as opportunities to interact with Act 2, Scene 4 from *The Diary of Anne Frank*.

1 Cite two examples of evidence in the text that show how Anne's attitude toward the outdoor environment has changed. **(RL.7.1)**

Anne: "Aren't the clouds beautiful? … It's funny… I used to take it all for granted … and now I've gone crazy about everything to do with nature."

2 What does Anne mean when she uses the phrase "in spite of everything?" **(RL.7.4; L.7.4a)**

Anne means that she does not let her opinion of people's goodness be affected by the happenings occurring in the world around her.

3 How are Anne's and Peter's feelings shaped by this scene's setting? **(RL.7.3)**

The attic where they have been hiding has limited Anne's and Peter's experience of the world. Anne has overcome it through imagination, but Peter is bitter.

4 Summarize: Write a summary of the scene's events. **(RL.7.2; W.7.9a)**

Anne and Peter tire of hiding in the attic. Anne tells how she imagines being outdoors. Peter tells how he gets angry when he thinks about being cooped up. Anne tries to convince Peter that things will get better someday, but impatient Peter wants it to happen now. As Anne and Peter resolve their disagreement, cars suddenly arrive outside.

5 Discuss in small groups: How does the playwright contrast Anne's and Peter's points of view? Use evidence from the dialogue and stage directions in your response. **(SL.7.1)**

Discussions will vary. Students might mention stage directions indicating Anne's and Peter's different tones of voice, as well as their choice of words.

Writing Activities

Write an Explanatory Essay (W.7.2, W.7.5)

- Have students analyze how elements such as setting and dialogue create dramatic tension in Act 2, Scene 4.

- Have students write an explanatory essay in which they identify the particular elements used and elaborate on how the elements contribute to the plot. Students should include quotations and other details from the text to support their explanations.

- Have partners exchange essays and edit each other's work. Students then revise their essays.

Dangling Modifiers (L.7.1c)

- Display this sentence: "Peter stands at the window, looking at the street below." Explain that the phrase "looking at the street below" modifies the sentence's subject. Ask who the subject is. (*Peter*)

- Ask students why the same phrase is a dangling modifier in this sentence: *Looking at the street below, traffic moves slowly.* (*It doesn't modify the subject.*) Have students correct the sentence.

- Then have students write two sentences, one with a dangling modifier and one with the dangling modifier corrected. Have volunteers share their sentences with the class.

LISTENING ACTIVITY (SL.7.6)

Listen Closely/Performance Reading and Listening

- In small groups, have students do a performance reading and listening of Act 1, Scene 2.

- Ask groups to assign roles: Anne, Mr. Frank, listening audience members.

- Remind students to adapt their speech to read the dialogue as if they were performing, following stage directions for speaking but not movements.

- Have audience members listen carefully and give compliments and suggestions.

DISCUSSION ACTIVITY (SL.7.1)

Talk in a Group/Discuss a Lost Scene

- Have students work in small groups to come up with a short scene that has been lost from *The Diary of Anne Frank*.

- Students draw on the scenes in the lesson as a basis for creating characters' dialogue, plot events, and setting.

- Students express their ideas clearly, building on the ideas of others.

- Allow time for groups to discuss their scenes.

MEDIA ACTIVITY (RL.7.7)

Be Creative/Film vs. Written Word

- Have students watch selected scenes from the film version of *The Diary of Anne Frank*.

- Familiarize students with film techniques, such as sound, lighting, and camera focus and angle.

- Guide a class discussion to compare and contrast the film version of the drama with the written version. Have a volunteer create a chart on the board tracking similarities and differences.

RESEARCH ACTIVITY (RL.7.9; W.7.8, W.7.9; SL.7.5)

Research and Present/Produce a Podcast

- Have students produce a podcast comparing and contrasting events that occurred in WWII with the fictional portrayal of events, characters, or setting in *The Diary of Anne Frank*.

- Students research events, in print and online, using effective search terms and identifying reliable sources. Students might include audio recordings of dialogue from the play, as well as audio from actual newscasts.

- Students share their podcasts with the class.

Analyzing Point of View

LESSON OBJECTIVES

- Analyze the techniques the author uses to develop the characters' and narrator's points of view.
- Contrast the points of view of different story characters and the narrator(s).

THE LEARNING PROGRESSION

- **Grade 6:** CCSS RL.6.6 requires students to focus on explaining how an author develops a narrator's or speaker's point of view.

- **Grade 7: CCSS RL.7.6 builds on the Grade 6 standard by considering the author's development of and contrasts among character and narrator points of view.**

- **Grade 8:** CCSS RL.8.6 requires students to broaden the rhetorical context by considering contrasts between the characters' and the audience's or reader's points of view.

PREREQUISITE SKILLS

- Use text evidence to determine the points of view of characters.
- Trace the development of a narrator's point of view in a text.

TAP STUDENTS' PRIOR KNOWLEDGE

- Tell students that they will be working on a lesson about how an author develops and contrasts different points of view of the narrator and characters. Ask students to explain what a narrator's or character's point of view is (*his or her attitude or perspective about story events and characters*).

- Review that the narrator is the one who tells the story and may be an observer or a story character. Ask why it is important to understand who is telling the story. If necessary, use the example of a courtroom testimony where the victim is likely to have a different point of view from the accused. Students might be more suspicious when hearing the supposed good intentions of an accused person if they knew the accused was the one telling the story.

- Point out that, just as a victim or accused person carefully tells his or her point of view, authors carefully describe characters' points of view. Looking closely at text evidence related to a character will help students learn what that character's point of view is and better get to know that character's motivations and personality traits.

Ready *Teacher Toolbox*

teacher-toolbox.com

	Prerequisite Skills	RL.7.6
Ready Lessons	✓	✓
Tools for Instruction		✓
Interactive Tutorials		✓

CCSS Focus

RL.7.6 Analyze how an author develops and contrasts the point of view of different characters or narrators in a text.

ADDITIONAL STANDARDS: RL.7.1, RL.7.2, RL.7.3, RL.7.4, RL.7.5, RL.7.7; L.7.4a, L.7.4b, L.7.4d, L.7.5a; W.7.1, W.7.3, W.7.4, W.7.5; SL.7.1, SL.7.4, SL.7.5 (*See page A39 for full text.*)

Part 1: Introduction

Lesson 16

AT A GLANCE

Students contrast the points of view of characters in an illustration. They will examine the evidence in the picture to note how a story is told is affected by who tells it.

STEP BY STEP

- Read aloud the first paragraph. Explain that point of view can also be described as perspective. Point of view is revealed through a character's words, thoughts, feelings, and actions. Encourage students to look at the illustration on page 153. Have them identify the main characters in the scene and describe how the same event would seem different if it were told from each character's point of view.

- Tell students that the chart shows how to contrast different characters' points of view by examining evidence. Stress that who tells the story affects how the story is told.

- Ask students to share examples of when they read a story where two or more characters had different points of view about the same situation.

- To reiterate how contrasting different points of view is a valuable reading strategy, share your own example. Remind students that when an author is specific about choosing or describing points of view, he or she is able to advance the plot and help readers understand the characters' actions and motivations.

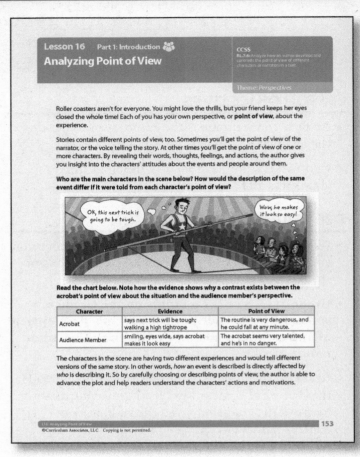

Genre Focus

Literary Texts: Allegories

Tell students that on page 156, they will read an allegory. Explain that an allegory is a work of fiction with two layers of meaning. One layer is literal, a simple story, while the other is abstract. An allegory usually features the following characteristics:

- Characters, setting, and other elements may represent abstract qualities.

- The purpose of the abstract layer is to convey truths, present criticisms, or teach life lessons.

- Sometimes an allegory is called an *extended metaphor*.

Have students share any allegories they have read or heard. You may also wish to share why you like a particular allegory yourself, such as *The Lord of the Rings* or the *Series of Unfortunate Events* books.

Explain that "The Stingy Artist" is an allegory. On the surface, it tells how a rich woman begrudgingly pays high fees for paintings by a seemingly greedy artist. However, the artist suffers this criticism for a worthy cause. In this instance, encourage students to discover the deeper meaning behind the artist's behavior.

Mention that "Places of Disinterest" is a realistic fiction story about a visit to an art museum and that the scene taken from *The Good Earth* comes from a classic novel.

AT A GLANCE

Students read a realistic fiction story about a trip to an art museum. They use text evidence to contrast the characters' points of view.

STEP BY STEP

- Invite volunteers to tell what they learned on the previous page about using evidence to contrast different points of view.

- Read aloud "Places of Disinterest."

- Then read the question: "How does the author contrast the points of view of the different characters?" Tell students you will use a Think Aloud to demonstrate a way of answering the question.

Think Aloud: I will reread the text to find evidence that tells about each character's point of view. In the first paragraph, I read that Blanca stared stonily out the car window, while Ramon beamed. What do these actions tell me about their feelings, or points of view, toward their museum trip?

- Direct students to the chart, and review how it helps to contrast the characters' points of view.

- Have students underline text evidence that suggests how Blanca feels and circle evidence that suggests how Ramon feels.

- Then point out the evidence in the chart about Blanca. Have students add evidence about Ramon.

Think Aloud: Now I can use what I learned about Blanca from her actions and dialogue in the text to decide how her interests and feelings affect her point of view about the family's outing to the museum.

- Have students fill in the Point of View column for Blanca in the chart.

- Discuss how the evidence they circled supports Ramon's point of view in the chart.

- Finally, have students respond to the question at the bottom of the page. Invite volunteers to share their responses with the class. (*Sample response: Ramon is interested in art and understands what the artists are trying to achieve. He enjoys his time at the museum much more than Blanca, who finds the museum boring.*)

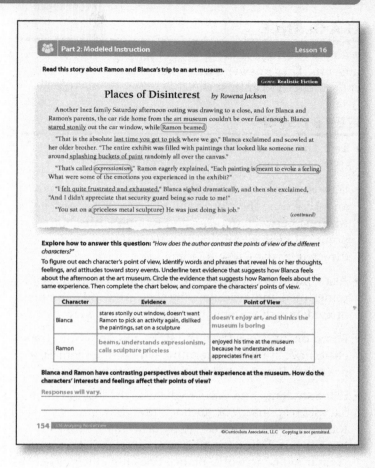

Tier Two Vocabulary: *Evoke*

- Direct students to the word *evoke* in paragraph 3. Ask them to identify context clues in the surrounding sentences that help them understand what *evoke* means. Remind them that context clues may appear in the same sentence as the unfamiliar word, or in sentences that come before or after the word. (*"a feeling," "emotions you experienced"*)

- Then have students explain what the word *evoke* means. (*"to bring to mind; to make aware of"*) Encourage them to use a dictionary to verify the meaning. **(RL.7.4; L.7.4a, L.7.4d)**

AT A GLANCE

Students continue reading about the visit to the art museum. They answer a multiple-choice question and cite evidence to contrast the characters' points of view.

STEP BY STEP

- Tell students that they will continue reading about the visit to the art museum.

- Have students read the rest of the passage and find and underline the words and phrases that show the contrast between Blanca's and Ramon's different points of view about the still-life paintings, as directed by the Close Reading.

- Ask volunteers to share the words and phrases they underlined and describe why they are good examples of evidence showing contrast in points of view.

- Based on evidence from the story and help from the Hint, have students determine which statement best describes Ramon's point of view about his sister.

- Place students into pairs to discuss the last question. Sample response: The author shows how much Ramon enjoys the museum by describing him as beaming and showing that he understands the "remarkable" artwork. Blanca does not enjoy either the art or the museum. She is angry and says her favorite part is the gift shop.

ANSWER ANALYSIS

Choice A is incorrect. Ramon does ask if Blanca noticed certain details, but he does not suggest he thinks his sister could be a painter.

Choice B is incorrect. Ramon does not push his sister to admit the art is valuable.

Choice C is correct. Ramon tries to point out ways his sister can notice and appreciate details in the artwork.

Choice D is incorrect. Ramon's questions suggest he has hope his sister will appreciate art, not that he is unsure.

> **ERROR ALERT:** Students who did not choose C may not have read the story carefully. Have them review the evidence that points to Ramon's point of view. Guide them to eliminate each incorrect choice because it is not supported by text evidence.

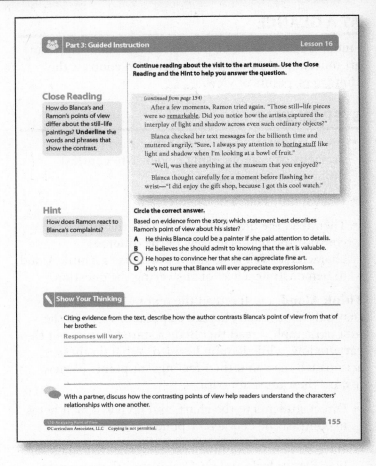

Tier Two
Vocabulary: *Remarkable*

- Direct students to the word *remarkable* in paragraph 1. Have them tell what the word means (*"worthy of attention"*) and identify context clues that help them to determine this meaning (*"captured the interplay of light and shadow"*). **(RL.7.4; L.7.4a)**

- To help students better understand the term, have them identify synonyms that have nearly the same meaning as *remarkable* and would fit in this context (*extraordinary, outstanding,* or *striking*).

AT A GLANCE

Students read a retelling of an ancient Zen tale. After the first reading, you will ask three questions to check your students' comprehension of the passage.

STEP BY STEP

- Have students read the passage silently without referring to the Study Buddy or Close Reading text.

- Ask the following questions to ensure students' comprehension of the text:

  What is the main plot in this story? (*Sakura asks Gessen to make her a painting, and Gessen and Sakura settle on a high fee. The painting is revealed at a dinner, where Sakura expresses her disdain about Gessen's greed. Unbeknownst to her, Gessen has been charging high fees to help poor villagers, and the reader learns that Sakura is the person who should be scorned.)*

  Why do the noblewoman and her guests scorn Gessen? (*They view him as shamelessly greedy.*)

  What did Gessen do with his earnings? (*He used all the money to help the people of his village who were suffering from famine. Once their needs were met, he never charged for a painting again.*)

- Ask students to reread the passage and look at the Study Buddy think aloud. What does the Study Buddy help them think about?

Tip: The Study Buddy reminds students that the dialogue between characters often reveals their points of view. Point out that students can better understand each character's perspective by the way he or she talks to and responds to other characters.

- Have students answer the questions and follow the directions in the Close Reading.

Tip: The Close Reading guides students to pay attention to the characters' feelings and motivations. Point out that when trying to understand a character's motivations, it is helpful to analyze the character's words and actions.

- Finally, have students answer the questions on page 157. Use the Answer Analysis to discuss correct and incorrect responses.

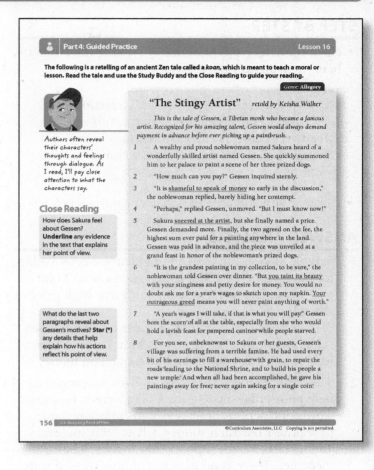

ELL Support: Prefixes

- Explain that many English words have prefixes. A prefix is a group of letters added to the beginning of a word to change its meaning.

- Direct students to the word *unveiled* in paragraph 5. Write the word on the board. Ask students to identify the prefix (*un-*) and the base word (*veil*). Explain that the prefix *un-* means "the opposite of." Tell students that adding the prefix *un-* to *veiled* has changed the meaning to "the opposite of veiled," or *uncovered*.

- Then ask students to determine the meaning of *unmoved* using what they have learned about the prefix *un-* ("*the opposite of moved or impressed*"). **(RL.7.4; L.7.4b)**

STEP BY STEP

- Have students read questions 1–3, using the Hints to help them answer those questions.

Tip: If students are struggling with question 2, direct them to find evidence in the text to support each answer choice. If they cannot find any evidence, then they can most likely eliminate that answer choice.

- Discuss with students the Answer Analysis below.

ANSWER ANALYSIS

1 Sample answer for Gessen—Evidence: keeps asking for money, spends money for a good cause; Point of View: does not feel it's wrong to charge high prices when it goes to a good cause
Sample answer for Sakura—Evidence: says Gessen is shameful, sneers and scorns him; Point of View: feels that it's shameful to be so fixated on money

2 The correct choice is D. Gessen uses his money to help poor villagers. Choice A is incorrect. Gessen's words and actions don't reveal his opinion about how others use their money. Choice B is incorrect. Text details do not support this answer. Choice C is incorrect. There is no mention of how Gessen feels about beauty in the text.

3 Sample response: Gessen and Sakura have very different points of view about the painter and his fees. Sakura believes it is shameful for him to bring up money, and she says that he is greedy. Gessen does not feel shame in charging so much to rich people. He suffers through their scorn because he knows the money is being spent to improve the lives of the poor villagers.

RETEACHING

Use a chart to verify the correct answer to question 2. Draw the chart below, and work with students to fill in the boxes. Sample responses are provided.

Character	Evidence	Point of View
Gessen	"used every bit of his earnings to fill a warehouse with grain, to repair the roads…"	feels money should be used to help others, not wasted

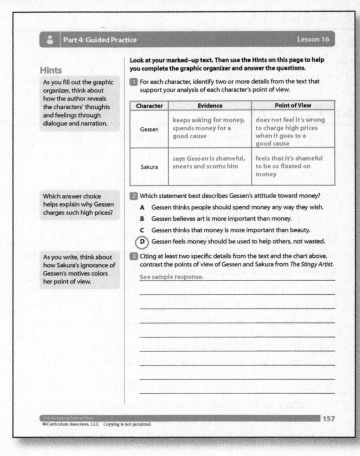

Integrating Standards

Use these questions to further students' understanding of "The Stingy Artist."

1 Analyze how Gessen's interactions with Sakura influenced events that took place in his village. *(RL.7.3)*

Because Gessen demanded a high price for his work, he and Sakura agreed upon "the highest sum ever paid for a painting." As a result, Gessen was able to use the payment to help the poor villagers who were starving.

2 Why do you think the author waits until the end of the allegory to tell readers that the artist used his profits to help people? *(RL.7.5)*

Sample response: Readers are intrigued that a monk is behaving so greedily, and suspense is built. Then, upon learning of the artist's secretive generosity at the end, readers are apt to reread the story to reevaluate the artist's character and derive new meaning from the whole story.

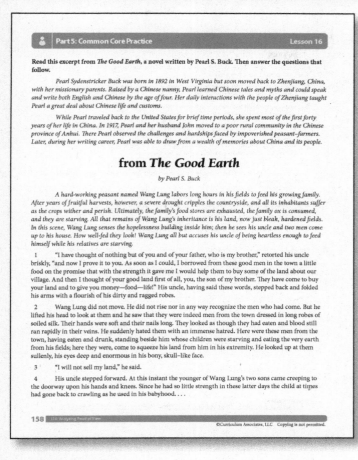

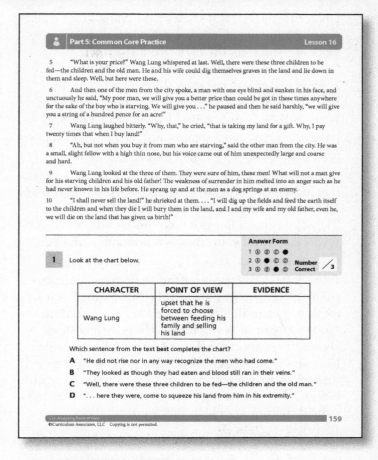

AT A GLANCE

Students independently read a longer passage and answer questions in a format that provides test practice.

STEP BY STEP

- Tell students to use what they have learned about reading closely and about using evidence to determine point of view to read the passage on pages 158 and 159.

- Remind students to underline or circle important points.

- Tell students to answer the questions on pages 159 and 160. For questions 1–3, they should fill in the correct circle on the Answer Form.

- When students have finished, use Answer Analysis to discuss correct responses and the reasons for them. Have students fill in the Number Correct on the Answer Form.

ANSWER ANALYSIS

1 Choice D is correct. It describes how Wang Lung feels about the men who are putting him in an awful position. Choice A is incorrect. It shows that Wang Lung doesn't know why the men have come, not that he is upset. Choice B tells that the men are well fed, not that they have come to ask Lung to sell his land. Choice C provides evidence of Lung's resignation as opposed to him being upset. **(DOK 2)**

Theme Connection

- How do all the passages in this lesson relate to the theme of new perspectives?

- How does each author use the perspective of the different characters to create drama and suspense?

2   Choice B is correct. It shows that Wang Lung feels taken advantage of. Choice A is incorrect. No evidence suggests the men think the uncle has Lung's interest at heart. Choice C is incorrect. No evidence suggests the men think Lung is easily fooled. Choice D is incorrect. The men don't treat Lung as if he is uncertain or indecisive. **(DOK 2)**

3   Choice C is correct. By not selling his land, Lung reveals how deeply he cherishes it. Choice A is incorrect. The uncle is selling out the family. Choice B is incorrect. Being dressed in robes is a reflection of Chinese clothing, not values. Choice D is incorrect. The offer is not a fair price, so this detail doesn't reveal a cultural value, nor is it honorable. **(DOK 3)**

4   Sample response: Wang Lung's responses reflect Pearl S. Buck's respect for the challenges faced by peasant-farmers in poor rural communities. Buck's experiences influence the story and are apparent in her treatment of Wang Lung's desperation. Buck shows her respect for Wang Lung as she describes his pain: "The weakness of surrender in him melted into an anger such as he had never known in his life before." She also recognizes how deeply the farmers valued their land, which they depended upon for their lives. **(DOK 3)**

Integrating Standards

Use these questions and tasks as opportunities to interact with the excerpt from *The Good Earth*.

1   How does the setting of this story affect the plot? **(RI.7.3)**

Because this story is set in rural China about 100 years ago, no public aid was available to help Wang Lung during the drought. As a result, the scene was set for people seeking to take advantage of the poor farmers. The plot develops around the city men's efforts to buy the farmland belonging to Wang Lung.

2   In paragraph 3 and in the final paragraph, the author chose to have Wang Lung say that he will not sell his land. Explain how these words have a greater impact by being repeated. **(RL.7.4)**

The author likely chose to use similar words in the beginning and at the end of the interaction to show how Wang Lung's feelings build and intensify. In the second instance, Lung shrieks the words and then continues to explain how he would rather starve than practically give away his land to such men.

3   Summarize: Write a brief summary of the passage. **(RL.7.2; W.7.4)**

Summaries may vary. Students should include that during a drought, Wang Lung and his family are starving. Men from the city come to offer to buy Wang Lung's land for an incredibly low price. Wang Lung refuses their offer, choosing to let his family starve rather than to sell it to them for such an unreasonable price.

4   Discuss in small groups: What inferences can you make about the characters in this story and their values? Use evidence to support your answers. **(SL.7.1)**

Discussions will vary. Encourage students to use evidence from the text to support their inferences and encourage students to pose relevant extension questions.

Writing Activities

Uncle's Point of View *(W.7.3, W.7.5)*

- Have students rewrite the scene from *The Good Earth* from the uncle's point of view. Encourage students to carefully consider how the narration might exclude or change some key details, while the dialogue would remain the same. Ask students to include clues about the uncle's thoughts, feelings, and motivations.

- Allow time for students to exchange their stories with a partner for discussion and peer evaluation.

Figurative Language *(L.7.5a)*

- Have students examine the following phrase from paragraph 7 of *The Good Earth*: "that is taking my land for a gift."

- Review with students that figurative language is the use of words in a way that is different from the literal meanings of the individual words. Ask students to explain what this example of figurative language means. (*Wang Lung compares the deal the men offer him to his giving them a gift. They are offering such as small amount of money that it seems to Lung as if he would be giving his precious land to them for free.*)

- Encourage students to identify and explain other examples of figurative language in this lesson's passages.

DISCUSSION ACTIVITY *(SL.7.1)*

Talk in a Group/Discuss Culture in Literature

- Have students read two or more fiction stories or novels by authors of diverse world cultures, such as *The Ink-Keeper's Apprentice, The Absolutely True Diary of a Part-Time Indian,* or *Esperanza Rising.*

- Remind students of how Pearl S. Buck drew from her experiences in China when she wrote *The Good Earth.* Then make available information about the cultural background of each author, especially details that are reflected in the story itself, such as relevant customs, values, and perspectives.

- Have small groups of students work to analyze how the culture of one author is reflected in his or her work. Ask them to determine how the author's cultural perspective influences story details. Ask: How do the setting and plot reflect the author's background? How does the author's perspective shape the different characters' points of view? Why? Have groups cite evidence to support their responses.

MEDIA ACTIVITY *(RL.7.7)*

Be Creative/Make a Venn Diagram

- Have students view the same scene they read in class from the 1937 film *The Good Earth.*

- After viewing the film's scene, have students complete a Venn Diagram that compares and contrasts the original book with the film version.

- In small groups, have students share their responses about the experiences of viewing a story and reading a story.

RESEARCH ACTIVITY *(W.7.1; SL.7.5)*

Research and Present/Present an Opinion

- Have students decide whether or not they think Wang Lung made the right decision by refusing to sell his land.

- Students must support their opinion with clear reasons and relevant evidence, and then present their opinion to the class along with multimedia components or another visual display to support their points.

- Have students write an argumentative essay to accompany their presentations.

SCORING GUIDE AND ANSWER ANALYSIS

Literature Passage Answer Analysis

1 Ⓐ Ⓑ ● Ⓓ   4A Ⓐ Ⓑ ● Ⓓ
2 ● Ⓑ Ⓒ Ⓓ   4B ● Ⓑ Ⓒ Ⓓ
3 Ⓐ Ⓑ ● Ⓓ   5 Ⓐ Ⓑ Ⓒ ●

1 Choice C is correct. The speaker describes how the flake of snow thinks ("Debates if it will go").

Choice A is incorrect. The speaker is not explaining or comparing sounds. Choice B is incorrect. The speaker does not use exaggeration to describe the way the flake of snow travels. Choice D is also incorrect. The speaker does not compare the flake of snow to the sky and clouds. (*RL.7.4; DOK 3*)

2 Choice A is correct. The word "debate" suggests trying to decide between two different positions; it makes the snowflake seem uncertain and hesitant.

Choice B is incorrect. The word "debate" makes the snowflake seem uncertain but not angry. Choice C is incorrect. While the word "debate" can sometimes mean a discussion between two people, in this case the snowflake is having a debate with itself; it is uncertain about which way to go. Choice D is also incorrect. The word "debate" does not suggest that the snowflake is playing with someone but that the snowflake is uncertain about which way to travel. (*RL.7.4; DOK 2*)

3 Choice C is correct. The use of rhyme creates a lilting, musical effect in the poem, like the lyrics of a song.

Choice A is incorrect. Although a poem will often convey emotions, the use of rhyme in this poem creates a musical effect. Choice B is incorrect. The effect of the rhyme scheme is not monotony, but music. Choice D is also incorrect. The rhyme creates a songlike or musical quality, and does not sound like a conversation. (*RL.7.4; DOK 3*)

4 **Part A:** Choice C is correct. Thomas has "always wanted to live in the city." Choice A is incorrect because it is Alec who questions Thomas's eagerness. Choices B and D also seem to describe Alec rather than Thomas. (*RL.7.6; DOK 3*)

Part B: Choice A is correct. It shows that Thomas is eager to move for a variety of reasons. Choice B shows Thomas's happiness, but it does not reflect directly on his feelings about the city. Choice C is said by Alec. Choice D only shows Thomas's skills as a salesman. (*RL.7.6; DOK 3*)

5 The correct choice is D. This sentence shows how the speaker has broadened her focus from the bleak winter sky to all of nature and humanity.

Choice A is incorrect. This phrase is part of the same idea presented in stanza 1—a bleak winter sky. Choice B is incorrect. This phrase completes the image of a bleak winter sky. Choice C is incorrect. Although this phrase adds something new to the bleak winter image—the wind—it does not signal a shift in the focus of the poem. (*RL.7.5; DOK 2*)

SAMPLE RESPONSES

Short Response

6 The poem's simple, sparse structure echoes the sparseness in the bleak winter day. The poem is very simple with only two stanzas. The first and third lines have eight beats; the second and fourth lines have six beats and rhyme with each other. This lean structure emphasizes the colorlessness of the winter day. *(RL.7.5; DOK 3)*

7 By using the word "diadem," or crown, the speaker shows that nature is grand or "royal." However, on days that are stormy or unpleasant, the grandness and beauty of nature are not apparent. Although the sky on this particular day is "low" and "mean" with a wind that "complains all day," the poet forgives Nature because it has off days, just as people do. *(RL.7.4; DOK 2)*

8 The author's use of dialogue reveals that the brothers have very different points of view. Tom sounds like a salesman when he talks to Alec and the children who come to the yard sale. He just wants to get rid of stuff and move away. He even tries to "sell" Alec on the great things about moving to the city. Alec's dialogue reveals that he cares about the little neighbor girl who asks about the bikes. When he says "miles of museums in the city," we see that he is unhappy about moving away. *(RL.7.5, RL.7.6; DOK 3)*

9 The setting of a yard sale in front of Tom and Alec's old home reveals the contrast between their feelings about moving. Tom reacts with boredom to the setting of the yard at the end of a dead-end street. He is tired of the quiet setting and eager to move to the city, which is "much more exciting." Alec reacts to the rock garden and swing set with fondness for both the place and the memories it evokes. He "doesn't know what it will be like to not live here anymore" and feels sad. The brothers react differently to the setting, revealing their opposing feelings about moving. *(RL.7.5, RL.7.6; DOK 3)*

Performance Task

10 Alec's monologue contributes to the meaning of the play because it reveals things that Alec would not say to Tom. In the monologue, Alec talks about the experiences and things that make his childhood home precious to him. These memories show that Alec has grown up in this place and that he connects strongly to it.

The details about designing and making the rock garden show that Alec prefers nature over a city environment. We realize that it will be hard for him to get used to living in an apartment. The grass and flowers of his yard and the quiet of the lane mean a lot to him.

People and family history are also important to Alec, which we find out in the monologue. He met his friend Janine in this yard, and this is clearly an important relationship for Alec. He recalls the fun he had camping with Tom and how Dad intervened in a scary situation. Through this speech, we find out that Alec is very sensitive to people and surroundings, which helps us understand why it will be hard for him to move away. *(RL.7.5, RL.7.6; DOK 3)*

SCORING RUBRICS

Short-Response Rubric

2 points   The response is accurate, complete, and fulfills all requirements of the task. Text-based support and examples are included. Any information that goes beyond the text is relevant to the task.

1 point   The response is partially accurate and fulfills some requirements of the task. Some information may be inaccurate, too general, or confused. Support and examples may be insufficient or not text-based.

0 points   The response is inaccurate, poorly organized, or does not respond to the task.

Performance Task Rubric

4 points   The response
- Fulfills all requirements of the task
- Uses varied sentence types and some sophisticated vocabulary
- Includes relevant and accurate details from the texts as well as text-based inferences
- Demonstrates a thorough understanding of the texts
- Maintains a clear focus and organization
- Is fluent and demonstrates a clear voice
- Uses correct spelling, grammar, capitalization, and punctuation

3 points   The response
- Fulfills all requirements of the task
- Uses simple sentences and grade-level vocabulary
- Includes relevant and accurate details from the texts
- Demonstrates a mainly literal understanding of the texts
- Maintains a mostly clear focus and organization
- Is fluent and demonstrates some sense of voice
- Uses mostly correct spelling, grammar, capitalization, and punctuation

2 points   The response
- Fulfills some requirements of the task
- Uses simple sentences, some fragments, and grade-level vocabulary
- Includes some relevant and accurate details from the texts
- Demonstrates some misunderstandings or gaps in understanding of the texts
- Attempts to maintain a clear focus and organization
- Is difficult to read, includes some inaccuracies, and demonstrates little or no sense of voice
- Contains some inaccurate spelling, grammar, capitalization, and punctuation that may hinder understanding

1 point   The response
- Fulfills few requirements of the task
- Uses sentence fragments and below-grade-level vocabulary
- Includes no details or irrelevant details to support the response
- Demonstrates very little understanding of the texts
- Does not establish a clear focus or organization
- Is difficult to read, contains many inaccuracies, and demonstrates no sense of voice
- Uses incorrect spelling, grammar, capitalization, and punctuation to an extent that impedes understanding

0 points   The response is irrelevant, poorly organized, or illegible.

Evaluating an Argument

Theme: *Energy and Our Future*

LESSON OBJECTIVES

- Evaluate the effectiveness of an argument by determining whether its claims are supported by relevant and sufficient evidence.

- Assess whether the author uses sound reasoning in making a claim.

THE LEARNING PROGRESSION

- **Grade 6:** CCSS RI.6.8 requires students to evaluate an argument by determining whether claims are supported with text evidence.

- **Grade 7: CCSS RI.7.8 builds on the Grade 6 standard by requiring students to consider whether the author uses sound reasoning to further the argument and to examine whether the evidence is relevant and sufficient.**

- **Grade 8:** CCSS RI.8.8 builds on the Grade 7 standard by focusing on the idea of evaluating the author's effectiveness in supporting claims by recognizing both relevant and irrelevant evidence within a text.

PREREQUISITE SKILLS

- Identify an author's argument.

- Understand that supporting evidence may include reasons, facts, and examples.

- Trace an author's argument by recognizing how specific claims contribute to the whole.

TAP STUDENTS' PRIOR KNOWLEDGE

- Tell students that they will work on a lesson about evaluating an argument in a text. Ask students what an argument in a text is. (*an opinion that the author wants readers to agree with*) Tell students that authors try to convince readers to agree with their stance by giving specific reasons, or claims, about why they believe their argument is correct or true. To show why each claim is valid, authors explain each claim in more detail by providing evidence, or proof, which includes reasons, facts, and examples.

- It is up to the readers to evaluate an argument. Ask students what *evaluate* means. (*judge whether or not the claims and evidence have a sound basis in logic and work together to create a strong argument*)

- Ask students how they decide if a particular movie, band, song, or video game is a good one. (*It captures your attention; it is about something you can relate to.*) Write several of their criteria on the board. Then explain that students have engaged in evaluating it. Tell them they can use the same process to evaluate what they read.

- Tell students that evaluating the arguments in the texts they read will help them to judge the merits of the author's stance as well as to develop their own opinions about a topic.

Ready *Teacher Toolbox*   teacher-toolbox.com

	Prerequisite Skills	*RI.7.8*
Ready Lessons	✓	✓
Tools for Instruction	✓	✓
Interactive Tutorials	✓	✓

CCSS Focus

RI.7.8 Trace and evaluate the argument and specific claims in a text, assessing whether the reasoning is sound and the evidence is relevant and sufficient to support the claims.

ADDITIONAL STANDARDS: **RI.7.1, RI.7.2, RI.7.4, RI.7.6, RI.7.7; L.7.4a, L.7.4c, L.7.4d, L.7.5b; W.7.1, W.7.4, W.7.5; SL.7.1, SL.7.2**
(*See page A39 for full text.*)

AT A GLANCE

By reading a paragraph on solar-powered cars, students analyze how an author constructs an argument. They learn that identifying claims and evidence will help them judge whether the argument is valid.

STEP BY STEP

- Read the first paragraph that includes the definitions of *argument, claims,* and *evidence.* Have students read the argument about solar-powered cars. Have them circle the claim, underline evidence, and cross out extra information that does not support the claim.

- Explain that the chart shows how the author has constructed the argument. Read the claim in the chart, and have students compare it to the text they circled. Discuss how students can tell that this is a statement the author believes to be true. Then read the three pieces of evidence in the chart, and have students compare them to the text they underlined. Discuss how each piece of evidence relates to the claim. Finally, have volunteers identify the information they crossed out and explain why it does not support the claim. (*The color of a car may be important to consumers, but it does not relate to the claim that research money should be used to develop affordable solar-powered cars.*)

- Have students give real-life examples of when they have made a claim they believed was true. Ask them to describe how they supported it with evidence.

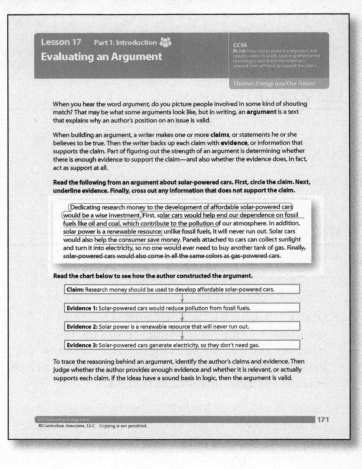

Genre Focus

Informational Texts: Speech

Tell students that in this lesson they will read a speech. Explain that a speech is a written talk, spoken and delivered to an audience.

Speeches have an introduction, a body, and a conclusion. In the body, facts and details are usually included to support the opinions or ideas of the speaker. In the conclusion, the speaker's opinions may be repeated to reinforce the ideas to the listener.

Speeches can have different purposes. They might be given to persuade the audience of an opinion, to convince them to take action, to inform about a topic, or simply to entertain.

Have students share any speeches they have read or heard. You may also wish to share why a speech you once heard had an impact on you.

Explain that the excerpt from "A Generational Challenge to Repower America" is a speech given by former Vice President Al Gore. This speech was given in 2008. In it, Gore proposes solutions to the energy crisis.

Tell students that they will also read an article about the importance of a law passed in California in 2012 to adopt the Advanced Clean Cars program as well as a persuasive essay about wind power. Discuss the difference between a written article or essay and a speech that is intended to be presented.

AT A GLANCE

Students read part of a speech by former Vice President Al Gore. They identify the claim he makes and the evidence used to support the claim.

STEP BY STEP

- Invite volunteers to tell what they learned on the previous page about analyzing an author's argument.

- Tell students that they will now analyze an author's argument in a speech.

- Read aloud the excerpt from "A Generational Challenge to Repower America."

- Then read the question: "This excerpt follows a section of the speech in which Gore makes claims about the dangers of relying on expensive foreign oil. What is Gore's claim in this part of the speech?"

- Tell students you will use a Think Aloud to demonstrate a way of answering the question.

Think Aloud: I know that a claim is a statement the speaker believes is true. I will reread to look for this statement. In the first sentence, I see that Al Gore makes a claim in the form of a question.

- Direct students to the chart and review that it is meant to show how the author has constructed his argument. Point out the claim in the first box.

- Have students underline facts in the text that relate directly to this claim.

Think Aloud: I will look for reasons and examples Gore includes to explain why he thinks we should use fuels that are cheaper, cleaner, and more accessible than foreign oil. In paragraph 2, I read that a small portion of solar energy could provide all of the electricity America uses. I read in paragraph 3 that wind power and geothermal energy could supply a lot of electricity. These three pieces of evidence all support this claim.

- Ask students to complete the chart with the evidence they underlined.

- Then have partners discuss the prompt at the bottom of the page. Ask volunteers to share their answers with the class.

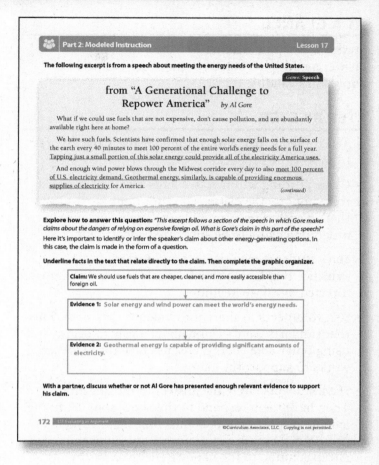

Tier Two Vocabulary: *Abundantly*

- Direct students to the word *abundantly* in paragraph 1. Ask students to tell what *abundantly* means in this sentence (*"in large amounts"*). Have them check the meaning in a dictionary and then confirm that it makes sense in this context.

- Work with students to name some related words (*greatly, hugely, generously*) and to understand that all the words have to do with more than enough. **(RI.7.4; L.7.4d)**

AT A GLANCE

Students continue reading Al Gore's speech. They answer a multiple-choice question and evaluate the argument's validity.

STEP BY STEP

- Tell students they will continue reading the excerpt from Al Gore's speech.

- Close Reading will help students focus on evidence that supports the claim. The Hint reminds students that an author must provide sufficient evidence in order for a claim to be supported adequately.

- Have students read the text and underline the evidence that Gore provides to support his claim, as directed by Close Reading.

- Ask volunteers to share the evidence they underlined that supports Gore's claim about a way to begin using renewable energy. Discuss how the evidence works to support the claim.

- Have students circle the answer to the question. Then have them respond to the Show Your Thinking. Sample response: Gore claims that solar, wind, and geothermal power can provide a quick, clean, and cheap solution to the nation's energy crisis by providing electricity, but he gives no facts, reasons, or other evidence as to why listeners should believe this to be true.

ANSWER ANALYSIS

Choice A is incorrect. Saying that the energy crisis holds us back doesn't explain why the best way to regain control is to use renewable energy to make electricity.

Choice B is incorrect. Gore is proposing a new energy strategy but doesn't explain why this way is best.

Choice C is correct. The evidence doesn't tell why the best way to use renewable energy is to make electricity.

Choice D is incorrect. Solar, wind, and geothermal power are forms of renewable energy.

> **ERROR ALERT:** Students who did not choose C may not have understood why Gore's claim is poorly supported. Review the evidence students underlined. Ask them to look for facts that explain *why* the best way to use renewable energy is to make electricity.

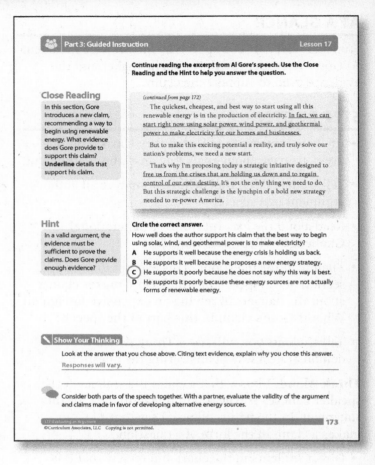

Tier Two Vocabulary: *Potential*

- Point out the word *potential* in paragraph 2. Explain that this word is used as a noun. Remind students that they can use context clues to help them determine the meaning of a word.

- Ask students to look at the surrounding words and concepts, and tell what *potential* means (*"the possibility of something happening"*). Work with students to help them understand which other phrases helped them figure out the meaning. (*"can start right now"*)

- Suggest that students look up *potential* in a dictionary or thesaurus to find synonyms. Ask, "What are some words that could be used in place of *potential*?" (*possibility, capability*) **(RI.7.4; L.7.4a, L.7.4c)**

AT A GLANCE

Students read an article twice about a newly adopted program in California. After the first reading, you will ask three questions to check your students' comprehension of the article.

STEP BY STEP

- Have students read the article silently without referring to the Study Buddy or Close Reading text.

- Ask the following questions to ensure students' comprehension of the text:

  What program does this article describe? (*The Advanced Clean Cars Program adopted by California.*)

  What is the author's opinion of this program? Explain. (*The author thinks this is a great program. Words such as "tremendous victory" and "rightly" suggest his point of view.*)

  What is the incremental change the program focuses on? (*requiring improved efficiency in internal combustion engines and their related emission systems*)

- Ask students to reread paragraph 1 and look at the Study Buddy think aloud. What does the Study Buddy help them think about?

Tip: The Study Buddy tells students that they will need to infer the author's claim in this text. Remind students that an inference is based on the details in the text combined with their own knowledge. Have students share their inferences.

- Have students reread the rest of the article. Tell them to follow the directions in the Close Reading.

Tip: The Close Reading helps students focus on evidence in the text. Review that evidence is facts and other information that supports a claim. Remind students to distinguish facts from the author's opinions. A fact is something that can be proven.

- Finally, have students answer the questions on page 175. Use the Answer Analysis to discuss correct and incorrect responses.

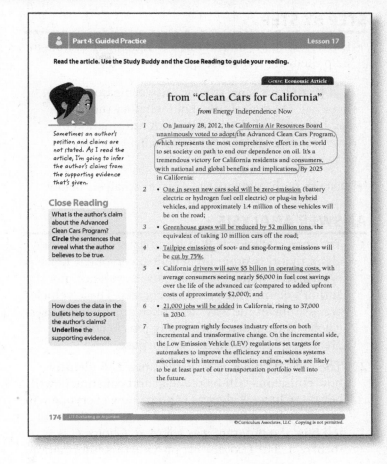

ELL Support: Compound Words

- Review with students that a compound word is made up of two smaller words. Often they can think about how the two smaller words might help them figure out the meaning of the compound word.

- Point out *greenhouse* in paragraph 2. Guide students to identify the two smaller words and talk about their meanings. Explain that some compound words mean something different from the two smaller words. *Greenhouse* does not mean "a house that is green." It is "a glass building which holds in heat where plants are grown."

- Tell students it is important to check the meaning of a compound word by using a dictionary. Have students use dictionaries to verify how *greenhouse* is used in the text (*relating to the greenhouse effect, which warms Earth's atmosphere*).

- Repeat for *tailpipe* in paragraph 3 (*"the rear section of a car's exhaust system"*). **(L.7.4d)**

STEP BY STEP

- Have students read questions 1–3, using the Hints to help them answer those questions.

Tip: If students have trouble answering question 3, encourage them to think about whether the author may have excluded any important information or have presented information in such a way that it adds bias.

- Discuss with students the Answer Analysis below.

ANSWER ANALYSIS

1   The correct choice is B. It summarizes the author's claim that this program benefits everyone. Choice A is incorrect. Reducing fuel costs is evidence, not the author's claim. Choice C is incorrect. These vehicles are just one of the ways to reduce greenhouse gases. Choice D is incorrect. Creating jobs is not its greatest achievement nor its purpose.

2   The correct choice is D. Paragraphs 2–6 identify how emissions will be reduced and consumers will benefit. Choice A doesn't support how everyone will benefit. Choice B is incorrect. The author does not tell how the program was adopted. Choice C is incorrect. The text doesn't provide this information.

3   Sample response: The author argues that the Advanced Clean Cars Program is a tremendous victory for California. He claims that the state and consumers will benefit from the increasing number of hybrid and zero-emissions vehicles and the increase in jobs as well as the regulations that reduce emissions and greenhouse gases. By creating cleaner, more efficient engines and emission systems, the program will help to reduce the nations' dependence on oil.

RETEACHING

Use a chart to verify the answer to question 2. Draw the chart below, and have students fill in the boxes. Sample responses are provided.

Claim: The Advanced Clean Cars Program benefits everyone.
Evidence 1: Reduce greenhouse gases.
Evidence 2: Reduce tailpipe emissions by 75%.
Evidence 3: Drivers save $5 billion in operating costs.

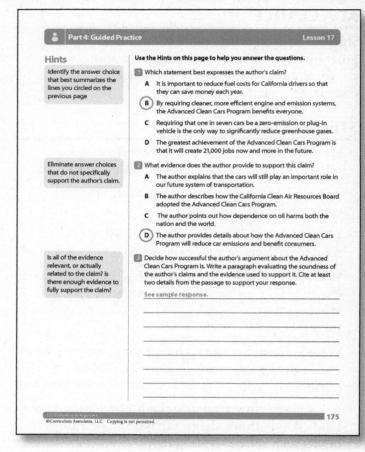

Integrating Standards

Use these questions to further students' understanding of "Clean Cars for California."

1   In paragraph 5, how does the author address evidence that supports the opposing view? **(RI.7.6)**

The author states evidence for the opposing view, that upfront costs will be about $2,000, and compares it to the cost savings to show how the savings are greater than the initial costs.

2   What would the author like to see happen to this program? How can you tell? **(RI.7.1)**

Sample response: I can infer that the author would like to see this program adopted by the rest of the United States and the world. The author states that this program "is a tremendous victory for California...with national and global benefits and implications." It makes sense that the author also thinks this program would benefit other states as well as countries worldwide.

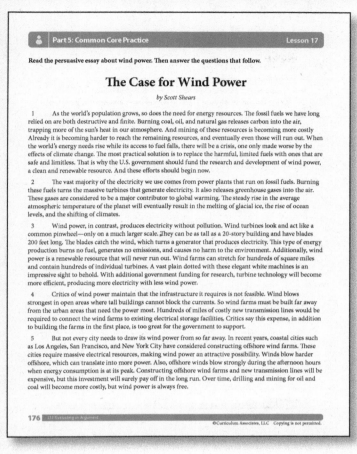

Part 5: Common Core Practice | Lesson 17

Read the persuasive essay about wind power. Then answer the questions that follow.

The Case for Wind Power

by Scott Shears

1   As the world's population grows, so does the need for energy resources. The fossil fuels we have long relied on are both destructive and finite. Burning coal, oil, and natural gas releases carbon into the air, trapping more of the sun's heat in our atmosphere. And mining of these resources is becoming more costly Already it is becoming harder to reach the remaining resources, and eventually even those will run out. When the world's energy needs rise while its access to fuel falls, there will be a crisis, one only made worse by the effects of climate change. The most practical solution is to replace the harmful, limited fuels with ones that are safe and limitless. That is why the U.S. government should fund the research and development of wind power, a clean and renewable resource. And these efforts should begin now.

2   The vast majority of the electricity we use comes from power plants that run on fossil fuels. Burning these fuels turns the massive turbines that generate electricity. It also releases greenhouse gases into the air. These gases are considered to be a major contributor to global warming. The steady rise in the average atmospheric temperature of the planet will eventually result in the melting of glacial ice, the rise of ocean levels, and the shifting of climates.

3   Wind power, in contrast, produces electricity without pollution. Wind turbines look and act like a common pinwheel—only on a much larger scale. They can be as tall as a 20-story building and have blades 200 feet long. The blades catch the wind, which turns a generator that produces electricity. This type of energy production burns no fuel, generates no emissions, and causes no harm to the environment. Additionally, wind power is a renewable resource that will never run out. Wind farms can stretch for hundreds of square miles and contain hundreds of individual turbines. A vast plain dotted with these elegant white machines is an impressive sight to behold. With additional government funding for research, turbine technology will become more efficient, producing more electricity with less wind power.

4   Critics of wind power maintain that the infrastructure it requires is not feasible. Wind blows strongest in open areas where tall buildings cannot block the currents. So wind farms must be built far away from the urban areas that need the power most. Hundreds of miles of costly new transmission lines would be required to connect the wind farms to existing electrical storage facilities. Critics say this expense, in addition to building the farms in the first place, is too great for the government to support.

5   But not every city needs to draw its wind power from so far away. In recent years, coastal cities such as Los Angeles, San Francisco, and New York City have considered constructing offshore wind farms. These cities require massive electrical resources, making wind power an attractive possibility. Winds blow harder offshore, which can translate into more power. Also, offshore winds blow strongly during the afternoon hours when energy consumption is at its peak. Constructing offshore wind farms and new transmission lines will be expensive, but this investment will surely pay off in the long run. Over time, drilling and mining for oil and coal will become more costly, but wind power is always free.

176   L17: Evaluating an Argument   ©Curriculum Associates, LLC Copying is not permitted.

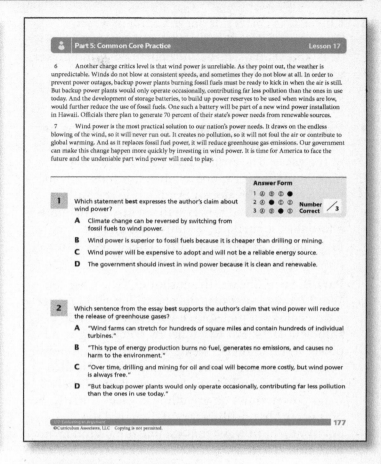

Part 5: Common Core Practice | Lesson 17

6   Another charge critics level is that wind power is unreliable. As they point out, the weather is unpredictable. Winds do not blow at consistent speeds, and sometimes they do not blow at all. In order to prevent power outages, backup power plants burning fossil fuels must be ready to kick in when the air is still. But backup power plants would only operate occasionally, contributing far less pollution than the ones in use today. And the development of storage batteries, to build up power reserves to be used when winds are low, would further reduce the use of fossil fuels. One such battery will be part of a new wind power installation in Hawaii. Officials there plan to generate 70 percent of their state's power needs from renewable sources.

7   Wind power is the most practical solution to our nation's power needs. It draws on the endless blowing of the wind, so it will never run out. It creates no pollution, so it will not foul the air or contribute to global warming. And as it replaces fossil fuel power, it will reduce greenhouse gas emissions. Our government can make this change happen more quickly by investing in wind power. It is time for America to face the future and the undeniable part wind power will need to play.

Answer Form
1 Ⓐ Ⓑ Ⓒ ●
2 Ⓐ ● Ⓒ Ⓓ   **Number Correct**   /3
3 Ⓐ Ⓑ ● Ⓓ

1 Which statement best expresses the author's claim about wind power?

A Climate change can be reversed by switching from fossil fuels to wind power.

B Wind power is superior to fossil fuels because it is cheaper than drilling or mining.

C Wind power will be expensive to adopt and will not be a reliable energy source.

D The government should invest in wind power because it is clean and renewable.

2 Which sentence from the essay best supports the author's claim that wind power will reduce the release of greenhouse gases?

A "Wind farms can stretch for hundreds of square miles and contain hundreds of individual turbines."

B "This type of energy production burns no fuel, generates no emissions, and causes no harm to the environment."

C "Over time, drilling and mining for oil and coal will become more costly, but wind power is always free."

D "But backup power plants would only operate occasionally, contributing far less pollution than the ones in use today."

©Curriculum Associates, LLC Copying is not permitted.   L17: Evaluating an Argument   177

AT A GLANCE

Students independently read a longer persuasive essay and answer questions in a format that provides test practice.

STEP BY STEP

- Tell students to use what they have learned about reading carefully and evaluating an argument to read the essay on pages 176 and 177.

- Remind students to underline or circle the author's claims and key evidence.

- Tell students to answer the questions on pages 177 and 178. For questions 1–3, they should fill in the correct circle on the Answer Form.

- When students have finished, use the Answer Analysis to discuss correct responses and the reasons for them. Have students fill in the Number Correct on the Answer Form.

ANSWER ANALYSIS

1 Choice D is correct. It summarizes the author's claims. Choice A is incorrect. The author doesn't claim climate change can be reversed. Choice B is incorrect. It does not include the author's claim about why the country should invest in wind power. Choice C is incorrect. It states the critics' claims. **(DOK 2)**

2 Choice B is correct. It explains why wind power will reduce greenhouse gas emissions. Choice A is incorrect. It states a fact about wind farms, but doesn't relate to emissions. Choice C only tells why wind power is more cost-effective. Choice D is incorrect. Less use of backup power plants would reduce emissions, but it doesn't describe how the use of wind power impacts greenhouse gases. **(DOK 2)**

Theme Connection

- How do all the passages in this lesson relate to the theme of energy and our future?

- What is one fact you learned from each passage?

3 Choice C is correct. It doesn't explain why the government should invest in wind power. Choices A, B, and D all describe the benefits of wind power, which supports the author's claim that the government should invest in this form of energy. *(DOK 2)*

4 **Part A:** The choice "Wind power is ecological" is supported by the most relevant and sufficient facts in the essay. The author says that advances will make wind power more reliable, but those advances have yet to be developed. And, while the author explains that wind power will eventually be more affordable, it currently requires significant investments in infrastructure. This makes wind power more expensive than other fuels.

Part B: Scott Shears, the author of "The Case for Wind Power," supports his claim that wind power is an ecological fuel source with relevant and sufficient facts. For example: By comparing wind power to fossil fuels, Shears states that wind power "produces electricity without pollution." He also indicates that, unlike the burning of fossil fuels, wind power emits no greenhouse gases. Finally, he points out that drilling for oil damages the environment in ways that establishing wind farms does not. *(DOK 3)*

---

3 Which piece of evidence from the text is **not** relevant to the author's claim?

A "Wind power, in contrast, produces electricity without pollution."

B "In addition, wind power is a renewable resource that will never run out."

C "A vast plain dotted with these elegant white machines is an impressive sight to behold."

D "Constructing offshore wind farms and new transmission lines will be expensive, but it is an investment that will surely pay off in the long run."

4 Below are three claims that one could make based on the essay "The Case for Wind Power."

CLAIMS	
	Wind power is reliable.
	Wind power is affordable.
X	Wind power is ecological.

Part A

Put an "X" by the claim that is supported by the most relevant and sufficient facts in "The Case for Wind Power."

Part B

Write a short paragraph with at least **three** details to show how the claim you chose in Part A is supported by relevant and sufficient facts in the essay.

See sample response.

_____

_____

_____

_____

_____

✓ **Self Check** *Go back and see what you can check off on the Self Check on page 170.*

178 L17: Evaluating an Argument   ©Curriculum Associates, LLC   Copying is not permitted.

Integrating Standards

Use these questions and tasks as opportunities to interact with "The Case for Wind Power."

1 What does a wind turbine do and look like? *(RI.7.1)*

A wind turbine looks and acts like a pinwheel. "The blades catch the wind, which turns a generator."

2 What are two central ideas that the author presents in this essay? *(RI.7.2)*

One central idea is that wind power is the most practical solution to the nation's energy problem. Another is that instead of being an unreliable and unrealistic alternative, wind power is cheaper, readily available, and does not harm the environment.

3 Describe the tone of this essay. How does the author's word choice impact this tone? *(RI.7.4)*

Sample response: The author creates a tone of mild urgency. Phrases such as "will be a crisis" and "make this change happen more quickly" help convey a sense that the government should take action right away.

4 Summarize: Write a brief summary of the passage. Be sure not to include personal opinions or judgments in your summary. *(RI.7.2; W.7.4)*

Summaries will vary. Sample response: The author claims the government needs to invest money in the development of wind power because this is a clean, renewable energy source. The author explains that although critics think wind power is expensive and unrealistic, it will pay off in the long run and will help reduce greenhouse gas emissions.

5 Discuss in small groups: How successful is the author's argument about why the government should invest in wind power? Evaluate the soundness of the author's claims and the evidence used to support it. *(SL.7.1)*

Discussions will vary. Students may point out that the author's argument is successful because he clearly states the opposition's claims and explains why the claims are invalid through use of sufficient evidence.

Writing Activities

Write an Argumentative Essay (W.7.1, W.7.5)

- Have students think about what they learned about energy and our future in this lesson.

- Challenge them to write an argumentative essay in which they state their own opinions about the use of renewable energy. Encourage them to cite evidence from each lesson passage in their writing.

- Have students work in pairs to revise their essays and strengthen their arguments by making sure they provide sufficient evidence to support their arguments.

Synonyms (L.7.5b)

- Point out the word *affordable* in the first sentence on page 171. Work with students to identify other words in this lesson's passages that have nearly the same meaning. (Examples include *not expensive, cheapest, cost savings, pay off in the long run,* and *free*).

- Point out that all these terms relate to the cost of things. Ask students to determine the differences in degree of meaning of each of these terms.

- Then have students write sentences using each of the terms to demonstrate the differences in meaning.

LISTENING ACTIVITY (SL.7.1, SL.7.2)

Listen Closely/Summarize

- Assign student pairs roles as speaker and listener.

- First, have the speaker read aloud from "The Case for Wind Power," pausing after each paragraph. Then have the listener summarize the paragraph.

- Have pairs reverse roles and repeat the activity until they have summarized the entire passage.

MEDIA ACTIVITY (RI.7.7)

Be Creative/Watch a Speech

- Direct students to a recording of former Vice President Al Gore's speech "A Generational Challenge to Repower America." Encourage students to watch the entire speech or the excerpt that they read in this lesson.

- Have students take notes as they listen.

- After viewing, have students discuss how the delivery of the speech impacts Gore's claims.

RESEARCH ACTIVITY (W.7.7, W.7.8; SL.7.1)

Address Problems Analytically

- Have students review the problems presented in "The Case for Wind Power." What are some challenges switching to wind power presents? Students may wish to work in small groups, pairs, or independently.

- Have students research more information about wind power, why it is considered a renewable energy source, and possible solutions to the problems that switching to wind power presents.

- Then ask students to use their research to write a persuasive speech about switching to wind power. Remind students that persuasive arguments include claims that are well supported with reasons and relevant evidence. Have students quote directly from their sources to support their claims and make a convincing argument.

- Have students present their speeches to the class.

- As time allows, guide a discussion about the solutions students presented. Encourage students to think creatively and build on each other's ideas to decide which of the solutions are the most effective and why.

Comparing and Contrasting Texts

LESSON OBJECTIVES

- Compare and contrast two informational texts on the same topic.

- Analyze the different ways authors present important information on the same topic by emphasizing different evidence or advancing different interpretations of similar facts.

THE LEARNING PROGRESSION

- **Grade 6:** CCSS RI.6.9 requires students to compare and contrast one author's presentation of events with that of another.

- **Grade 7: CCSS RI.7.9 builds on the Grade 6 standard by requiring students to compare and contrast how authors writing on the same topic shape their presentations of key information by emphasizing different evidence or interpreting facts differently.**

- **Grade 8:** CCSS RI.8.9 requires students to analyze a case in which two or more texts provide conflicting information on the same topic and identify where the texts disagree on matters of fact or interpretation.

PREREQUISITE SKILLS

- Determine central ideas and how they are developed.

- Identify an author's purpose and point of view.

- Analyze how the text structure chosen for a passage organizes and develops ideas.

- Compare and contrast authors' text presentations.

TAP STUDENTS' PRIOR KNOWLEDGE

- Tell students they will be working on a lesson about comparing and contrasting texts. Review with students what compare and contrast means. (*to tell how two or more things are alike and different*)

- Remind students that they often compare and contrast things in their own lives. Have students suggest examples. (*music, clothing*)

- Explain that one way to compare and contrast texts is to analyze the ways in which different authors present information and evidence on the same topic.

- As an example, ask students to describe the evidence they would use to support each side of a debate about school uniforms or another common issue. Then point out how students emphasized different evidence depending upon the side they supported.

- Another way students can analyze texts is by noting how authors advance different interpretations of facts. An interpretation is an explanation of what something means. Ask students how they might interpret the fact that a fire truck is parked by the school. (*It's there for a fire, a drill, or an inspection.*)

- Point out that comparing and contrasting texts will help students understand each author's interpretation of the evidence. It will also help them to better understand the points of view surrounding informational topics they read.

Ready *Teacher Toolbox*

teacher-toolbox.com

	Prerequisite Skills	RI.7.9
Ready Lessons	✓	✓
Tools for Instruction	✓	
Interactive Tutorials		✓

CCSS Focus

RI.7.9 Analyze how two or more authors writing about the same topic shape their presentations of key information by emphasizing different evidence or advancing different interpretations of facts.

ADDITIONAL STANDARDS: RI.7.1, RI.7.3, RI.7.4, RI.7.5, RI.7.6, RI.7.7, RI.7.8; L.7.1a, L.7.4a, L.7.4b, L.7.4c, L.7.4d; W.7.1, W.7.5, W.7.8; SL.7.1, SL.7.4 (*See page A39 for full text.*)

AT A GLANCE

Through a cartoon, students can see that two different people might have very different thoughts about the same topic. They learn to compare and contrast when reading texts about the same topic.

STEP BY STEP

- Read the first paragraph, and discuss with students the example of two artists creating two different artworks about the same topic, depending on their purposes. Encourage students to study the cartoon and think about the differences in how each character reacts to the poster.

- Explain that the chart shows several facts about global warming. Using the characters' reactions to the poster, discuss which facts would have been chosen by each character for his or her report. Then have students read the last paragraph and compare it to their conclusions.

- Ask students to discuss other real-life situations when they have compared and contrasted two texts about the same topic, such as movie reviews or articles about sporting events.

- Reinforce the value of comparing and contrasting as a reading strategy. Describe two informational texts you have read about the same topic and explain what you learned from comparing and contrasting details emphasized in them.

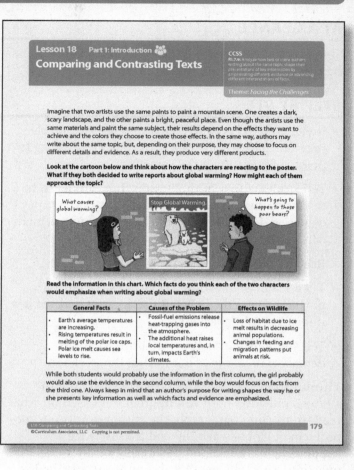

Genre Focus

Informational Texts: Persuasive Essay

Tell students that in this lesson they will read informational texts. One type is a persuasive essay, in which the writer offers an opinion and then gives claims supported with evidence, including facts, examples, and reasons.

The purpose of a persuasive essay is to convince readers to agree with the author's perspective.

Based on this information, ask students to discuss persuasive writing they have read. What was the writer trying to convince them to agree with? Were they persuaded after reading? Why or why not?

Explain that "Water for the World" is a persuasive essay. The writer's purpose is to persuade the reader to agree with the writer's opinion about a practical solution to water shortages.

Explain that the accounts "Global Warming: Why?" and "The Side Effects of Warming" are informational texts meant to inform the reader.

Tell students that "Some Simple Water Science" is a factual report that is also meant to inform the reader.

"Big Fish in Troubled Waters" and "Protecting the Oceans, One Choice at a Time" are scientific accounts about declining fish populations. Again, the writers' purpose is to use facts to inform the reader.

AT A GLANCE

Students compare and contrast two informational texts on the same topic.

STEP BY STEP

- Invite volunteers to tell what they learned on the previous page about comparing and contrasting two points of view about the same topic.

- Tell students that in this lesson they will learn how to determine the way the author's purpose shapes the choice of details emphasized in an account, which can help them compare and contrast.

- Read aloud "Global Warming: Why?"

- Then read the question: "How does the author's purpose shape the focus of the account and the key information he presents?"

- Tell students you will use a Think Aloud to demonstrate a way of answering the question.

Think Aloud: The account doesn't exactly tell the author's purpose, but I can figure it out based on what I read. In the first paragraph, the author points out the problem of global warming and asks why it's happening. In the second paragraph, he answers that question. This tells me that the author is writing to explain why global warming occurs.

- Direct students to the chart. Point out that it will help them organize details to compare and contrast the focuses of two different texts.

Think Aloud: Based on the information in these two paragraphs of this text, I think the author's main focus is to inform readers about what global warming is and what causes this rise in Earth's temperature. He explains the process to help clarify this information for readers.

- Have students write the focus of this account in the first column of the chart. Invite volunteers to share their answers with the class.

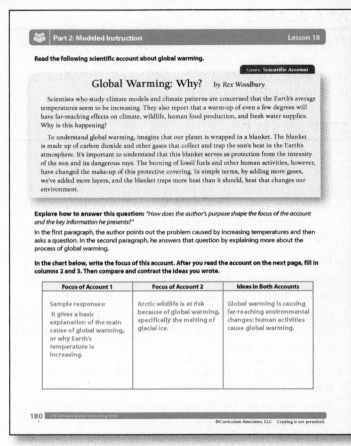

ELL Support: Regular Plural Nouns

- Explain to students that nouns name people, places, or things. Students can look at the endings of nouns to know *how many*.

- Point out the regular plural nouns *models* and *patterns* in paragraph 1. Discuss with students how the plural was formed (*add* s) and tell how many (*more than one*).

- Direct attention to *gases* in paragraph 2. Have students tell how the plural was formed (*add* es).

- Then point out the word *supplies* in paragraph 1. Have students identify the singular form of this noun (*supply*). Ask them to describe how the plural is formed (*change* y *to* i *and add* es). Explain that this is a common spelling change for singular nouns that end in *-y*. **(L.7.1)**

AT A GLANCE

Students read another account about global warming. Then they compare and contrast the two accounts.

STEP BY STEP

• Tell students they will read another account about global warming.

• Close Reading helps students identify key information and compare it to the information they read in the previous account. The Hint will help them contrast the two accounts.

• Have students read the account and underline facts that are similar to the first account and write an asterisk after facts unique to this account, as directed by Close Reading. Explain that this technique will help them compare and contrast the two accounts.

• Ask volunteers to share the facts they marked. Discuss how these facts help identify how the two accounts are similar and different. Then have students complete the chart on the previous page, circle the correct answer to the question on page 181, and write a response to Show Your Thinking.

• Place students in pairs to discuss the question at the bottom of the page. Point them toward the last sentence in the second account as evidence for the author's purpose.

ANSWER ANALYSIS

Choice A is correct. The first account tells about the cause of global warming, while the second explains an effect of it.

Choice B is incorrect. The first account does not describe any possible solutions.

Choice C is incorrect. The second account talks about both glacial ice and polar bear habits.

Choice D is incorrect. The second account warns of climate changes and other future problems.

ERROR ALERT: Students who did not choose A might not have read the accounts carefully enough. Point out that the second account talks about many of the ideas listed in the other answer choices. Only answer A describes what both accounts tell about.

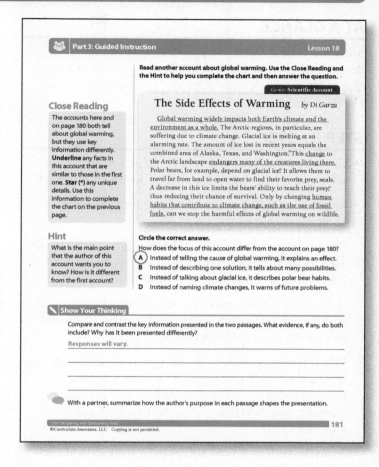

Part 3: Guided Instruction Lesson 18

Read another account about global warming. Use the Close Reading and the Hint to help you complete the chart and then answer the question.

Genre: Scientific Account

The Side Effects of Warming by Di Garza

Close Reading
The accounts here and on page 180 both tell about global warming, but they use key information differently. **Underline** any facts in this account that are similar to those in the first one. **Star (*)** any unique details. Use this information to complete the chart on the previous page.

Global warming widely impacts both Earth's climate and the environment as a whole. The Arctic regions, in particular, are suffering due to climate change. Glacial ice is melting at an alarming rate. The amount of ice lost in recent years equals the combined area of Alaska, Texas, and Washington. This change to the Arctic landscape endangers many of the creatures living there. Polar bears, for example, depend on glacial ice. It allows them to travel far from land to open water to find their favorite prey, seals. A decrease in this ice limits the bears' ability to reach their prey, thus reducing their chance of survival. Only by changing human habits that contribute to climate change, such as the use of fossil fuels, can we stop the harmful effects of global warming on wildlife.

Hint
What is the main point that the author of this account wants you to know? How is it different from the first account?

Circle the correct answer.
How does the focus of this account differ from the account on page 180?
A Instead of telling the cause of global warming, it explains an effect.
B Instead of describing one solution, it tells about many possibilities.
C Instead of talking about glacial ice, it describes polar bear habits.
D Instead of naming climate changes, it warns of future problems.

Show Your Thinking
Compare and contrast the key information presented in the two passages. What evidence, if any, do both include? Why has it been presented differently?
Responses will vary.

With a partner, summarize how the author's purpose in each passage shapes the presentation.

L18 Comparing and Contrasting Texts
©Curriculum Associates, LLC   Copying is not permitted.   181

Tier Two Vocabulary: *Impacts*

• Direct students to the verb *impacts* in the first sentence. Ask them to list the context clues they can use to determine the meaning of the word. (*"suffering," "change," "melting"*) Ask them to figure out what *impacts* means. (*"has an effect on"*)

• Ask what other words would make sense in place of *impacts* (*affects, influences*).

• Then have students look up the word *impacts* in a dictionary to find other meanings. Ask them to use the word in sentences to explore the other meanings. (**RI.7.4; L.7.4a, L.7.4d**)

AT A GLANCE

Students read a scientific account twice about desalination. After the first reading, you will ask three questions to check your students' comprehension of the passage.

STEP BY STEP

- Have students read the report silently without referring to the Study Buddy or Close Reading text.

- Ask the following questions to ensure students' comprehension of the text:

Describe the kind of water that is scarce. (*Fresh water used by people and other living things is scarce. Only 2.5 percent of Earth's water is fresh water.*)

How did scientists discover the desalination technique? (*Scientists spent years studying a special membrane in seabirds' throats.*)

What is reverse osmosis? (*Reverse osmosis is a process in which two different types of molecules become separated and more concentrated. In the salt water example, salt molecules are separated from water molecules.*)

- Ask students to reread the passage and look at the Study Buddy think aloud. What does the Study Buddy help them think about?

Tip: The Study Buddy reminds students to focus on how the author's purpose influences the key information used in the report. Encourage students to mark text and write margin notes to help them identify and connect the key information to the central ideas and the author's purpose

- Have students answer the questions and follow the directions in the Close Reading.

Tip: The Close Reading continues to guide students in identifying important information about desalination. Students may have difficulty grasping the scientific process explained in this text. Remind them that they can reread and summarize the process in their own words to help them understand the scientific concepts the author presents.

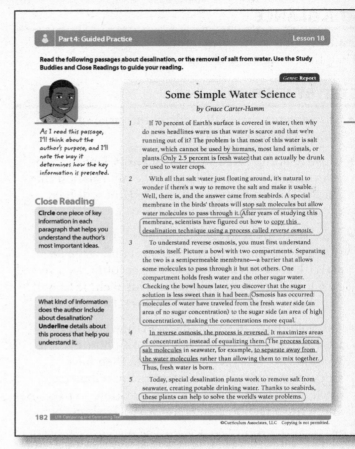

Tier Two Vocabulary: *Concentration*

- Direct students to the word *concentration* in paragraph 3. Tell students that *concentration* is a multiple-meaning word. Have them look up definitions of the word in a dictionary. (*"the act of focusing attention," "the amount of a substance in a given space"*)

- Then ask them to use the report's context to determine the meaning of *concentration* as it is used here. (*"the amount of a substance in a given space"*) Note the use of the word's technical meaning in this instance. (**RI.7.4; L.7.4c**)

AT A GLANCE

Students read a persuasive essay about desalination twice. After the first reading, you will ask questions to check students' comprehension of the passage.

STEP BY STEP

- Have students read the essay silently without referring to the Study Buddy or Close Reading text.

- Ask the following questions to ensure students' comprehension of the text:

  Why is water important according to this text? (*It is essential for life. It is needed for drinking, for growing crops, and for taking care of livestock.*)

  Why is our supply of fresh water dwindling? (*The world population has tripled, and the demand for fresh water has greatly increased.*)

  How is desalination helpful? (*It helps provide clean, safe, fresh water for people to use.*)

- Ask students to reread the passage and look at the Study Buddy think aloud. What does the Study Buddy help them think about?

Tip: The Study Buddy tells students to think about the key information and the focus of the essay as they read. This will help them understand how the information here is presented differently than in the report they read earlier.

- Have students answer the questions and follow the directions in the Close Reading.

Tip: The Close Reading guides students to identify key information in the text that is similar to the previous report and information that is new. Remind students that comparing and contrasting texts on the same topic will enable them to gain a broader understanding of it. This in turn will help students to better distinguish between accurate facts and misinformation or bias in an article, which helps them determine whether or not a source is reliable.

- Finally, have students answer the questions on page 184. Use the Answer Analysis to discuss correct and incorrect responses.

ELL Support: Suffixes

- Explain to students that many English words have suffixes. A suffix is a group of letters added to the end of a word to change its meaning. Work with students to show how the meaning of a word changes with a suffix.

- Point out the word *potful* in paragraph 4. Help students identify the suffix (*-ful*) and the base word (*pot*). Explain that the suffix *-ful* means "full of." Tell students that adding the suffix *-ful* to pot changes the meaning to a "full pot."

- Point out the suffix *-able* in *usable* in paragraph 4. Discuss that adding the suffix *-able* changes *use* to mean "able to be used." Note that *use* drops the *e* to add a suffix; explain that adding suffixes to some words requires a spelling change to the base word.

- Have students find another word with a suffix in this passage and explain how the suffix helps them understand the word's meaning. (*Sample response:* limitless, *"without limits"*). **(L.7.4b)**

STEP BY STEP

- Have students read questions 1–3, using the Hints to help them answer those questions.

Tip: The Hints remind students to look back at each text to compare and contrast the facts and important ideas presented. Point out that this will help them remember how the texts are similar and different, making it easier for them to answer the questions.

- Discuss with students the Answer Analysis below.

ANSWER ANALYSIS

1 The correct choice is D. The first text informs, and the second explains a solution to the crisis. Choice A is incorrect because both passages describe the limits on water resources. Choice B sums up only the first passage. Choice C is incorrect. The first passage does not present pros and cons.

2 The correct choice is B. Reverse osmosis is discussed in both texts; however, the first text explains the process. Choice A is incorrect in stating that both authors talk about how people need water to survive. Choice C is incorrect. The first passage doesn't include the fact about 1.1 billion people. Choice D is incorrect in stating that the first passage discusses challenges.

3 Sample response: Both passages discuss the importance of desalination as a way to increase our supply of drinkable fresh water. However, "Some Simple Water Science" uses facts about desalination to explain the science behind the process, while "Water for the World" uses facts about water scarcity, population growth, and desalination itself to suggest that we need to increase the number of desalination plants to help solve the water problem.

RETEACHING

Use a chart to organize an answer to question 3. Draw the chart below, and work with students to fill in the boxes. Sample responses are provided.

"Some Simple Water Science"	Both	"Water for the World"
explains desalination process	discuss desalination to increase fresh water supply	tells how desalination can help solve the water crisis

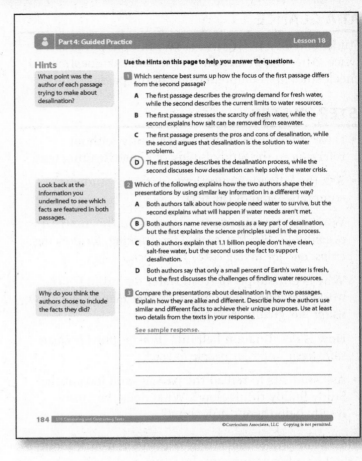

Integrating Standards

Use these questions to further students' understanding of "Some Simple Water Science" and "Water for the World."

1 According to "Some Simple Water Science," how have seabirds influenced scientists? **(RI.7.3)**

Scientists have studied seabirds because they have a membrane in their throats that is semipermeable and enables them to remove salt from sea water. The membrane allows water to pass through it but keeps out salt. Understanding how this membrane works has helped scientists develop the desalination process.

2 What is the author's purpose for writing "Water for the World?" **(RI.7.6)**

His purpose is to persuade the reader to agree with his perspective about the need to solve the world's water crisis by increasing the number of desalination plants.

Read both scientific articles about endangered fish. Then answer the questions that follow.

from "Big Fish in Troubled Waters"

by Stephen Ornes, Science News for Kids

1   You may have heard the popular saying "there are always more fish in the sea." But as a number of new studies show, the truth of that statement depends on the kind of fish. Fish populations are changing, and not necessarily for the better.

2   Consider the case of big, predatory fish. These giants, like sharks and cod, devour other, smaller fish. Big fish are an important part of the marine ecosystem—which includes the ocean and all the things living in it—because they keep down the numbers of smaller fish. Without fish that eat other fish, populations of smaller swimmers could swell. More of these smaller fish would devour more plants, leaving less vegetation for other organisms—or for future fish.

3   As fierce and ferocious as predators can be, they're no match for fishing technology. Many people love to eat predatory fish like sharks, cod and tuna. According to two new, large studies, these giant predators are becoming scarce. One study shows how the populations are decreasing; the other shows how fishing hauls, or the amount of fish caught, have changed. Together, the studies suggest that overfishing threatens the creatures near the top of the marine food chain.

4   In one study, Villy Christensen and his colleagues looked at 200 past studies of marine life to learn how fish populations have changed over time. Christensen is a fisheries expert at the University of British Columbia in Vancouver. The oldest studies his team looked at dated to 1880; the most recent were published in 2007. In these 200 studies, researchers counted and described all the different types of life in small oceanic ecosystems.

5   Christensen presented the team's findings in February at the 2011 meeting of the American Association for the Advancement of Science in Washington, D.C. He reported that between 1910 and 1970, the numbers of big predators decreased slowly. In 1970, their populations really started to drop. Around that time, fishing ships began using new tools that led to catching more fish. The numbers have been falling quickly ever since.

6   Now, the number of these big fish in the ocean is very low. Christensen reported that today there is only about one-third as many of the large, fish-eating fish as there was in 1910. That means for every three you might have found in 1910, now you would only find one. Christensen said the future looks increasingly dismal for these giants.

7   "We see no indication that things are improving," Christensen told the audience. "It's a pretty bleak situation."

8   While Christensen looked at the problem from the perspective of the fish, Reg Watson approached it from the perspective of the fishermen. Watson, a biologist also at the University of British Columbia, studied the increase in fishing in recent decades. Like Christensen, Watson reported his findings at the AAAS meeting.

9   In the middle of the 20th century, Watson reported, fishing boats didn't venture far from home—and most fish were caught near the shore. That wasn't true in the 1980s. By then, he said, fishing had moved farther from shore, into the open oceans, and it was helped by the development of new tools and technologies. These advances helped a lot: In the 1990s, fisherman hauled in five times as much fish, by weight, as they had in the middle of the century. But since the 1990s, something has changed. Despite new technologies and more effort, fishing operations have not continued to boost their hauls. If there are fewer fish in the sea, fishing companies may have a hard time keeping up with the demand for fresh fish.

10   The studies by Watson and Christensen don't paint a promising picture for sea predators. These scientists studied historical data to understand the present, and this research is needed to forecast the future of fish and fishing. And the forecast doesn't look good: Large predator fish are becoming harder to find—and there may not be more in the sea for long.

Protecting the Oceans, One Choice at a Time

by Oscar Seever

1   When the US Department of Agriculture (USDA) introduced new dietary guidelines in 2010, one of its key recommendations was to eat seafood twice a week. Seafood is higher in protein and lower in fat than other animal proteins. Also, many fish and shellfish are rich in omega-3 fatty acids. Omega-3s have been shown to have many health benefits, including the support of heart health. If all Americans were to follow this recommendation, however, consumption of seafood in the United States would double.

2   While this would be great for people's health, it could pose a problem for the world's oceans. Current fishing practices are already reducing the populations of many seafood species to the point of collapse. If we want to have access to seafood well into the future, we must take steps to preserve and renew the ocean's bounty and encourage others around the world to do the same. Action from world governments will be vital to sustain seafood populations in the oceans that cover three-quarters of Earth's surface. But there is something you can do as an individual, too. You can exercise the power of your fork and avoid eating seafood with populations that have become endangered.

3   When choosing which seafood to buy and eat, there are two important factors to consider, the species of fish and where it was caught. The bluefin tuna is critically endangered and has been overfished all over the world, largely due to its popularity as a sushi fish. This huge fish, which can grow to be 10 feet long and weigh 1,400 pounds, is popular with fisherman—just one fish can be sold for up to $100,000. But if enough people avoid this fish, the demand would go down. Fishermen wouldn't have as much reason to catch them. Tuna fans can still feed their cravings by choosing more abundant bigeye or yellowfin tuna.

4   The Atlantic halibut is another large fish, which can grow to be 9 feet long and 1,000 pounds. It is particularly vulnerable to overfishing due to its long lifespan. It can live to be 50 years old, and it doesn't reach reproductive maturity until it is between 10 and 14. Halibut caught before they reach maturity never get a chance to reproduce, damaging the entire population. The United States has banned Atlantic halibut fishing in its waters. However, it cannot regulate fishing practices on the "high seas," the large areas of ocean outside of any individual country's control. Luckily, there is a good alternative to Atlantic halibut, its relative the Pacific halibut.

AT A GLANCE

Students independently read two longer scientific accounts and answer questions in a format that provides test practice.

STEP BY STEP

- Tell students to use what they have learned about reading closely, comparing and contrasting texts, and analyzing details to read the scientific accounts on pages 185–187.

- Remind students to underline or circle important details in each text.

- Tell students to answer the questions on pages 187 and 188. For questions 1–3, they should fill in the correct circle on the Answer Form.

- When students have finished, use the Answer Analysis to discuss correct responses and the reasons for them. Have students fill in the Number Correct on the Answer Form.

ANSWER ANALYSIS

1   Choice D is correct. The first article explains the effects of overfishing, while the second persuades readers to make careful decisions about meals. Choice A is incorrect. It makes accurate statements but does not sum up how the articles' focus differs. Choice B is incorrect. The second article does not explain where to find information about fish that are rich in Omega-3s. Choice C is incorrect. The second article does not explain the connection between the creatures in the ocean food chain. **(DOK 3)**

Theme Connection

- How do all the passages in this lesson relate to the theme of facing the world's challenges?

- What is one fact or idea you learned about facing the world's challenges from each passage in this lesson?

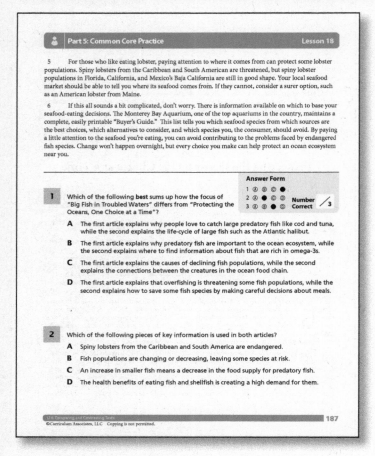

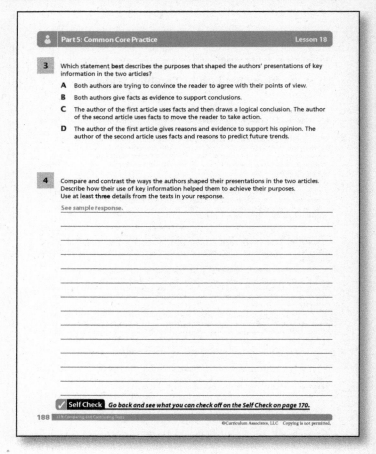

---

2 Choice B is correct. Both articles discuss the changing fish populations. Choice A is incorrect because the first article makes no mention of spiny lobster populations. Choice C is a false statement. An increase in smaller fish would increase the food supply for predatory fish. Choice D is incorrect because only the second article discusses the health benefits of eating fish. *(DOK 2)*

3 Choice C is correct. Both articles use facts, and the first draws a logical conclusion while the second is trying to move the reader to take action. Choice A is incorrect because only the second article is trying to persuade the reader. Choice B is incorrect because only the first article uses facts to support a conclusion. Choice D is incorrect because the opposite is true. The first article predicts future trends and the second article gives reasons to support an opinion. *(DOK 3)*

4 Sample response: Both authors are concerned about endangered fish populations. The author of the first article focuses on the results of two studies that show the decline of large predator fish. In the second article, the author focuses on endangered food fish, including predator fish, to tell how people can avoid adding to the problem by making wise seafood choices. The focus on scientific studies in the first article makes the author's presentation more factual. The author's focus on how people can affect endangered fish populations in the second article makes the author's presentation more persuasive. *(DOK 4)*

Integrating Standards

Use these questions and tasks as opportunities to interact with "Big Fish in Troubled Waters" and "Protecting the Oceans, One Choice at a Time."

1 In "Big Fish in Troubled Waters," what examples of big, predatory fish does the author include? **(RI.7.1)**

Examples of big, predatory fish include sharks, cod, and tuna.

2 In "Big Fish in Troubled Waters," how effectively does the author support the claim that fish populations are changing for the worse? **(RI.7.8)**

Sample response: The author supports the claim effectively by providing ample, relevant evidence such as information from several scientific studies, including from a well-respected scientist.

3 In "Protecting the Oceans, One Choice at a Time," what can you infer the author thinks about his audience based on the phrase "If this all sounds a bit complicated"? **(RI.7.1)**

It seems the author expects that his audience will be unable to remember so many different details about endangered fish species and alternative meal choices.

4 How does the first paragraph of "Protecting the Oceans, One Choice at a Time" contribute to the development of the author's overall message? **(RI.7.5)**

This paragraph informs readers that the demand for fish has increased since the government issued dietary guidelines that encourage people to eat more fish. This helps set up the author's argument that when taking these guidelines into consideration, people should avoid eating fish that is endangered.

5 Discuss in small groups: How do these two articles increase your knowledge about the endangered fish population? What information have you learned, and what questions do you still have? **(SL.7.1)**

Discussions will vary. Encourage students to cite key information from both articles that increased their understanding of the topic.

Writing Activities

Write an Argumentative Essay (W.7.1, W.7.5)

- Have students review the information presented in each of this lesson's passages. What environmental challenges are people facing? What are some ways to help solve these challenges?

- Challenge students to write an argumentative essay in which they describe the three challenges they read about and present their opinions about how to solve these challenges.

- Have students work in small groups to revise their writing and make sure their arguments are persuasive, supporting them with relevant reasons and evidence.

Prepositional Phrases (L.7.1a)

- Review with students that prepositions are words that show the relation between other words in a sentence. Common prepositions include *after, at, of, between, under.* Explain that a prepositional phrase serves to modify another element in the sentence.

- Have students identify the prepositional phrase in the first sentence of "Water for the World. *(for life)* What does it modify? *(ingredients)* Have students identify and describe the function of other phrases in this article.

LISTENING ACTIVITY (SL.7.3)

Listen Closely/Listen for Details

- Have student pairs take turns reading aloud paragraphs from "Protecting the Oceans, One Choice at a Time."

- After each paragraph is read, the listener should identify the details that he or she heard.

DISCUSSION ACTIVITY (SL.7.1)

Talk in a Group/Discuss Challenges

- Have students work in small groups to discuss the information they learned about global warming from "Global Warming: Why?" and "The Side Effects of Warming."

- Have students discuss the following questions: What is global warming? What causes it, and what are its effects? What are ways that people can help reduce the effects of global warming? Challenge groups to come up with a list of ways that they, as students, can work to minimize their contribution to global warming.

- Have groups present their lists to the class and discuss which ideas are most effective and simple to do.

MEDIA ACTIVITY (RI.7.9)

Be Creative/Create a Cartoon

- Have students review the cartoon on page 179. Remind them that they had to analyze which character might emphasize different facts when writing about global warming.

- Invite students to create cartoons that require the reader to analyze which character might emphasize different facts about the same topic.

- Have students exchange cartoons and discuss which character would emphasize which facts when writing about a particular topic.

RESEARCH ACTIVITY (RI.7.7; W.7.8; SL.7.4)

Research and Present/Compare and Contrast

- Have students use the Internet to find a video of Villy Christensen, the scientist discussed in "Big Fish in Troubled Waters."

- After studying the video, have students write a report in which they analyze how the video and the article they read in this lesson portray the subject of overfishing. In their reports, students should address how the medium affects the impact of the words. Have students share their reports.

SCORING GUIDE AND ANSWER ANALYSIS

Informational Passage Answer Analysis

1 Ⓐ ● Ⓒ Ⓓ   4 Ⓐ Ⓑ Ⓒ ●

2 Ⓐ Ⓑ Ⓒ ●   5 ● Ⓑ Ⓒ Ⓓ

3 Ⓐ Ⓑ ● Ⓓ

1   Choice B is correct. The statement describes a clear benefit for homeowners: reducing their heating and electricity bills.

Choice A is incorrect. The statement just describes the process of how fluid breaks up shale rock. Choice C is incorrect. It does not describe a benefit. The pollution of drinking water and the harmful effects of fracking on the environment is a risk. Choice D is also incorrect because it describes how the chemicals contaminate the ground water that it seeps into; this is not a benefit of fracking. **(RI.7.8; DOK 3)**

2   Choice D is correct. While this statement is in the first passage, the author of the second passage claims that the jobs created from the demand for shale gas are not high-paying or safe. She says that these jobs are unsafe because many workers have been diagnosed with lung cancer.

Choice A is incorrect. Only the first passage mentions that some businesses have left the United States because of the high cost of fuel. Therefore, we do not know if the author of the second passage disagrees. Choice B is incorrect. The second passage does not mention this fact. Therefore, we do not know if this author disagrees. Choice C is also incorrect. Both passages note that jobs will be created because of the demand for shale gas. Therefore, the author of the second passage does not disagree with this statement. **(RI.7.9; DOK 3)**

3   Choice C is correct. The author of "The Benefits of Shale Gas" is the only one to say that shale gas is the cleanest of all fossil fuels and that burning shale gas releases less carbon dioxide into the air than burning coal or oil.

Choice A is incorrect. Only the author of "Stop the Fracking!" discusses truck traffic. Choice B is incorrect. Both authors discuss the process of hydraulic fracturing, but only the author of "The Benefits of Shale Gas" mentions that burning shale gas is cleaner than burning coal or oil. Choice D is also incorrect. Only the author of "Stop the Fracking!" discusses open pits. The author of "The Benefits of Shale Gas" is the only one to say that shale gas is the cleanest of all fossil fuels and that burning shale gas releases less carbon dioxide than burning coal or oil. **(RI.7.9; DOK 2)**

4   Choice D is correct. These sentences point out a way that fracking harms the environment, so they support the author's main argument.

Choice A is incorrect. The author's main argument is that fracking harms the environment and people, so it does not matter whether these sentences are about the process of drilling for shale gas. Choice B is incorrect. The author's main argument is not about taxpayers being affected by hydraulic fracturing; it's about hydraulic fracturing harming the environment and people. Choice C is also incorrect. The author's main idea is not just about the contamination of drinking water; it's about all the harmful effects of fracking. **(RI.7.8; DOK 3)**

5   Choice A is correct. The author of "The Benefits of Shale Gas" acknowledges that the fluid used in hydraulic fracturing contains chemicals that can contaminate water, but he says that "the risk of this happening is extremely small." The author of "Stop the Fracking!" says that groundwater has been contaminated "with nearly every well that gas companies have drilled."

Choice B is incorrect. The author of the first passage says that the fluid contains a small amount of chemicals. The author of the second passage says that about 40,000 gallons of chemicals are mixed into about 8 million gallons of fluid. Therefore, the fluid does not consist mostly of chemicals. Choice C is incorrect. The author of "The Benefits of Shale Gas" says that the risk of contamination can be eliminated "if gas companies do not drill near drinking-water sources." He is not saying that gas companies do not drill near drinking-water sources. The author of "Stop the Fracking!" does not say that gas companies almost always drill near drinking-water sources. Choice D is also incorrect. The author of the second passage says that contaminated water is unsafe, but the author of the first passage does not say it is safe. **(RI.7.9; DOK 3)**

SAMPLE RESPONSES

Short Response

6 The author of "The Benefits of Shale Gas" explains that burning shale gas is good for the economy because shale gas costs less than other types of fuel. This is relevant evidence. He says that before gas companies had the technology to access shale gas, the cost of fuel was very high. This led some businesses to relocate to other countries where gas was more affordable. The author states that businesses won't do this in the future because of the low cost of shale gas, and some businesses that have relocated to other countries might return to the United States. But he has no proof that this will happen. This is not sufficient to support his claim that burning shale gas would be good for the economy. *(RI.7.8; DOK 3)*

7 **Part A:** The first choice, "Fracking contaminates groundwater," is best supported by the most relevant and sufficient evidence. The second choice is supported by some evidence, but not as much as the first choice. The essay actually argues against the idea that fracking creates high-paying jobs. *(RI.7.8; DOK 3)*

Part B: Sentences that students choose will vary. Sample sentences are below.

Sentence 1: "Reports show that more than 1,000 people have suffered serious illnesses and/or death from drinking water that was contaminated due to fracking."

Sentence 2: "About 40,000 gallons of chemicals are mixed into this fluid; some of these chemicals are carcinogens, or chemicals known to cause cancer." *(RI.7.8; DOK 3)*

8 Both the author of "The Benefits of Shale Gas" and the author of "Stop the Fracking!" explain that fluid is used to break up shale rock. The author of "The Benefits of Shale Gas" says that the fluid consists of water and sand and a small amount of chemicals, but the author of "Stop the Fracking!" is more specific. She explains that the process uses up to 8 million gallons of fluid, and that 40,000 gallons of chemicals are mixed into this fluid. She also mentions the hazards of open pits, which the first author does not. *(RI.7.9; DOK 4)*

Performance Task

9 Students may select either essay as the stronger one. **Possible response:** I think that the author of "Stop the Fracking!" presents a stronger argument than the author of "The Benefits of Shale Gas" because she provides statistics and information to make her point. She also discusses topics that the other author does not.

Both essays define and explain the process of hydraulic fracturing. However, while the author of the first essay admits that fracking has contaminated drinking water in some instances, the author of the second essay says that more than 1,000 cases have been reported of people who have become ill or died from drinking water that has been contaminated because of fracking. The author of the first essay explains that some chemicals are added to the fluid used in fracking. However, the author of the second essay is once again more specific, noting that 40,000 gallons of chemicals are added to the 8 million gallons of fluid.

The author of "Stop the Fracking!" also discusses problems related to fracking that the author of "The Benefits of Shale Gas" does not. For example, she explains that truck traffic from fracking damages rural roads and costs taxpayers a great deal of money. She also mentions what happens to farmers' land and drinking water after fracking has taken place. She even notes that the Environmental Protection Agency (EPA) is investigating the effects of fracking. These topics aren't discussed in "The Benefits of Shale Gas." For these reasons, I think that "Stop the Fracking!" is a much stronger essay than "The Benefits of Shale Gas." *(RI.7.8, RI.7.9; DOK 4)*

SCORING RUBRICS

Short-Response Rubric

2 points The response is accurate, complete, and fulfills all requirements of the task. Text-based support and examples are included. Any information that goes beyond the text is relevant to the task.

1 point The response is partially accurate and fulfills some requirements of the task. Some information may be inaccurate, too general, or confused. Support may be insufficient or not text-based.

0 points The response is inaccurate, poorly organized, or does not respond to the task.

Performance Task Rubric

4 points The response
- Fulfills all requirements of the task
- Uses varied sentence types and some sophisticated vocabulary
- Includes relevant and accurate details from the texts as well as text-based inferences
- Demonstrates a thorough understanding of the texts
- Maintains a clear focus and organization
- Is fluent and demonstrates a clear voice
- Uses correct spelling, grammar, capitalization, and punctuation

3 points The response
- Fulfills all requirements of the task
- Uses simple sentences and grade-level vocabulary
- Includes relevant and accurate details from the texts
- Demonstrates a mainly literal understanding of the texts
- Maintains a mostly clear focus and organization
- Is fluent and demonstrates some sense of voice
- Uses mostly correct spelling, grammar, capitalization, and punctuation

2 points The response
- Fulfills some requirements of the task
- Uses simple sentences, some fragments, and grade-level vocabulary
- Includes some relevant and accurate details from the texts
- Demonstrates some misunderstandings or gaps in understanding of the texts
- Attempts to maintain a clear focus and organization
- Is difficult to read, includes some inaccuracies, and demonstrates little or no sense of voice
- Contains some inaccurate spelling, grammar, capitalization, and punctuation that may hinder understanding

1 point The response
- Fulfills few requirements of the task
- Uses sentence fragments and below-grade-level vocabulary
- Includes no details or irrelevant details to support the response
- Demonstrates very little understanding of the texts
- Does not establish a clear focus or organization
- Is difficult to read, contains many inaccuracies, and demonstrates no sense of voice
- Uses incorrect spelling, grammar, capitalization, and punctuation to an extent that impedes understanding

0 points The response is irrelevant, poorly organized, or illegible.

Comparing Text to Other Media

LESSON OBJECTIVES

- Understand the differences between, and the benefits of, written, visual, and audio versions of a text.

- Compare and contrast a text to a multimedia version of the same material; examine how the medium affects the way the reader or viewer responds to the content.

THE LEARNING PROGRESSION

Grade 6: CCSS RI.6.7 requires students to combine information from different media sources and "develop a coherent understanding of the topic."

Grade 7: CCSS RI.7.7 builds on the Grade 6 standard by requiring students to compare and contrast a text to an audio, video, or multimedia version of the text, "analyzing each medium's portrayal of the subject."

Grade 8: CCSS RI.8.7 requires students to "evaluate the advantages and disadvantages" of using different mediums to present a topic or idea.

TAP STUDENTS' PRIOR KNOWLEDGE

- Ask students whether they would rather read about a sports event in the newspaper, listen to it on the radio, or watch it live or on TV. Most students will probably choose the live or televised game. Ask them why, pointing out all these mediums would tell key moments and players from the game and who won.

- Students might argue that newspaper articles don't let you experience the game as it's happening. And when they actually watch a game, they can hear and see details that wouldn't come across if they were just listening—the players' movements, the referee's calls, the reactions of the coaches and the crowds.

- Point out that different media have played important roles in our society. First radio, then TV, and now the Internet have dramatically affected how we receive information, how we interact with others, and how we react to what we're hearing and seeing.

- Tell students that in this lesson, they will be learning more about how the medium through which information is delivered can affect the message itself. They will also read part of a famous speech and view the speech online to compare the effect each medium has on the audience.

▪ **Ready** *Teacher Toolbox*		*teacher-toolbox.com*
	Prerequisite Skills	*RI.7.7*
Ready Lessons	✓	✓
Tools for Instruction		
Interactive Tutorials		✓

CCSS Focus

RI.7.7. Compare and contrast a text to an audio, video, or multimedia version of the text, analyzing each medium's portrayal of the subject (e.g., how the delivery of a speech affects the impact of the words).

ADDITIONAL STANDARDS: *RI.7.10; SL.7.2, SL.7.4*

AT A GLANCE

Students will be asked to consider how the way in which information is presented can be as important as the content itself. They will then compare and contrast the text and video of a famous speech to see the benefits of both versions, and also to see just how big a difference the choice of a medium can make.

STEP BY STEP: PAGE 197

- Ask students if they have ever heard the phrase "the medium is the message." Ask what they think it means. Then tell them that it was coined by Marshall McLuhan, a professor who was considered the world's foremost expert in media theory. The phrase meant that the medium through which information (the message) was delivered so strongly influenced the perception of the message that the medium and the message became the same thing.

- Read the first two paragraphs of the introduction with students. Explain that the Kennedy-Nixon debates marked the first time TV played a major role in American politics, and the first time voters were able to see candidates compete. 70 million people tuned in to watch, and at voting time, half the voters said that the debates had influenced their opinion.

- Explain to students that they are about to read, and then watch, Kennedy's inaugural address. Ask them to consider the differences between reading a speech and seeing it presented. Then go through the bulleted items in the chart and ask students if they agree with these benefits, or have anything to add. Also ask them to predict the kinds of things they might later add under "Limitations."

- **Discussion:** Have students complete the discussion activity in pairs or small groups.

STEP BY STEP: PAGE 198

- Explain to students that at age 43, Kennedy was the youngest man ever elected president. To Americans, he represented a new, more youthful generation to lead the country. A hero in World War II, Kennedy was elected when both world politics and American culture were changing rapidly.

- Remind students that one of the benefits of reading a speech is that they can examine word choices and the writing structure. Read the directions on page 198.

Tell students to underline any phrases or ideas that make an impact on them as they read the excerpt.

- When students have finished reading and underlining phrases in the text, have them share in small groups the lines and phrases that made an impact on them.

- Next, direct students to the web site of the John F. Kennedy Presidential Library and Museum—http://www.jfklibrary.org/Asset-Viewer/BqXIEM9F4024nt Fl7SVAjA.aspx—where they can view his inaugural address. (The portion that matches the text excerpt begins at time stamp 13:05.) Have them play the video three times. First, have them listen only. Is Kennedy's delivery—the tone and volume and emotion—what they expected?

- Now have students watch the speech. The first time, allow them to sit back and experience it as the crowd would have. Next, have them view it again and take notes on Kennedy's facial expressions, his gestures, and how the crowd responded.

- Finally, have students look again at the text in their book and review what they underlined. Discuss how Kennedy's delivery affected the impact of the words. Did he emphasize the same things with his voice or with gestures that they felt were important when reading it? Did his delivery make them feel differently about what they were hearing?

- Finally, return to the written speech. Explain that reading a speech can provide another way to appreciate it. Point out Kennedy's use of alliteration in phrases such as "Same high standards of strength and sacrifice" and "lead the land we love." Direct attention to the careful construction of Kennedy's address, which shows up in balanced phrases such as these:

  - I do not shrink from this responsibility, I welcome it

  - Whether you are citizens of America or citizens of the world

  - With a good conscience our only sure reward, with history the final judge

- **Discussion:** Have students form small groups to discuss how they felt when reading the speech excerpt as opposed to when they were watching and hearing Kennedy deliver it. What are the limitations to each experience? Would they suggest that other viewers read the speech first or simply watch the video of the speech? Why?

MAKE A STATEMENT (SL.7.4)

- Have students write a short (3–4 paragraph) speech about an issue they feel strongly about (the environment, school lunches, animal cruelty, etc.). Tell them to write the speech with the intent of delivering it to the class, and to mark the speech to show what they would emphasize with their voice or gestures.

- Ask for volunteers to present their speech. Then, either pass out hard copies of each student speech to the entire class or put each one on an interactive whiteboard for the entire class to read right before the speech is delivered. Have students read each speech before the speaker presents it to the class. Ask the class to compare the differences between the text version of the speech and the speech as it is delivered by the student.

IN THE NEWS (SL.7.2)

- Have students choose a current national news story that interests them. Topics can range from politics to entertainment to natural disasters.

- Have students find a print article on the topic and take notes on what they learn. Then have them watch a television news show on the same subject. Finally, have students find the same story online.

- After they are done exploring all three sources, have students write a short assessment of which source made them feel most informed about the topic, which held their interest more, and how the different mediums affected their reaction to and understanding of the story.

TWEETS, BLOGS, AND MORE (RI.7.7)

- New forms of media appear on an almost daily basis. Have students list as many different types as possible: blogs, texts, social networking sites like Facebook, Twitter, Skype, YouTube, etc.

- Divide students into groups and have them choose four of these mediums to compare, using the copymaster on page 184. Direct them to write the mediums they choose across the top of the chart.

- Next, have students analyze each medium, covering each of the questions listed in the chart. Afterwards, ask them which forms they think are most useful and whether they affect the way we interact with others positively, negatively, or both.

- As an additional topic of conversation, you may wish to point out that businesses, advertisers, entertainers, and politicians are also using new media to get their messages across. Have students find and discuss examples, and consider how they are affected by those messages.

THE KING'S SPEECH (RI.7.10)

- Provide students with some background on King George VI, who was king of England from December, 1936, until his death. The former Duke of York had a pronounced stammer, which suddenly became a critical issue in the 1920s, when radio became an important way through which world leaders communicated with people around the globe. When the duke realized he was to be king, he became determined to overcome the stammer that he knew would prevent him from inspiring his people and gaining their confidence.

- Reproduce the speech "In this grave hour," which the king delivered on September 3, 1939, as England prepared to go to war. (A PDF can be found at www.royal.gov.uk/pdf/georgevi.pdf)

Have students read, mark, and discuss it as they did with Kennedy's inaugural speech. Then direct them to listen to the speech in the BBC archives at http://www.bbc.co.uk/archive/ww2outbreak/7918.shtml

- In small groups, have students discuss why it was so critical for the king to be able to deliver this speech on the radio rather than just have it printed in newspapers.

Name_____ Date_____

DIRECTIONS: Write the names of four types of media across the top of the chart. The compare and contrast them by adding information to answer each question listed.

Who uses it, and what is its purpose?				
How does it work?				
What types of content does it contain?				
What are some benefits and drawbacks?				

After filling out the chart, discuss which mediums you think are the best or most useful. Also discuss whether you think each medium has had a positive or negative affect on communication. Compare your conclusions with those of other groups.

Comparing and Contrasting Genres

LESSON OBJECTIVES

- Compare and contrast a fictional portrayal of a particular time, place, or character with a historical account of the same period.

- Analyze the techniques an author uses to incorporate historical information in a fictional text.

- Recognize the ways in which fictional texts alter history.

THE LEARNING PROGRESSION

- **Grade 6:** CCSS RL.6.9 requires students to compare and contrast texts in different forms or genres without specifically considering the ways in which fictional texts alter history.

- **Grade 7: CCSS RL.7.9 requires students to recognize the ways in which fictional texts connect with and diverge from historical texts. By comparing and contrasting a fictional portrayal with a historical account of the same period, students recognize the function, possibilities, and limitations of historical fiction.**

- **Grade 8:** CCSS RL.8.9 has students broaden their consideration of how fiction renders new material from existing works by analyzing modern fiction drawn from religious texts and traditional stories.

PREREQUISITE SKILLS

- Identify similarities in the way that two or more texts in different genres deal with the same theme or topic.

- Identify differences in the way that two or more texts in different genres deal with the same theme or topic.

TAP STUDENTS' PRIOR KNOWLEDGE

- Tell students they will be working on a lesson about comparing and contrasting fictional and historical accounts of the same period.

- Ask students if they can think of any movies they have seen that are based on real people or events. (*Examples include* The Social Network, *about Mark Zuckerberg, and* Titanic, *a retelling of the sinking of an "unsinkable" luxury liner.*)

- Then discuss some historical fiction students may be familiar with, such as *Number the Stars* by Lois Lowry and *Riding Freedom* by Pam Munoz Ryan.

- Explain that although some people and main events in each movie or book are real, details, characters, and dialogue are fictionalized, or made up, by the author in order to make an interesting, dramatic, or exciting book or movie that people will read or see.

- Ask students what the point is of fictionalizing historical events. (*It's an entertaining way of presenting important events that people may then want to learn more about.*)

- Point out that although historical fiction is a valid form of literature, readers must always be aware that what they are reading is fiction, which uses and alters historical facts to suit the author's purpose.

Ready *Teacher Toolbox* — teacher-toolbox.com

	Prerequisite Skills	RL.7.9
Ready Lessons	✓	✓
Tools for Instruction		
Interactive Tutorials		✓

CCSS Focus

RL.7.9 Compare and contrast a fictional portrayal of a time, place, or character and a historical account of the same period as a means of understanding how authors of fiction use or alter history.

ADDITIONAL STANDARDS: **RL.7.1, RL.7.2, RL.7.3, RL.7.4, RL.7.7; L.7.1, L.7.4a, L.7.4b, L.7.5a; W.7.5, W.7.7, W.7.9a; SL.7.1, SL.7.6** (*See page A39 for full text.*)

AT A GLANCE

Through an illustration of a real person in a historical setting, students are introduced to the idea of fictionalizing history. They learn ways in which authors alter historical events to create works of fiction.

STEP BY STEP

- Read the definitions of *historical fiction* and *historical account.* Then encourage students to examine the illustration of Martin Luther King Jr., and think about which details are real and which are made up.

- Ask volunteers to tell which details in the picture are real. Then ask other volunteers to tell which details they think are made up and how they know. (*Real: Martin Luther King, Jr. library. Made-up: the young woman who is an admirer of Martin Luther King Jr., the young woman's thoughts; although many young people met and interacted with him, there is no way to know with historical accuracy what people thought when they met him.*)

- Explain that the chart shows how writers use historical facts to create works of fiction. Read the first column and compare the information listed to the details in the illustration. Then read the second column and discuss how the illustration of Martin Luther King Jr. and the young woman is an example of altering historical facts to create an appealing image.

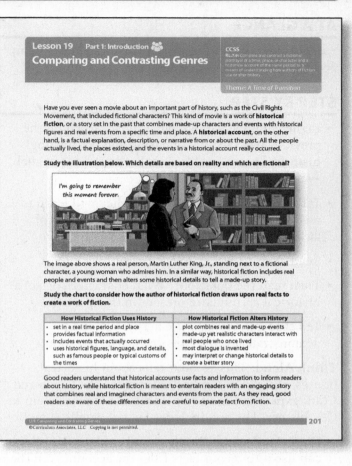

Genre Focus

Informational Texts: Historical Accounts

Tell students that in this lesson they will read informational texts. One type of informational text is a historical account, or a written account of a historical event. It usually includes the following characteristics:

- It is based on evidence from historical documents and other primary sources. Examples of primary sources are the written journals that Lewis and Clark kept during their expedition to explore uncharted territory west of the Mississippi River.

- It may narrate, summarize, interpret, or synthesize information taken from one or more primary sources created during a particular time period.

Based on these characteristics, ask students to describe some historic accounts they have read. What historical events were explained, and what did students notice about the accounts? Were any artifacts or illustrations included, and if so, how did they relate to or clarify the facts presented?

Explain that this lesson features two historical accounts. "Journey to the Pacific" details how the Lewis and Clark expedition reached the Pacific Ocean. "Orphan Train Riders" tells of the efforts of a fledgling social agency to relocate orphaned children living on New York City streets in the mid-1800s. Then a speech by a famous suffragist highlights the gains made by the Women's Rights Movement by 1893.

AT A GLANCE

Students identify and record the historical facts in an account about the Lewis and Clark expedition.

STEP BY STEP

- Invite volunteers to tell what they learned on the previous page about comparing and contrasting historical events and fictionalized versions of such events.

- Tell students that in this lesson they will learn to recognize a historical account and the kinds of factual details characteristic of the genre.

- Read aloud "Journey to the Pacific."

- Then read the question: "What characteristics of a historical account are present in this passage?"

- Tell students you will use a Think Aloud to demonstrate a way of answering the question.

Think Aloud: This account tells about historical figures, real places, and actual events. The Lewis and Clark expedition is an important and famous event in U.S. history. The text includes factual details about it.

- Direct students to the chart and explain that they can use it to record facts from the account. Tell them that they will read a fictional story on the next page about the same events, and the chart will help them to compare and contrast the two texts.

Think Aloud: The first paragraph includes the date the expedition began and facts about who ordered it, what its purpose was, and some of the explorers' experiences. I will record these details in the chart. The passage goes on to say that the explorers mistook the Columbia River for the Pacific Ocean. That is surprising—and a detail I would like to confirm. That should be easy. Many nonfiction books and articles have been written about Lewis and Clark. The journals they wrote as they traveled are also available.

- Have students record facts from the account in the first column of the chart.

- Finally, have partners discuss how to confirm that the expedition did mistake the Columbia River for the Pacific Ocean, as recounted in the text.

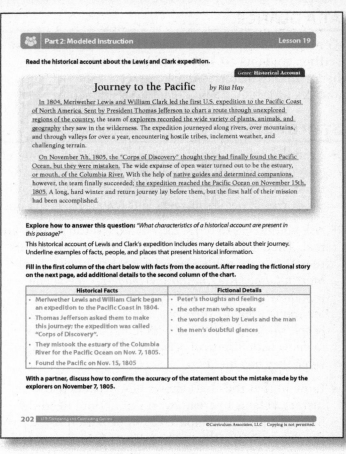

Tier Two Vocabulary: *Expanse*

- Read the second sentence of Paragraph 2. Point out the word *expanse*. Tell students the word comes from a Latin word, *pandere*, meaning "to spread." Ask what prefix they see in the word and what it means. (*ex-, meaning "out," "away from"*)

- Based on the meanings of the word parts, ask students what they think the noun *expanse* might mean. (*"something that spreads out"*)

- Ask what context clues in the sentence help to confirm the word's meaning. (*"wide, open water," "mouth of the Columbia River"*)

- Based on these clues, ask what *expanse* means. (*"a wide and open surface"*) **(RL.7.4; L.7.4a, L.7.4b)**

AT A GLANCE

Students read a fictional story based on the main event described in "Journey to the Pacific." They identify and record fictional details. Then they answer a multiple-choice question and analyze the details that helped them select the correct answer.

STEP BY STEP

• Tell students they will read a fictional account about the Lewis and Clark expedition.

• Close Reading helps students focus on what is fact and what is fiction. The Hint will help them consider the answer choices carefully. Have students read the passage and mark the historical facts and the fictional details, as directed by the Close Reading.

• Ask volunteers to share the facts they underlined and the details they starred. Discuss how they decided what was fact and what was fiction.

• Have students fill in the second column of the chart on page 202. Then have students compare the details in both columns. What fictional details were added to the story? Why were they added? How do they affect readers' understanding of the events?

• Have students circle the answer to the question and complete page 203. Then discuss their responses and their ideas about the advantages of reading each type of account.

ANSWER ANALYSIS

Choice A is incorrect. Peter is a fictional character.

Choice B is incorrect. It cites dialogue from the story that is most likely fictional.

Choice C is incorrect. No facts support this idea.

Choice D is correct. It is the only choice that states a fact also presented in "Journey to the Pacific."

ERROR ALERT: Students who did not choose D may have overlooked the direction to refer to facts presented in the previous passage. Remind students that "Sighting the Pacific" is fiction and that minor characters—not the historical figures—are usually invented by the author. They are not factual. Neither is most dialogue in this genre.

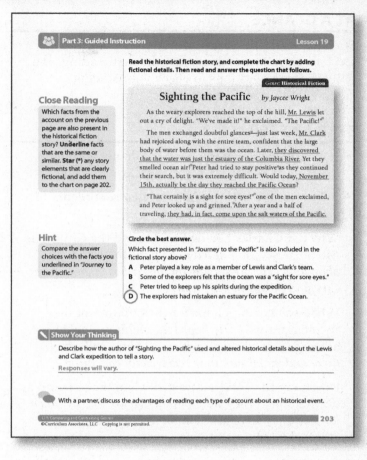

ELL Support: Idioms

• Tell students that the English language includes many expressions known as idioms. Explain that an idiom is a phrase with a meaning different from the meanings of its individual words.

• Discuss some examples of idioms, such as "in one ear and out the other," "shake a leg," and "seeing red." Tell students idioms are examples of informal language and are often used in conversation and written dialogue.

• Point out the first sentence in the last paragraph. Tell students "a sight for sore eyes" is an idiom. Ask, "What is the 'sight' referred to in the expression?" (*the Pacific Ocean*) Explain that the explorers' eyes are not really sore, or hurting. In the context of the story, ask students what "That certainly is a sight for sore eyes!" means. (*After traveling for a long time, the men are relieved and happy to finally see the Pacific Ocean.*) **(RL.7.4; L.7.4a, L.7.5a)**

AT A GLANCE

Students read a historical account twice about the Orphan Train Movement. After the first reading, you will ask three questions to check your students' comprehension of the passage.

STEP BY STEP

- Have students read the passage silently without referring to the Study Buddy or Close Reading text.

- Ask the following questions to ensure students' comprehension of the text:

  Why did Charles Loring Brace found the Children's Aid Society? (*He wanted to help the thousands of abandoned children living on the streets of New York City find homes in the country.*)

  What was Loring's hope for the children of the "orphan trains"? (*He hoped the children would be adopted by good people who would love and care for them and make sure they received an education.*)

  How were the children treated when they arrived at a destination? (*They were put on display like livestock for sale; they were poked and prodded; siblings were often split up.*)

- Ask students to reread paragraph 1 and look at the Study Buddy think aloud. What does the Study Buddy help them think about?

Tip: The Study Buddy reminds students that the passage is a historical account and to look for important facts and historical details about the people and events. Being able to identify the genre of a text will improve students' understanding of it.

- Have students read the rest of the passage. Tell them to follow the directions in the Close Reading.

Tip: Close Reading helps students identify details that make this passage a historical account. Have students think about how they would summarize the important facts of this account to help them check that they understand what they read.

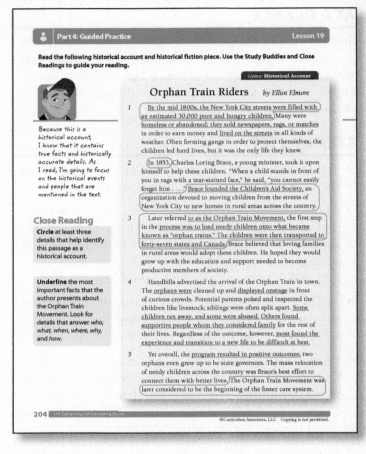

Tier Two
Vocabulary: *Abandoned*

- Point out the word *abandoned* in paragraph 1. Students may be familiar with this word in the context of an "abandoned house." Ask them how they would describe an abandoned house. (*empty, deserted, rundown*)

- Tell students these are valid synonyms for the word. Elicit that for something to be truly abandoned, there has to have been someone who was originally responsible for it, someone who has given up on it and no longer takes care of it.

- Have students read the first two sentences of the passage. Given the context and what they know, ask how they would define *abandoned children*. (*"children whose parents or guardians have given up responsibility for them and no longer provide them with food or shelter"*) **(RL.7.4; L.7.4a)**

AT A GLANCE

Students read a historical fiction story twice about the Orphan Train Movement. After the first reading, you will ask three questions to check your students' comprehension of the passage.

STEP BY STEP

- Have students read the passage silently without referring to the Study Buddy or Close Reading text.

- Ask the following questions to ensure students' comprehension of the text:

  Why were Robbie and his sister put on the train by the Children's Aid Society people? (*Their parents had died, and the children were living by themselves on the streets of New York City.*)

  Why do you think the two orphans were so confused and terrified by the time they were seated in the hall? (*Sample responses: Their trip had been long and tiring; they knew nothing about the location, the strangers looking them over, or what their fate would be; they did not know if they would be separated.*)

  Why does the orphan girl claim that her luck held? (*The couple took both Robbie and his sister into their home and raised them just like family members.*)

- Ask students to reread paragraph 1 and read the Study Buddy think aloud. How does it help them?

Tip: Point out that this text tells about two fictional children who lived through the orphan train experience. Ask students to look for facts about the Orphan Train Movement that have been used in this story. Which facts have been left out or altered?

- Have students read the rest of the story. Tell them to follow the directions in the Close Reading.

Tip: Remind students that this passage is a work of fiction. The important historical facts and events referred to may be accurate, but characters, settings, and plot events are often invented. Being able to distinguish fact from fiction is an essential skill for readers to develop, particularly when reading historical fiction.

- Finally, have students answer the questions on page 206. Discuss the Answer Analysis to discuss correct and incorrect responses.

ELL Support: Regular Past-Tense Verbs

- Review with students that the past tense of most verbs is formed by adding -*ed* or -*d* to the base form of the verb. Have students find examples of regular past tense verbs formed this way in paragraph 1. (*boarded, advised*) Ask what the present tense of each verb is. (*board, advise*)

- Explain that for a one-syllable verb ending in a single consonant, they must double the final consonant before adding -*ed*. Ask students to find an example of such a past tense verb in paragraph 3. (*blurred*) Ask what the present tense of *blurred* is. (*blur*) **(L.7.1)**

- Point out that for verbs ending in a consonant plus *y*, they must change the *y* to *i* before adding -*ed*, as in *cry, cried*.

STEP BY STEP

- Have students read questions 1–3, using the Hints to help them answer those questions.

> **Tip:** Tell students to clearly label the historical and the fictional texts so as not to confuse them. For questions 1 and 2, guide students to eliminate choices based on answers that only describe one of the passages, since the questions ask about both.

- Discuss with students the Answer Analysis below.

ANSWER ANALYSIS

1 The correct choice is D. Paragraph 4 in "Orphan Train Riders" says the transition to a new life was difficult. "The Train to Somewhere" illustrates this fact with negative details. Choice A is incorrect. The story doesn't mention handbills. Choice B contradicts the historical account. Choice C does not reflect enough of the girl's experience.

2 The correct choice is B. The author alters historical details through fictional characters. Choice A is incorrect. The story does not mention when the Children's Aid Society was formed. Choice C is incorrect. The story doesn't mention the families' beliefs. Choice D is incorrect. The story is about the orphan train experience.

3 Sample response: The author used details from the actual experiences of orphans on the orphan trains, including that children were rescued by the Children's Aid Society off the streets of NYC and were sent away on trains to be taken in and adopted by strangers. The made-up details of the girl's experience illustrate the uncertainty and confusion expressed by those who actually lived it. The author altered details to describe the experiences of two imaginary children. She provided a happy ending to the story, which was not always the case in reality.

RETEACHING

Use a chart to answer question 3. Draw the chart below, and work with students to fill in the boxes.

Historical Facts	Fictional Details
Abandoned children were rescued from NYC by the Children's Aid Society. Transition was difficult.	siblings ride on train girl terrified of being separated from brother adopted by caring family

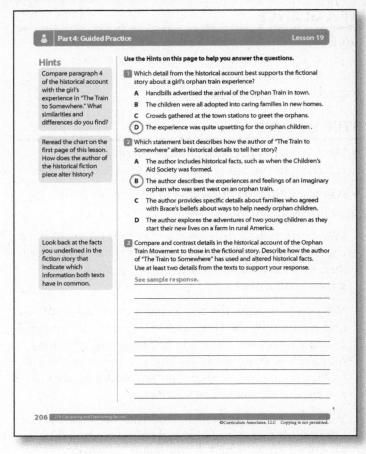

Hints

Compare paragraph 4 of the historical account with the girl's experience in "The Train to Somewhere." What similarities and differences do you find?

Reread the chart on the first page of this lesson. How does the author of the historical fiction piece alter history?

Look back at the facts you underlined in the fiction story that indicate which information both texts have in common.

Use the Hints on this page to help you answer the questions.

1 Which detail from the historical account best supports the fictional story about a girl's orphan train experience?

  A Handbills advertised the arrival of the Orphan Train in town.

  B The children were all adopted into caring families in new homes.

  C Crowds gathered at the town stations to greet the orphans.

  D The experience was quite upsetting for the orphan children .

2 Which statement best describes how the author of "The Train to Somewhere" alters historical details to tell her story?

  A The author includes historical facts, such as when the Children's Aid Society was formed.

  B The author describes the experiences and feelings of an imaginary orphan who was sent west on an orphan train.

  C The author provides specific details about families who agreed with Brace's beliefs about ways to help needy orphan children.

  D The author explores the adventures of two young children as they start their new lives on a farm in rural America.

3 Compare and contrast details in the historical account of the Orphan Train Movement to those in the fictional story. Describe how the author of "The Train to Somewhere" has used and altered historical facts. Use at least two details from the texts to support your response.

See sample response.

_____

_____

_____

_____

_____

_____

_____

_____

Integrating Standards

Use these questions to further students' understanding of "Orphan Train Riders" and "The Train to Somewhere."

1 Summarize the conditions that led Charles Loring Brace to form the Children's Aid Society. **(RL.7.2)**

In the mid 1800s, thousands of abandoned children were living on the streets of New York City. They fended for themselves by selling whatever they could. Life was hard, and the children formed gangs to protect themselves.

2 The girl in "The Train to Somewhere" says, "My heart was in my throat." Explain what this phrase means and what mood it sets. **(RL.7.4)**

It means that the girl is nervous about the trip. Her heart is pounding so hard it feels as if it has jumped into her throat. The phrase sets a mood of fear and anxiety.

Read the following speech and historical fiction story. Then answer the questions that follow.

from "The Progress of 50 Years"

by Mrs. Lucy Stone

Lucy Stone was a well-known suffragist in the Women's Rights Movement. Forced to pay for her own education, she was the first woman from Massachusetts to earn a college degree and gained fame for not changing her name after marrying Henry B. Blackwell in 1855. Stone continued to fight for equality for women throughout her career. The following is an excerpt from her last public speech, presented to the Congress of Women at the World's Fair in 1893.

1   Fifty years ago the legal injustice imposed upon women was appalling. Wives, widows and mothers seemed to have been hunted out by the law on purpose to see in how many ways they could be wronged and made helpless. A wife by her marriage lost all right to any personal property she might have. The income of her land went to her husband, so that she was made absolutely penniless. If a woman earned a dollar by scrubbing, her husband had a right to take the dollar. . . . It was his dollar. If a woman wrote a book the copyright of the same belonged to her husband and not to her. The law counted out in many states how many cups and saucers, spoons and knives and chairs a widow might have when her husband died. I have seen many a widow who took the cups she had bought before she was married and bought them again after her husband died, so as to have them legally. The law gave no right to a married woman to any legal existence at all. Her legal existence was suspended during marriage. She could neither sue nor be sued. If she had a child born alive the law gave her husband the use of all her real estate as long as he should live, and called it by the pleasant name of "the estate by courtesy." When the husband died the law gave the widow the use of one-third of the real estate belonging to him, and it was called the "widow's encumbrance." While the law dealt thus with her in regard to her property, it dealt still more harshly with her in regard to her children. No married mother could have any right to her child, and in most of the states of the Union that is the law to-day. But the laws in regard to the personal and property rights of women have been greatly changed and improved, and we are very grateful to the men who have done it.

2   We have not only gained in the fact that the laws are modified. Women have acquired a certain amount of political power. We have now in twenty states school suffrage for women. Forty years ago there was but one. Kentucky allowed widows with children of school age to vote on school questions. We have also municipal suffrage for women in Kansas, and full suffrage in Wyoming, a state larger than all New England.

3   The last half century has gained for women the right to the highest education and entrance to all professions and occupations, or nearly all. As a result we have women's clubs, the Woman's Congress, women's educational and industrial unions, the moral education societies, the Woman's Relief Corps, police matrons . . . colleges for women, and co-educational colleges and the Harvard Annex, medical schools and medical societies open to women, women's hospitals . . . women as a power in the press, authors, women artists, women's beneficent societies and Helping Hand societies, women school supervisors, and factory inspectors and prison inspectors, women on state boards of charity, the International Council of Women, the Woman's National Council, and last, but not least, the Board of Lady Managers. And not one of these things was allowed women fifty years ago, except the opening at Oberlin. By what toil and fatigue and patience and strife

and the beautiful law of growth has all this been wrought? These things have not come of themselves. They could not have occurred except as the great movement for women has brought them out and about. They are part of the eternal order, and they have come to stay. Now all we need is to continue to speak the truth fearlessly, and we shall add to our number those who will turn the scale to the side of equal and full justice in all things.

A Widow's Burden

by Hanna Ingram

1   Though Sarah loved her parents, she began to worry as soon as she received word that her mother and father were coming to the farm for a visit. She hadn't told them the news about Elijah's estate, and she wondered how she would fit everyone at the table during mealtime. In truth, that problem was small compared to her other burdens, but she could do little to remove a single one.

2   Sarah missed her husband Elijah terribly. Last winter, he had caught a chill and died from it. This left Sarah to manage the farm alone. She and her girls could have coped, but a few months ago, her stepson Brad had shown up at her door, court order in hand. He was laying claim to two-thirds of Elijah's farm, his rightful inheritance. Being a woman meant she was only entitled to one third of her husband's property; her stepson was "kind" enough to let her keep the cabin and a small plot of land for a garden. The rest of the farm would be sold. Sarah only hoped she could grow enough to feed her girls and find work in town.

3   Just focusing on her parents' visit brought Sarah more heartache. It was so unfair. As a widow, she was entitled to so little of Elijah's estate, and Brad had claimed most of the furniture, the extra plates, and the silverware, silverware she'd received from her grandmother. She was left with four place settings and four chairs—just enough for herself and the girls for each meal. She had done some mending for Mr. Molloy with the intention of earning enough money to buy back the plates and a chair or two, but she'd had to spend the money on flour, sugar, and more pins.

4   Sarah tidied the house nervously as she waited for her parents to arrive. The last time she had seen them, Elijah was still alive. Soon she saw a distant cloud of dust from their wagon as it rolled up the road. The children ran behind it toward the house, and Sarah greeted her parents fondly. Setting aside her own worries, Sarah began chatting about family and friends.

5   At last, the family sat down to eat. Sarah's two oldest girls withdrew quietly, knowing that they were to eat later so as to share their seats and place settings with their grandparents. As Sarah served the dinner she could ill afford, her mother watched her with concern.

6   "Why aren't we all eating together, dear?" her mother asked. "And what is on your mind?"

7   Sarah hesitated, but then she decided to tell the truth. "As a widow, I am only entitled to a few of the things Elijah and I once shared, and Elijah's son Brad has claimed the rest. That's why my home is so bare. We have so little now that Elijah is gone."

8   Her father shook his head sadly. "What about the farm?" he asked.

AT A GLANCE

Students independently read two longer passages and answer questions in a format that provides test practice.

STEP BY STEP

- Tell students to use what they have learned about reading closely and noting how writers alter historical facts to read the passages on pages 207–209.

- Remind students to underline or circle important facts and fictional details.

- Tell students to answer the questions on pages 209 and 210. For questions 1–3, they should fill in the correct circle on the Answer Form.

- When students have finished, use the Answer Analysis to discuss correct responses and the reasons for them. Have students fill in the Number Correct on the Answer Form.

ANSWER ANALYSIS

1   Choice A is correct. The author of "A Widow's Burden" has taken the fact, included in Stone's speech, that a widow was entitled to only one-third of her husband's estate and built a story around it. Choices B and C are inaccurate. Choice B implies that Sarah and her mother attended Stone's speech; the story does not say this. And rather than accept her fate, as choice C says, Sarah and her parents decide to fight to get back her farm. Choice D, while a valid statement, does not describe how the author of the story altered fact to create fiction. **(DOK 3)**

Theme Connection

- How do all the passages in this lesson relate to the theme of a time of transition?

- What is one fact or idea from an account in this lesson that you found especially interesting? Why?

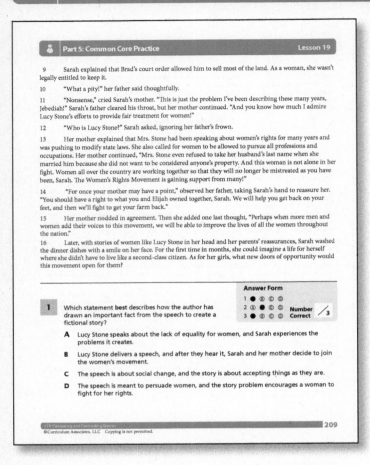

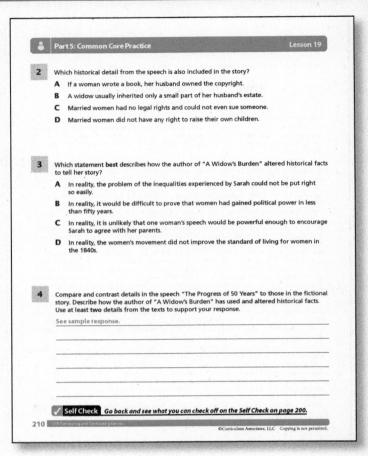

2 Choice B is correct. That a widow was entitled to only one-third of her husband's estate is the fact from Stone's speech around which the story, "A Widow's Burden," is built. Choices A, C, and D are accurate, but these facts are not used in the story. There is no mention in the story of copyright law, of the fact that married women could not sue, nor that mothers did not have any right to their children. **(DOK 2)**

3 Choice A is correct. According to Stone's speech, it took fifty years for women to begin to gain equality and legal justice. It is unlikely that Sarah's problem over the inheritance of the farm could be easily resolved. The optimistic note at the end of the story is probably not realistic. Choice B is incorrect. While the statement could be considered accurate, the story does not specifically refer to women's political power. The speech, on the other hand, indicates that by 1893, women were only just beginning to gain political power. Only one state, Wyoming, had full suffrage for women. Choice C is incorrect because it does not connect to any

historical fact in the speech. Choice D may be an accurate statement since the women's movement probably did not exist in any organized way in the 1840s, but no date is given in the story, so this statement is irrelevant. **(DOK 3)**

4 Sample response: Lucy Stone's speech provides a first-hand historical account of the inequalities, beliefs, and attitudes that resulted in the Women's Rights Movement. Sarah's story, the historical fiction piece, reflects the unfairness of the inheritance laws by illustrating the problems such laws created for an imaginary woman living in the 1800s. Most women actually living in those times would not have had as much sympathy or help from their parents, nor would their problems be dealt with as quickly or easily. **(DOK 4)**

Integrating Standards

Use these questions and tasks as opportunities to interact with "The Progress of 50 Years" and "A Widow's Burden."

1 Summarize the gains achieved by women in education and career opportunities as listed in paragraph 3 of Lucy Stone's speech. **(RL.7.2)**

Women had gained admittance to higher education, and institutions and societies had been established for women. Women could now hold more jobs such as authors, police matrons, artists, and managers.

2 Analyze how the setting contributes to the plot development of "A Widow's Burden." **(RL.7.3)**

The setting is in the mid 1800s on a small farm. A few pieces of furniture and some dishes are all that Sarah rightfully owns after her husband's death. These details highlight Sarah's plight at being allowed to inherit only one-third of her husband's estate, a common predicament in those times. They help drive events, such as Sarah's daughters not being able to eat with their family and her parents' shock.

3 What kind of people do you think Sarah's mother and father are? **(RL.7.1)**

They are sympathetic and supportive parents. The mother is knowledgeable about the women's movement, and even though he seems reluctant to agree with his wife, the father admits that Sarah has suffered an injustice. They vow to help her.

4 Discuss in small groups: In 1893, at the time of Lucy Stone's speech, only one state had granted full suffrage, or the right to vote, to women. In 1920 the nineteenth amendment to the Constitution was passed, allowing women to vote. Why do you think it took another 27 years for all women to be allowed to vote? **(SL.7.1)**

Discussions will vary. Encourage students to consider the state of women's legal status in the mid 1800s as recounted in Stone's speech and the realities illustrated in "A Widow's Burden." Point out that all attempts to change the status quo are prolonged, as values and customs are hard to change.

Writing Activities

Evaluate Texts Based on Criteria *(W.7.9a)*

- Have students reflect upon the three sets of paired passages in the lesson and the topics they cover: Lewis and Clark, the Orphan Train Movement, and the Women's Rights Movement. Ask students to interpret and make connections between the fictional passages in these pairs and the cultural perspective and eras described in the historical accounts. Work with students to establish criteria for successfully using historical facts to tell a story. Criteria may include using many historically accurate facts, describing an era-appropriate setting, and creating believable characters, dialogue, and events.

- Have students write a response to literature in which they evaluate one or more of the fictional texts by expressing their opinion about its quality. Was it successful at accurately incorporating historical facts to tell a story? In what way? Which is the most successful? Why?

- Remind students to introduce their opinion, support it with logical reasons and evidence, and organize their writing logically. Allow time for students to work in groups to comment on and revise their writing.

- Then guide a class discussion about students' opinions, reviewing how they used the established criteria to make their arguments.

LISTENING ACTIVITY *(SL.7.1)*

Listen Closely/Ask and Answer Questions

- Have students review "The Progress of 50 Years" and "A Widow's Burden." Have them write several questions about the passages that can be answered from the text. Challenge students to include at least one question that requires synthesis of the information from both passages.

- Have students work in small groups to ask and answer each other's questions. Listeners must pay close attention to the questions and cite evidence from the text in their answers.

DISCUSSION ACTIVITY *(SL.7.1)*

Talk in a Group/Talk About Lewis and Clark

- Have student recall facts about the Lewis and Clark expedition—how it came about, its purpose, its leaders, the routes traveled, the contributions of Sacajawea, and the challenges they faced.

- Then have students form small groups to discuss this expedition, which came to represent the pioneering spirit of America.

- Ask groups to write a statement explaining the group's assessment—positive or negative—of the expedition's historical significance.

MEDIA ACTIVITY *(RL.7.7)*

Be Creative/Compare and Contrast Versions

- Have students watch a portion of an educational film about the orphan train movement. Encourage students to take notes as they watch the film.

- After viewing, have students discuss how the techniques used in film, such as lighting, sound, and camera focus, affect their understanding of the information. Compare the experience to reading a historical account and fictional story about the same event.

RESEARCH ACTIVITY *(W.7.5, W.7.7; SL.7.6)*

Research and Present/Write a Report

- Have students to use the information in the two accounts of the Orphan Train Movement to write a report about this episode of American history.

- Ask student to research additional information to include in their reports, such as the movement's benefits and controversies, personal accounts of people who lived through the experience, famous people who were part of it, or the movement's lasting effects.

- Have students review their reports with partners and revise them based on feedback.

SCORING GUIDE AND ANSWER ANALYSIS

Literature Passage Answer Analysis

1 ● Ⓑ Ⓒ Ⓓ   4 Ⓐ Ⓑ ● Ⓓ

2 Ⓐ Ⓑ ● Ⓓ   5A Ⓐ ● Ⓒ Ⓓ

3 Ⓐ Ⓑ Ⓒ ●

1 Choice A is correct. In "The Fateful Journey," the author includes details about the difficult trip to America.

Choice B is incorrect. The author doesn't list the cities that the immigrants are going to. Choice C is incorrect. The author explains that the family boards a steamship, but he doesn't give details. Choice D is also incorrect. The author writes that the family left from Bremen, Germany, a city that was mentioned in "Moving to America," but he doesn't describe it. *(RL.7.9; DOK 3)*

2 Choice C is correct. "A Fateful Journey" is a fictional story with made-up characters. These characters use invented dialogue when they speak. Invented dialogue would not be a part of a factual account such as "Moving to America."

Choice A is incorrect. "A Fateful Journey" is about an important event in the life of a girl and her family, but it does not give the date. Dates are found only in the factual account. Choice B is incorrect. "A Fateful Journey" has dialogue between the characters, but it does not have famous quotations. Part of a famous quotation on the Statue of Liberty is found in the factual account. Choice D is also incorrect. Both passages describe conditions faced by travelers on the ocean. *(RL.7.9; DOK 2)*

3 Choice D is correct. The detail about Bremen was mentioned in both passages. "Moving to America" uses Bremen as an example of a busy immigration port. In "A Fateful Journey," Maryana and her family travel to Bremen to catch their ship.

Choice A is incorrect. The detail about the high cost of tickets is included only in "Moving to America." The characters in "A Fateful Journey" do not mention the ticket cost. Choice B is incorrect. The detail about some immigrants coming from Greece is suggested in "A Fateful Journey." However, "Moving to America" does not

specifically mention that immigrants came from Greece. Choice C is also incorrect. The detail about passengers sleeping in bunk beds is suggested in "A Fateful Journey." However, "Moving to America" does not specifically mention this detail. *(RL.7.9; DOK 3)*

4 Choice C is correct. In "Moving to America," the author notes that most immigrant groups feuded with one another. The author of "A Fateful Journey" does not give this fact. Rather, the immigrants in the boat sing together and become friends.

Choice A is incorrect. In "Moving to America," the author states that many immigrants traveled to the United States. This is reflected in "A Fateful Journey," in which the author describes a large crowd of immigrants packed into the steamship. Choice B is incorrect. In "Moving to America," the author notes that many immigrants found jobs in coal mines. This fact appears in "A Fateful Journey" when a woman says her husband migrated to America and worked in a coal mine. Choice D is incorrect. In "Moving to America," the author explains that immigrants came from throughout Europe. The author of "A Fateful Journey" reflects this fact by stating that the immigrants in steerage were speaking many languages. *(RL.7.9; DOK 3)*

5 **Part A:** Choice B is correct. "Moving to America" describes the transatlantic voyage as "extremely unpleasant," and "A Fateful Journey" calls the crossing "long and difficult." All other choices are true of "Moving to America" only. *(RL.7.9; DOK 3)*

Part B: Students' choice of sentences will vary. Sample sentence: "Most were made to travel in steerage—a crowded, uncomfortable area in the lower part of a ship." *(RL.7.9; DOK 3)*

Part C: Students' choice of sentences will vary. Sample sentence: "'Welcome to steerage,' said a gruff attendant, leading them to some cramped bunk beds." *(RL.7.9; DOK 3)*

SAMPLE RESPONSES

Short Response

6 In "A Fateful Journey," Mikhail tells his daughters that Uncle Pyotr emigrated to the United States and started a large textile company where he became very wealthy. This might be true, but it seems unlikely based on the facts in "Moving to America." The factual article states that most immigrants had to work at difficult and dangerous jobs. Most did not have the money or other resources to start their own companies. *(RL.7.9; DOK 4)*

7 In "A Fateful Journey," Maryana believes that arriving in the United States means the end of her family's problems. However, in "Moving to America," the author writes that immigrants faced many more challenges in their new country. Many immigrants had to take hard, dangerous jobs in coal mines, railroads, and factories. At the same time, some Americans treated them poorly, and different immigrant groups were at odds with one another. *(RL.7.9; DOK 4)*

8 In both "Moving to America" and "A Fateful Journey," the authors show that steamship tickets were very important to immigrants. In "Moving to America," the author calls these tickets "precious." He also writes that immigrants had to pay a great deal of money for each ticket. In "A Fateful Journey," Mikhail displays his family's ticket and says that it is their "future" and their way to get to the "land of opportunity." *(RL.7.9; DOK 4)*

Performance Task

9 "A Fateful Journey" is a fictional story about a real historical period. The author tells an entertaining story while teaching some important lessons about history.

The author starts with historically accurate facts and details, such as the long journey to the port of Bremen and the steamships in the harbor. The real-life experiences of immigrants traveling to the United States become the backdrop for a story about a fictional family and their own experiences. Details about the conditions on the ship, arriving in a new country, searching for work, all affected the lives of real people as well as the fictional characters in the story. These details give the story an authentic feel.

Writers of historical ficton can choose the historical details that help tell a good story. For example, in real life, immigrants were detained at Ellis Island and examined before being admitted into the US. This detail is not in the fictional story. The historical account emphasizes how difficult and unpleasant the voyage was and notes that immigrants would sometimes fight among themselves. In "A Fateful Journey" the immigrants are laughing, dancing, and singing. The impact of the author's choices is that the story is a much more upbeat and cheerful picture of immigrant life than the historical account. *(RL.7.9; DOK 4)*

SCORING RUBRICS

Short-Response Rubric

2 points The response is accurate, complete, and fulfills all requirements of the task. Text-based support and examples are included. Any information that goes beyond the text is relevant to the task.

1 point The response is partially accurate and fulfills some requirements of the task. Some information may be inaccurate, too general, or confused. Support and examples may be insufficient or not text-based.

0 points The response is inaccurate, poorly organized, or does not respond to the task.

Performance Task Rubric

4 points The response
- Fulfills all requirements of the task
- Uses varied sentence types and some sophisticated vocabulary
- Includes relevant and accurate details from the texts as well as text-based inferences
- Demonstrates a thorough understanding of the texts
- Maintains a clear focus and organization
- Is fluent and demonstrates a clear voice
- Uses correct spelling, grammar, capitalization, and punctuation

3 points The response
- Fulfills all requirements of the task
- Uses simple sentences and grade-level vocabulary
- Includes relevant and accurate details from the texts
- Demonstrates a mainly literal understanding of the texts
- Maintains a mostly clear focus and organization
- Is fluent and demonstrates some sense of voice
- Uses mostly correct spelling, grammar, capitalization, and punctuation

2 points The response
- Fulfills some requirements of the task
- Uses simple sentences, some fragments, and grade-level vocabulary
- Includes some relevant and accurate details from the texts
- Demonstrates some misunderstandings or gaps in understanding of the texts
- Attempts to maintain a clear focus and organization
- Is difficult to read, includes some inaccuracies, and demonstrates little or no sense of voice
- Contains some inaccurate spelling, grammar, capitalization, and punctuation that may hinder understanding

1 point The response
- Fulfills few requirements of the task
- Uses sentence fragments and below-grade-level vocabulary
- Includes no details or irrelevant details to support the response
- Demonstrates very little understanding of the texts
- Does not establish a clear focus or organization
- Is difficult to read, contains many inaccuracies, and demonstrates no sense of voice
- Uses incorrect spelling, grammar, capitalization, and punctuation to an extent that impedes understanding

0 points The response is irrelevant, poorly organized, or illegible.

Comparing Media Techniques

LESSON OBJECTIVES

- Compare and contrast the effect on the reader or audience of print and filmed versions of the same story.

- Analyze the techniques used in the filmed version of a written story (e.g. camera angles, lighting, sound, and editing).

THE LEARNING PROGRESSION

Grade 6: CCSS RL.6.7 requires students to analyze storytelling elements to compare and contrast "the experience of reading a story, drama, or poem to listening to or viewing an audio, video, or live version of the text."

Grade 7: CCSS RL.7.7 builds on the Grade 6 standard by requiring students to compare and contrast written and visual versions of texts by "analyzing the effects of techniques unique to" film or stage versions of stories.

Grade 8: CCSS RL.8.7 requires students to analyze how faithful a filmed or stage version of a story is to the original text, "evaluating the choices made by the director or actors."

TAP STUDENTS' PRIOR KNOWLEDGE

- Ask the class for examples of well-known books that have been turned into movies (e.g., the *Twilight* or *Hunger Games* series; *Coraline*). Discuss some of the ways the movie version is different from the original print version. Ask students what they liked about each version.

- Explain that an author uses carefully chosen words and images, along with storytelling conventions such as conflict and suspense, to create the characters and details of the world in which his or her story takes place. A movie director has a number of other tools that can be used to tell the story, including camera shots, sound effects, sets, and editing techniques. While both use similar storytelling conventions, film directors must decide how to use all of the other tools at their disposal to create the desired effect on the viewer.

- Tell students they will look at several important techniques used by film directors to tell a story, and they will think about how those techniques might have a different effect on the viewer than the experience of reading a print version of the story.

■ **Ready** *Teacher Toolbox*		teacher-toolbox.com
	Prerequisite Skills	**RL.7.7**
Ready Lessons	✓	✓
Tools for Instruction		
Interactive Tutorials		✓

CCSS Focus

RL.7.7 Compare and contrast a written story, drama, or poem to its … filmed … version, analyzing the effects of techniques unique to each medium (e.g., lighting, sound, color, or camera focus and angles in a film).

ADDITIONAL STANDARDS: *W.7.3; SL.7.4, SL.7.5*

AT A GLANCE

By focusing on the techniques used by film directors to tell a story, students will be better able to compare the experience of reading a story to reading the print version.

STEP BY STEP: PAGE 219

- Have a volunteer read the introduction on page 219 aloud to the class. Explain that even though writers and directors use similar conventions of storytelling, their tools and techniques are very different. Writers must create every detail of a story with words, while film directors use a variety of techniques to create the settings, characters, and plot line of a story.

- Read the lines above the chart on page 219. Be sure students understand the format of the chart. Explain that the "Techniques" on the left are standard tools that film directors use; that the "Characteristics" column explains each technique; and that the "Effect on Viewer" column describes how each technique might impact someone watching a movie.

- **Camera Shots:** Explain to students that a film director chooses camera shots based on what he or she wants the viewer to see. To demonstrate, have students create a rectangle shape using the thumb and second finger of each hand, and then view the classroom through that "lens." Point out how this affects what they see and know at any give moment. Then review the bullet points in the chart, asking students for examples from movies they've seen.

- **Editing:** Tell students that filmmakers use editing to set the pace of a scene in the same way writers might use sentence length to create pace on the page. At a tense point in a film, a director might use many cross–cuts to depict the actions and increase the pace of the film. To depict time passing, a director might choose a slow dissolve from one scene to another.

- **Set Design:** Discuss the fact that directors may shoot a scene "on location," in a real setting, or on a set that is built (or computer generated) from scratch. Details and props are added to create the right environment for the story.

- **Lighting & Sound:** Explain that film directors use lighting to create mood or to focus the viewer's attention on something. Directors also use sound effects to enhance a scene. During a chase scene, for example, a filmmaker might include exaggerated breathing sounds to convey a character's panic.

- Point out that in addition to these techniques, directors must also consider casting, costuming, and performances. While writers must describe characters, they can depend on readers to enhance those details with their own imaginations. Filmmakers must make decisions about each detail.

- For the activity, you may wish to choose several compelling scenes from appropriate movies and show them to the whole class. Have students create a viewer's log using the copymaster found on page 202 of this Teacher's Guide, and ask them to jot down the techniques they notice as they watch.

STEP BY STEP: PAGE 220

- Ask students to remember the first time they saw a villain in a movie they viewed. Use the elements from the chart on page 219 to fuel the discussion. What do they recall about the camera shots? How was lighting used? Were there unusual sound effects? Discuss how the various techniques directors use affected the way they perceived the villain.

- Read aloud the introduction to the passage from Ray Bradbury's *Something Wicked This Way Comes* on page 220, and point out that students will be expected to complete the Director's Notes at the bottom of the page.

- Direct students to read the passage, circling words and phrases the author used to help create a specific mood. (*crouched, crept, dry autumn field, all black, quiet, whispered, shadow–faced*) List the words and phrases on the board, and discuss their impact.

- Tell students they are now going to assume the role of a filmmaker and make decisions about how to effectively bring this scene to the screen. Tell them to first write their goal for the scene, then jot down notes in the chart on page 220. Explain that their notes should reflect the techniques in the chart on page 219 and the effects of these techniques on a viewer.

- When students have completed their Director's Notes, ask pairs of students to exchange their notes and compare choices. Ask them to discuss how the different decisions would affect the scene and the viewer, and how their movie versions would compare to the passage they read.

VIDEO TRAILER *(SL.7.5)*

- Challenge students to plan a scene for a video trailer that would be used to sell one of their favorite books. The trailer would focus on a highlight from the book, and should be exciting enough to "hook" viewers and make them want to read the story.

- Suggest that students plan their trailer by creating a storyboard that includes a sketch of what's happening in each shot, a description of the type of shot used, and notes about camera shots, sound effects, lighting, and sets.

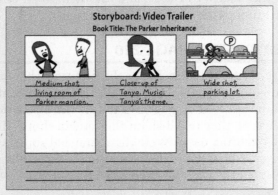

- When students have completed their storyboards, ask them to work in small groups to share the original passage and their storyboard ideas. How effective does the group think the trailer will be, and why?

NOVELIZATION *(W.7.3)*

- Explain to students that sometimes when a movie is very successful, a book version of that movie is written. These are called novelizations.

- Tell students that they are being hired to write a novelization of a movie. Have them choose one scene or memorable moment from a movie they know well and try to write the scene as it would appear in a book. (Encourage students to select a movie that is not already based on a book they have read, if possible.) Ask them to watch the scene and make notes on the setting, what happens in the scene, and how the actors perform as the characters.

- Remind the students that as they write their novelization, they need to use vivid and detailed language to capture the movie scene in print. If

there is dialogue in the scene, they may choose to use direct quotes from the movie, or modify it as needed. The important thing for students to remember is that a novelization uses words to capture the images and action movie viewers see, and provides readers with as similar an experience as possible.

- Ask students to share their novelizations with the class by reading them aloud. Also ask them to discuss the challenges of creating a scene that's as powerful on the page as it was on the screen.

PAGE VERSUS STAGE *(RL.7.7)*

- Have students compare and contrast the original print version of a story with the movie version and decide which was more successful in terms of the effect on the reader/viewer. The analysis should include:

  - an overall opinion about how successful the filmmaker was in translating the written story to the big screen

  - specific comments about how character, mood, plot, and setting were conveyed in each version

  - supporting details about the techniques the filmmaker used to present the story

- Ask students to share their analyses in small groups.

THE PERFECT SONG *(SL.7.4)*

- Explain that sometimes when you read a book or story you think of the perfect song to accompany a scene. Have students think of the perfect song for the soundtrack to a scene in the movie version of a book they've read. Tell students that they will need to find a memorable scene or moment from a book and choose a song that they think would fit or enhance a filmed version.

- Tell students that the song must be appropriate to discuss in class.

- Have volunteers present their music choices to the class. Students will need to provide their classmates with a short synopsis of what happens in the book or story before playing the song they've chosen. They should explain clearly to the class their rationale for choosing the song.

Name____________________ Date____________

DIRECTIONS: Select a short scene from a film, one that you found particularly effective. Watch the scene several times, noting the techniques that the director used to create mood, get a sense of place, enhance action, or deepen understanding of the characters in some way. Record what you see in the chart below. Include not only what you saw but how it affected you.

Description of Scene: ____________________

____

Set Design	Camera Shots
Lighting and Sound	**Editing**

Other techniques, such as casting, costuming, and performances:

Cut along the dotted line.

Ready® Common Core Language Handbook

The **Ready Common Core** Language Handbook was created to help students develop proficiency with the Common Core State Standards for Language. Each lesson uses scaffolded instruction, beginning with an introduction and guided practice and then moving students into fully independent practice of the skills and strategies behind the Common Core.

Conventions of Standard English

Knowledge of Language

Vocabulary Acquisition and Use

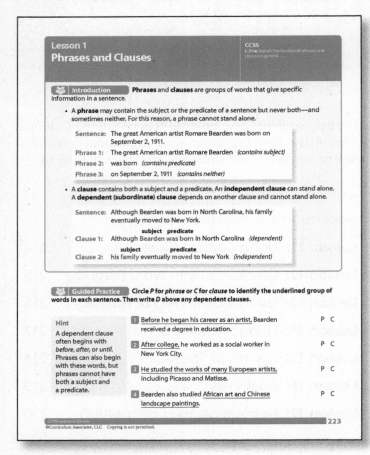

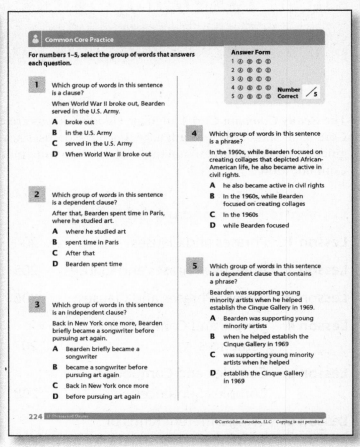

Lesson 1: Phrases and Clauses

Guided Practice, page 223

1   C, with D written above

2   P

3   C

4   P

Common Core Practice, page 224

1   D

2   A

3   A

4   C

5   B

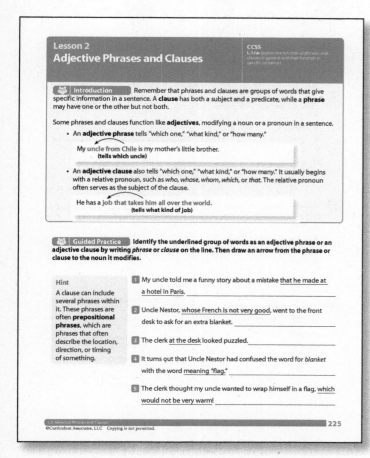

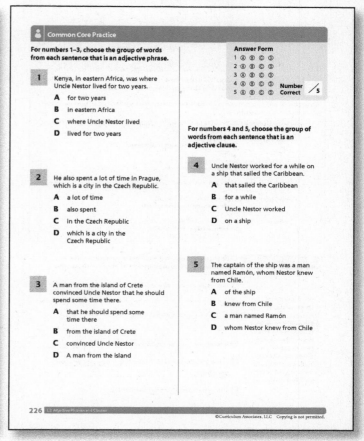

Lesson 2: Adjective Phrases and Clauses

Guided Practice, page 225

1   clause; arrow points to *mistake*

2   clause; arrow points to *Uncle Nestor*

3   phrase; arrow points to *clerk*

4   phrase; arrow points to *word*

5   clause; arrow points to *flag*

Common Core Practice, page 226

1   B

2   C

3   B

4   A

5   D

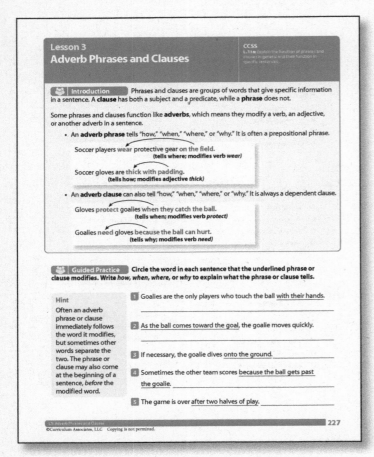

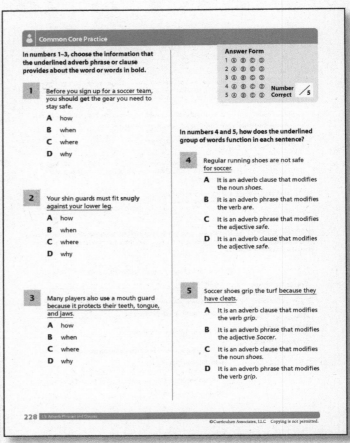

Lesson 3: Adverb Phrases and Clauses

Guided Practice, page 227

1 touch: how

2 moves: when

3 dives: where

4 scores: why

5 over: when

Common Core Practice, page 228

1 B

2 C

3 D

4 C

5 A

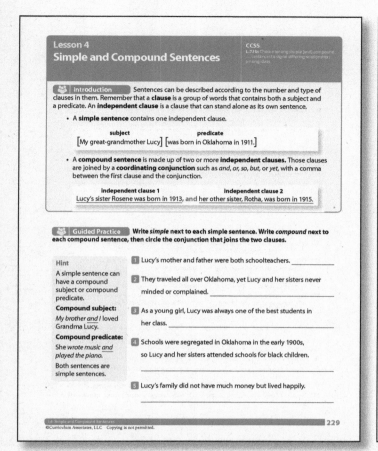

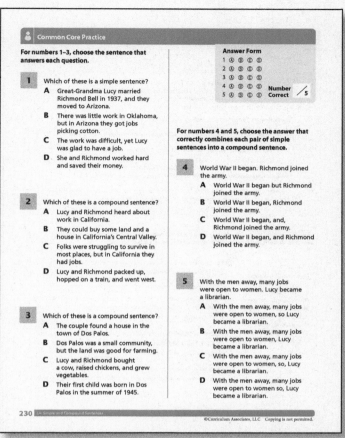

Lesson 4: Simple and Compound Sentences

Guided Practice, page 229

1 simple

2 compound: yet

3 simple

4 compound: so

5 simple

Common Core Practice, page 230

1 D

2 C

3 B

4 D

5 A

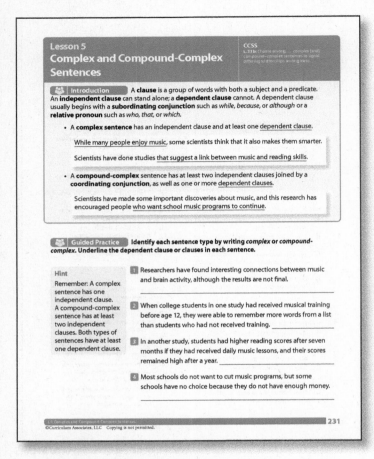

Lesson 5: Complex and Compound-Complex Sentences

Guided Practice, page 231

1 complex: although the results are not final

2 complex: when college students in one study had received musical training before age 12; who had not received training

3 compound-complex: if they had received daily music lessons

4 compound-complex: because they do not have enough money

Common Core Practice, page 232

1 D

2 C

3 D

4 B

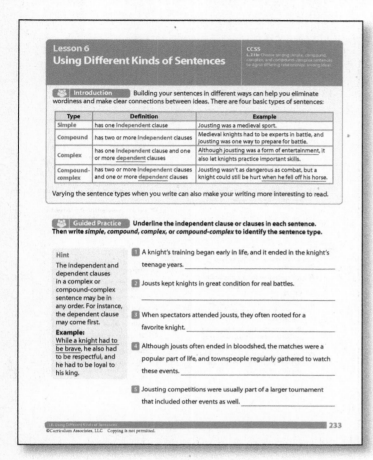

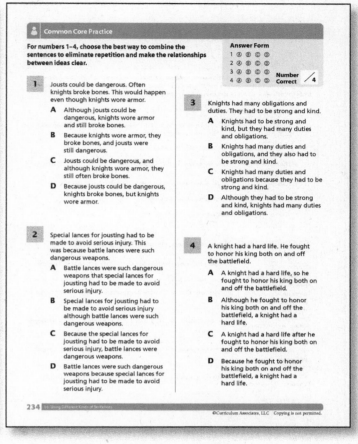

Lesson 6: Using Different Kinds of Sentences

Guided Practice, page 233

1 A knight's training began early in life; it ended in the knight's teenage years: compound

2 Jousts kept knights in great condition for real battles: simple

3 they often rooted for a favorite knight: complex

4 the matches were a popular part of life; townspeople regularly gathered to watch these events: compound-complex

5 Jousting competitions were usually part of a larger tournament: complex

Common Core Practice, page 234

1 C

2 A

3 B

4 D

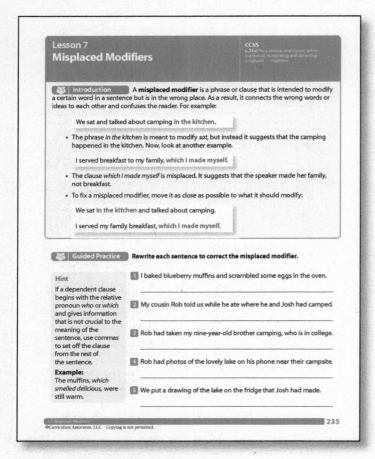

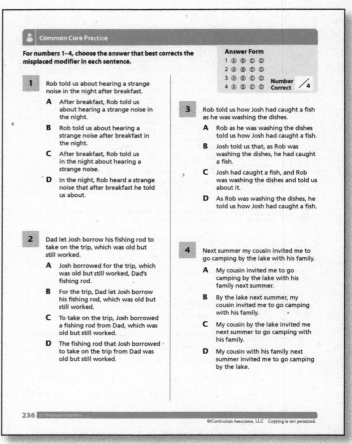

Lesson 7: Misplaced Modifiers

Guided Practice, page 235

Responses may vary. Sample answers:

1 I baked blueberry muffins in the oven and scrambled some eggs.

2 While he ate, my cousin Rob told us where he and Josh had camped.

3 Rob, who is in college, had taken my nine-year-old brother camping.

4 Rob had photos on his phone of the lovely lake near their campsite.

5 On the fridge, we put a drawing that Josh had made of the lake.

Common Core Practice, page 236

1 A

2 B

3 D

4 A

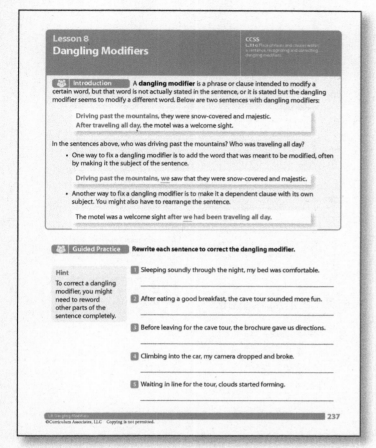

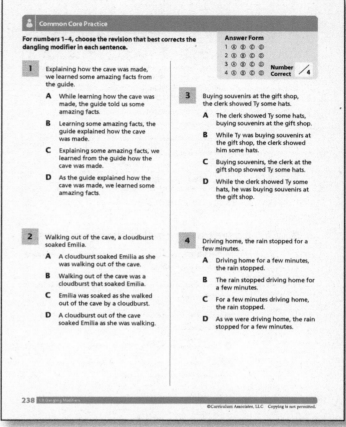

Lesson 8: Dangling Modifiers

Guided Practice, page 237

Responses will vary. Sample answers:

1 Sleeping soundly through the night, I was comfortable in my bed.

2 After I ate a good breakfast, the cave tour sounded more fun.

3 Before we left for the cave tour, we got directions from the brochure.

4 Climbing into the car, I dropped my camera and broke it.

5 As we waited in line for the tour, clouds started to form.

Common Core Practice, page 238

1 D

2 A

3 B

4 D

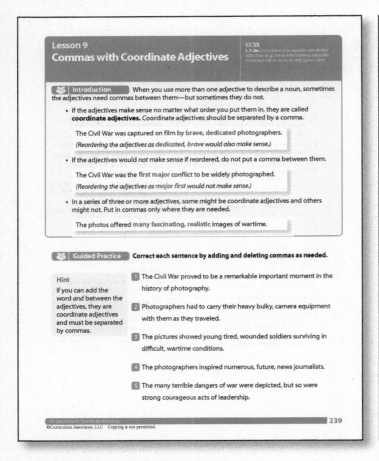

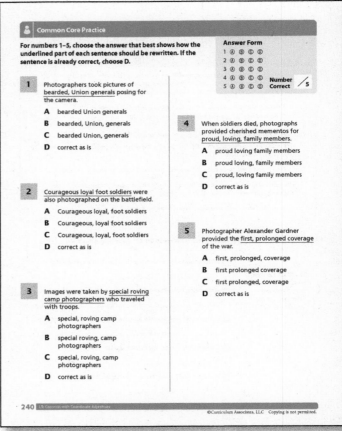

Lesson 9: Commas with Coordinate Adjectives

Guided Practice, page 239

1 The Civil War proved to be a remarkable, important moment in the history of photography.

2 Photographers had to carry their heavy, bulky, camera equipment with them as they traveled.

3 The pictures showed young, tired, wounded soldiers surviving in difficult, wartime conditions.

4 The photographers inspired numerous, future, news journalists.

5 The many terrible dangers of war were depicted, but so were strong, courageous acts of leadership.

Common Core Practice, page 240

1 A

2 B

3 D

4 C

5 B

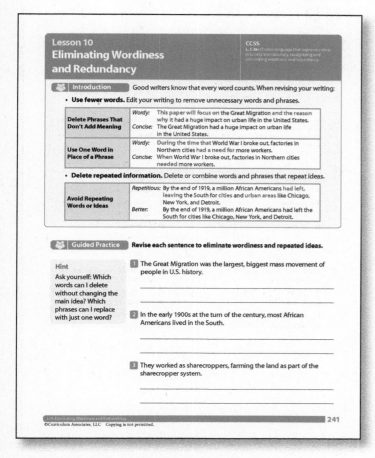

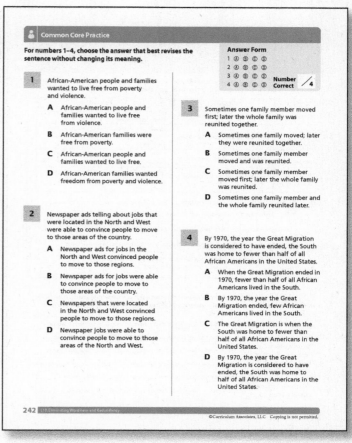

Lesson 10: Eliminating Wordiness and Redundancy

Guided Practice, page 241

Responses will vary. Sample answers:

1 The Great Migration was the largest movement of people in U.S. history.

2 In the early 1900s, most African Americans lived in the South.

3 They worked as sharecroppers, farming the land.

Common Core Practice, page 242

1 D

2 A

3 C

4 A

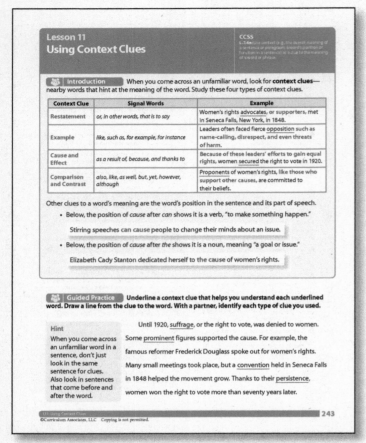

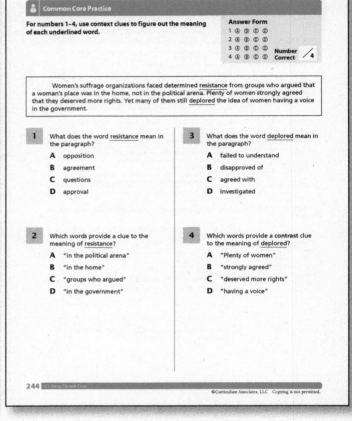

Lesson 11: Using Context Clues

Guided Practice, page 243

Responses will vary. Sample answers:

1 suffrage: or the right to vote (restatement)

2 prominent: For instance, the famous reformer Frederick Douglass (example)

3 convention: Many small meetings took place, but (contrast)

4 persistence: Thanks to . . . women won the right to vote more than seventy years later. (cause and effect)

Common Core Practice, page 244

1 A

2 C

3 B

4 B

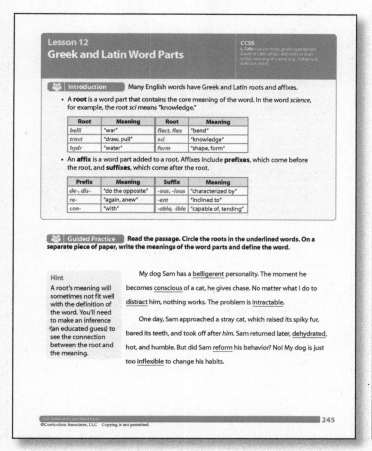

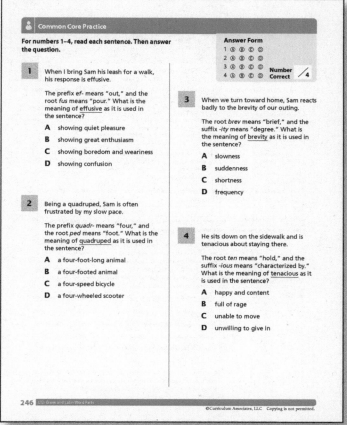

Lesson 12: Greek and Latin Word Parts

Guided Practice, page 245

Responses will vary. Sample answers:

(belli)gerent: root *belli* means "war"; suffix *-ent* means "inclined to"; *belligerent* means "aggressive"

con(sci)ous: prefix *con-* means "with"; root *sci* means "knowledge"; suffix *-ious* means "characterized by"; *conscious* means "aware"

dis(tract) prefix *dis-* means "do the opposite"; root *tract* means "draw, pull"; *distract* means "to change the focus of attention"

in(tract)able: root *tract* means "draw, pull"; suffix *-able* means "capable of, tending"; *intractable* means "hard to control"

de(hydr)ated: prefix *de-* means "do the opposite"; root *hydr* means "water"; *dehydrated* means "having lost fluid"

re(form): prefix *re-* means "again, anew"; root *form* means "shape"; *reform* means "to change for the better"

in(flex)ible: root *flex* means "bend"; suffix *-ible* means "capable of"; *inflexible* means "incapable of change"

Common Core Practice, page 246

1 B

2 B

3 C

4 D

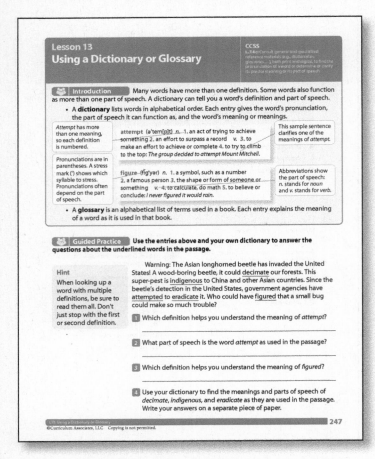

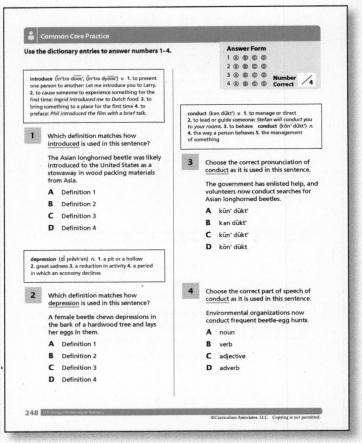

Lesson 13: Using a Dictionary or Glossary

Guided Practice, page 247

1 definition 3, "to make an effort to achieve or complete"

2 verb

3 definition 5, "to believe or conclude"

4 Responses will vary. Sample answers: decimate: verb; to destroy a large part of something indigenous: adjective; originating in a place, native eradicate: verb; to get rid of

Common Core Practice, page 248

1 C

2 A

3 B

4 B

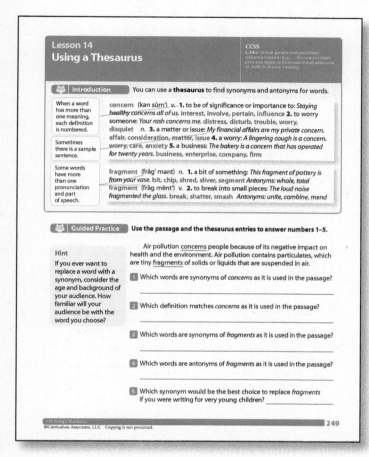

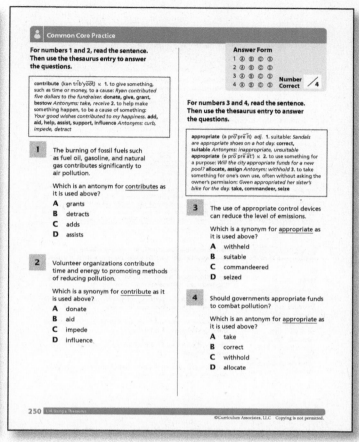

Lesson 14: Using a Thesaurus

Guided Practice, page 249

1 distress, disturb, trouble, worry, disquiet

2 definition 2, "to worry someone"

3 bit, chip, shred, sliver, segment

4 whole, total

5 bits

Common Core Practice, page 250

1 B

2 A

3 B

4 C

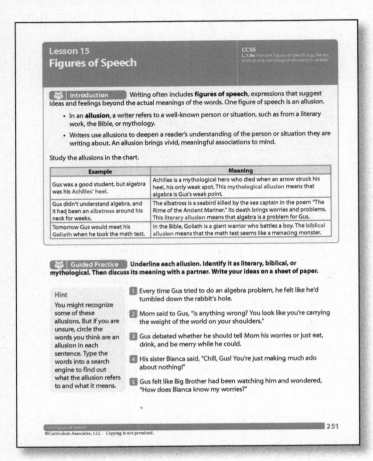

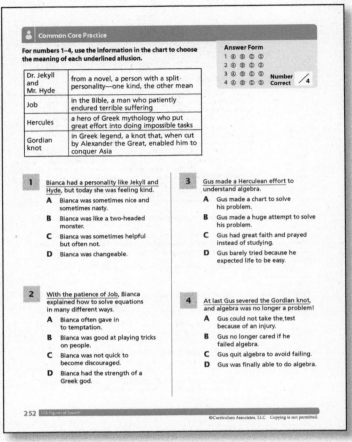

Lesson 15: Figures of Speech

Guided Practice, page 251

1 down the rabbit's hole: literary

The allusion to *Alice's Adventures in Wonderland* means that Gus felt like he was in a strange land (i.e., extremely disoriented) whenever he tried to do algebra.

2 carrying the weight of the world on your shoulders: mythological

The allusion is to Atlas, who had to carry the world on his shoulders. This means that Gus seems to be weighed down by a big problem.

3 eat, drink, and be merry: biblical

The allusion refers to the parable of the rich fool, in which Christ describes a rich farmer who saves his wealth for a later time but who dies before enjoying it. The allusion means that Gus wonders if he might as well enjoy himself, because tomorrow he'll have bigger problems when he fails his math test.

4 much ado about nothing: literary

The allusion refers to Shakespeare's play *Much Ado About Nothing*. It means that Gus is making a big fuss about something that isn't important.

5 Big Brother: literary

The allusion refers to the character of Big Brother, a dictator in George Orwell's dystopian novel *Nineteen Eighty-Four*. In this dystopia, the propagandistic slogan "Big Brother is watching you" is everywhere. The allusion means that Gus feels like his sister's been spying on him because she knows what he is worried about.

Common Core Practice, page 252

1 A

2 C

3 B

4 D

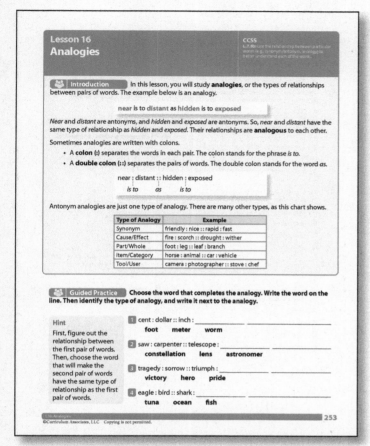

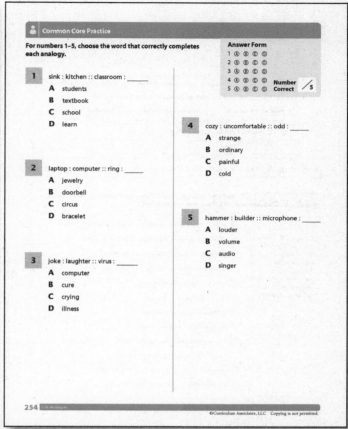

Lesson 16: Analogies

Guided Practice, page 253

1 foot; part/whole

2 astronomer; tool/user

3 pride; cause/effect

4 fish; item/category

Common Core Practice, page 254

1 C

2 A

3 D

4 B

5 D

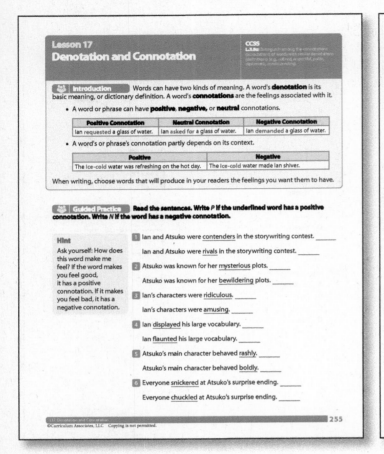

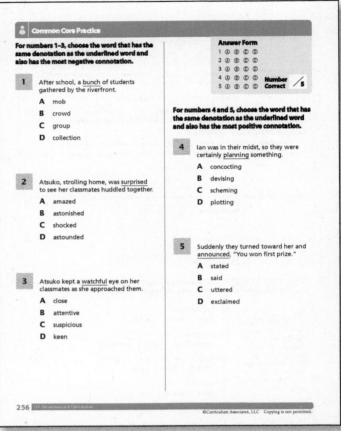

Lesson 17: Denotation and Connotation

Guided Practice, page 255

1 contenders: P
   rivals: N

2 mysterious: P
   bewildering: N

3 ridiculous: N
   amusing: P

4 displayed: P
   flaunted: N

5 rashly: N
   boldly: P

6 snickered: N
   chuckled: P

Common Core Practice, page 256

1 A

2 C

3 C

4 A

5 D